The Perennial Philosophy

Series

World Wisdom
The Library of Perennial Philosophy

The Library of Perennial Philosophy is dedicated to the exposition of the time-less Truth underlying the diverse religions. This Truth, often referred to as the *Sophia Perennis*—or Perennial Wisdom—finds its expression in the revealed Scriptures as well as the writings of the great sages and the artistic creations of the traditional worlds.

The Perennial Philosophy provides the intellectual principles capable of explaining both the formal contradictions and the transcendent unity of the great religions.

Ranging from the writings of the great sages of the past, to the perennialist authors of our time, each series of our Library has a different focus. As a whole, they express the inner unanimity, transforming radiance, and irreplaceable values of the great spiritual traditions.

The Betrayal of Tradition: Essays on the Spiritual Crisis of Modernity appears as one of our selections in the Perennial Philosophy series.

The Perennial Philosophy Series

In the beginning of the Twentieth Century, a school of thought arose which has focused on the enunciation and explanation of the Perennial Philosophy. Deeply rooted in the sense of the sacred, the writings of its leading exponents establish an indispensable foundation for under-standing the timeless Truth and spiritual practices which live in the heart of all religions. Some of these titles are companion volumes to the Treasures of the World's Religions series, which allows a comparison of the writings of the great sages of the past with the perennialist authors of our time.

The Betrayal of

𝕿radition

Essays on the
Spiritual Crisis of Modernity

Edited by

Harry Oldmeadow

World Wisdom

The Betrayal of Tradition: Essays on the Spiritual Crisis of Modernity
© 2005 World Wisdom, Inc.

For complete bibliographic information on the articles
in this anthology, please see the the Acknowledgments section
at the end of the book, pp. 365-67

Library of Congress Cataloging-in-Publication Data

The Betrayal of Tradition: Essays on the spiritual Crisis of Modernity / edited by
Harry Oldmeadow.
    p. cm. – (The library of perennial philosophy)
Includes bibliographical references and index.
ISBN 0-941532-55-0 (pbk. : alk. paper)
1. Modernism (Christian Theology) 2. Tradition (Theology)
 I. Oldmeadow, Harry, 1947- II. Series.
 BT82.B45 2005
 202–dc22

                                                                    2004022095

Printed on acid-free paper in Canada

For information address World Wisdom, Inc.
P.O. Box 2682, Bloomington, Indiana 47402-2682

www.worldwisdom.com

Tradition speaks to each man the language he can comprehend, provided he wishes to listen. The latter proviso is crucial, for tradition, let it be repeated, cannot "become bankrupt"; rather is it of the bankruptcy of man that one should speak, for it is he that has lost all intuition of the supernatural and the sense of the sacred. It is man who has let himself be deceived by the discoveries and inventions of a falsely totalitarian science ... [M]an has ended by being submerged by his own creations; he will not realize that a traditional message is situated on quite a different plane or how much more real that plane is ... Tradition is abandoned, not because people are no longer capable of understanding its language, but because they do not wish to understand it, for this language is made to be understood till the end of the world ...

FRITHJOF SCHUON

TABLE OF CONTENTS

INTRODUCTION:

SIGNS OF THE TIMES AND THE LIGHT OF TRADITION

The title of this anthology alerts us to the spiritual crisis of modernity and to its root cause: the betrayal of tradition. That there is indeed a spiritual crisis will hardly be denied by anyone who has pondered the condition of the contemporary world. We need not rehearse the whole catalogue of inter-related symptoms, but here are a few of the more conspicuous: ecological catastrophe, a material sign of the rupture between Heaven and Earth; a rampant materialism and consumerism, signifying a surrender to the illusion that man can live by bread alone; the brutal extirpation of traditional cultures by the runaway juggernauts of "modernization"; political barbarities on an almost unimaginable scale; a religious landscape dominated by internecine and inter-religious strife and by the emergence of aggressive fundamentalisms in both East and West; social discord, endemic violence and dislocations of unprecedented proportions; widespread alienation, ennui and a sense of spiritual sterility amidst the frenetic confusion and din of modern life; the loss of any sense of the sacred, even among those who remain committed to religious forms. These "signs of the times"—and the inventory is by no means exhaustive—are plain enough to those with eyes to see. No amount of gilded rhetoric about "progress," the "miracles" of modern science and technology, or the "triumphs of democracy" (to mention just three shibboleths of modernity) can hide the fact that our age is tyrannized by an outlook inimical to our most fundamental needs, our deepest yearnings, our most noble aspirations. More problematic is the question of how we arrived at this state of affairs and in which direction we might turn for some remedy.

In the luminous essay with which this volume opens, Frithjof Schuon observes: "That which is lacking in the present world is a profound knowledge of the nature of things; the fundamental truths are always there, but they do not impose themselves because they cannot impose themselves on those unwilling to listen." Those truths, so often derided in the modern world, can be found in tradition—and by this term we mean something very different from the jaundiced senses it has accumulated in the modern mentality ("the blind observance of inherited customs," and the like). St. Augustine speaks of "wisdom uncreate, the same now that it ever was, the same to be forevermore."[1] This timeless wisdom has carried many names: *philosophia perennis, Lex Aeterna, Hagia Sophia, Din al-Haqq, Akalika Dhamma,* and *Sanatana Dharma* are among the better known. In itself this truth is formless and beyond all conceptualizations. Any attempt to define it is, to borrow a metaphor, like trying to catch the river in a net. This universal wisdom, in existence since the genesis of time and the spiritual patrimony of all humankind, can also be designated as the Primordial Tradition. René Guénon refers to "... the Tradition contained in the Sacred Books of all peoples, a Tradition which in reality is everywhere the same, in spite of all the diverse forms it assumes to adapt itself to each race and period ..."[2] In this sense tradition is synonymous with a perennial philosophy or wisdom which is eternal, universal and immutable. The Primordial Tradition or *sophia perennis* is of supra-human origin and is in no sense a product or evolute of human thought. It is the birthright of humanity. All the great religious teachings, albeit in the differing vocabularies appropriate to the spiritual economy in question, affirm just such a principle. Recall Krishna's declaration, in the *Bhagavad Gita,* of the pre-existence of his message, proclaimed at the dawn of time.[3] Likewise Christ, speaking in his cosmic function as incarnation of the Truth, states, "Verily, verily, I say unto you, before Abraham was, I am."[4] "Tradition," then, in its most pristine sense is this primordial Truth and as such takes on the status of a first cause, a cosmic datum, a principial reality woven into the very fabric of the universe and ingrained in the human spirit.

"Tradition" also has a secondary meaning, directly pertinent to our theme. Etymologically it simply means "that which is transmitted." Here the term cannot be equated with a formless and

---

[1] Quoted in S. Radhakrishnan, "Fragments of a Confession," in *The Philosophy of Sarvepalli Radhakrishnan,* ed. P.A. Schilpp (New York: Tudor, 1952), p. 80.

[2] R. Guénon in *La Gnose,* 1909, quoted in Whitall Perry, *A Treasury of Traditional Wisdom* (London: Allen & Unwin, 1971), p. 20.

[3] *Bhagavad Gita* IV.5.i.

[4] *St John* VIII.58.

immutable Truth but is, rather, that Truth as it finds formal expression, through the medium of a divine Revelation, in the myths, doctrines, rituals, symbols, and other manifestations of any religious culture. As Lord Northbourne has observed, "Tradition, in the rightful sense of the word, is the chain that joins civilization to Revelation."[5] In this context "tradition" becomes more or less synonymous with "religion," always with the proviso that it is integral, orthodox religions of which we speak. Let us also not forget that,

> When people talk about "civilization" they generally attribute a qualitative meaning to the term, but really civilization only represents a value provided it is supra-human in origin and implies for the civilized man a sense of the sacred ... A sense of the sacred is fundamental for every civilization because fundamental for man; the sacred—that which is immutable, inviolable, and so infinitely majestic—is in the very substance of our spirit and of our existence.[6]

Traditional societies are grounded in an awareness of this reality. Society itself represents nothing of permanent or absolute value but only insofar as it provides a context for the sense of the sacred and the spiritual life which it implies.

At radical odds with Tradition, in all of its senses, stands the world of modernity and the Promethean philosophy which underpins it. For want of a better word we might call the dominant worldview of the post-medieval West "modernism" (not to be confused with the more restricted meaning sign-posting certain artistic and literary movements in the early 20th century). For present purposes the term comprises the prevalent assumptions, values and attitudes of a worldview fashioned by the most pervasive intellectual and moral influences of recent European history, an outlook in conformity with the *Zeitgeist* of the times. One might classify the constituents of modernism under any number of different schemata. Lord Northbourne typifies it as "anti-traditional, progressive, humanist, rationalist, materialist, experimental, individualist, egalitarian, free-thinking, and intensely sentimental."[7] Seyyed Hossein Nasr gathers these tendencies together under four general marks of modern thought: anthropomorphism (and by extension, secular-

[5] Lord Northbourne, *Religion in the Modern World* (London: J.M. Dent, 1963), p. 34.

[6] Frithjof Schuon, *Understanding Islam* (London: Allen & Unwin, 1976), p. 33.

[7] Lord Northbourne, *Religion in the Modern World*, p. 13.

ism); evolutionist progressivism; the absence of any sense of the sacred; an unrelieved ignorance of metaphysical principles.[8]

Modernism is nothing less than a spiritual disease which continues to spread like a plague across the globe, destroying traditional cultures wherever they are still to be found. Although its historical origins are European, modernism is now tied to no specific area or civilization. Its symptoms can be detected in a wide assortment of inter-related "mind sets" and "-isms," sometimes involved in cooperative co-existence, sometimes engaged in apparent antagonism, but always united by the same underlying assumptions. Scientism, rationalism, relativism, materialism, positivism, empiricism, evolutionism, psychologism, individualism, humanism, existentialism— these are some of the prime follies of modernist thought. The pedigree of this family of ideas can be traced back through a series of intellectual and cultural upheavals in European history and to certain vulnerabilities in Christendom which left it exposed to the subversions of a profane science. The Renaissance, the Scientific Revolution and the so-called Enlightenment were all incubators of ideas and values which first ravaged Europe and then spread throughout the world like so many bacilli. Behind the bizarre array of ideologies which have proliferated in the last few centuries we can discern a growing and persistent ignorance concerning ultimate realities and an indifference, if not always an overt hostility, to the eternal verities conveyed by tradition. Not without reason did William Blake characterize the modern worldview as "Single Vision," a horizontal understanding of reality which strips the "outer" world of its mystery, its grandeur and its revelatory function, and denies our human vocation as the "arks of God."

The contrast between tradition and modernity is a motif to be found in many of the essays in this anthology. The contrast is likely to be most illuminating when it is informed by the following considerations:

> When the modern world is contrasted with traditional civilizations, it is not simply a question of seeking the good things and the bad things on one side or the other; good and evil are everywhere, so

---

[8] See S.H. Nasr, "Reflections on Islam and Modern Thought," *The Islamic Quarterly* 23, no. 3 (1979): 119-131.

that it is essentially a question of knowing on which side the more important good and on which side the lesser evil is to be found. If someone says that such and such a good exists outside tradition, the answer is: no doubt, but one must choose the most important good, and it is necessarily represented by tradition; and if someone says that in tradition there exists such and such an evil, the answer is: no doubt, but one must choose the lesser evil, and again it is tradition that embodies it. It is illogical to prefer an evil which involves some benefits to a good which involves some evils.[9]

No one will deny that modernity has its compensations, though these are often of a quite different order from the loudly trumpeted "benefits" of science and technology—some of which are indubitable but many of which issue in consequences far worse than the ills which they are apparently repairing. Furthermore, many so-called "advances" must be seen as the poisoned fruits of a Faustian bargain which one day must come to its bitter conclusion. What indeed is a man profited if he gain the whole world but lose his own soul? On the other hand, one real advantage of living in these latter days is the ready access we have to the spiritual treasuries of the world's religious and mythological traditions, including esoteric teachings which hitherto have been veiled in secrecy.

Many of our contributors are traditionalists who cleave uncompromisingly to the *sophia perennis*—we need only mention such towering figures as René Guénon, Ananda Coomaraswamy, Frithjof Schuon, and Titus Burckhardt. Readers unfamiliar with their work will find here an introduction to some of the most sagacious thinkers of the last century. However, the anthology is not intended as a compendium of traditionalist thinkers alone but embraces a variety of viewpoints and perspectives, united by the conviction that the modern world stands in the most urgent need of the wisdom of the ages. *The Betrayal of Tradition* complements the other volumes already published by World Wisdom in the Perennial Philosophy series, especially *Science and the Myth of Progress* (edited by Mehrdad M. Zarandi) and *Every Branch in Me* (edited by Barry McDonald).

It is my hope that the juxtaposition of essays by traditionalists

---

[9] Frithjof Schuon, *Light on the Ancient Worlds* (London: Perennial Books, 1966), p. 42.

and other eminent contemporary thinkers will illuminate some common ground and thereby help to dispel the false charges sometimes leveled at traditionalists that they are dusty obscurantists "out of touch" with the contemporary world, that they want to "wind back the clock," that they are romantic reactionaries escaping into an idealized past. The essential message of tradition is timeless and thus ever new, ever fresh, and always germane to both our immediate condition and to our ultimate destiny. As Schuon remarks, a "nostalgia for the past" is, in itself, nothing; all that is meaningful is "a nostalgia for the sacred" which "cannot be situated elsewhere than in the liberating 'now' of God."[10]

HARRY OLDMEADOW
Bendigo, Australia

---

[10] Frithjof Schuon, "On the Margin of Liturgical Improvisations," in *The Sword of Gnosis*, ed. J. Needleman (Baltimore: Penguin, 1974), p. 353.

1

TRADITION AND MODERNITY

The modern mentality itself, in everything that
characterizes it specifically as such … is no more
than the product of a vast collective suggestion,
which has operated continuously for several
centuries and has determined the formation
and progressive development of the anti-traditional spirit … [T]he very idea of tradition has
been destroyed to such an extent that those who
aspire to recover it no longer know which way to
turn…

RENÉ GUÉNON

"No Activity Without Truth"*

Frithjof Schuon

The purpose of this congress is of the most extreme importance, since it concerns, directly or indirectly, the destiny of mankind. In the face of the perils of the modern world, we ask ourselves: What must we do? This is an empty question if it be not founded upon antecedent certainties, for action counts for nothing unless it be the expression of a knowing and also of a manner of being. Before it is possible to envisage any kind of remedial activity, it is necessary to see things as they are, even if, as things turn out, it costs us much to do so; one must be conscious of those fundamental truths that reveal to us the values and proportions of things. If one's aim is to save mankind, one must first know what it means to be a man; if one wishes to defend the spirit, one must know what is spirit. "Before doing, one must be," says the proverb; but without knowing, it is impossible to do. "The soul is all that it knows," as Aristotle said.

In our time one has often heard it said that in order to fight against materialism, technocracy, and pseudo-spiritualism, a new ideology is needed, one capable of standing up to all seductions and assaults, and of galvanizing those of good will. Now, the need for an ideology or the wish to oppose one ideology to another is already an admission of weakness, and anything undertaken on this basis is false and doomed to fail. What must be done is to counter false ideologies with the truth that has always been and that we could never invent since it exists outside us and above us. The present-day world is obsessed with "dynamism", as if this constituted a "categorical imperative" and a universal remedy and as if dynamism had any meaning or positive efficacy outside truth.[1]

No man in possession of his faculties could have the intention of merely substituting one error for another, whether "dynamic" or

---

* Editor's Note: A talk composed for a congress in Japan in 1961.

[1] In popular language this is called "putting the cart before the horse." We recall that during the Depression, one spoke of "creating a mystique of recovery"; as if the fatalities of industrialism were imaginary maladies, curable through autosuggestion, and as if autosuggestion could transform subjective chimeras into objective realities.

not; before speaking of force and effectiveness one ought to speak of truth and nothing else. A truth is effective to the extent that we assimilate it; if the truth does not confer on us the strength we need, this only goes to prove that we have not really grasped it. It is not for truth to be dynamic, but for us to be dynamic in function of a true conviction. What is lacking in today's world is a penetrating and comprehensive knowledge of the nature of things; the fundamental truths are always there, but they are not obvious for those who are unwilling to accept them.

It is obvious that we are concerned here, not with the quite external data with which experimental science can possibly provide us, but with realities which that science does not and indeed cannot handle and which are transmitted through quite a different channel, notably that of mythological and metaphysical symbolism. The symbolical language of the great traditions of mankind may indeed seem arduous and baffling to some minds, but it is nevertheless perfectly intelligible in the light of the orthodox commentaries; symbolism—this point must be stressed—is a real and rigorous science, and nothing can be more naïve than to suppose that its apparent naïvety springs from an immature and "prelogical" mentality. This science, which can properly be described as "sacred," quite plainly does not have to adjust itself to the modern experimental approach; the realm of revelation, of symbolism, of pure and direct intellection, stands in fact above both the physical and the psychic realms, and consequently it lies beyond the scope of so-called scientific methods. If we believe we cannot accept the language of traditional symbolism because to us it seems fanciful and arbitrary, this shows we have not yet understood that language, and certainly not that we have advanced beyond it.

Nothing is more misleading than to pretend, as is so speciously done in our day, that the religions have compromised themselves hopelessly in the course of the centuries and that their role is now over. If one knows what a religion really consists of, one also knows that the religions cannot compromise themselves and that they are independent of human abuses; in fact, nothing men do is able to affect the traditional doctrines, symbols, or rites, so long of course as human actions remain on their own level and do not attack sacred things. The fact that a man may exploit religion in order to support national or private interests in no wise affects religion as message and patrimony. In Japan, Shinto, for example, was eventually made to serve political ends, but it was in no wise compromised in itself by this fact, nor could it be. Its symbols, rites, traditions, moral code, and doctrine remain what they always were, from the "Divine Epoch" down to our own times; and as for an exhausting of the religions, one might speak of this if all men had by now become saints or Buddhas. In that case only could it be admitted that the religions were exhausted, at least as regards their forms.

Tradition speaks to each man the language he can comprehend, provided he wishes to listen. The latter proviso is crucial, for tradition, let it be repeated, cannot "become bankrupt"; rather is it of the bankruptcy of man that one should speak, for it is he that has lost all intuition of the supernatural and the sense of the sacred. It is man who has let himself be deceived by the discoveries and inventions of a falsely totalitarian science; that is to say, a science that does not recognize its own proper limits and for that same reason misses whatever lies beyond those limits.

Fascinated alike by scientific phenomena and by the erroneous conclusions he draws from them, man has ended by being submerged by his own creations; he will not realize that a traditional message is situated on quite a different plane or how much more real that plane is, and he allows himself to be dazzled all the more readily since scientism provides him with all the excuses he wants in order to justify his own attachment to the world of appearances and to his ego and his consequent flight from the presence of the Absolute in any form.

People speak of a duty to make oneself useful to society, but they neglect to ask the question whether that society does or does not in itself possess the usefulness that a human society normally should exhibit, for if the individual must be useful to the collectivity, the latter for its part must be useful to the individual, and one must never lose sight of the fact that there exists no higher usefulness than that which envisages the final ends of man. By its divorce from traditional truth—as primarily perceivable in that "flowering forth" that revelation is—society forfeits its own justification, doubtless not in a perfunctorily animal sense, but in the human sense. This human quality implies that the collectivity, as such, cannot be the aim and purpose of the individual but that, on the contrary, it is the individual who, in his solitary station before the Absolute and in the exercise of his supreme function, is the aim and purpose of the collectivity. Man, whether he be conceived in the plural or the singular, or whether his function be direct or indirect, is like "a fragment of absoluteness" and is made for the Absolute; he has no other choice before him. In any case, one can define the social in terms of truth, but one cannot define truth in terms of the social.

Reference is often made to the "selfishness" of those who busy themselves with salvation, and it is said that instead of saving oneself one ought to save others; but this is an absurd kind of argument, since either it is impossible to save others, or else it is possible to save them but only in virtue of our own salvation or of our own effort toward salvation. No man has ever done a service to anyone else whatsoever by remaining "altruistically" attached to his own defects. He who is capable of being a saint but fails to become such certainly will save no one else; it is sheer hypocrisy to conceal one's own weakness and spiritual lukewarmness behind a screen of good works believed to be indispensable and of absolute value.

Another error, closely related to the one just pointed out, consists in supposing that contemplative spirituality is opposed to action or renders a man incapable of acting, a belief that is belied by all the sacred scriptures and especially by the Bhagavad Gita. In Japan the example of saints such as Shotoku Taishi, Hojo Tokimune, Shinran Shonin, and Nichiren proves—if proof is needed—that spirituality is neither opposed to action nor dependent upon it, and also that spirituality leads to the most perfect action whenever circumstances require it, just as it can also, if necessary, turn away from the urge to action when no immediate aim imposes the need for it.

To cut off man from the Absolute and reduce him to a collective phenomenon is to deprive him of all right to existence qua man. If man deserves that so many efforts should be spent on his behalf, this cannot be simply because he exists, eats, and sleeps or because he likes what is pleasant and hates what is unpleasant, for the lowest of the animals share this same modality without therefore being considered our equals and deserving to be treated accordingly. To the objection that man is distinguished from the animals by his intelligence, we will answer that it is precisely this intellectual superiority that the social egalitarianism of the moderns fails to take into account, so much so that an argument that is not applied consistently to men cannot then be turned against the animals. To the objection that man is distinguished from animals by his "culture" we will answer that the completely profane and worldly "culture" in question is nothing more than a specifically dated pastime of the human animal; that is to say, this culture can be anything one pleases, while waiting for the human animal to suppress it altogether. The capacity for absoluteness that characterizes human intelligence is the only thing conferring on man a right of primacy; it is only this capacity that gives him the right to harness a horse to a cart. Tradition, by its otherworldly character, manifests the real superiority of man; tradition alone is a "humanism" in the positive sense of the word. Anti-traditional culture, by the very fact that it is without the sense of the Absolute and even the sense of truth—for these two things go together—could never confer on man that unconditional value and those indisputable rights that modern humanitarianism attributes to him *a priori* and without any logical justification.

The same could also be expressed in another way: When people speak of "culture", they generally think of a host of contingencies, of a thousand ways of uselessly agitating the mind and dispersing one's attention, but they do not think of that principle that alone confers lawfulness on human works; this principle is the transcendent truth, whence springs all genuine culture. It is impossible to defend a culture effectively—such as the traditional culture of Japan, which is one of the most precious in the world—without referring it back to its spiritual principle and without seeking therein the sap that supports life. Agreement as between cultures means agreement on spiritual principles; for truth, despite great differences of expression, remains one.

Many people of our time reason along the following lines: The religions—or the differing spiritual perspectives within a given religion—contradict one another, therefore they cannot all be right; consequently none is true. This is exactly as if one said: Every individual claims to be "I", thus they cannot all be right; consequently none is "I". This example shows the absurdity of the anti-religious argument, by recalling the real analogy between the inevitable external limitation of religious language and the no less inevitable limitation of the human ego. To reach this conclusion, as do the rationalists who use the above argument, amounts in practice to denying the diversity of the knowing subjects as also the diversity of aspects in the object to be known. It amounts to pretending that there are neither points of view nor aspects; that is to say, that there is but a single man to see a mountain and that the mountain has but a single side to be seen. The error of the subjectivist and relativist

7

philosophers is a contrary one. According to them, the mountain would alter its nature according to whoever viewed it; at one time it might be a tree and at another a stream. Only traditional metaphysics does justice both to the rigor of objectivity and to the rights of subjectivity; it alone is able to explain the unanimity of the sacred doctrines as well as the meaning of their formal divergences.

In sound logic, to observe the diversity of religions should give rise to the opposite conclusion, namely: since at all periods and among all peoples religions are to be found that unanimously affirm one absolute and transcendent reality, as also a beyond that receives us according to our merit or knowledge—or according to our demerit and ignorance—there is reason to conclude that every religion is right, and all the more so since the greatest men that have walked the earth have borne witness to spiritual truths. It is possible to admit that all the materialists have been mistaken, but it is not possible to admit that all the founders of religions, all the saints and sages, have been in error and have led others into error; for if one had to admit that error lay with them and not with those who contradicted them, mankind itself would cease to offer any interest, so that a belief in progress or in the possibility of progress would become doubly absurd. If the Buddha or Christ or a Plotinus or a Kobo Daishi were not intelligent, then no one is intelligent, and there is no such thing as human intelligence.

The diversity of religions, far from proving the falseness of all the doctrines concerning the supernatural, shows on the contrary the supra-formal character of revelation and the formal character of ordinary human understanding; the essence of revelation—or enlightenment—is one, but human nature requires diversity. Dogmas or other symbols may contradict one another externally, but they concur internally.

Howbeit, it is easy to foresee the following objection: even if it be admitted that there is a providential and inescapable cause underlying the diversity of religions and even their exoteric incompatibility in certain cases, ought we not then to try to move beyond these differences by creating a single universal religion? To this it must be answered first that these differences have at all times been transcended in the various esotericisms and second that a religion is not something one can create for the asking. Every attempt of this kind would be an error and a failure, and this is all the more certain inasmuch as the age of the great revelations closed centuries ago.

No new religion can see the light of day in our time for the simple reason that time itself, far from being a sort of uniform abstraction, on the contrary alters its value according to every phase of its development. What was still possible a thousand years ago is so no longer, for we are now living in the age known to Buddhist tradition as "the latter times". However, what we are able to do and must do is to respect all the religions—but without any confusion of forms and without asking to be fully understood by every believer—while waiting till Heaven itself wills to unite those things that now are scattered. For we find ourselves on the threshold of great upheavals, and what man himself has neither the power nor the right to realize will be realized by Heaven, when the time for it shall be ripe.

The world is full of people who complain that they have been seeking but have not found; this is because they have not known how to seek and have only looked for sentimentalities of an individualistic kind. One often hears it said that the priests of such and such a religion are no good or that they have brought religion itself to naught, as if this were possible or as if a man who serves his religion badly did not betray himself exclusively; men quite forget the timeless value of symbols and of the graces they vehicle. The saints have at all times suffered from the inadequacy of certain priests; but far from thinking of rejecting tradition itself for that reason, they have by their own sanctity compensated for whatever was lacking in the contemporary priesthood. The only means of "reforming" a religion is to reform oneself. It is indispensable to grasp the fact that a rite vehicles a far greater value than a personal virtue. A personal initiative that takes on a religious form amounts to nothing in the absence of a traditional framework such as alone can justify that initiative and turn it to advantage, whereas a rite at least will always keep fresh the sap of the whole tradition and hence also its principial efficacy—even if men do not know how to profit thereby.

If things were otherwise or if spiritual values were to be found outside the sacred traditions, the function of the saints would have been, not to vivify their religion, but rather to abolish it, and there would no longer be any religion left on earth, or else on the contrary there would be religions by the million, which amounts to the same thing; and these millions of personal pseudo-religions would themselves be changing at every minute. The religions and their orthodox developments—such as the various traditional schools of Buddhism—are inalienable and irreplaceable legacies to which nothing essential can be added and from which nothing essential can be subtracted. We are here, not in order to change these things, but in order to understand them and realize them in ourselves.

Today two dangers are threatening religion: from the outside, its destruction—be it only as a result of its general desertion—and from the inside, its falsification. The latter, with its pseudo-intellectual pretensions and its fallacious professions of "reform", is immeasurably more harmful than all the "superstition" and "corruption" of which, rightly or wrongly, the representatives of the traditional patrimonies have been accused; this heritage is absolutely irreplaceable, and in the face of it men as such are of no account. Tradition is abandoned, not because people are no longer capable of understanding its language, but because they do not wish to understand it, for this language is made to be understood till the end of the world; tradition is falsified by reducing it to flatness on the plea of making it more acceptable to "our time", as if one could—or should—accommodate truth to error. Admittedly, a need to reply to new questions and new forms of ignorance can always arise. One can and must explain the sacred doctrine, but not at the expense of that which gives it its reason for existing, that is to say, not at the expense of its truth and effectiveness. There could be no question, for instance, of adding to the Mahayana or of replacing it by a new vehicle, such as would necessarily be of purely human invention; for the Mahayana—or shall we say Buddhism?—is infinitely sufficient for those who will give themselves the trouble to look higher than their own heads.

One point that has been already mentioned is worth recalling now because of its extreme importance. It is quite out of the question that a "revelation", in the full sense of the word, should arise in our time, one comparable, that is to say, to the imparting of one of the great sutras or any other primary scripture; the day of revelations is past on this globe and was so already long ago. The inspirations of the saints are of another order, but these could in any case never falsify or invalidate tradition or intrinsic orthodoxy by claiming to improve on it or even to replace it, as some people have suggested. "Our own time" possesses no quality that makes it the measure or the criterion of values in regard to that which is timeless. It is the timeless that, by its very nature, is the measure of our time, as indeed of all other times; and if our time has no place for authentic tradition, then it is self-condemned by that very fact. The

Buddha's message, like every other form of the one and only truth, offers itself to every period with an imperishable freshness. It is as true and as urgent in our day as it was two thousand years ago; the fact that mankind finds itself in the "latter days", the days of forgetfulness and decline, only makes that urgency more actual than ever. In fact, there is nothing more urgent, more actual, or more real than metaphysical truth and its demands. It alone can of its own right fill the vacuum left in the contemporary mentality—especially where young people are concerned—by social and political disappointments on the one hand and by the bewildering and indigestible discoveries of modern science on the other. At the risk of repetition let the following point be stressed, for to doubt it would be fatal: to search for an "ideology" in the hopes of filling up that vacuum—as if it were simply a matter of plugging a hole—is truly a case of "putting the cart before the horse". It is a case of subordinating truth and salvation to narrowly utilitarian and in any case quite external ends, as if the sufficient cause of truth could be found somewhere below truth. The sufficient cause of man is to know the truth, which exists outside and above him; the truth cannot depend for its meaning and existence on the wishes of man. The very word "ideology" shows that truth is not the principal aim people have in mind; to use that word shows that one is scarcely concerned with the difference between true and false and that what one is primarily seeking is a mental deception that will be comfortable and workable, or utilizable for purposes of one's own choosing, which is tantamount to abolishing both truth and intelligence.

Outside tradition there can assuredly be found some relative truths or views of partial realities, but outside tradition there does not exist a doctrine that catalyzes absolute truth and transmits liberating notions concerning total reality. Modern science is not a wisdom but an accumulation of physical experiments coupled with many unwarrantable conclusions; it can neither add nor subtract anything in respect of the total truth or of mythological or other symbolism or in respect of the principles and experiences of the spiritual life.

One of the most insidious and destructive illusions is the belief that depth psychology (or in other words psychoanalysis) has the slightest connection with spiritual life, whose teachings it persistently falsifies by confusing inferior elements with superior. We cannot be too wary of all these attempts to reduce the values vehicled by tradition to the level of phenomena supposed to be scientifically controllable. The spirit escapes the hold of profane science in an absolute fashion. It is not the positive results of experimental science that one is out to deny (always assuming that they really are positive in a definite sense) but the absurd claim of science to cover everything possible, the whole of truth, the whole of the real; this quasi-religious claim to totality moreover proves the falseness of the point of departure. If one takes into account the very limited realm within which science moves, the least one can say is that nothing justifies the so-called scientific denials of the beyond and of the Absolute.

If it is essential to distinguish between the realm of religion or traditional wisdom and that of experimental science, it is also essential to distinguish between the intellect, which is intuitive, and reason, which is discursive; reason is a limited faculty, whereas the intellect opens out upon the Universal and the Divine. For metaphysical wisdom, reason only possesses a dialectical, not an enlightening, usefulness; reason is not capable of grasping in a concrete way that which lies beyond the world of forms, though reason is able to reach further than imagination. All ratiocination condemns itself to ignorance from the moment it claims to deal with the roots of our existence and of our spirit.

We all know that the need to account for things in terms of causality, as felt by modern man, is apt to remain unsatisfied in the face of the ancient mythologies; but the fact is that attempts to explain the mythological order with the aid of reasonings that are necessarily arbitrary and vitiated by all sorts of prejudices are bound to fail in any case. Symbolisms reveal their true meaning only in the light of the contemplative intellect, which is analogically represented in man by the heart and not by the brain. Pure intellect—or intuition and supra-rational intelligence—can flower only in the framework of a traditional orthodoxy, by reason of the complementary and therefore necessary relationship between intellection and revelation.

The fundamental intention of every religion or wisdom is the following: first, discernment between the real and the unreal, and then concentration upon the real. One could also formulate this intention in these terms: truth and the way, *prajñā* and *upāya*, doctrine and its corresponding method. One must know that the Absolute or the Infinite—whatever may be the names given it by respective traditions—is what gives meaning to our existence, just as one must know that the essential content of life is the consciousness of this supreme reality, a fact that explains the part to be played by continual prayer; in a word we live to realize the Absolute. To realize the Absolute is to think of it, under one form or another as indicated by revelation and tradition, by a form such as the Japanese *nembutsu* or the Tibetan *Om mani padme hum* or the Hindu *japa-yoga*, not forgetting the Christian and Islamic invocations, such as the Jesus Prayer and the *dhikr* of the dervishes. Here one will find some very different modalities, not only as between one religion and another but also within the fold of each religion, as can be shown, for instance, by the difference between Jodo Shinshu and Zen. However this may be, it is only on the basis of a genuine spiritual life that we can envisage any kind of external action with a view to defending truth and spirituality in the world.

All the traditional doctrines agree in this: from a strictly spiritual point of view, though not necessarily from other much more relative and therefore less important points of view, mankind is becoming more and more corrupted; the ideas of "evolution", of "progress", and of a single "civilization" are in effect the most pernicious pseudo-dogmas the world has ever produced, for there is no newfound error that does not eagerly attach its own claims to the above beliefs. We say not that evolution is nonexistent, but that it has a partial and most often a quite external applicability; if there is evolution on the one hand, there are degenerations on the other, and it is in any case radically false to suppose that our ancestors were intellectually, spiritually, or morally our inferiors. To suppose this is the most childish of "optical delusions"; human weakness alters its style in the course of history, but not its nature. A question that now arises is as follows: Seeing that humanity is decaying inescapably and seeing that the final crisis with its cosmic consummation as foretold in the sacred books is inevitable, *what then can we do?* Does an external activity still have any meaning?

To this it must be answered that an affirmation of the truth, or any effort on behalf of truth, is never in vain, even if we cannot measure beforehand the value or the outcome of such an activity. Moreover we have no choice in the matter. Once we know the truth, we must live in it and fight for it; but what we must avoid at any price is to let ourselves bask in illusions. Even if, at this moment, the horizon seems as dark as possible, one must not forget that in a perhaps unavoidably distant future the victory is ours and cannot but be ours. Truth by its very nature conquers all obstacles: *Vincit omnia veritas.*

Therefore, every initiative taken with a view to harmony between the different cultures and for the defense of spiritual values is good, if it has as its basis a recognition of the great principial truths and consequently also a recognition of tradition or of the traditions.

"When the inferior man hears talk about Tao, he only laughs at it; it would not be Tao if he did not laugh at it.... [T]he self-evidence of Tao is taken for a darkness." These words of Lao-tzu were never more timely than now. Errors cannot but be, as long as their quite relative possibility has not reached its term; but for the Absolute errors have never been and never shall be. On their own plane they are what they are, but it is the Changeless that shall have the final say.

A MATERIAL CIVILIZATION*

René Guénon

From all that has been said so far it already seems to follow clearly that those Orientals who reproach modern Western civilization with being a purely material one are fully justified; it is certainly in this direction exclusively that its development has taken place, and from whatever point of view one may look at it, one is always faced with the more or less direct consequences of this materialization. Nevertheless, there still remains something to add to what we have said on the subject and in the first place it is necessary to explain the different ways in which a word like "materialism" can be understood: if we use it to describe the contemporary world, various people, who do not believe themselves to be materialists at all while at the same time claiming to be modern in their outlook, will not fail to protest in the belief that this is sheer calumny; some further explanation therefore is required in order to forestall any ambiguity which might arise on the subject.

It is a significant fact that the word "materialism" itself dates back only as far as the eighteenth century; it was invented by the philosopher Berkeley, who used it to denote any theory admitting the real existence of matter; it is hardly necessary to say that it is not this use of the word which concerns us here, the question of the existence of matter not being in dispute. Soon afterwards the same word took on a more restricted meaning, which it has retained ever since: it came to denote a conception according to which nothing exists at all except matter and its derivatives; and it is important to emphasize the novelty of such a conception and the fact that it is essentially a product of the modern outlook, corresponding therefore at least to a part of its inherent tendencies.[1] But it is above all

---

* Editor's Note: Chapter 7 of *The Crisis of the Modern World,* first published in the French original in 1927.

[1] Prior to the eighteenth century there were "mechanistic" theories, from Greek atomism down to Cartesian physics, but mechanism should not be confused with materialism, despite certain affinities which may have subsequently brought about a kind of fellowship between them [Editor's Note: A footnote included in the Arthur Osborne translation, but not present in the Marco Pallis translation].

in a different and much wider, though at the same time quite definite sense that we propose to speak of "materialism" in the present chapter; the word is here taken as referring to an entire mental outlook, of which the conception we have just described amounts to no more than one manifestation among many others, being in itself independent of any philosophical theory. This mental outlook is one which consists in more or less consciously giving preponderance to things belonging to the material order and to preoccupations relating thereto, whether these preoccupations still retain a certain speculative appearance or whether they remain purely practical ones; and it cannot be seriously denied that this is, in fact, the mental attitude of the great majority of our contemporaries.

The whole of the "profane" science which has been developed during the course of recent centuries is confined to the study of the sensible world: its horizon is bounded exclusively by that world and its methods apply within that sphere only; but these methods have been proclaimed "scientific" to the exclusion of all others, an attitude which amounts to repudiating the existence of any science not dealing with material things. Among those who think thus, and even among those who have devoted their lives especially to the sciences in question, there are however many who would refuse to call themselves "materialists" or to accept the philosophical theory which bears that name; there are even some who readily profess a religious faith, the sincerity of which is beyond question; yet their scientific outlook does not differ appreciably from that of avowed materialists. From the religious point of view it has often been debated whether modern science ought to be denounced as atheistical or as materialistic, but this question, more often than not, has been wrongly framed; it is quite apparent that such a science does not deliberately profess either atheism or materialism, and that it is content to ignore certain things as a result of its preconceptions, though without formally denying them as this or that philosopher might do; in connection with modern science, therefore, one can only speak of a *de facto* materialism, or of what we would willingly term a practical materialism; but the evil is then perhaps all the more serious in that it penetrates deeper and is more widely diffused.

A philosophical attitude can be something quite superficial, even among "professional" philosophers; furthermore, there are certain mentalities which shrink from an actual negation, but which can accommodate themselves to an attitude of complete indifference; and this is the most dangerous attitude of all, since in order to deny something it is still necessary to think about it to some extent, however slightly, whereas an attitude of indifference makes it possible to avoid giving any thought to it whatsoever. When an exclusively material science sets itself up as the only possible science and when men have got into the habit of accepting as an unquestionable truth the doctrine that no valid knowledge can exist apart from it, and when all the education which is imparted to them tends to inculcate the "superstition" of that science (or "scientism" as it should then be termed), how can such men fail to be anything but materialists in practice, or in other words, how can they fail to have all their preoccupations turned in the direction of matter?

It seems that nothing exists for modern man other than what can be seen and touched; or at least, even if they admit theoretically that something else may exist they hasten to declare it not merely unknown but "unknowable," which absolves them from having to give it further thought. If nevertheless some persons still are to be found who try to form some kind of idea of an "other world," relying as they do on nothing but their imagination they picture it in the likeness of the terrestrial world and transfer to it all the conditions belonging to that world, including space and time and even a sort of "corporeality"; in speaking elsewhere of spiritualistic conceptions we have given some very striking examples of this kind of grossly materialized representation; but if the beliefs there referred to represent an extreme case in which this particular feature is exaggerated to the point of caricature, it would be a mistake to suppose that spiritualism and the sects more or less akin to it retain the monopoly of this kind of thing. Indeed, in a more general way, the intrusion of the imagination into realms where it can yield no useful results, and which ought normally to remain closed to it, is a fact which in itself shows very clearly how incapable modern Westerners have become of raising themselves above the realm of the senses; there are many who do not know how to distinguish between "conceiving" and "imagining," and some philosophers, such as Kant, go so far as to declare "inconceivable" and "unthinkable" everything that is not capable of representation. In the same way everything that goes by the name of "spiritualism" or "idealism" usually amounts to no more than a sort of transposed materialism; this applies not only to what we have described as "neo-spiritualism," but also to philosophical spiritualism, although the latter considers itself to be the very opposite of materialism. The fact is that spiritualism and materialism, in the philosophical sense of these expressions, have no significance apart from one another: they are simply two halves of the Cartesian dualism, whose radical separation has been turned into a kind of antagonism; and, since then, the whole of philosophy has oscillated between these two terms without being able to pass beyond them. Spiritualism, in spite of its name, has nothing to do with spirituality; its conflict with materialism can be of no interest to those who place themselves at a higher standpoint and who see that these opposites are fundamentally very near to being equivalent, their supposed opposition reducing itself, on many points, to a merely verbal disagreement.

The moderns, generally speaking, cannot conceive of any other science except that which deals with things that can be measured, counted, or weighed, material things that is to say, since it is to these alone that the quantitative point of view is applicable; and the claim to reduce quality to quantity is most characteristic of modern science. In this direction the stage has been reached even of supposing that there can be no science at all, in the real sense of the word, except where it is possible to introduce measurement, and that there can be no scientific laws except those which express quantitative relations; Descartes' "mechanism" marked the birth of this tendency, which has grown more and more pronounced ever since, the rejection of Cartesian physics notwithstanding, for it is not a tendency connected with any particular theory but with an altogether general conception of scientific knowledge. Nowadays people try to apply measurement even in the field of psychology, which lies beyond its reach from its very nature; they end by ceasing to understand that the possibility of measurement rests solely upon a property inherent in matter, namely its indefinite divisibility, unless indeed it be supposed that the same property is to be found in everything that exists, which amounts to materializing everything. As we have already remarked, it is matter which is the principle of division and pure multiplicity; the predominance attributed to the quantitative point of view, and extended, as we have already shown, to the social domain, does therefore indeed constitute materialism in the sense mentioned above, although it need not necessarily be connected with philosophical materialism, which, as a matter of fact, it preceded historically in the course of development of the tendencies inherent in the modern outlook. We will not dwell upon the error of seeking to reduce quality to quantity or upon the inadequacy of all those attempts at explanation conforming more or less to the mechanistic type; that is not our present purpose and we will only remark, in this connection, that even within the sensible order a science of this type has but little connection with reality, of which the greater part must necessarily lie outside its scope.

While speaking of "reality" another fact should be mentioned, which might easily be overlooked by many, but which is very significant as a sign of the mentality we are describing: we refer to the habit of using the word "reality" exclusively to denote reality belonging to the sensible order. As language is the expression of the mentality of a people or of a period, one must conclude from this that for those who speak in this manner everything that cannot be grasped by the senses is illusory and even totally non-existent; it is possible that they are not fully conscious of the fact, but this negative conviction is none the less the underlying one, and if they assert the contrary one may be sure that this assertion is only the expression of some much more superficial element in their mentality, although they happen not to be conscious of the fact, and that their protest may even be a purely verbal one. If this should seem to be an exaggeration one has only to try and ascertain, for example, what the supposed religious convictions of a great many people amount to; a few notions learnt by heart in a purely academic and mechanical way without any real assimilation, notions to which they have never given any serious consideration, but which they retain in their memory and repeat on occasion because they form part of a certain formal and conventional attitude, which is all they are able to understand by the word religion. We have already referred to this "minimizing" of religion, of which the "verbalism" we mentioned represents one of the latest phases: it is this which explains why many so-called "believers" in no wise fall short of the "unbelievers" in the matter of practical materialism; we shall return to this question later, but first we must conclude our investigation of the materialistic nature of modern science, since this is a subject that requires to be treated from various angles.

Attention must once again be drawn to a point that has been mentioned earlier; the modern sciences do not possess the character of disinterested knowledge, nor does their speculative value, even for those who believe in it, amount to much more than a mask behind which purely practical considerations lie concealed, one which makes it possible nevertheless to retain the illusion of a false intellectuality. Descartes himself, in working out his physics, was already primarily concerned with extracting from it a system of mechanics, medicine, and morality, and a still greater change came with the spread of the Anglo-Saxon empiricism; moreover, the prestige of science in the eyes of the general public rests almost solely upon the practical results it makes attainable because, here again, it is a question of things that can be seen and touched. We have said that pragmatism represents the final outcome of all the modern philosophy and marks the lowest stage in its decline; but outside the philosophical field there also exists, and has already existed for a long time, a diffused and unsystematized pragmatism which is to philosophical pragmatism what practical materialism is to philosophical materialism, and which merges into what people generally call "common sense." This almost instinctive utilitarianism is inseparable, moreover, from the materialistic tendency: common sense consists in not venturing beyond the terrestrial horizon, as well as in not paying attention to anything devoid of an immediate practical interest; it is "common sense," above all, that regards the world of the senses as alone being real and admits of no knowledge beyond what proceeds from the senses; and even this limited degree of knowledge is of value in its eyes only in so far as it allows of satisfying material needs and also sometimes because it feeds a certain kind of sentimentalism, since sentiment, as must be frankly admitted at the risk of shocking contemporary "moralism," really is very closely related to matter. No room is left in all this for intelligence, except in so far as it may consent to be put to the service of practical ends, acting as a mere instrument subordinated to the requirements of the lowest or corporeal portion of the human individual, "a tool for making tools," to quote a significant expression of Bergson's: "pragmatism" in all its forms amounts to a complete indifference to truth.

Under these conditions industry can no longer by considered simply as an application of science, one of which science in itself ought to remain completely independent; it becomes the very object and justification of science, so that in this realm also we find that the normal relations have been reversed. What the modern world has devoted its entire energy to bringing about, even when it has claimed to be pursuing science in its own way, is really nothing but the development of industry and machinery; and in thus seeking to dominate matter and to mold it to their purposes, men have only succeeded, as we said at the beginning, in turning themselves into its slaves; for not only have they restricted their intellectual ambitions—if it is permissible to use such an expression in this instance—to the invention and construction of machines, but they have also ended by turning into mere machines themselves. Indeed "specialization," so enthusiastically advocated by certain sociologists under the name of a "division of labor," has imposed itself not only upon scholars but also upon technicians and even ordinary laborers, and for the latter all intelligent work has thereby been rendered impossible; very different from the craftsmen of former times, they have become no more than servants of machines, forming as it were a single unit with them; in a purely mechanical way they are obliged to repeat continually certain prescribed movements, which never vary and are always performed in the same way, so as to avoid the slightest loss of time; at least such are the requirements of those American methods which are considered to represent the most advanced stage of "progress." The fact is that it is solely a question of producing the greatest possible quantity; quality receives scant attention and it is quantity alone that counts; we are brought back once more to the same conclusion that we had already reached in other fields: modern civilization can justly be described as a quantitative civilization, which is only another way of saying that it is a material civilization.

To convince oneself more completely of the truth of this statement one has only to notice the tremendous influence exerted nowadays by economic factors alike on the lives of peoples and of individuals; industry, commerce, finance, these seem to be the only things that count; and this agrees with what we have already remarked elsewhere about the only surviving social distinctions being based upon material wealth. Politics appear to be altogether dominated by economics and commercial competition exercises a preponderant influence upon the relations between peoples; it may be that this is only so in appearance and that these factors are not so much causes as means of action; but the selection of such means clearly indicates the nature of the age which finds them opportune.

Moreover, our contemporaries are convinced that it is economic conditions that dictate historical events almost exclusively, and they even imagine that this has always been the case; a theory has even been invented according to which everything is explainable in terms of economic factors alone, and it bears the significant name of "historical materialism." Here also may be seen the effect of one of those processes of suggestion to which we have already referred, the power of which is all the greater in that they correspond with the tendencies of the general mentality; and the result in this case is that economic factors have really come to decide almost everything that occurs in the social sphere. It is doubtless true that the masses have always been led in one way or another, and it could be said that their part in history consists primarily in allowing themselves to be led, since they represent a predominantly passive element, a *materia* in the Aristotelian sense of the word; but in order to lead them today it is sufficient to possess oneself of purely material means, taking the word matter this time in its ordinary sense, and this clearly shows to what depths the present age has sunk; and at the same time these same masses are made to believe that they are not being led, but that they are acting spontaneously and governing themselves, and the fact that they believe this to be true gives an idea of the extent of their unintelligence.

As economic factors have been mentioned, we will take the opportunity to draw attention to an all too common illusion on the subject, which consists in imagining that relations established in the field of trade can serve to draw people closer together and bring about an understanding between them, whereas in reality the effect is just the contrary. Matter, as we have often pointed out, partakes essentially of the nature of multiplicity and division, and is therefore a source of struggle and conflict; similarly, whether it be a case of peoples or of individuals, the economic sphere remains and cannot but remain one of a rivalry of interests. In particular the West cannot count upon industry, any more than upon modern science which is inseparable from it, to supply a basis for an understanding with the East; if Orientals get to the point of accepting this industry as a troublesome, though transitory, necessity—and for them it could hardly amount to more than that—it will only be as a weapon enabling them to resist the invasion of the West and to safeguard their own existence. It is important to understand that things could not well be otherwise: those Orientals who resign themselves to the prospect of economic competition with the West, in spite of the repugnance they feel for this kind of activity, can only do so with one purpose in mind, namely to rid themselves of a foreign domination based on brute force, on the material power, that is to say, which industry places at its disposal; violence calls forth violence, but it should be recognized that it is not the Orientals who have solicited conflict in this field.

Furthermore, apart from the question of relations between East and West, it is easy to see that one of the most conspicuous results of industrial development is the continual perfecting of engines of war and the formidable increase in their powers of destruction. This alone should be enough to shatter the pacifist dreams of certain admirers of modern "progress"; but these dreamers and "idealists" are incorrigible and their credulity seems to know no bounds. Certainly the "humanitarianism" at present so much in vogue does not deserve to be taken seriously; but it is strange that people should talk so much about putting an end to war at a time when the ravages it causes are greater than they have ever been before, not only because the means of destruction have been multiplied, but also because, since wars are no longer fought between comparatively small armies composed entirely of professional soldiers, all the individuals on both sides are flung against each other indiscriminately, including those who are least qualified to carry out this kind of function. Here again is a typical example of present-day confusion, and it is truly amazing, for anyone who cares to think about it, that a "mass call-up" or "general mobilization" should have come to be considered quite a natural thing and that, with very few exceptions, the minds of all should have accepted the idea of an "armed nation." In this also one can see a result of the belief in the power of numbers alone: it is in keeping with the quantitative character of modern civilization to set in motion enormous masses of combatants; and at the same time in this way the demands of "equalitarianism" are satisfied as well as by means of such institutions as "compulsory education." Let it be added that these generalized wars have only been made possible by the arising of another specifically modern phenomenon, that is to say by the formation of "nations," a consequence, on the one hand, of the destruction of the feudal system, and, on the other, of the simultaneous disruption of the higher unity of medieval Christendom; and, without pausing to consider a subject that would carry us too far afield, let it be pointed out that matters have been made still worse, by the refusal to recognize any spiritual authority, which, under normal conditions, should be an effective arbiter, occupying a position, as it must do of its very nature, above all the conflicts pertaining to the political order. Repudiation of the spiritual authority is in its way also an example of practical materialism; and even those people who in theory claim to recognize such an authority, refuse in practice to allow it any real influence or any power of intervention in the social sphere, exactly in the same way that they fence off religion from the concerns of their everyday existence; whether in public or in private life, it is the same mental attitude that prevails.

Even admitting that material development offers certain advantages, though only from a very relative standpoint, it may well be asked whether, in view of such consequences as we have just been describing, those advantages are not heavily outweighed by other disadvantages. We are not thinking of the many things of incomparably greater worth that have been sacrificed for the sake of this one type of development, of the higher forms of knowledge that have been forgotten, of the intellectuality that has been destroyed and the spirituality that has disappeared; simply taking modern civilization for what it is in itself it can well be maintained that, if the advantages and disadvantages of what has been brought about were to be compared, the result might even so, on balance, prove to be a negative one. Inventions, which at present go on being multiplied with ever-increasing momentum, are all the more dangerous because they call into play forces the real nature of which is completely unknown to the very people that make use of them; and this demonstrates conclusively the worthlessness of modern science from the explanatory point of view, as knowledge that is to say, even when limited to the physical sphere: at the same time the fact that these considerations in no wise cause practical applications to be restrained proves that this science is far from being disinterested and that it is industry which is the only real object of its researches. As the danger of these inventions—even of those not purposely designed to play a fatal part where mankind is concerned, and which nevertheless cause so many catastrophes, not to mention unsuspected disturbances in the terrestrial environment—as this danger, we say, will no doubt continue to grow to an extent that is difficult to foretell, it is permissible to suppose, without too much improbability, that it is perhaps by this means that the modern world will succeed in bringing about its own destruction, unless it can check its present breakneck course while there is yet time.

As far as modern inventions are concerned, however, it is not enough to criticize them on the grounds that they are dangerous, and we must go further than that; people speak of the "benefits" of what they have become accustomed to call "progress," and which one might agree to describe thus so long as care is taken to point out clearly that the progress is of a purely material kind; but are not these so highly esteemed "benefits" largely deceptive? Today men claim that they are increasing their "welfare" by this means; in our belief this goal which they are aiming at, even if it actually were to be attained, is not worth the expenditure of so great an effort; but, at the same time, it seems extremely debatable whether it is being attained. In the first place, the fact should be taken into account that not all men have the same tastes or the same needs and that there are still some who, in spite of everything, might wish to avoid the modern restlessness and mania for speed, but who are no longer in a position to do so; can anyone presume to maintain that it is a "benefit" to these people to have imposed upon them what is so entirely contrary to their own nature? The answer will be given that such people are few in number nowadays, and therefore that there is every justification for regarding them as a negligible minority, just as also in the field of politics the majority arrogates to itself the right to crush minorities, which, in its eyes, have evidently no right to exist, since their very existence runs counter to the "equalitarian" passion for uniformity. But, if one takes mankind in its entirety instead of limiting one's view to the inhabitants of the Western world, the question assumes a different aspect; has not the majority of a moment ago now become a minority? But it is no longer the same argument which is made to serve in this case and, by a peculiar contradiction, it is in the name of their "superiority" that the "equalitarians" seek to impose their own civilization on the rest of the world, and to cause trouble among people who have never asked them for anything; and as this "superiority" exists solely in a material sense it is only natural that it should be imposed by the crudest means. Let there be no mistake about it: if the general public accepts the pretext of "civilization" in all good faith, there are some for whom it amounts to no more than mere moralist hypocrisy, a cloak for their designs of conquest and economic ambition; but what strange times indeed, when so many men allow themselves to be persuaded that they are making a people happy by reducing them to subjection, by robbing them of what is most precious in their eyes, namely their own civilization, by compelling them to adopt customs and institutions which were intended for another race, and by coercing them into assuming the most distasteful occupations in order that they may perforce come to acquire things for which they have not the slightest use! That however is the position today: the modern West cannot tolerate the idea that men should prefer to work less and be content to live on little; as quantity alone counts, and as everything that eludes the grasp of the senses is held moreover to be nonexistent, it is taken for granted that anyone not producing material things must be an "idler"; without even taking into account the criticism commonly leveled at the Orientals on this score, one has only to observe the attitude adopted by Europeans towards their own contemplative orders, even in supposedly religious circles. In such a world there is no longer any room for intellectuality or for what is of a purely inward nature, for those are things which can neither be seen nor touched, weighed nor counted; there is only room for outward action in all its forms, including those most completely devoid of meaning. Furthermore it is not surprising that the Anglo-Saxon passion for "sport" gains more and more ground every day; the ideal of the modern world is the "human animal" who has developed his muscular strength to the utmost; its heroes are the athletes, should they even be brutes; it is they who awaken the popular enthusiasm and it is their exploits that command the passionate interest of the crowd; a world in which such things are possible has indeed sunk low and would seem to be nearing its end.

However, let us put ourselves for a moment in the position of those who pin their hopes to the ideal of material welfare and who therefore rejoice at all the improvements to life furnished by modern "progress"; are they quite sure that they are not being made dupes? Is it true that men are happier today than they used to be simply because they command swifter means of transport and other things of that kind, or because of their more agitated and complicated mode of life? The truth would appear to be quite the contrary; disequilibrium cannot be the condition of any real happiness; moreover, the more needs a man has the greater likelihood there is of his lacking something, and consequently of his being unhappy; modern civilization aims at creating ever greater and greater artificial needs, and, as we have already remarked, it will always create more needs than it can satisfy, because, once launched upon such a course, it becomes exceedingly difficult to pull up, and, indeed, there is no reason for pulling up at one stage rather than at another. It was no hardship for people to do without things that did not exist and which they could never have even dreamed of; now, on the contrary, they are bound to suffer when deprived of those things, since they have grown accustomed to regarding them as necessities, with the result that they have in fact really become necessary to them. Consequently, with all the power at their disposal, they struggle to acquire whatever can procure them material satisfactions, the only kind they are capable of appreciating; they become absorbed in "making money," because it is money which enables them to obtain these things, and the more they possess the more they desire because they are continually discovering fresh needs, until this pursuit becomes their only aim in life. Hence that ferocious competition which certain "evolutionists" have raised to the dignity of a scientific law under the name of the "struggle for existence," the logical result of which is that only the strongest, in the most narrowly material sense of the word, have a right to exist. Hence also the envy and even hatred with which those possessed of wealth are regarded by those who are not so endowed; how could men to whom equalitarian theories have been preached fail to react when all around they see inequality in the most material order of things, the order to which they are bound to be most sensitive? If modern civilization is destined to collapse some day under the pressure of the disorderly appetites it has aroused in the masses, one would have to be blind indeed not to perceive therein the just punishment of its fundamental vice, or, to express oneself without recourse to moral phraseology, the repercussion of its own action in that same sphere in which it was exercised. It is written in the Gospel: "All they that take the sword shall perish by the sword"; those who unloose the brute forces of matter will perish, crushed by those same forces, of which they are no longer masters when they rashly set them in motion, and which they cannot claim to hold back indefinitely once launched on their fatal course; forces of nature or forces of mass man, or both in combination, it makes little difference, because in either case it is the laws of matter which come into play and which will inexorably destroy those who believed it possible to manipulate them without themselves rising superior to matter. The Gospel also says: "If a house be divided against itself, that house cannot stand"; this saying too is directly applicable to the modern world with its material civilization, which cannot fail, from its very nature, to provoke strife and division in all directions. The conclusion is only too easy to draw and further considerations need not be elaborated in order to enable one, without fear of deception, to predict a tragic end to the present world, unless a radical change, amounting to a complete reversal of direction, should intervene within a very short time.

We are well aware that some people will reproach us with having omitted to mention, while describing modern civilization and its materialism, certain elements which seem at least to mitigate it to a certain extent; and indeed, if none such existed it is highly probable that this civilization would have perished miserably long since. We do not therefore in any way dispute the existence of such elements, but at the same time we must not let ourselves fall into illusions; on the one hand, it would be incorrect to include under this heading the various philosophical movements bearing labels such as "spiritualism" or "idealism," or anything among contemporary tendencies that takes the form of "moralism" or "sentimentalism"; we have already sufficiently discussed these questions and we will simply recall the fact that, from our point of view, these attitudes of mind are not less profane than a theoretical or practical materialism and are in reality much less far remote from it than might appear at first sight; on the other hand, if some remnants of true spirituality have been preserved, that can only be in spite of the modern outlook and in opposition to it. As far as strictly Western elements are concerned, it is in the religious sphere only that these remnants of spirituality are still to be found; but we have already pointed out how shrunken has become the conception of religion at the present time, and what a shallow and mediocre idea even believers themselves have formed of it and to what an extent it has been emptied of its intellectuality, which is but one and the same thing as true spirituality; under these conditions, if certain possibilities still remain, they scarcely do so more than latently, and their effective influence at present amounts to very little. The vigor of a religious tradition is nevertheless to be admired when, though withdrawn into a kind of virtuality, it survives in spite of all the attempts made during several centuries to stifle and annihilate it; and, if one pauses to think about it, it will be apparent that there is something about a resistance of this kind implying the presence of a more than human power; but, once again let it be repeated, the tradition in question does not belong to the modern world, nor does it form one of its component elements, but is the exact opposite of all its tendencies and aspirations. It is necessary to say this openly and not look for deceptive reconciliations; between the religious point of view, in the true sense of the word, and the modern attitude of mind there can be nothing but antagonism; any compromise can but serve to enfeeble the former and strengthen the latter, nor will the hostility of the modern mentality be lessened on that account, since it cannot help desiring the total destruction of everything in mankind that reflects a reality superior to the human.

It is said that the modern West is Christian, but this is a mistake: the modern outlook is anti-Christian because it is essentially anti-religious; and it is anti-religious because, in a still wider sense, it is anti-traditional; it is this that gives it its particular character and causes it to be what it is. Assuredly, something of Christianity has passed over even into the anti-Christian civilization of our time, with the result that its most "advanced" representatives (as they style themselves in their own special language) cannot help having undergone and continuing to undergo, involuntarily and perhaps unconsciously, a certain Christian influence, if only an indirect one; this is so because a break with the past, however radical, can never be altogether complete and such as to preclude all continuity. We will go further and say that everything of any value still to be found in the modern world came to it from Christianity, or at any rate through Christianity, which brought with it the whole heritage of former traditions and has kept that heritage alive, in so far as the conditions of the West permitted, and still bears its latent possibilities within itself; but, even among those calling themselves Christians, is there anyone at the present time who retains a full consciousness of these possibilities? Where, even in Catholicism, are to be found the men who understand the deeper meaning of the doctrine they profess outwardly, and who are not simply content with "believing" in a more or less superficial way, sentimentally rather than through the intelligence, but who really "know" the truth of the religious tradition which they claim for their own? One would indeed welcome some evidence of the existence of at least a few such people, for that would be the greatest and perhaps the only hope of salvation for the West; but it must be admitted that up to the present time none have made themselves known; can it be supposed that, like certain sages of the East, they live apart in some inaccessible retreat, or must this last hope be finally abandoned? The West was Christian in the Middle Ages but is so no longer; if it be said that it might become so again, there is no one who can desire this more fervently than ourselves, and may it come about in a shorter time than all that is to be seen around would lead one to suppose; but let no man delude himself on the subject; if this should happen, the modern world will have had its day.

TRADITION AND THE INDIVIDUAL*

Brian Keeble

The idea of tradition has long preoccupied the modern mind. No doubt the sense of its loss as well as the realization of its importance for the ordering and orientation of human affairs are the cause of this concern. This being said, however, tradition is seldom understood in its primal sense. In the anti-traditional milieu that is the modern world, the word is misused in ways both deliberate and unconscious. The word "tradition" is now likely to figure in the dismissal of any custom or practice whose meaning is no longer understood, or in conjunction with any matter that is deemed to be out of date and irrelevant to modern interests. In fact, the modern mind is founded upon a relentlessly progressive stance according to which tradition is more or less thought of as the corpse of the past and is best disposed of, the sooner the better.

But for all that the modern mind cannot relinquish entirely the idea of tradition and has at times taken some pains to distinguish and define it. Of equal importance has been the problem—one might say the anxiety—of establishing a true relationship between tradition and the individual. This relationship necessarily accompanies the idea of tradition since it is one of the primary functions of a tradition, in relation to culture, to unite in a common principle that which would otherwise appear to be an unending stream of unrelated ideas and events.

During the early part of this century a number of writers whose views on tradition were subsequently to prove influential tackled the subject in books and essays. Perhaps the best known of these was T.S. Eliot's essay "Tradition and the Individual Talent," in which he seemed to many to have established the terms and extent of the subject from the modern point of view. Far less widely known was the more profound notion of tradition formulated by René Guénon, A.K. Coomaraswamy, Frithjof Schuon and others. Whereas Eliot's

---

* Editor's Note: Chapter 2 of *Conversing with Paradise*.

notion of tradition was drawn up on the basis of European culture, the idea of tradition that we find in the works of Guénon and his associates is founded on the universal metaphysical principles that have been the perennial bedrock of the world's religions. We will return later to Eliot's more familiar ideas. For the moment let us take a closer look at this perennial notion of tradition and its relationship with history and the individual.

The word "tradition," like many other words one can offer as examples of extreme semantic depreciation in contemporary usage, being allowed to mean almost anything inevitably comes to mean almost nothing.[1] The difficulty is here compounded simply because the concept of tradition contains a superabundant richness of connotations such as to make neatness of definition, even if it were desirable, near to impossible. It is the same with tradition as with all things whose origin needs to be traced back to Revelation. The problem remains one of grasping the ontological mystery of the passage from essence to manifestation—from beyond the realm of time and space to the world of continuous generation and decay.

The word "tradition" (from the Greek *paradidormi*, Latin *traditio*) indicates a transmission, a handing over, a handing down of something. Clearly such a transmission must involve some sort of language, whether written or pronounced. The *what* and the *how* of this transmission comprise the two primary aspects of tradition. The content of tradition implies a vertical axis of descent as to its transhuman and integrative principle while its *modus operandi* implies a horizontal chain of transmission whose continuity is other than the historical process of change itself. It is important not to confuse the content and transmission of tradition with the temporal succession of history, since to do so is to impoverish the very means by which man is attached to the sacred.

---

[1] Of the word "myth," for example, we have at the one extreme Coomaraswamy's "myth embodies the nearest approach to absolute truth that can be stated in words," and at the other the *Shorter Oxford Dictionary*'s "a purely fictitious narrative": this last eliciting from David Jones, "a bloody lie in fact ... that is about the limit in loss of meaning." Elsewhere, with his characteristic eye to the incarnational quality of history, he glosses the word as follows: "To conserve, to develop, to bring together, to make significant for the present what the past holds, without dilution or any deleting, but rather by understanding and transubstantiating the material, this is the function of genuine myth, neither pedantic nor popularizing, not indifferent to scholarship, nor antiquarian, but saying always: 'of those thou has given me have I lost none' (John 17:12)" (*Epoch and Artist* [London, 1959], p. 243).

Indeed, both content and transmission must remain attached to their transcendent principle if tradition is to be saved from an "evolution" in which it becomes something other than what is potential to it "in the beginning." Being a form of initiation, a tradition must be transmitted in conformity with the integral meaning and possibility of the principle it expresses and from which it derives its being (Christian Love; Moslem Unity; Buddhist Self). Assuredly a tradition can "develop," for it is a living thing, but such development is always an extension and an application of its principle as opposed to its assimilation to any purely historical process. Any such assimilation can result in the weakening of the ontological links that bind a tradition to its reflection in a civilization and a culture, since in the very act of transmission there remains the possibility of dissolution and involvement with profane knowledge and conceptions.

Tradition, then, is far from being an accumulation of human endeavor and fabrication even if it does have a history. Even if we grant that the embodiment of a tradition in a civilization is colored and conditioned by the characteristics of a particular historical period, none the less we have to recognize that the atemporal, supra formal principle of a tradition, that which gives it its power to unite in a common understanding the diversity of what is scattered throughout time and place, is proof enough that a tradition, though it is in time, is not of it. Which is to say a tradition has both a transcendent and an immanent aspect. It is in virtue of its Divine principle that attachment to and immersion in a tradition becomes a mode of internal witness which provides the objectification that lifts the human subject clear of what would be a meaningless succession of historical events, and from which no individual could otherwise ever hope to extricate himself. Insofar as man makes "sense" of history, or strives to do so, he depends upon the effective reality of this supra formal principle to save himself from being engulfed by the determinism that is the relentless flow of actions and events. It is the realization of this internal witness which preserves that Truth, the knowledge of which "will make you free" (John 8:32), and which reveals the atemporal criteria by which temporal movement can be measured.

To understand tradition as meaning simply the continuity of history comes about as the result of an error that could hardly be made were it not for the prevailing conception of man as being, to all intents and purposes an autonomous, soulless being trapped in an existential isolation that acknowledges only the dualistic claims of mind against matter. This post-Cartesian conception discards outright the soul as the active organ of spiritual perception. Its proper role denied, what hope is there that the soul can act as the ever-present witness to those internal qualities that elude the funeral cortège of time? He who seeks possession of a living tradition understands the need to free himself from the illusion that the "archives" of the past represents the vital substance of a tradition. For him the regeneration of the soul alone permits in turn the renewal of a tradition. It is in the soul that the association of a tradition with change escapes the impotence of being interpreted exclusively in terms of all that man himself has contributed to the wreckage of historical time. Otherwise there could be no possibility of spiritual renewal, only the sterility and the deception of the customary and the commonplace. Only in the subtle ontology of its integral perceptions can the soul recognize those qualitative essences whose forms cheat that inner death that insists that past experience can never be freed from what made it the past.

All of which presupposes that there is no such thing as a profane tradition. Profanity is the desacralization of tradition. There is no tradition apart from the Divine and its earthly reverberations: Tradition as such. And this latter is not a sort of amalgam and summation of all the differing traditions that have been revealed to man, completing and perfecting them in a way each of them is incapable of doing on its own. Insofar as man has access to the Divine he does so by way of a tradition; that is, he is immersed in ways of being and doing that have been determined by a spiritual principle addressed to that portion of mankind it is his destiny to belong to. In other words, he cannot hear the "music" of Tradition as such apart from the "performance" of a tradition.

To say that tradition must be rigorously dissociated from all that threatens to lose it among the contents of history, is another way of saying that a tradition must be capable of preserving for us the objective norm by which we can know who we are apart from that which merely happens to us. Despite whatever clues may be offered by thoughts, actions, and reactions to external events, to seek to define man purely in terms of his thinking and his acting will impoverish the human self-image because such a definition must shelve the question of the ultimate nature of the subject who thinks and acts.[2]

---

[2] For a discussion of the principal dangers and delusions of self knowledge from the perspective of a tradition—in this case the Sufi tradition of Islam—see William Chittick, *Sufism, A Short Introduction* (Oxford: Oneworld, 2000), Chapter 4, "Self Help."

Just as appearances are logically of something that is "hidden," so the ultimate selfhood of the person is "masked" by the protean abundance of his or her thoughts and actions. It is the indistinct subject that gives coherence to the psycho-physical existence of the individual, a subject that can obviously never become an object of knowledge so far as the individual knowing subject is concerned. The individual subject can be understood in this light to possess a defining essence that is never simply the cumulative body of psycho-physical states which are in reality so many modes of the hidden subject. The existence of the indistinct subject allows us to speak of man as being able to know, in any objective sense, Truth, the divine immanence at the root of consciousness. It is essentially the purpose of tradition to safeguard the divine immanence of consciousness, as it is formally the purpose of tradition to participate in the transcendent dimension of truth throughout human thought and action. Vladimir Lossky states the case precisely.

> Tradition is the unique mode of receiving [the Truth]. We say specifically unique mode and not uniform mode, for to Tradition in its pure notion there belongs nothing formal. It does not impose on human consciousness formal guarantees of the truths of faith, but gives access to the discovery of their inner evidence. It is not the content of Revelation, but the light that reveals it; it is not the word, but the living breath which makes the words heard at the same time as the silence from which it came; it is not the Truth, but a communication of the Spirit of Truth outside which the Truth cannot be received.[3]

It becomes clear that tradition presupposes the spiritual nature of intelligence, and stands over and against the dissipating forces of spiritual, moral, and artistic improvisation for their own sake. As a mode of spiritual inheritance and cultural preservation, tradition stands guard over the coherence and the integrity of inspiration, thought, and action by means of ritual action, mythical thought patterns, and archetypal forms of symbolic expression. Thus it aligns man with the reverberations of the Spirit in the human soul, and which await actualization in some form by means of the individual's inborn gifts.

---

[3] Vladimir Lossky, *In the Image and Likeness of God* (London, 1975), pp. 151-52.

Tradition, then, is the intrinsic mode of a specific body of revealed knowledge, and as such is the integral ontological light by which what is potential to the Divine is realized in human consciousness. Like all metaphysical knowledge, tradition takes account of the inexpressible, the silence that makes possible the Word, the void that makes possible all manifestation. Tradition permits intelligence to hold a mirror to the Infinite in order to recognize—in accordance with cosmic principles—its affinity with it. Which is why tradition cannot be impoverished or fabricated from merely human means since it is only by the light of tradition that man is able to understand the ultimate truth of his subjective nature, a nature whose limitations, in terms of that light, are a state of unknowingness that cannot, by mere recourse to itself, overcome its own ignorance.

Inasmuch as a tradition is that light "outside which the Truth cannot be received," it represents a perspective by which the human subject may see beyond those very conditions and limitations that make him the individual he is. It implies immutable criteria not only with respect to intelligence but to the objectivity of the knowing subject's ultimate knowledge as well. It may be that nothing is known except in the mode of the knower, but there can be no certainty as to the objective truth of the knower's knowledge of himself unless a distinction is possible between Intellect as such and its reflection in the individual mind. To lump together discursive thought, intuition, and imagination as faculties of a vaguely defined "mind," and then to suppose that the operations of this "mind" have their sources entirely within individual subjective consciousness, is to degrade and diminish both Truth and intelligence. As Frithjof Schuon has pointed out, this subjective hypothesis harbors a fundamental inconsistency:

> That man can never pass beyond what is "subjective" and human is the most gratuitous and contradictory of hypotheses. Who then defines "human subjectivity" as such? If it is human subjectivity itself which does so, then there is no such thing as objective knowledge and no definition is possible; if something other than this subjectivity does so, then it is clearly wrong to say that man cannot pass beyond it. It is clear that no definition has value apart from its objectivity, that is to say apart from absence of error; on the other hand one cannot seek to enclose the Universe in the "subjective

and human" while at the same time admitting of a point of view beyond this same subjectivity which can consequently define it.

By the same token it is clear that human subjectivity as such can no more be said to think for itself than one can say that an eye can see vision. For, as Schuon continues,

> If it is a man who defines himself, what objective value can be attached to this definition? And, if there is no objective value, no transcendent criterion, why think? If it is enough to be a man in order to be in the right, why seek to refute human errors?[4]

If the objective status of Truth and its proper relationship to the human subject is to be maintained, then the apparent subjectivity of all modes of individual thought must be seen as projected upon a consciousness without individuality and without plurality, namely, the Divine Intellect, which intelligence reflects and embodies. In every effort of individual communication a consciousness without plurality is by definition invoked. All the sacred traditions teach how the many individual dispositions of mind are in essence consubstantial with the supra-human Intellect that transcends the "separateness" of individual thought and provides the true and ultimate ground of an understanding in common.

*

T.S. Eliot certainly expressed the standpoint of the modern mind, with its characteristic sense of its own religious disorientation, when he wrote in "Tradition and the Individual Talent": "… tradition cannot be inherited, and if you want it you must obtain it by great labor." In stressing the great labor that the acquisition of tradition requires, Eliot in part echoes the view of W.B. Yeats (in *The Celtic Twilight*), who none the less approached the matter from a very different perspective:

> In a society that has cast out imaginative tradition, only a few people—three or four thousand out of millions—favored by their own

[4] Frithjof Schuon, *Spiritual Perspectives and Human Facts*, trans. Macleod Matheson (London: Perennial Books, 1954), pp. 16-17.

characters and by happier circumstances, and only then after much labor, have understanding of imaginative things, and yet "the imagination is the man himself."[5]

The idea that one has to labor in order to possess tradition is itself symptomatic of modern man's spiritual disorientation. Within the matrix of a society in which the institutions, rituals, and social structures are themselves the embodiment and expression of metaphysical truth, man has no more to labor to understand tradition than the fish has to labor to "understand" water. Tradition is simply the natural element in which he has his being.

In an important sense, however, Yeats's understanding is the inverse of Eliot's. For Yeats, tradition is immanent and fundamental to man's nature. For Eliot—who thought that tradition "cannot be inherited," despite his claim that it "involves ... the historical sense ... which is a sense of the timeless as well as the temporal"—tradition is external to man, something added to his effort to produce a culture and which has its roots in the notion of the contemporaneous value of man's cultural "successes" (Eliot's word). It is really a view dominated by time, and insofar as it implicitly formulates a philosophy of human intelligence, it attempts to trace the relationship between tradition and the individual mind from past phases of man's cultural history. Indeed, on the basis of this derivation, Eliot went on to develop his theory of creative depersonalization, with its agent the "objective correlative."

In all this the spiritual roots of tradition are obscured and impoverished. Man cannot arrive at criteria of immutable value on the basis of anything so vague as a sense of the contemporary relevance of bits and pieces of his own created past. By what trans cultural principle is such a sense to be ordered? What man does can only be valued in the light of what man is—which points to the need, in all cultural activity, to take into account the non discursive essence of the intelligence and the uncreated essence of the individual being.

Doubtless "Tradition and the Individual Talent" does not represent Eliot's most mature reflections on the subject, but we are here

---

[5] *Mythologies* (London, 1932), pp. 14.

concerned primarily with its important and widespread influence. Even when he came to reconsider the essay, as he did in *After Strange Gods* (1934), he could only redefine tradition as "rather a way of feeling and acting which characterizes a group throughout generations; and that it must be, or that many of the elements in it must be, unconscious." In such a definition the question of the suprahuman source of tradition is put aside so that all criteria of objectivity and permanence guaranteed by that source come to seem determined by the contingencies of human experience.[6] With his insistence that it involves the "historical sense," and by his inclination to see tradition as belonging in some way to "cultural success" Eliot unavoidably adulterates the notion of tradition. In his view the appeal of tradition is not to those metaphysical principles that are the ever-abundant source of eternal reality and wisdom, but to such externalities of human effort as shape the world of cultural history.

On Eliot's terms it is evidently not a question of the degree to which metaphysical principles are ever present realities of knowing and being. What is absent from his formulation is that genuine interior bond by which the archetypal reality draws back to itself, through the experience of the individual, what is originally intrinsic to it.

The limitations of Eliot's conclusions were perhaps predetermined; firstly, by his concern to define the nature and place of tradition from within the confines of a particular perspective of modern European thought; and secondly, and more importantly, by an intellectual standpoint whose foundations rested on the post Renaissance "humanist" culture rooted in post-Cartesian dualism. The underlying assumptions of his formulation were shaped by a history and a culture whose understanding of the terms "truth," "reality," "knowledge," as well as its tacit human self-image, were themselves anti-traditional. The history and the culture on which he implicitly draws are characterized by their deviation from those metaphysical and spiritual norms whose effective existence attaches the individual to the Divine reality. At least at the time of writing his essay, Eliot precluded the possibility of such an attachment, for his

---

[6] This illustrates the inversion of values, so prevalent in modern thought, whereby explanation proceeds from "below upward" instead of "above downwards." See René Guénon, *The Reign of Quantity and the Signs of the Times*, trans. Lord Northbourne (London, 1953).

formulation of tradition, as he admitted, halted "at the frontier of metaphysics." At which point the poet had arrived at the threshold of tradition.

Against the earlier view of Eliot the critic we must balance the more comprehensive and later view of Eliot the poet.[7] Because his earlier poems are so readily valued for their "modernity" and "originality," the deeper achievement of his later poetry is sometimes overlooked. In an age that has succumbed to the superstition of "thinking for oneself" the apparent freedom of a trackless desert must seem preferable to following a path that is overgrown through neglect. One can only suppose this to be the premise of those who regard Eliot's retreat to the Church and his "falling back" upon religion as a sign of weakness. It surely is the case that Eliot discovered in his maturity that the way to the truth had been trodden by countless generations throughout history and yet is not to be found in history.

We can certainly point to the poetry as reflecting the gradual development of its author's understanding of the relationship between tradition as a unique mode of truth and the individual consciousness. The shift of emphasis can be traced from the nightmarish autonomy of Prufrock's post-Cartesian psychic world, through the ambivalent subjectivity of Tiresias who

> throbbing between two lives,
> Old man with wrinkled female breasts

"sees all" and "foresuffers all," who is thus no character yet unites all the other characters of *The Waste Land*, to the universal consciousness enunciated in Heraclitus, "Although the Logos is common the many live as though they had private understanding" (which forms an epigraph to "Burnt Norton" and the implications of which are a recurring theme in *Four Quartets*).

The illusion of individual autonomy that each self-experience creates consists precisely in limiting subjective intelligence to operating exclusively within the continuum of events in the space time world. In the impotence of Prufrock we can discern the morbid

---

[7] Eliot was later to study Sanskrit and comparative religion as well as confessing to the influence of A.K. Coomaraswamy and Frithjof Schuon.

dilemma of the "thinking individual" who, on the basis of a private psycho-mental awareness, is locked in the passive, self-enclosed network of thoughts that places his identity at the mercy of their own evermore reflexive and attenuated inter-relationships:

> Do I dare
> Disturb the Universe?
> In a minute there is time
> For decisions and revisions which a minute will reverse

Only tradition in its primal sense can provide the transcendent dimension whereby the seemingly independent reality of the isolated "I" is both recognized and vanquished, for only in that "unique mode" of intelligence safeguarded by tradition can there be found the means of discernment to objectify the human subject and so bind it back to that innate principle which itself links man to all that is above subjectivity as such. Only in such a context is the passage away from private and habitual experience illuminated, and the limitations that psycho-physical awareness imposes upon the mind overcome. As Eliot acknowledges in "The Dry Salvages":

> Men's curiosity searches past and future
> And clings to that dimension. But to apprehend
> The point of intersection of the timeless
> With time, is an occupation for the saint—
> No occupation either, but something given
> And taken, in a lifetime's death in love,
> Ardor and selflessness and self-surrender.

More concerned with elaborating knowledge than with wisdom, with mental concepts than with metaphysical discernment, with intellectual sophistication rather than with truth, that "searching curiosity" that Eliot speaks of, which absorbs the mind into the mirrored surface of its own protean experience, at the same time obscures the uncreated essence of the Intellect upon which, like a screen, all knowledge and experience are projected. In "East Coker" Eliot acknowledged,

> There is, it seems to us,
> At best, only a limited value
> In the knowledge derived from experience.

> The knowledge imposes a pattern, and falsifies,
> For the pattern is new in every moment
> And every moment is a new and shocking
> Valuation of all we have been.

When the content of that "knowledge derived from experience" is studied for what it can be made to yield on its own terms, it is as if, mesmerized by its own subjective prolongations, the mind is too bemused ever to question the objective status of that which occupies it. In the sapiential context of tradition, however, the divine ground of consciousness is admitted at the outset as the *modus operandi* of all intellectualization and the necessity for its actualization is taken for granted as the necessary condition of objective knowledge.

There is a need, then, to acknowledge that the ultimate referent of the subject, like an indistinct dimension, stands apart from its reflection in discursive thought, an identity made manifest in the humility of recognizing the infinite and common essence of all being, as Eliot likewise acknowledges in the same poem:

> The only wisdom we can hope to acquire
> Is the wisdom of humility: humility is endless.

For the action of humility destroys at the roots all those notions derived from subjective "thinking," whose web is so cunningly woven in the postulation of its own self centered reality. Humility attacks the illusory identification of the knowing subject with subjectivity itself, for only in the plenitude of the moment when the Knower is the sole object of all knowledge is the only possible wisdom achieved—the chasm between knowing and being finally bridged. Again, from Eliot's "East Coker":

> In order to arrive there,
> To arrive where you are, to get from where you are not,
> You must go by a way wherein there is no ecstasy.
> In order to arrive at what you do not know
> You must go by a way which is the way of ignorance.
> In order to possess what you do not possess
> You must go by the way of dispossession.
> In order to arrive at what you are not
> You must go through the way in which you are not.
> And what you do not know is the only thing you know

> And what you own is what you do not own
> And where you are is where you are not.

In the uncreated essence of all subjectivity is the sole objective end: "In my beginning is my end."

So we conclude that the importance of Eliot's views on tradition are to be found not in their formulation in his earlier critical writings but as they are expressed later in his *Four Quartets*. Here they are at their most profound and mature. Indeed, here, as near as ever he did, the poet implicitly declares himself an anti modernist.

*

It is the earthly destiny of man to return from whence he came— God. As Frithjof Schuon has observed: "The substance of human knowledge is Knowledge of the divine Substance." On the evidence of the cultures of the sacred traditions we find every indication we could need to confirm the universality of the link between human history and the plane of divine energies whose imprint, by means of the eternal archetypes, determines the norms of cultural meanings and values. Everywhere we look in traditional cultures we see the spiritual adventures of man, those preludial journeys that prepare him for the life beyond the particular "time" and "place" of his earthly existence. Everywhere there is the constant attempt, founded upon spiritual knowledge, to understand the phenomenal world's transparency in relation to its divine source. For traditional man everywhere the generated world is instinct with the sacred reality of the Spirit. For him, as Blake wrote, "Eternity is in love with the production of time." As with all things of a spiritual nature it comes down to the state of preparedness of the individual, for "nothing is known except in the mode of the knower." This "mode of the knower" involves more than merely subjective experience, for such experiences would be nothing were it not for the objective status of the intellect. Discursive intelligence, mirroring and "making sense" of phenomenal reality, has need of a point of reference beyond that reality in order to set the seal of meaning on what it discovers. The ultimate as well as logical context for an understanding of the world of time and space is one in which their origin beyond time and space is taken into account. Time can have no beginning in time; space no extensive reality from space itself. If we believe that the reality that lies beyond the world of empirical experience is unknowable, which we do, if only unwittingly, in taking an exclusively quantifiable view of things, then the intelligence must abandon what appears at all times to be its immediate and ultimate objective: to "take in" that which is, in order to distinguish the real from the illusory, truth from falsehood.

India and the Modern World[*]

Kathleen Raine

When life ceases to have value and meaning, no material wealth, no political or economic measures can save us. I would like to speak to you from the heart. When time is so short, why waste it in anything less than heart's truth?

In the past I have spoken from my small store of learning as a Blake scholar. But today I will speak for myself, here and now, to you who share this hour on Earth with me. And yet, in speaking so, I hope I am also speaking for all those poets whose words I have inherited with the English language, and for all those known and unknown forbears from whom I have received, for my brief lifetime, words. For words come to us laden with the wisdom and the folly, the loves and the secret thoughts of all the ancestors, known and unknown, who in their days received, enriched, and bequeathed to us these words, laden with all it is that we human beings have known, wondered, sought for, in our days on Earth. We receive, and we transmit, enriched or impoverished, the great human heritage of language.

I speak of words, of language, because I have spent my years studying and delighting in, above all, poetry. I have written poems, some of which I hope will go on their way in the great river of life to which each of us adds our drop—the perpetual choir to which we add our voices. I see it so, as a river, a music, which flows on. It is not the poets but the poetry, not the musicians but the music, which flows on. It is better to be a very small fish in that great river that flows into the ocean, than the biggest fish in some small rock-pool of history, or some goldfish-bowl of popular fashion.

So if you are wondering in whose name and by what right I speak, it is in the name of the English region of the universal kingdom of the imagination. That well-loved promoter of the arts, Herbert Read, wrote a book entitled *The Politics of the Unpolitical,* and I am among these. My only political opinion is that politics cannot

---

[*] Editor's Note: A talk given at the Indira Gandhi National Center for the Arts, Delhi, 1989.

set the world to rights, much less give us reasons why we are here on Earth, what the purpose and the chief end of our lives is. At best it can organize the flow of events but cannot pronounce on the values and meanings by which we live.

As the Irish poet and mystic, George Russell, used to say, the art is to conform "the politics of time" with "the politics of eternity." And Shelley was only recording what every civilization has proved, that the poets are "the unacknowledged legislators of the world."

Unacknowledged because the words of poets form no part of political debate, and in more modern terms are not the language of the press and the media; rather they are secret words spoken not from our transient mortal selves on transient issues, but from the heart, and to the heart, from the immortal and universal spirit all share.

So my only credentials are those of a poet, least in a long succession, and I speak in the name of that invisible kingdom of the imagination, here at the heart of the supreme civilization of the imagination, India. All know who have come within sight of the India of the imagination that India has, more fully than any civilization on Earth, past or present, embodied the highest and most all-embracing realization of our human scope. My friend, your great philosopher-novelist Raja Rao, unfolded to me, many years ago, what he understood by the eternal India. India, he said, is not a nationality, it is a state of mind. I think he said "mind"; or perhaps it was "a state of being." It was, as I heard it, like an invitation: "Reach that India if you can; it is open to all who can attain it." The eternal India is the place of arrival.

India is infinite and inexhaustible, not because in India more or greater works of art, architecture, sculpture, music, and poetry are to be found. But what is unmatched elsewhere is that in all traditional Indian art there is that infinite dimension. I include, of course, those greatest of all works, the Upanishads and other works of Indian spiritual wisdom, including those of Buddhism and of the other religions of India. But not these alone; also Indian poetry, dance, sculpture, designs of textiles and crafts, embody the dimension of infinity, and whatever takes us into that inexhaustible mystery is in itself inexhaustible. It is, in a word, sacred art.

The severance of art from the sacred, did not, in India, as in the West, take place at any level—or only since Western influence reached India.

Dr. Kapila Vatsyayan, on her recent visit to London, attempted to explain to an audience of students of architecture the significance of the formula "zero plus one divided by three": what, we Westerners wonder, is the difference between zero plus one divided by three, and one divided by three? None that we can see. Yet in terms of Indian mathematics that zero is all-important, since it opens into the inexhaustible infinity, the source of all numbers and manifestation. This fertile zero is not present in secular art. Modern Western civilization as a whole lacks that immeasurable zero opening into other dimensions of the unknown, unknowable, all-sustaining, mysterious, inexhaustible source of the daily epiphany of creation, source also of the marvels we ourselves create. It is in this sense that the eternal India is all-embracing.

As for political, economic, and industrial India, this may not be so. Quite the contrary: in these fields the roads seem to lead the other way, ending, I suppose, in California. Or Disneyland, since the way down is easier than the steep ascent. Perhaps this must be so; each of us seeks what we lack. The materially poor East lacks what we in the West can provide; while our spiritually destitute materialist civilization looks to the Orient.

Spiritually, it is we in the West who are in want, and it is to the inexhaustible plenty of India that so many in the Western world are now turning. We have discovered very late the truth of the words of Jesus, that "Man shall not live by bread alone." That fullness of spiritual knowledge has flowered elsewhere and in other times, but as one looks round the world it is evident that the light has been extinguished in one country after another, but that that treasury of universal wisdom, however imperiled by other influences, is still India's. And if India is lost, all is lost. For the greatest economic prosperity, the most prestigious and profitable multinationals cannot sustain a civilization in the absence of wisdom.

It is not in the streets of affluent London—or New York or Dallas—that faces of radiant beauty and the joy of life are to be seen. The rich, in England as in America—as in all countries where our modern materialist civilization has prevailed, take their quiet desperation to the psychiatrists who have supplanted among those for whom "God is dead" the work of the church; and the poor seek solace in drugs and an outlet in violence. Even our politicians are calling for a return to "basic values" in sheer panic—whatever basic values may be in a godless world. Suddenly everyone has noticed that we have lost some element—an essential element to well being that money cannot supply—but what that lost element is, we no longer remember. And if you in India succumb to those same forces you too will lose a treasure beyond price which hitherto you have preserved intact through thousands of years of civilization. And for the sake of the whole world may it not be lost!

What are these basic values that we know only that we have lost? And how have we, in the materially powerful West, come to lose them? I have friends who go so far as to condemn the great development of science itself, out of hand. Some trace the deviation from the universal and unanimous tradition of wisdom back to Aristotle, some to the Renaissance. W.B. Yeats wrote that "the mischief began at the end of the seventeenth century, when Man became passive before a mechanized nature." It is regrettable that the great scientific development of these three centuries was grounded in a severance between observer and observed, which led to the view of nature as a lifeless, autonomous, mechanized order, apart from the observing mind.

I am not one of those who condemn science out of hand—indeed, perhaps Western science has been our greatest gift to the world. The study of nature, from its most minute to its vast spaces presents a marvel of ordered harmony that should fill us with awe. Great minds have contributed to this achievement. The scientific exploration of the "appearances" of nature is now perhaps complete, astronomy cannot go beyond the known cosmos nor physical measurement pursue nature further into the labyrinths of the minute world where measurability itself vanishes. The achievement is immense, but in its realization we are again confronted with the unknown immeasurable. The natural universe is a part of reality but not, as the Western popular mind still believes, the whole.

Every civilization is grounded in certain premises, some inspiring vision, and completes the cycle set in motion by that seminal vision, its rise, flowering, and withering, scattering the seed of perhaps some new civilization elsewhere and in the future. The French metaphysician René Guénon has described our own era as "the reign of quantity." In his many books, Guénon exposed its shortcomings and called for a return to sacred tradition.

What then is the inherent flaw that time has shown in the prestigious development of the natural sciences, which has been the great achievement of Western civilization? The separation of observer and object presented itself very clearly in the fifteenth century use of optical perspective in paintings of the Italian Renaissance, and later in the development of microscope and telescope during the seventeenth century in which Yeats saw science developing in such a way as to make the mind only the passive observer of phenomena, not itself an agent. The great virtue of the scientific mind is its total commitment to truth without preconceptions, political or religious. Nor are the value judgments of feeling or belief allowed to interfere with the total commitment to truth so conceived, to the measurable, objective world interpreted in the light of reason.

Such a dedication is admirable in itself and perhaps served to purge European civilization of a certain amount of credulous superstition. But feelings and values are also aspects of reality and a science of nature based on measurement alone describes a part but not the whole; nor is our civilization, which has grown and flourished on the basis of materialism, a complete civilization; its limitations are becoming ever more apparent. What is more, it seems that pure science has increasingly given place to the service of technology, and technology in turn deviated from its true function—which is to serve human well-being—to the service of the profit motive, creating wants where none exist, in order to sell the products of the machines it has brought into being. Whereas every spiritually based civilization has placed the highest value not on multiplying wants but on reducing desire for material possessions.

The materialist ideology leads to the nihilism which afflicts so many in the modem world: for the logical pursuit of a mode of knowledge which deliberately—conscientiously even—excludes values and meanings from its definition of truth and reality reduces humankind itself to a valueless and meaningless accident in a mechanistic universe. And that is the message of much contemporary art, literature, and philosophy. That powerful and truthful painter, Francis Bacon, has shown us the hell of modern Man when seen as an accident in a universe without meaning.

Standing as we do on the farthest frontier of material knowledge our choice lies between the *nihil* of negativity and the abundant Nothing of the mystics, source and sustainer of all worlds. We have discovered that the truth of science is a partial truth—and our souls are unsatisfied, and our world itself threatened. It is to India that the most advanced thinkers of the West, in philosophy, in theology, and indeed in mathematical and scientific studies "arrive." But because the central teaching of India is the presence of the divine in every human soul, in every created being, in every particle of dust, this wisdom gives dignity no less to the poor and simple than to the brilliant and gifted, since our human dignity lies not in what we achieve but in what we are. Let it not be forgotten that Mahatma Gandhi's message was to restore dignity to the poorest and most unvalued people. Human dignity lies in the presence of the divine in all and is therefore not relative but absolute. Nothing can compensate for the sense of failure of the unsuccessful, played on continually by the media of the television age, dazzling the poor with a never-never land of fabulous wealth, a dream fabricated by Mammon.

Nor was it Mahatma Gandhi alone in India who spoke alike to rich and poor, to the successful and to the losers. Sri Aurobindo indeed addresses the learned in their own language, but the love of Ramana Maharshi was given alike to all, and so to this day men and women of all castes and creeds flow towards India's ashrams and not from India alone but also from the affluent West. For I am not speaking of a past golden age, but of this century, for there have been, and are, holy men, known and hidden, here and now, as you well know. Surely the most unloved people in the world today are inhabitants of those "inner city areas" where the unemployed losers in the affluent West have nothing to hope for from the society we have created for the production and promotion of material goods. Nor does the Communist ideal of an equal distribution of material wealth answer the deep needs of the human soul by providing less and less material wealth for more and more people.

I think often of an image from Kabir, who wrote that all know of the drop in the ocean, but what of the ocean in the drop—that zero, that inexhaustible source, known alike to mystic and to mathematician. When the great founder of the Neoplatonic school, Plotinus, wrote, "There is nothing higher than the truth," it was of this perennial wisdom he was speaking, a golden thread that has woven its way through every civilization.

We live on the frontiers not only of the unknown but of the unknowable. But at the same time the knowable of mental worlds is a great coherent universe which India has explored with the same dedication as the West has explored nature. The truths of science are not creeds or opinions, they are always open to revision in the light of new discoveries; and neither do India's philosophers deal in creeds and opinions, but with the exploration of the immeasurable universe of mind.

It is this whole vast world that we in the West have to rediscover, and that is why we turn to India. Please God you do not reject or forget the sacred heritage of your civilization of the mind and the imagination just at the time when the whole world has never needed that knowledge as we do now, not as something to be added when all material needs have been met, but as essential to our survival as civilized human beings. Never has the world needed India as now. When life ceases to have value and meaning, no material wealth, no political, or economic measures can save us.

2

PERENNIAL TRUTHS AND MODERN COUNTERFEITS

Corruptio optimi pessima
ANCIENT ADAGE

Religion has been grossly sentimentalized and humanized, distorted and even perverted, and sometimes reduced to little more than a kind of idealism or ideology competing with profane ideologies for the same ends ...

LORD NORTHBOURNE

ANCIENT BELIEFS OR MODERN SUPERSTITIONS:

THE SEARCH FOR AUTHENTICITY*

Rama P. Coomaraswamy

I

The greatest problem facing those who believe in the possibility of truth and who set out to seek it seriously, is the absence—or supposed absence—of any criteria by which to be certain that what we find is the real thing. With several major religions and between 5 to 20,000 cults all offering us various and often exclusive options, how are we to choose, or more precisely, discern? Caught as we are in the toils of *Maya*—or as a Catholic would put it, with our intellects wounded and our wills weakened by the Fall of Adam, how can we, by ourselves and without external help, ever be sure that we are avoiding delusion? We can of course embrace the skeptics' position and give up the struggle. But as an old gloss of Plato says, "skepticism is easy, unbelief is for the mob." But for those who are not yet intellectually dead, the question still remains: by what authority do we live and die? Are there authentic well-springs of truth, or is truth simply a matter of our own personal gut feelings, our psychological experiences, and what works for us?

The first problem to be faced is whether truth is an objective or a subjective entity. Is there such a thing as objective truth—truth which has always been and always will be the same—unchanging and constant—hence a truth which is absolute? Now, either words have meaning or they don't. If truth is only a matter of personal taste, if one is convinced that all reality is relative, there is hardly any point in continuing either discussion or search. One is caught in the vicious circle of proclaiming that the only truth is that there is no truth.

In the last analysis we have only three possible sources for authenticity. We have the Ancient Teachings which are—or so I

* Editor's Note: Revised version of a talk given to the Himalayan International Institute of Yoga Science and Philosophy of the USA, June 1988.

assume—embodied in the great religious traditions of the world.[1] We have our own gut feelings or psychological experience as to what is true. And we have some mixture of these two extremes. Either we accept objective criteria, or we accept subjective criteria, or we create a mixture that for some reason or another we find personally satisfactory. The latter is also, needless to say subjective.

It is only when we accept the possibility of objective truth that we can look to the Ancient Teachings as a possible authentic source. Unfortunately, we live in a very superstitious age. The so-called "age of enlightenment"—a phrase which certainly appeals to man's egoity—is more appropriately described by the Ancient Teachings as the *Kali Yuga*, the age of darkness, or in Catholic terminology, "the latter days." This brings us to two of the most powerful superstitions which we accept—indeed they could almost be called the "dogmas" of modernity—namely evolution and progress. Most of us are convinced that mankind has evolved over the centuries, and continues to evolve with each generation. Do we not consider our ancestors as somewhat primitive, backward and superstitious? The very word "superstitious" makes us think of a medieval European peasant fingering her beads before some miraculous shrine of the Madonna, or of a Hindu *brahman* refusing untouchables access to the temple precincts. The last person we would think of as superstitious is a Harvard professor or a prominent scientist.

The problem with being superstitious is that it tends to blind us to the truth. If we are convinced something false is true, we are hardly likely to seek beyond its confines for a source of authenticity. If we are to look to Ancient Teachings as embodied in the great religious traditions of the world as a possible source of authentic and objective truth, the first thing we must do is abandon our modern superstitious belief in progress and evolution. As we shall see, there are a host of other superstitious beliefs that may also have to be abandoned. Among these are included our modern view of the nature of man, our false egalitarian concepts, our socialist and utopian ideals, our familial attitudes, our moral or rather our unmoral codes, our belief in science, and our attitude towards religion.

[1] The author would like to make it clear that it is not his intent to advocate any kind of syncretism in religion.

I well remember how my college friends—and later, how some of my professional colleagues—looked upon my being Catholic. I was accused of no longer thinking for myself. Now the idea that it is a good thing to think for oneself is another modern superstition. To put the matter into clearer focus, I would ask you to imagine a classroom of mathematical students telling the teacher that they disagreed with his answers because they were doing mathematics "for themselves." No, thinking for oneself is not a healthy thing to do. What we must do is learn, not to think for ourselves, but to think correctly. It is the function of the Ancient Teachings to help us do just that, but it takes both work and discipline. We do of course have the freedom to think for ourselves—we can think any way we want. But we do not have a right to do so, for error never has rights. Like murder: we are free to murder anyone we want, but we certainly do not have a right to do so.

We no longer accuse religious adherents of failing to think for themselves. The current allegation is that they have allowed themselves to be brainwashed. Brainwashing implies that one's thoughts and attitudes can be influenced, if not controlled, by external forces. Both religions and cults—to say nothing of political systems—are accused of using various techniques to bring this about. Have those individuals who adhere to the Ancient Teachings as embodied in the great religious traditions in their integrity allowed themselves to be brainwashed? Before answering this question, allow me to point out that we are all to some degree brainwashed. Every day our minds are bombarded by the news media, by television which the average American watches for over 60 hours a week, by popular novels, and by those with whom we are in daily contact. There is no doubt in my mind but that most if not all of these entities embrace an anti-religious, liberal-humanistic, socialist, and more or less skeptical-atheistic viewpoint. Moreover, the stresses of modern life are such that, in what little free time we have left, most of us expose ourselves to the media in a completely passive and non-critical manner. We in essence let the newscaster and politicians and writers of Book-of-the-Month Club novels tell us how to think, and pride ourselves that we are thinking for ourselves. If we do not see this as brainwashing, it is because these sources pander to our egos and we find the offered pablum both acceptable and pleasant. On the other hand, a mother who teaches her ancestral faith to her children and the *brahman* who insists on ritual purity and caste restrictions are also guilty of brainwashing. But here many find the process highly objectionable.

Let us for a moment consider our own educational backgrounds. What formation did we bring with us from our homes? Most parents today have been so effectively brainwashed by the liberal and agnostic ethos of our times, that they no longer have, and hence cannot convey, any value system or set of fixed beliefs, to their offspring—unless of course you consider material success a belief system. And so it is that most children leave the home with a sort of *tabula rasa*—or worse, a belief in the world of the television screen. According to published statistics, every Saturday 16 ½ million children spend an hour and a half watching Graystone or the Mutant Ninja Turtles. Sociologists call television the "third parent." Unfortunately, it is often the only parent.

And so, it is with considerable relief that children are sent off to school. Here formal brainwashing is initiated. The process starts in kindergarten where boys are made to play with dolls and girls with swords—this in order, to use the jargon of modern psychology, "to teach them to avoid stereotypes." Through a variety of techniques such as "values clarification" they are taught to reject their parents' values—assuming they were inculcated with some—under the guise of developing their own, usually those of the teacher or those being promoted by various governmental agencies. This process is called "desatilization." Throughout the next ten years they are taught to be good little evolutionists, socialists, and how to use the gift of sex without responsibility. And then they go to college, which is the *sine qua non* for entrance into a modicum of economic success. Once again, they pay a steep price—the price being paid is more than fees for tuition—it is the subjecting of our minds to yet another process of indoctrination. As my father[2] once said—and this is the forties—it is almost impossible for someone to graduate from college without a severe degree of intellectual impairment.

And so to the question: are religious adherents brainwashed? I think the answer to this question must be phrased in terms of "thinking correctly" and of embracing "correct values." If the Ancient Teachings are an authentic source of truth, and if we make them our own, then we are like the student of mathematics who

---

[2] Ananda K. Coomaraswamy.

learns to calculate correctly. Such a student is not brainwashed, because he knows how to do his sums correctly. The truth, our submission to the truth, and our making it "our own," is in the last analysis our only protection against both brainwashing and self-delusion.

II

Man does not live in a vacuum. Everyone—even the convinced atheist—has what we can call a "belief system," that is to say, a series of convictions that determine how he lives his life. Now every belief system can be characterized by three things: by its "creed" or what is believed, by its "cult" or manner of worship, and by the "code" or rules for behavior which it practices or advocates.

Let us consider the belief system—the creed, cult, and code of the average college graduate. What does he believe? I think it fair to say that he is convinced that there is no such thing as absolute truth—that all truth is subjective, and hence relative. Hence it is that, in common parlance, he no longer says "I know," but only that "I feel" something to be true. He believes that evolution is a law of nature applicable to all realms of experience. Everything evolves, not only man, but knowledge, society, and even God! I remember my six year old son coming home one afternoon from school and announcing with pride that he no longer believed in God! I asked him what he believed in then and he answered "E ... oh, how do you say that word?" Fortunately I was able to convince him otherwise. But evolution is inculcated in our children's minds from the cradle. Have you ever looked at a nature show on television? The pictures are marvelous but the message is driven home repeatedly. Everything from the tiger's stripes to the giraffe's neck evolved. Every child knows who Darwin is. How many have heard of Gautama the Buddha or John the Baptist?

Evolution is of course quite absurd from both the scientific and philosophical viewpoint. From the scientific viewpoint: not only is there absolutely no proof in favor of evolution; all the evidence is against it. Geology, biology, genetics and all other scientific disciplines speak to the fixity of the species and to the impossibility of transformism. No intermediary forms between species have been found. There is much talk of "missing links." The problem with missing links is that they are missing! To believe in evolution is to

59

believe that the greater can come out of the less; it is to believe that energy can be created *in sui generis,* it is to believe that things happen by "chance" in the sense that chance is a random possibility. Probability theory tells us that the chance of one evolutionary step occurring is so remote as to be impossible. Yet evolutionists tell us many such steps have occurred. The most amazing thing about evolution is that scientists who admit all this continue to believe in evolution—they are truly men of deep but blind faith. It is not bushman, but rather modern man who believes in the blind forces of nature and who should be labeled an animist!

Philosophically, evolution is also absurd. If it were true, it would be as impossible for man to step outside the evolutionary stream in order to examine the process that "developed" him as it would be for a computer to examine the creator. As the Oxford philosopher, Sir Karl Popper, points out: "If Darwinism is right, then any theory is held because of a certain physical structure in the holder—perhaps of his brain. Accordingly we are deceiving ourselves and are physically so determined as to deceive ourselves whenever we believe that there are such things as arguments or reasons for anything. Purely physical conditions, including our physical environment, make us say or accept whatever we say or accept."

Implicit in evolutionary theory is the denial of free will. As Huxley says, "the fundamental proposition of evolution" is that "the whole world, living and not living, is the result of the mutual interaction, according to definite laws, of the forces possessed by the molecules of which the primitive nebulosity of the universe was composed." After all, how can "something"—notice, I did not say "someone," which is the product of rigid laws, laws which control its future development and which has no freedom to step outside the evolutionary process—how can this "something" act independently of these laws? How can this thing have a free will for which it is responsible? Evolutionist Jonas Salk admits as much. He openly admits that his polio vaccine works against the evolutionary process of natural selection. The only way he can explain his drive to develop this vaccine is that he was genetically programmed to do so. Here one comes upon another conundrum, and one interestingly enough shared by socialists for whom evolution takes the form of historical determinism. If man's life is determined by evolution or by history, how can he be "free"? Yet both evolutionists and historical determinists proclaim man is free to help the process on its way towards perfection and an earthly utopia. Socialists go even further. They punish man for his failure to do so, and in the name of their socialist ideation have killed millions more than all the wars of the last three centuries.

To think this way, as the psychiatrist Karl Stern has said, "is crazy" in the sense that decompensated schizophrenics are crazy. I have called evolution a superstition—indeed, it is the grand-daddy of all modern superstitions. Allow me to give you a definition of "superstition" taken from an older edition of Webster's New International Dictionary:

> An irrational abject state of mind ... proceeding from ignorance, unreasoning fear of the unknown or mysterious morbid scrupulosity, a belief in magic or chance, or the like, misdirected or unenlightened religion or interpretation of nature ... a fixed irrational idea, a notion maintained in spite of evidence to the contrary.

Who are some of the more dominant "gurus" of the modern world, and what do they believe? Freud, Adler, Fromm, Maslow, Rogers and Jung—are or were, all of them, evolutionists and consequently atheists. They tell us that what is called "intelligence" consists of "reason," the ability to deal with abstractions, the capacity to learn, and the ability to handle new situations. Now reason apart—and enormous amounts of energy are expended in an attempt to prove that animals reason—all these abilities are to be found in lower forms of life. Hence it is not surprising to find Darwin telling us that "animals have an intellect of different proportions," and that "man's intellectual faculties have been mainly and gradually perfected through natural selection ..." Similarly, we are told that man's motivations and beliefs have their origin in his "subconscious," a term for which there are innumerable definitions and which is best defined as a kind of "cesspool of evolutionary memory." Again, we are told that man's ultimate motives are a search for security, pleasure, or what they call "self activation" through the meeting of "meta-needs." Truth is what is true for the individual; beauty is what gives pleasure; love the fulfilling of "biological urges." At the cost of denying both logic and experience, all that is qualitative in man is declared to be genetically determined—that is, determined by evolution—and hence is reduced to the measurable and thus to matter. Everything falls under this aegis. Rousseau held that savage man progressed to "civilized" man. Huxley gave this progression his scientific blessing. "Nature's great progression is from the formless to the formed—from the inorganic to the organic—from blind force to conscious intellect and will." If one can accept these premises it is easy to be persuaded that man is but a higher form of matter and that Superman is on the way. Those who think otherwise are dismissed as "dreamers"—as if matter could dream—who for all their efforts produce nothing materially beneficial.

Let one thing be quite clear. One cannot logically believe in evolution and also believe in God. Every scientist and every theologian worthy of his hire will admit to this. You will hear much talk about theistic or mitigated evolution—the idea that God works through evolution. If such were the case, then God would be very upset with any one who interfered with natural selection. How dare we treat the sick child or feed the poor and hungry? These are but nature's way of weeding out the weak. How dare we stop wars when they are so highly successful in controlling the population explosion? Let's face it. It would be stupid to pray to a God whose only answer to prayer would have to be "let natural selection or the 'punctured equilibrium' solve your problem." No scientist ever came up with the idea that God worked through evolution. Theologians did so. And why? Because they wanted to appear to be up to date and "scientific."

Now, I have spent a long time on the creedal issue of evolution because we will never look to the Ancient Teachings as a source of authentic truth unless we abandon our superstitious belief in evolution and progress. By definition, no evolutionary process can provide us with authenticity—and surely this is reasonable. After all, an evolutionary process is a changing process and anything that is spiritually authentic cannot change.

No wonder the Ancient Teachings are unanimous in declaring that all creation is the result of God's activity and not of evolution. The Church insists on a *creatio ex nihilo*, and the Vedas teach that "being is engendered from non-being." And they are even clearer in specifying that man, society, and above all truth, are not subject to any evolutionary process.

Let us return to our college graduate who sees himself—in so far as he troubles to look at himself at all—as made in the image of an amoeba. Having dealt with his fundamental creedal premises, what can we say of his manner of worship? For modern man no "cult"—

no form of worship—is possible unless it be the worship of materialism or of that lesser "self" which we refer to when we call someone selfish. What besides the evolutionary process or man, which is its highest product, is there to worship? As Karl Marx said: "Humanism is the denial of God and the total affirmation of man." This then is the foundation of modern humanism.

Finally, we come to "code." Here the rule of thumb is expediency. Everything is allowed providing it doesn't hurt the other—but in point of fact, self interest usually takes precedence. Consider adultery—and certainly adultery is not a rare phenomenon in our society. When we sleep with our neighbor's wife we loudly proclaim that such activities between consenting adults hurt no one. But what of the offended party? Or again, we claim that abortion hurts no one—and rapidly proclaim that the fetus is no one.

This then is the "uncreed," the "uncult" and the "uncode" of modern man. We can summarize it as being progressive, evolutionist, anthropocentric or man-centered, and void of metaphysical principles. What is of interest is that so many major religious bodies have adopted this *weltanschauung* or world view. At the risk of offending certain Catholics, let me say that these are precisely the principles which Vatican II embraces and which form the foundation on which the post-Conciliar Church rests. The Ancient Teachings—what the Hindus call *Sanatana Dharma*, what St. Augustine called "Wisdom uncreate, the same now as it ever was and ever will be," are unanimous in being diametrically opposed to such attitudes. They are not progressive, but rather static, because while sin may change its style, it can never alter its nature. Indeed, they are anti-progressive, because they hold that man has fallen from his former high estate. Born to a Golden Age, a Garden of Eden, men living in the *Kali Yuga* or "latter days" are degenerate. Again, the great traditions are unanimous in declaring that all creation is the result of God's direct action—*ex nihilo*, as the Catholics put it: "being engendered from non-being," as the Vedas put it; and they are unanimous in proclaiming that man is created, not in the image of an amoeba, but in the image of God. All are theocentric rather than anthropocentric. All teach that man *qua* man can never be a sure source of truth, that man's dignity does not lie in his self-validating abilities, but rather from his adherence to God's truth. Finally, all claim and can demonstrate that they are based on solid metaphysical principles—which is to say, a consistent doctrine dealing, not only with conditioned and quantitative experience, but also with universal possibility. The two extremes are like oil and water. They cannot be mixed. To accept the one is to reject the other. In which fundamental set of ideas are we to find truth and authenticity?

III

Turning to the Ancient Teachings, we find that the most striking thing that all the religions have in common is their claim—right or wrong—to be based on a Revelation—what the Hindus call *Sruti*. At some time God—an *Avatar*—or a Messenger appeared on earth and gave man a specific "creed," "cult," and "code"—or to use oriental terminology, a doctrine and a method. Moreover, they all hold this Revelation to be fixed, complete, and unalterable. The Vedas are fixed once and for all. New insights into the teachings of the Buddha may occur, but the Buddha is not providing his followers with a continuous revelation—one that evolves and progresses with the course of time. Mohammed is called the "Seal of the Prophets," by which is understood that he has provided the last and final revelation in the Abrahamic line. Muslims do not hold that the Archangel Gabriel is still revealing passages in the Quran. The Torah can be interpreted, but Moses is not currently sending us any messages. In passing it should be noted that none of the great founders of religions claimed to be discovering or revealing new truths. Jesus spoke of fulfilling, not changing the law and proclaimed that he taught, not his own, but his Father's doctrine. The Buddha said that he himself only "followed the ancient path," and added that "whoever pretends that I preach a doctrine wrought by my own reasoning and argumentation shall be cast out." Mohammed claimed to be returning to the religion of Abraham. And does not Krishna tell us in the Bhagavad Gita that he comes down to earth when *dharma* grows cold?

Religions have another criterion in common. Their revelations arc often somewhat elliptical—or appear to be such to our darkened and *Kali Yuga* intellects. Hence it is that religions provide official interpreters—be they saints or sages. The Hindus have what is called *smriti* as well as the writings of such individuals as Shankaracharya—to say nothing of the Kanchi Guru who is his living descendant. The Muslims have the commentaries on the Quran such as those of Ibn Arabi and al-Ghazali. The Jews have the Haftoras as well their Rebbes—those authorized to give current interpretations. The Christians have Church Fathers, Doctors, and what is called the "Teaching Magisterium." And what characterizes authenticity in all these living sources is that their teachings in no way depart from that of their predecessors and, ultimately, in no way depart from the original Revelation.

Yet another aspect of fixed Revelation is "cult." Forms of worship in a religion are never man-made. They are determined by God or His representative. Consider the *agnihotra* or Vedic fire sacrifice. Do you think this was made up by some old men in the forest—what today would be called a consilium of theologians—wishing to dupe the poor peasants out of their hard-earned money, or to placate the lightning? And the same is true of the prayers used by the Muslims and of the true and ancient Catholic Mass.

Similarly with regard to "code." It is Christ Himself who determined that divorce was forbidden to his followers though permitted to the Jews. The practice of Mohammed and his judicial decisions along with the Quran provide the basis for Muslim law. The laws of Man were not put together by a conference of businessmen, lawyers, and politicians.

The very word "religion" means that which "binds," that which ties us to the Origin and Center. That is why an intact religion is always traditional, for tradition means to hand on or hand down. And what is handed down other than the original revelation? Thus all religions speak of "orthodoxy" and "heresy"—oh, how we moderns hate those words! "Orthodoxy" is defined as pure faith and sound belief—that which is in conformity with the original revelation. Heresy is a departure from this as a result of picking and choosing what we will or will not believe. Heresy, as the Buddhists say, is like "a worm in the heart of a lion."

Another important fact is that there are no secret doctrines in religions. There are teachings which are not readily available, or which are phrased in obscure fashions so as to avoid "casting pearls before swine," but they are not secret as such. All the sacred texts of the Hindus have been published—you might have to learn Sanskrit, but they are not hidden. Of course one has need of certain things to access these sources: one has to have certain intellectual and moral qualifications; one needs guidance and hence a guru; and one needs initiation which is a ritual act that ties one to the *Avatar* or founder of the religion and ultimately to God. Now if this offends our egalitarian prejudices, allow me to ask you if you would allow a person who had not trained under a skilled teacher to perform surgery on you. I rather doubt it. Certainly, there are anatomical texts and descriptions of operations published in the medical literature, but one still needs certain qualifications, guidance, and training to access them. Why should religion be different?

It should be abundantly clear by now that religions provide us with objective criteria. Gurus and spiritual directors are not judged on the basis of their charismatic personalities, but on the degree to which they conform to the truth of the religion in question, on the degree that they themselves are perfect conduits or vehicles for the truth. Every ritual act on the part of the Catholic priest is *persona Christi*. We confess, not to Father Bob, but to Christ. It is Christ who in the person of the priest effects the consecration in Mass.

Religions not only provide us with objective criteria, but even more, they all share a view of man which is vastly different from that of the modern psychologist. The premises that reason uses can be derived from four possible sources: measurable phenomena (science), feelings, intellection, or Revelation. These sources then are both internal and external, both superior and inferior—intellection and Revelation being of a higher order than reason. Judgment or discernment is part of intellection and hence can look at a reasoned conclusion to determine whether or not it is true. However, our intellects are darkened because of the Fall, and hence we stand in need of Revelation.

Modern psychologists tell us that reason is the highest product of the evolutionary process. Now, clearly, truth does not depend on reason. We do not say something is true because it is logical, but rather that it is logical because it is true. This presupposes a still higher faculty of judging or, to use the term of St. Thomas Aquinas, "discernment." Modern philosophers attempt to get around this problem by speaking of "rational principles," but forget that principles can never be derived from discursive logic. Reason cannot prove its own validity, for principles must be grasped intuitively and suprarationally. As Aristotle said, "one does not demonstrate principles, but one perceives directly the truth thereof..." To make use of scholastic terminology, it is the pure intellect which is the *habitus principiorum*, while reason is only the *habitus conclusionum*. Man then possesses reason and with it language, only because, unlike animals, he has access in principle to suprarational vision. It is this suprarational vision, intellection or insight that gives man, not only discernment, but certitude: certitude in his own existence as a being, confidence in the functional capacity of reason, the ability to discriminate between what is real and what is unreal, what is true and what is false. Intellection is a kind of "seeing," a seeing with the "Third Eye," and not a conclusion, and it is this that opens to man the possibility of metaphysical certitude.

It should be clear that intellection has nothing to do with mental agility. This is well evidenced by what psychiatrists call "idiot savants"—people who can function like a computer, but who are incapable of thinking, much less intellection. But if all men are endowed with an intellect, why is it that all men do not see clearly? The various religions answer this differently. Christianity and the Semitic religions see the intellect as "clouded" and the will as "weakened" by the Fall. This does not mean that man is deprived of them, but only that they don't work as well as they should. Hinduism explains the same situation by what is called *Maya* and portrays sin in terms of ignorance. This is precisely why a Revelation is required. Adam, or man living in the Golden Age, required no Revelation as his intellect was clear and he "walked and talked with God." We, however, especially as we approach the end of the *Kali Yuga*, are desperately in need of a guidance, which is preciscly why there is Revelation.

If the religions provide man with objective criteria, they also hold that man is capable of objectivity. Man is capable of using his intellect to determine what is objectively real and of discriminating between this and what is illusory. This requires on his part a certain act of the will. Man must choose to accept these objective criteria or reject them, and must suffer the consequences which flow from this choice. With freedom comes responsibility. This ability to exercise the intellect and the will are qualities man shares with God and hence man is said to be made in the "image of God." By exercising them correctly, we participate in the divine life. Modern man, seeing himself as made in the "image of an amoeba," does not believe it is possible to know Truth, or God who is the essence of Truth, much less desire Him. Hence he does not believe he is responsible to anything other than his fellow amoebas. And this brings us to another principle that all religions have in common: man is responsible and hence when he dies he will be rewarded or punished in accord with how he uses both his intellect and his free will. This principle is inculcated in a variety of ways. The Semitic religions speak of hell and heaven. Hinduism speaks of the transmigration of the soul, of the need to be born again myriads of times in myriads of worlds prior to being once again given that central opportunity which is man's to achieve—*moksha* or liberation. Buddhism describes this as the "round of existence."

Again, all the religions are agreed that in man there is a hierarchy in which what is higher must rule over what is lower, in which ultimately the *Atman* must rule over the ego and the various passions. As the Bhagavad Gita teaches, it is Krishna who must control and drive the chariot lest the passionate horses, being left unbridled, should run amuck. Putting this in other terms, all the religions advocate a spiritual life whose goal is the sanctification of the individual. All this speaks to the fact that the religions inculcate a strict moral code, not as an end in itself, but as predispositive towards the true and proper ends of man.

Now clearly the religions are agreed on the need of prayer to sanctify our lives. Not only individual prayer whose purpose is to obtain particular favors and to purify the soul, but also prayers that express man's gratitude, resignation, regret, resolution, and praise. Man always has grounds for gratitude. Resignation is the acceptance in advance of the non-fulfillment of some request. Regret or contrition: the asking of pardon, and the desire to remedy some transgression. Praise signifies not only that we relate every value to its ultimate Source, but also that we see every trial in terms of its necessity and usefulness.

Another mode of prayer is meditation where the contact between man and God becomes one between intelligence and Truth. Where prayer is subjective and volitive, meditation is objective and intellectual—in the language of Vedanta it is called *vichara* or "investigation" leading to *viveka* or the discrimination between what is Real and what is unreal. But the individual who follows a path of meditation does so within the cultural milieu of a given tradition which provides him with canonical prayers and presumes all the attitudes that volitive prayer implies as a sort of substratum, *japa yoga* or the invocation of the Divine Name, embracing all these attitudes.

All religions relate back to the Center or Origin, a Golden Age when the Founder "walked upon earth," a sort of *Ram Raj*, and hence see the present era as one of a falling away or degeneracy. Now in view of this, it is not surprising that none of the religions are utopian. One must however make distinctions, for all the religions envision man's life on earth as one to be patterned after a divine model—this precisely in order that our sojourn or exile here below can be one which directs us and leads us to a life above. Here we come to another important point: modern man and the "cultic ethos"—if I can utilize such a phrase—dream of creating a perfect society on earth, a society that is, as T.S. Eliot says, "so perfect that no one will ever need to be good." Modern man has, so to speak, re-oriented himself and, instead of looking "above," he looks "ahead." The religions know that an earthly utopia is an absurd dream. Even in the Garden of Eden a snake existed—or, as Scripture tells us, "God alone is good." The fundamental error of those imbued with the utopian imperative is their mechanistic belief that if one changes the nature of society it will change the nature of man. But every man is a kingdom unto himself and must make the choice of whether or not he wishes to conform to that image in which he is created. Yet all this does not mean that man should not, in con-formity with his nature and with simple good sense, attempt to over-come the evils he encounters in the course of life—this requires no injunctions, either divine or human. Putting it simply, one does not have to be a sage to know enough to come in out of the rain. But to attempt to establish a certain state of well-being with God in view is one thing, and to seek to institute a perfect state of happiness on earth apart from God is quite another. In any event, the latter aim is foredoomed to failure precisely because the lasting elimination of our miseries is dependent not on ourselves, but on our conforming to the Divine Equilibrium and upon our establishing the Kingdom of God within our own souls. As long as men have not realized a sanctifying "inwardness," the abolition of earthly trials is impossible, for, as the Buddha taught, we can never eliminate, sorrow, sickness, old age, and death. It is not only impossible, it is not even desirable, because the sinner—exteriorized man—has need of suffering in order to expiate his faults and tear himself away from sin; in order to escape that very "outwardness" from which sin derives. From the spiritual point of view, which alone takes account of the true cause of our calamities, a society "perfect" in the worldly sense, a society with the maximum of comfort and so-called "justice," would, if the final ends of man were frustrated, be one of the most evil societies conceivable. Those who dream of liberating man from his age-old frustrations are in fact the ones who are imposing on him the most radical and irreparable of all frustrations. The *Civitas Dei* and worldly Progress as envisaged by modern man can never merge.

What kinds of social order do the religions advocate? Basically, one patterned after the Gods—Thy Kingdom come—*Ram Raj jaya.* Such is not capitalism and certainly not socialism. On the contrary, all the traditions envision one which modern economists would describe as "distributism" or what I like to call "sufficientism"—that is, the widest possible distribution of private property providing people with enough to live in dignity such as is appropriate to their station in life. Without private property there can be no freedom. Usury, which is at the heart of modern economics, is forbidden by every religious tradition. It also envisions a non-industrial society, one in which "the artist is not some special kind of man, but each person is a special kind of artist." People in such societies were organized into guilds which functioned not only to protect their members, but also to insist on a high standard of production. The term "masterpiece" was thus applied to the work that an apprentice produced at the end of his period of training and which, when so judged by the guild, gave him the license to open his own shop.

Now, religions are further agreed on several other matters. All are agreed in considering the family as the basic structure of society. Catholics envision it as a mini-Church where the father has as his exemplar God. As Arjuna says in the Gita, "in the destruction of a family, the immemorial family traditions perish; in the perishing of traditions, lawlessness overcomes the whole family ... the abode of the men whose family customs are extinguished is everlastingly in hell." This is one of the reasons the various traditions surround the sexual act with so many taboos or restrictions. This is not the only reason, because fundamentally, the sexual act is seen as a sacred act, one performed in the imitation of the Gods. All the Ancient Teachings insist upon a strict morality—not as an end in itself, but as predispositive to the proper ends of man. Just as he has the "freedom" to think for himself, so also, he has the freedom to act for himself. But he has no "right" to misbehave, and when he does, he loses his dignity. Man is only dignified when he conforms to the Divine Image. Lacking this he behaves like an animal.

Religions display another feature. They are exclusive. They all claim to provide mankind with everything that is needed to save his soul and know his true nature. However much they may appreciate or admit that other religions have elements of truth, they clearly are anti-syncretic. None of them advocates the creation of a single world religion. And there is good reason for this. Inevitably anyone who attempts to syncretize religions abandons objectivity and indulges his personal feelings and becomes his own judge of truth. If we are to let syncretism have its free play, we will all end up drinking wine like Christians and having four wives like Muslims. There is no divine or heavenly mandate for such an approach. Along with this anti-syncretic attitude is another of equal importance. One is required to accept the totality of any given religion. One cannot be half a Muslim—one cannot accept the Hadiths of the Prophet Mohammed and reject the Quran. Similarly, Catholicism teaches that to reject one dot of revealed truth is to reject the whole body of Revelation. One cannot pick and choose.

One last question: are there Ancient Teachings available to us outside the great religions? The answer is both "yes" and "no." "Yes" in the sense that one might turn, for example, to the ancient Egyptian religion. But "no" in the sense that one would not have access to the totality of that religion, and "no" because every religion demands ritual participation as a prerequisite for participation in the Truth.

And so we are brought back to our original thesis: Ancient Teachings or Modern Superstitions—the Search for Authenticity. We have demonstrated that the revelations provide us with objective criteria and that man is capable of objectivity. We have basically three alternatives open to us. Either there is an absolute objective truth outside ourselves, or a relativistic subjective truth drawn from within us, or some mixture of the two. If we accept objective truth and use our innate ability to discern between what is real and what is unreal, we are forced to turn to the Ancient Teachings as incorporated in the great religious traditions. There simply is no other objective source. If we declare ourselves to be the source of what is true for us, or pick and choose between this and the former alternative, to accepting only those Ancient Teachings which we like, we are placed in the position of a physician who treats himself or a lawyer who is his own advocate. However, since we are dealing neither with our physical health nor our money, but rather with our soul, we are in essence declaring that we will be our own spiritual guides. There is an ancient oriental saying that "he who takes himself as his spiritual guide, takes Satan as his guru." The latter alternative is, as Catholic apologists were prone to say, a situation in which "every man becomes his own Pope."

A final caveat: when we look to the Ancient Teachings, we must be absolutely sure that it is the Ancient Teachings we access. Thus with regard to Hinduism, translations by academics trained in the skeptical and positivistic views of the modern West, and unfamiliar with Christian theology, can hardly be expected to produce metaphysically accurate works that can be trusted. The comment also applies to many Hindu translators who derive their training from the same Western sources. The same applies to Catholicism and every other religion. One can no more find true Hindu doctrine in the writings of Krishnamurti and Aurobindo than one can find true Catholic doctrine in the writings of Hans Küng and Karl Rahner.

Now, from the point of view of the Ancient Teachings man is placed in this world so that he can know (*jnana*), love (*bhakti*) and serve (*karma*) God and thereby save his soul (*moksha*). The unfolding of human potential can only follow two alternate courses. Either man conforms to the image in which he is created, and as the early Church Fathers said, "divinizes" himself—and this is what the Ancient Teachings and methods help him to do—or he makes himself the source of both doctrine and method, remains attached to his prideful ego and self-validating psychological experience, and condemns himself to a perpetual migration through interminable samsaric hells. Our human potential can be summed up in two simple alternatives, "sanctity" or "damnation," *moksha* or the interminable round of existence. Heaven or Hell. In the last analysis, nothing else matters.

Satyam aevam jayati—Veritas vincit omnia.

FAITH AND MODERNITY

Karen Armstrong

In the Western world, a strong belief in the objective truths of religion, which are viewed as incontrovertible, demonstrable facts, is regarded as essential to the life of faith. When asking if somebody is religious, people often inquire: "Does he or she believe?" as though accepting certain creedal propositions was the prime religious activity. Indeed, faith is equated with belief, but this equation is of recent provenance. Originally the meaning of the word "faith" was akin to trust, as when we say that we have faith *in* a friend or an ideal. Faith was not an intellectual position but a virtue: it was the careful cultivation, by means of the rituals and myths of religion, of the conviction that, despite all the dispiriting evidence to the contrary, life had some ultimate meaning and value. The Latin word *credo* (translated now as "I believe") seems to have derived from the phrase *cor dare*: to give one's heart. The Middle English word *beleven* meant to love. When Christians proclaimed: *credo in unum Deum*, they were not so much affirming their belief in the existence of a single deity as committing their lives to God. When St. Anselm of Canterbury prayed in the eleventh century: *credo ut intellagam* ("I have faith in order that I may understand"),[1] he was not blindly submitting to the doctrines of religion in the hope that one day these incredible assertions would make sense to him, if he abdicated his critical intelligence. His prayer should really be translated: "I commit myself in order that I may understand." The meaning of dogma would only be revealed when he lived a fully Christian life, embracing its mythology and rituals wholeheartedly. This attitude is foreign to modernity. Today people feel that before they live a religious life, they must first satisfy themselves intellectually of its metaphysical claims. This is sound scientific practice: first you must establish a principle before you can apply it. But it is not the way that religion has traditionally worked.

In the modern world, faith has come to mean an acceptance of creedal truths as objective facts. When people find that they are not

[1] Anselm of Canterbury, *Proslogion*, 2.

convinced by the so-called "proofs" of God's existence, they think that they have lost their faith. Because the doctrines of religion cannot be demonstrated logically and empirically, they seem untrue. Our Western modernity has led us to an entirely different notion of truth, and, as a result, we can no longer be religious in quite the same way as our ancestors. Our scientifically oriented society has lost the sense of the symbolic, which lay at the heart of all pre-modern faith. In the perspectives of tradition, where every earthly reality was a replica of its celestial archetype, the symbol was inseparable from the transcendent reality to which it directed our attention. Likeness denoted presence, in rather the same way as the son of a deceased friend brings his father into the room with him and, at the same time, makes us newly conscious of our loss and distance from the dead and makes us yearn towards the departed. For traditional faith, Christ was present in this way in the eucharistic symbols of bread and wine. Once the Protestant reformers stated that the eucharist was *only* a symbol, and essentially separate from Christ, the modern spirit had declared itself.

In the traditional world, there were two recognized ways of thinking, speaking, and acquiring knowledge, which scholars have called *mythos* and *logos*.[2] Both were essential to humanity; neither was considered superior but both were regarded as complimentary, each with its special area of competence. Myth related to what was thought to be timeless and constant; it looked back to the origins of life, to the beginnings of culture, and to the deepest levels of the mind. Myth was not concerned with practical matters, but with meaning. Unless we find some significance in our lives, human beings fall very easily into despair. The *mythos* of a society provided people with a context that made sense of their day-to-day existence. It directed their attention to the eternal and universal. It was also rooted in what we would call the unconscious mind. The various mythological stories were not intended to be taken literally, but can perhaps be understood as a primitive form of psychology. When people told stories about heroes who descended into the underworld, struggled through labyrinths, or fought with monsters, they were bringing to light the obscure regions of the subconscious

---

[2] See, for example, Johannes Sloek, *Devotional Language*, trans. Henrik Mossin (Berlin and New York, 1996), pp. 53-96.

realm, which is not accessible to purely rational investigation. Because of the dearth of myth, many now resort to the techniques of psychoanalysis to help them to come to terms with their inner world.

Myth could not be demonstrated by logical proof; its insights were more intuitive and similar to those acquired by means of art. Myth only became a reality when it was embodied in cult, rituals, and ceremonies which worked upon the worshipers esthetically, evoking within them a sense of sacred significance and enabling them to apprehend the deeper currents of existence. Myth and cult were so inseparable that it is a matter of scholarly debate which came first: the mythical narrative or the cult that was attached to it. Myth was also associated with mysticism, the descent into the *psyche* by means of structured disciplines of focus and concentration which have been developed in all cultures as a means of acquiring insight that lies beyond the reach of reason. The words "myth" and "mysticism" are both related etymologically to the Greek *musteion*: to close the mouth or the eyes.[3] They are both, therefore, associated with experience that is silent, obscure, and not amenable to the clarity of truths which are self-evident or rationally demonstrable. But without a cult or mystical practice, the truths of mythology make no sense, and seem arbitrary and incredible. In rather the same way, a musical score remains opaque to most of us and needs to be interpreted instrumentally before we can appreciate its beauty and intuit the "truth" that the music is trying to convey.

In the pre-modern world, people had a different view of history, which was not seen as a chronological sequence of unique events but a way of expressing truths that were timeless, constant realities. Hence history would tend to repeat itself: in the Bible, the people of Israel pass miraculously through a sea, which has opened to let them cross dry-shod, on at least two occasions. Historical narratives were composed precisely to bring out this eternal dimension, and were not designed to relate what actually happened.[4] They attempted to define the meaning of an event. Thus we do not know what really occurred when the ancient Israelites escaped from Egypt and

---

[3] John Macquarrie, *Thinking About God* (London, 1957), p. 34.

[4] Sloek, *Devotional Language*, pp. 73-74; Thomas L. Thompson, *The Bible in History: How Writers Create a Past* (London, 1999), pp. 15-33.

passed through the Sea of Reeds. The biblical tale has been deliberately written up as a myth, and linked with other stories about rites of passage, immersion in the deep, and gods splitting a sea in two to bring a new reality into being. Thus well-meaning, modern attempts to explain the story (by referring to the frequency of flash-flooding in the region, for example) are entirely misplaced. The myth has become central to Jewish identity by means of ritual. Every year the Passover *Seder* brings this strange story into their lives and helps them to make it their own. Indeed, the *Haggadah* reminds worshipers that every single Israelite must regard himself or herself as a member of the generation that escaped from slavery in Egypt and passed through the Sea of Reeds. One could say that unless an historical event is mythologized and ritualized in this way, it cannot be religious. The cult and the mythical narrative liberate the original incident from the confines of its historical period and make it a timeless reality in the lives of the faithful. To ask whether the Exodus from Egypt took place exactly as recounted in the Bible or to demand historical or scientific evidence to prove that it is factually true is a modern attitude that mistakes the nature and purpose of this story.

In the same way, St. Paul made the historical Jesus into a myth by means of such rites as baptism and the eucharistic meal. In baptism, he explained to his Roman converts, the Christian entered into the death of the Messiah in the hope of rising again with him to new life;[5] when they broke bread and drank wine in memory of Jesus, as he had instructed his disciples, Christians "proclaimed the death of the Lord," making it ritually present again, and thus making it a redemptive factor in the lives of those present.[6] Indeed, Paul makes it clear that Christians were not concerned any longer with the historical Jesus, who lived "according to the flesh." They now know the Christ in a different, more spiritual way.[7] To this day, Catholics are taught that the Mass recreates the sacrifice of Calvary in a mystical manner, lifting this distant event from the first century and making it a living reality by means of the stylized cultic actions of the priest. In the Islamic tradition, the rites and practices

[5] Romans 6:3-11.

[6] 1 Corinthians 11:23-28.

[7] 2 Corinthians 5:16.

of the Law liberate the Prophet Muhammed from the seventh century: by imitating the way the Prophet lived, loved, prayed, washed, ate, and worshiped, Muslims hope, by cultivating his external *sunnah*, to acquire his attitude of perfect surrender (*islam*) to God; in a real but trans-rational way, the Prophet thus lives again in every devout Muslim, who has internalized Muhammed and made him part of his or her very being. Shii Muslims do the same with Imam Husain, when they reproduce the circumstances of his death in their passion plays and ritual dirges; when they march in mourning processions through the street on the fast day of *Ashura*, the anniversary of Husain's martyrdom, they promise to join his struggle against tyranny and injustice. The rites have made the historical tragedy of Husain's murder at Kerbala a potent myth, which expresses the Shii sense of an unseen but constant battle for justice that lies at the core of human existence.

But in the traditional world, *logos* was equally important. *Logos* was the rational, pragmatic, and scientific thought that enabled men and women to function effectively in the world. Our modernity may have reduced our understanding of *mythos*, but we are very familiar with *logos*, which is the basis of our society. Unlike *mythos*, *logos* must relate accurately to the factual evidence and correspond to external mundane reality if it is to be effective. It must work efficiently in the ordinary world. We use this logical, discursive reasoning when we have to make things happen, get something done, or persuade other people to adopt a particular course of action. *Logos* is practical. Unlike myth, which looks back to the beginnings and to the foundations, *logos* forges ahead and tries to discover something new: to elaborate upon old insights, achieve a greater control over our environment, invent something novel, or find something fresh.[8]

In the pre-modern world, both *mythos* and *logos* were regarded as indispensable. We have always needed science, even if only to make an arrow sharp or effective, or to find the best way of harvesting our crops.

It was the discipline of *logos* which enabled rulers to govern society efficiently, to arrive at satisfactory political decisions, and to succeed in battle. *Mythos* could do none of these things, but it was also

[8] Sloek, *Devotional Language*, pp. 50-52, 68-76.

considered essential for humanity. We are beings that fall very easily into despair. Unlike other animals, we fret about the human condition, are haunted by the fact of our mortality, and distressed beyond measure by the tragedies that flesh is heir to. As soon as men and women became recognizably human, they began to create religions, at the same time and for the same reasons as they created works of art: the myths and cults of tradition gave their lives a sense of sacred significance which made them worthwhile; they provided the context within which they could pursue their *logos*-driven activities.

But *mythos* and *logos* were essentially distinct, and it was held to be dangerous to confuse mythical and rational discourse. They had separate jobs to do. Myth was not reasonable; its narratives were not expected to be demonstrated empirically. You were not supposed to make *mythos* the basis of a pragmatic policy. If you did so, the results could be disastrous, because what worked well in the inner world of the *psyche* was not readily applicable to the affairs of the external world. When, for example, Pope Urban II summoned the First Crusade in 1095, his plan belonged to the realm of *logos*. He wanted the knights of Europe to stop fighting one another and tearing the fabric of Western Christendom apart, but instead to expend their energies instead in a war in the Middle East and so extend the power of the Roman church. But when this military expedition became entangled with folk mythology, biblical lore, and apocalyptic fantasy, the result was catastrophic, practically, militarily, and morally. Throughout the long Crusading project, it remained true that whenever *logos* was in the ascendant, the Crusaders prospered. They performed well on the battlefield, created workable colonies in the Middle East, and learned to relate more positively with the local Muslim population. But whenever the Crusaders made a mythical or mystical vision the basis of their policies, they were usually defeated and committed terrible atrocities.[9]

Yet *logos* also had its limitations. It could not assuage human pain or sorrow. Rational discourse could make no sense of tragedy. Faced with the natural catastrophes and man-made atrocities which punctuate human life, reason is silent and has nothing to say. A sci-

[9] Karen Armstrong, *Holy War: The Crusades and their Impact on Today's World* (London, 1988; London and New York, 1991), pp. 3-75, 147-274.

entist could make things work more efficiently and could discover astounding new facts about the physical world, but he could not explain the meaning of life. *Logos* could not answer our anguished questions about the ultimate value of human life. That was the preserve of myth or cult.[10]

In the traditional worldview, faith had a different meaning. People did not, for example, read their scriptures in a literal manner. After the Jews were expelled from Spain in 1492, some of the exiles found comfort in the teaching of Isaac Luria (1524-1572), who evolved a new creation myth, which bore no relation to the creation story in the Book of Genesis. But to Luria's disciples, the new myth made perfect sense. They were still reeling with the shock and trauma of exile, and Luria's version of creation resonated deeply with this experience. It began with an act of voluntary exile. In order to make room for the world, the infinite, inaccessible, and omnipresent god (which Jewish mystics call *Ein Sof*: "Without End") shrank into itself, evacuating, as it were, a region within itself in order to make a space for the physical universe. In its compassionate desire to make itself known in and by its creatures, *Ein Sof* had inflicted exile on a part of itself. Unlike the orderly creation described in Genesis, this was a violent process of primal explosions, disasters, and false starts, which seemed to the Spanish exiles a more accurate picture of the cruel world they had experienced. At an early stage, *Ein Sof* had tried to fill the vacuum it had created with light, but the "vessels" or "pipes," which were supposed to channel this divine light shattered under the strain. Sparks of heavenly light remained trapped in the world of matter; everything was now in the wrong place, and Luria's disciples imagined the *Shekhinah*, the Presence that is the closest we come to an apprehension of the divine in this life, wandering through the world, a perpetual exile, yearning to be reunited with the Godhead.[11]

If the mystics of Safed had been asked if they believed that this had really happened, they would have considered it an inept question. The primordial events described in such *mythos* were not simply incidents that had happened once in the remote past; they were also occurrences that happened all the time. They pointed to the

---

[10] Sloek, *Devotional Language*, p. 143.

[11] Gershom Scholem, *Major Trends in Jewish Mysticism* (London, 1955), pp. 245-280.

fundamental truths and laws that underlay phenomena and historical happenings. The Spanish Jews would probably have replied that exile was a basic law of existence. All over the world, Jews were uprooted aliens; even the Gentiles experienced loss, disappointment, and a sense that they were not quite at home in the world, and Luria's creation myth revealed this in a wholly new way. The exile of the *Shekhinah* and their own lives as refugees were not two separate realities, but were one and the same, since exile was inscribed in the very Ground of being—even in God itself. Today people would be disturbed by such a flagrant departure from scripture, yet Luria's vision became a mass-movement, the only theological system to win such general acceptance among Jews all over the world at this time.[12] A literal reading of Scripture is a modern preoccupation. In the traditional world, Jews, Christians, and Muslims all relished highly allegorical, inventive, and esoteric interpretations of the sacred text. Since God's word was infinite, it was capable of multiple readings. So Jews were not distressed, as many modern people would be, by Luria's divergence from the plain meaning of the Bible. His myth spoke to them with authority because it explained their lives and provided them with meaning.

But despite the power of its symbolism, Lurianic Kabbalah would not have become so popular had it not been expressed in ritual and meditative disciplines. Jews who followed Luria's vision would make night vigils, rising at midnight, weeping, and rubbing their faces in the dust. These ritual gestures helped them to express their sense of grief and trauma, and linked them with their exiled God. They would lie awake all night, calling out to God like lovers, lamenting the pain of separation which is at the heart of the experience of exile. There were penitential disciplines—fasting, lashings, rolling in the snow—which were believed to hasten the end of this divine exile. Kabbalists would go for long hikes through the countryside, wandering like the *Shekhinah*, and acting out their sense of homelessness.[13] But Luria insisted that there was to be no

---

[12] Gershom Scholem, *Sabbetai Sevi: The Mystical Messiah* (London and Princeton, 1973), pp. 23-25; R.J. Weblowsky, "Messianism in Jewish History," in Marc J. Saperstein (ed.), *Essential Papers in Messianic Movements in Jewish History* (New York and London, 1992), p. 48.

[13] R.J. Weblowsky, "The Safed Revival and Its Aftermath," in Arthur Green (ed.), *Jewish Spirituality*, 2 Vols., (London, 1986, 1999), II, pp. 15-19.

unhealthy wallowing. His mystics must work through their sorrow in a disciplined stylized way, until they achieved a measure of joy. The midnight rituals always ended with a meditation on the reunion of the *Shekhinah* with *Ein Sof,* and, consequently, the end of the separation of humanity from its divine source. The mystic was told to imagine that every one of his limbs was an earthly shrine for the Divine Presence.[14] They were also taught the techniques of concentration (*kawwanot*), which helped them to become aware of the divine spark of light within their own selves and which filled them with bliss and rapture. These mystical disciplines and cultic rituals filled Jews with joy at a time when the world seemed alien and cruel.[15] Rational thought cannot assuage our sorrow. After the Spanish disaster, Jews found that the logical discipline of philosophy, which had been popular among the Spanish Jews, could not address their pain.[16] To make life bearable, the exiles turned from *logos* to *mythos,* which enabled them to make contact with the unconscious sources of their sense of loss, and anchored their lives in a vision that bought them comfort.

Without a cult, without prayer and ritual, myths and doctrines seem arbitrary and meaningless. Without the special rites he devised, Luria's creation story would have remained a conoclcuu, bizarre fiction. Faith is only possible in such a liturgical, prayerful context. Once people were deprived of that type of spiritual activity, they would lose their faith. This is what happened to some of the Jews who elected in 1492 to stay behind in Spain and convert to Christianity. This had been the choice offered to Jews by Ferdinand and Isabella, the Catholic monarchs of Spain, when they signed the Edict of Expulsion. While many of these Jewish converts to Christianity became fervent and even influential Catholics, many never fully made the transition to the new faith. This was hardly surprising, since, once they had been baptized, they were scrutinized

---

[14] Gershom Scholem, *On the Kabbalah and its Symbolism* (New York, 1965), p. 150.

[15] Laurence Fine, "The Contempla5

tive Practice of Yehudim in Lurianic Kabbalah," in Green (ed.), *Jewish Spirituality,* II, pp. 89-90; Louis Jacobs, "The Uplifting of the Sparks in Later Jewish Mysticism," in *Jewish Spirituality,* II, pp. 108-111.

[16] R.J. Weblowsky, "The Safed Revival and Its Aftermath," p. 17; Jacob Katz, "Halakah and Kabbalah as Competing Disciplines of Study," in Green (ed.), *Jewish Spirituality,* II, pp. 52-53.

by the Inquisition, and lived in constant fear of arrest on the flimsiest of charges. Ever watchful for any signs of a convert lapsing back into Judaism (such as refusing to eat shellfish or work on the Sabbath), this scrutiny by the Inquisition could mean imprisonment, torture, death, or, at the very least, the confiscation of the suspects' property.[17] As a result, some of the converted Jews became alienated from religion altogether. They could not identify with the Catholicism which made their lives a misery, and, since there was no practicing Jews left in the Iberian peninsula, Judaism itself became a distant, unreal memory. Even if the converts wished to practice Judaism in secret, they had no means of learning about Jewish law or ritual practice. In consequence, some were pushed into a religious limbo. Long before secularism, atheism, and religious indifference became common in the rest of Europe, we find instances of these essentially modern attitudes among the Marrano Jews of the Iberian peninsula.[18] Some of the Jewish converts did try to adhere to Judaism in secret, but because they did not know how to pray, or to perform the rites of the Law, their "Judaism" bore little relation to the reality.

Because those closet Jews did not know how to pray or how to perform the rites correctly, they fell back perforce on reason, creating a form of rational deism, not dissimilar to the philosophical religion that became popular in Europe during the eighteenth century Enlightenment.[19] In the seventeenth century, some of these secret Jews escaped from the Iberian peninsula and fled to Amsterdam, where Jews were allowed to practice their faith openly and without persecution. But when they encountered a real Jewish community, a few of them were appalled. The laws and customs of Judaism seemed senseless and barbaric. They had studied modern sciences in Iberia, such as logic, physics, mathematics, and medicine. The abstruse dietary laws and the rituals of purification seemed barbaric and meaningless to these sophisticated Jews, who found it difficult to accept the explanations of the rabbis because they had become accustomed to thinking things out rationally for

---

[17] Paul Johnson, *A History of the Jews* (London, 1986), pp. 225-29.

[18] Yirmanyahu Yovel, *Spinoza and Other Heretics, I: The Marrano of Reason* (Princeton, 1989), pp. 91, 93, 102.

[19] *Ibid.*, pp. 75-76.

themselves.[20] To an outsider, many of the laws and customs of the Torah seem bizarre: they make sense only in a cultic context which had been denied to the secret Jews of Spain. Two of these Jewish refugees from the Spanish inquisition achieved notoriety in Amsterdam, because they found it quite impossible to adapt. In the early seventeenth century, one Uriel Da Costa was expelled three times from the Jewish community of Amsterdam: he had written a treatise attacking Jewish law, declaring that he believed only in human reason and the laws of nature. As an excommunicate, he lived an isolated, miserable life, jeered at by children in the street, and shunned by Jews and Christians alike. In 1640, he finally shot himself in the head.[21] In 1657, the rabbis were forced to expel Juan da Prado, who had been horrified by the Judaism he had discovered in Amsterdam. In Portugal, he had belonged to the Jewish underground, fighting for his right to think and worship as he chose, but his idea of Judaism was entirely idiosyncratic. Why did Jews think that God had chosen them alone, he demanded of the Amsterdam rabbis; was it not more logical to think of God as the First Cause rather than as a personality who had dictated a set of barbarous, absurd laws?[22] To Jews such as Prado and da Costa, the *mythos* of Judaism seemed nonsensical, because they approached it from the standpoint of reason, outside the liturgical context that alone could endow it with significance and spirituality. Many modern people have a similar problem, when they confront the mythology of religion with *logos* alone. They do not meditate, perform rituals, or take part in any ceremonial liturgy, and find that the myths of religion are senseless, barbaric, and incredible.

At the same time as da Costa and Prado were struggling with the mythology of Judaism, modernity was slowly and painfully coming to birth in Europe. It was a long and complex process, but by the eighteenth century, the people of Europe and America had achieved such astonishing success in science that they began to think that *logos* was the only path to truth and began to discount *mythos* as false and superstitious. The new world that was being created contradicted the dynamic of the old mythical spirituality. Our

[20] *Ibid.*, pp. 51-52.
[21] *Ibid.*, pp. 42-51.
[22] *Ibid.*, pp. 57-73.

religious experience in the modern world has changed, and because an increasing number of people regard scientific rational-ism alone as true, they have often tried to turn *mythos* into faith in *logos*, even though in the pre-modern world it was always considered dangerous to conflate the two.

We can see the dearth of mythical thinking in the philosophy of the French scientist René Descartes (1596-1650), who was only able to speak in *logoi*. For Descartes, the universe was a lifeless machine, the physical world inert and dead. It could yield no information about the divine: the sole living thing in the cosmos was the human mind, which could find certainty only by turning in upon itself. We could not even be sure that anything besides our own doubts and thoughts exists. Descartes was a devout Catholic, and he wanted to satisfy himself about God's existence. But he could not submit to the rhythms of *mythos*, so deeply was he involved in the disciplines of rational thought. Where myth had always looked back to the pri-mordial beginnings, Descartes was a child of *logos*, which is always pressing forward and seeking something new. He could not there-fore go back to the imaginary past of myth and cult. Nor could he rely on the insights of the old prophets and holy texts. A man of the new age, he would not accept received ideas. The scientist, he believed, must make his mind a *tabula rasa*. Truth could only be sup-plied by mathematics or by such self-evident propositions as "What's done cannot be undone." Since the way back was closed, Descartes could only inch his way painfully forward.

One evening, sitting besides a wood stove, Descartes evolved the maxim: *Cogito ergo sum*: "I think, therefore I am." This, he main-tained, was self-evident and certain. The only thing of which we could be certain was our mind's experience of doubt. But doubt showed the imperfection of the human mind, and the very notion of "imperfection" would make no sense if we did not have a prior notion of "perfection." Since a perfection that did not exist would be a contradiction in terms, God—the Ultimate Perfection—must exist.[23] This so-called proof is unlikely to convince a modern skep-tic. It shows the impotence of reason, when it is not backed up by prayer and ritual, when faced with ultimate issues. Descartes, sitting beside his stove, in his cold, empty world, locked into his own uncer-

[23] Cf. René Descartes, *Discourse on Method*, II.6.19.

tainty, and uttering a "proof" which is little more than a mental conundrum embodies the spiritual dilemma of modern humanity, which has lost the traditional understanding of the role and truth of *mythos*.

We can see how impossible it was for a man of reason to think mythically in the case of the British scientist Sir Isaac Newton (1642-1727), who was perhaps the first fully to make rigorous use of the new scientific methodology of experimentation and deduction. But this total immersion in the world of *logos* made it impossible for Newton to appreciate that other, more intuitive forms of perception might also offer human beings a form of truth. He was a deeply religious man; in the course of his studies, as he contemplated what he believed to be the scientific laws that governed the universe, he used to cry aloud: "O God, I think Thy thoughts after Thee!"[24] But for Newton, mythology and mystery were primitive and barbaric: "'Tis the temper of the hot and superstitious part of mankind in matters of religion," he once wrote irritably, "ever to be fond of mysteries and for that reason to like best what they understand least."[25]

Newton became almost obsessed with the desire to purge the Christian faith of its mythical doctrines. He became convinced that the arational dogmas of the Trinity and the Incarnation were the result of a fourth century conspiracy. While working on his magnum opus *Philosophiae Naturalis Principia*, he was also hard at work on a treatise called *The Philosophical Origins of Gentile Theology*, which argued that Noah had founded a superstition-free religion which had no revealed scriptures, no doctrines, but only a Deity which could be known through the contemplation of the natural world in a rational manner. Later generations had corrupted this pure faith, and imposed the abominable doctrines of Trinitarianism upon the Church by forging the evidence. Newton was now so thoroughly imbued with pure *logos* that he could not see that the Greek Orthodox theologians of the fourth century had devised the doctrine of the Trinity precisely as *mythos*. As Gregory of Nyssa, one of

[24] Richard Tarnas, *The Passion of the Western Mind: Understanding the Ideas that Have Shaped Our World View* (New York and London, 1991), p. 300.

[25] Richard S. Westfall, "The Rise of Science and the Decline of Orthodox Christianity: A Study of Kepler, Descartes, and Newton," in David C. Lindberg and Ronald L. Numbers (eds.), *God and Nature: Historical Essays on the Encounter Between Christianity and Science* (Berkeley, Los Angeles, and London, 1986), p. 231.

the doctrine's creators, had explained, the three hypostases of Father, Son, and Spirit were not objective facts but simply "terms that we use" to express the way in which the "unnamable and unspeakable" divine nature adapts itself to the limitations of our human minds. It made no sense outside the cultic context of prayer, contemplation, and liturgy.[26] But Newton could only see the Trinity in rational terms, had no understanding of the role of myth, and was therefore obliged to jettison the doctrine. The difficulty that many Christians today experience with trinitarian theology, which is the crux of Greek Orthodox spirituality, show that they share Newton's bias in favor of scientific rationalism.

Hitherto, in the perspectives of tradition, *mythos* and *logos* had always been seen as complimentary. Now for the first time in human history, they were beginning to be seen as incompatible. But even though *logos* can provide us with great gifts on the practical level, it is incapable of yielding a sense of sacred significance or of addressing the ultimate questions. At a time when science and unfettered rationality were forging brilliantly ahead, life was becoming meaningless for an increasing number of people, who for the first time were having to live without mythology. The British philosopher Thomas Hobbes (1588-1679) believed that there was a God, but for all practical purposes, God might just as well not exist. God, Hobbes thought, had revealed himself at the beginning of history and would do so again at its End, but until that time we had to get along without him, and wait for him in the dark.[27] For the French mathematician Blaise Pascal (1623-1662), an intensely religious man, the emptiness and the "eternal silence" of the infinite universe opened up by modern science inspired pure terror:

> When I see the blind and wretched state of men, when I survey the whole universe in its deadness and man left to himself with no light, as though lost in this corner of the universe without knowing who put him there, what he has to do, what will become of him when he dies, incapable of knowing anything, I am moved to terror, like a man transported in his sleep to some terrifying desert

---

[26] Gregory of Nyssa, "*To Alybius: That There Are Not Three Gods.*"

[27] Joshua Mitchell, *Not By Reason Alone: Religion, History, and Identity in Early Modern Political Thought* (Chicago, 1993), pp. 58, 61.

island, who wakes up quite lost with no means of escape. I marvel that so wretched a state does not drive people to despair.[28]

Reason and *logos* had never been deemed capable of assuaging such existential terror. As a result of the modern jettisoning of *mythos*, despair and alienation of the sort so eloquently described by Pascal have been a part of the modern experience.

By the end of the nineteenth century, scientific rationalism had been so astoundingly successful that an increasing number of scientists, who could command a large popular following, maintained dogmatically that reason must be the sole criterion of truth. As T.H. Huxley (1825-1895), who popularized Darwin's ideas, explained, people would have to choose between mythology and science. There could be no compromise: "one or the other would have to succumb after a struggle of unknown duration."[29] Truth was now narrowed down to what is "demonstrated and demonstrable,"[30] which, religion aside, would exclude the truths told by art or music. For a man like Huxley, there was no other path. Reason alone was truthful and the dogmas of religion were truthless, because they could not be proved logically and empirically. Once religious truth was treated as though it were rational *logos*, it became incredible. This was perceived by Friedrich Nietzsche (1844-1900), who declared in *The Gay Science* (1882) that God was dead. He told the parable of a madman running one morning into the marketplace crying "I seek god!" When the amused bystanders asked if he imagined that God had emigrated or taken a holiday, the madman glared. "Where has God gone?" he demanded. "We have killed him—you and I! We are all his murderers!"[31] In an important sense, Nietzsche was right. Without myth, cult, ritual, and prayer, the sense of the sacred evoked only by these means inevitably dies. By making "God" a wholly notional truth, struggling to reach the divine by intellect alone, as some modern believers were attempting to do in the new age, modern men and women had killed it for themselves.

[28] Blaise Pascal, *Pensées*, trans. A.J. Krailsheimer (London, 1966), p. 209.

[29] Quoted in Peter Gay, *A Godless Jew: Freud, Atheism, and the Making of Psychoanalysis* (New Haven and London, 1987), pp. 6-7.

[30] T.H. Huxley, *Science and Christian Tradition* (New York, 1896), p. 125.

[31] Friedrich Nietzsche, *The Gay Science* (New York, 1974), p. 181.

The whole dynamic of their future-oriented culture had made the traditional ways of apprehending the sacred psychologically impossible. Like the Iberian Jews, who had been forced to convert to Christianity and tried to hold on to their Judaism in secret, they had been thrust into a religious limbo, and many people imbued with the rational ethos of modernity experienced the truths of religion as tenuous, arbitrary, and incomprehensible.

Nietzsche's madman believed that the death of God had torn humanity from its roots, thrown the earth off course, and cast it adrift in a pathless universe. Everything that had once given human beings a sense of ultimate direction had vanished. "Is there still an above and below?" he had asked. "Do we not stray, as though through an infinite nothingness." A profound terror, a sense of meaningless rage and fear of annihilation has become a part of the modern experience. Modernity has been enthralling, empowering, and liberating for those of us who are fortunate enough to live in the privileged sectors of the world. But without a faith that life has some ultimate value, human existence becomes prey to despair. The terrible icons of our century, Auschwitz, Rwanda, Bosnia, and Kosovo, give us a chilling glimpse of a world in which all sense of sacredness has been lost. To recover our sense of the divine, however we choose to formulate it, we need somehow to recover our sense of *mythos*, reinstating it as the partner of scientific *logos*.

THE LOGIC OF MYSTERY AND THE NECESSITY OF FAITH

Timothy Scott

For the person of simple religious faith the sense of being irrational in the light of modern science can sometimes occasion embarrassment. Such people often find themselves believing in a science based on the seen and the knowable, yet having faith in the unseen and the unknowable. Inevitably they feel themselves caught in a contradiction. The scientism of the modern era claims a rational view of reality. Up against this rationality it places what it takes to be the often incongruous demands of religious faith. However, it is a gross error to suggest that rationality and faith-based perspectives are irreconcilable. Faith, fully understood, is conformity to Truth. Rational thought is a mode of perception of truth and as such faith is rational, or more to the point, rationality is an aspect of faith. This without denying an element of mystery in faith; for mystery, properly understood, is a *sine qua non* of Reality, which is to say, it is a logical imperative. By contrast, the modern scientific claim to objectivity can be shown to be intrinsically unsound and anti-rational. Here it suffices to show that it involves a contradiction of first principles.

This essay presents a comparison of the religious and the modern understandings of the nature of Reality. The aim is to show that it is only from the metaphysical perspective—the intellectual understanding of the religious viewpoint—that Reality can be understood in a manner that is logically sound. According to this position faith is fundamental to an understanding of the nature of Reality. However the necessity of faith provides no excuse for being anti-rational. On the one hand, as St. Anselm famously put it, one is obliged to believe in order to be able to understand (*credo ut intelligam*); on the other hand, to say human is to say intelligence and thus the right to use this intelligence. In fact, our right to intelligence is nothing less than an obligation to apply it to its full extent and thus to its limit. That which is limited implies that which limits and, *ipso facto*, that which is "beyond." Yet the limit of intelligence does not imply a failing in its power but in fact the very opposite, for this limitation, as such, supplies our intelligence with its highest function: the intimation of that which is greater than ourselves.[1]

Credo ut intelligam. Yet, from a certain perspective, it is equally true to say that "with understanding one is obliged to believe." In the words of Ananda Coomaraswamy, "One must believe in order to understand, and understand in order to believe. These are not successive, however, but simultaneous acts of the mind."[2] But this does not mean that subjective intellection can act on its own behalf without the objectifying light of the divine Intellect that manifests Itself through Revelation. As Frithjof Schuon remarks, "One can neither conceive of a Saint Augustine without the Gospels, nor a Shankaracharya without the Veda."[3]

Faith is both rational and supra-rational; this latter and infinitely higher aspect of faith in no way implies a denial of the former. In the first case, the necessity of faith, arising from the logical place of mystery in the structure of Reality, means that faith is fundamentally rational, at least if we are to use this term in the sense of being logical, practical and common-sensical. In the second case, the fulfillment of faith involves an understanding of a level of Reality beyond that accessible to rational thought. It is in this second sense that we might say that faith is non-rational, but this is simply to say that it is not commensurate with rational thought by virtue of transcending it.

*

The person of religious sensibility has faith in a reality both seen (immanent: "in the world") and unseen (transcendent: "in heaven"). For the strict rationalist, belief is limited to what can be "seen" and measured. It is thus better to refer to this mindset as empirical rather than rational, for the rational faculty, as a mode of our intelligence, is limited only by its scope and in this limitation it alludes to that which exceeds it; by contrast, the strictly empirical mind is limited by the boundaries it imposes upon itself in denying any

---

[1] In this way the limit of indefinite space implies the Infinite.

[2] A. Coomaraswamy, *Selected Papers Vol.2: Metaphysics*, ed. R. Lipsey (Princeton: Princeton University Press, 1977), p. 8.

[3] F. Schuon, *Stations of Wisdom* (Bloomington, IN: World Wisdom Books, 1995), p. 44.

other reality. For the empiricist what cannot be measured, *ipso facto*, does not exist.

The study of the empirical world of and for itself does have certain benefits as long as it is recognized for what it is. But it cannot answer any so-called "questions of existence," and it is this presumption with which we are here concerned. Here it suffices to note that the empirical mindset rests on a fundamental flaw: it seeks to explain the greater by the lesser. For the empiricist a thing can only be the sum of its parts. The empirical ideology proposes to answer the question of reality by exhausting the measure of the universe. Yet the very mentality that produced empiricism has proceeded to demonstrate the ultimate impotence of the purely empirical methodology when Reality is considered at the quantum level. Heisenberg's Uncertainty Principle and Bohr's Copenhagen Interpretation lead to the realization that "uncertainty and fuzziness are intrinsic to the quantum world and not merely the result of our incomplete perception of it."[4] For physicists the "staggering conclusion" of all this is that consciousness is not merely an observer in the dynamics of the universe, but an active participant.[5]

A cautionary note: we must not be fooled into thinking that these new sciences bring the answer to the "meaning of existence." It is sometimes claimed that the new sciences "prove" what was once only primitively intuited (and here both "primitive" and "intuition" have a pejorative coloring). With this "proof" is claimed a victory for modern intellectualism over the traditional acceptance of faith. Let us simply say, without wishing to understate the gravity of this point, that these new sciences bear the seed of a danger more subtle than the simplistic bludgeonings of the empiricist, for they introduce the deceit of the counterfeit; but this is another question.[6]

The empiricists want a reality that can be pegged down. Yet, at the same time they posit a reality constantly in flux, as new "facts"

[4] P.C.W. Davies and J.R. Brown (eds.), *The Ghost in the Atom* (Cambridge: Cambridge University Press, 1989), p. 12. The unsatisfactory and implicitly negative notions of "uncertainty" and "fuzziness" are positively expressed through the religious conception of "mystery."

[5] D. Reanney, *The Death of Forever: A New Future for Human Consciousness* (Melbourne: Longman Cheshire, 1992), p. 25.

[6] On the modern counterfeit of traditional understanding, the "Great Parody," see René Guénon, *The Reign of Quantity & The Signs of the Times* (Middlesex: Penguin Books, 1972), Chapters 38 & 39.

are discovered and old theories abandoned. One must keep in mind that a fact that can eventually be disproved is precisely not a fact. Undoubtedly there are many sincere scientists who readily admit that the scientific ideology is based upon hypotheses and not facts; however, we are far from being concerned with the integrity of those for whom science constitutes an expertise, but instead take issue with the scientism that has become the pseudo-religion of our age.

Mathematically speaking, the empiricists attempt to explain the line as a sum of points and, moreover, to explain this in terms of measure. On the one hand, any single point is indefinitely small, and indefinitely large for that matter. Thus the line is made up of an indefinitude of points, which is to say that any attempt to truly know the line by measure is futile. On the other hand, a point, in itself, can not be said to have a quality of magnitude and thus does not lengthen the line of which it is the principle;[7] this again discounts the idea of a purely quantitative measure of the line.[8] Moreover, as noted above, attempts at measure are influenced by the subjectivity of the measurer. If one sets out to understand a line as the sum of its points then one must start at a point. From the first point the next point is considered with respect to this starting point. However, when one moves on to the next point the relationship is changed and the "original" point is no longer the same point, as it now lacks the element of the measurer's experience of it. Hence this method of understanding can never be more than a subjective approximation. This is not to say that an approximation may not have value as a working figure, but simply that the line cannot be "known," in any absolute sense, by measure.

The growth of the modern mindset was solidified with Descartes' *cogito ergo sum*, with the Cartesian plane becoming the basis for modern measurement. With this statement the modern mindset, which can be traced from the Renaissance onwards, was truly born. Descartes' *cogito* signaled a shift in our perceptive start-

---

[7] This is a point made by Meister Eckhart, *Par. Gen.* prop. 20. See *Meister Eckhart: The Essential Sermons, Commentaries, Treatises, and Defense*, trans. E. Colledge and B. McGinn (New Jersey: Paulist Press, 1981), p. 100. See further, Albert the Great, *On Indivisible Lines* 5-6 and, of course, Euclid's *Geometry*.

[8] On the argument against the modern idea of quantitative measure see René Guénon's, *The Reign of Quantity & The Signs of the Times*, Ch. 4.

ing point from the evidentness of the divine Object to the individual recognizing subject. The error of this shift should be obvious.
To use a well-known metaphor: it is as if one were to try to see the
faculty of sight with the eye. Still, the irrationality of this notion will
be apparent only to those who can see beyond empiricism.

*

For all traditional peoples, which is to say religious peoples, the
starting point is obvious: God Is; Reality Is; Being Is; the Absolute Is.
Thus Descartes' famous proposition is, in a sense, an inversion of
what should appear obvious: "Being is, therefore I think." Even this
is not precise; better to say, "Being is Consciousness." The traditional mind starts from the evidentness of Reality and in the light of
this truth is able to understand existence. The modern mind starts
from individual existence, with all its subjective prejudices, and
from there attempts to construct a reality. The traditional mind is
inward looking; it bases itself on one true Center, a Principle,
untainted by its effect, from which everything else can be logically
deduced. The modern mind is outward looking; it seeks to measure
the extent of that which is not only indefinite, and thus immeasurable, but also constantly affected by this act of measuring. At the risk
of delving into the modern psyche, one is tempted to say that the
empiricists are compelled to continue looking "outwards," regardless of any sense of the futility of this method that they might feel,
for they have tied their whole notion of self to this methodology.
What has been said regarding the empirical perspective will not
change the minds of those who proclaim it; one cannot argue someone into a position of faith. It is enough to show that the empirical
method is essentially irrational. We must now turn to the religious
or traditional understanding of Reality to determine the logical
consistency of this perspective.

God is both Being and Beyond-Being, and this we may call the
absoluteness of God. To say that Being is ontologically evident is a
pleonasm, but one that is helpful. Similarly, the Absolute is logically evident. Beginning from this position we may explain the universe and the meaning of our existence. Unlike the modern
scientific method, this explanation is not a progression outwards
into the absurd but, instead, it is like the opening of a multifoliate
rose, revealing layers of petals that have been there all along. Within

this unfolding we find the logical place of mystery and the necessity of faith.

While modern science is the science of physics, the *scientia sacra* of traditional understanding is the science of metaphysics.[9] "In metaphysics," says Schuon, "it is necessary to start from the idea that the Supreme Reality is absolute, and that being absolute it is infinite. That is absolute which allows of no augmentation or diminution, or of no repetition or division; it is therefore that which is at once solely itself and totally itself. And that which is infinite is not determined by any limiting factor and therefore does not end at a boundary; it is in the first place Potentiality or Possibility as such, and *ipso facto* the Possibility of things, hence Virtuality."[10] Here we must not make the modern error of confusing the term "infinite," which refers to that which is beyond the finite, with the term "indefinite," which refers to the perpetual extension of the finite. The Absolute, in the full sense of this term, is identical with All-Possibility or the Infinite, and in this it is the Supreme Perfection or the Good. In fact, as Schuon remarks, "there is no need to consider a trinity formed by the aspects 'Good,' 'Absolute,' 'Infinite'; but rather, what ought to be said is that the Sovereign Good is absolute and, therefore, that it is infinite."[11]

All-Possibility, by definition, includes the possibilities of Being and Non-Being. Regarding the idea of "Non-Being" Plato says that "it is really impossible to speak of Non-Being or to say anything about it or to conceive it by itself, but it is inconceivable, not to be spoken of or mentioned, and irrational."[12] Note again that Non-Being is "irrational" only insomuch as it is not commensurate with the rational domain, which exists within the domain of Being. Ontological Potentiality is *a* possibility of the All-Possibility and thus identical in essence if not extent; that is to say, Potentiality is identical to Possibility without limiting Possibility to Potentiality. Similarly, Being is identical with the Absolute without limiting the

---

[9] On the *scientia sacra* see S.H. Nasr, *Knowledge and the Sacred* (Edinburgh: Edinburgh University Press, 1981), Ch. 4.

[10] F. Schuon, *Survey of Metaphysics and Esoterism* (Bloomington, IN: World Wisdom Books, 2000), p. 15.

[11] F. Schuon, *Survey of Metaphysics and Esoterism*, pp. 22-23.

[12] *Sophist* 238 c.

Absolute to Being. Thus one talks of the Absolute as "Beyond-Being." Consider this extended analogy: the Absolute is a sea within which there is a glass of water, which here stands for Being. Furthermore, the glass is itself an illusion, its substance being also water; here one might consider the glass as formed of ice, which in substance, if not in state, is still water, and this is to recognize that illusion is a state and not a substance. The water in the glass and the water of the sea are identical in substance but not in extent. One might say that there is a difference or discontinuity in extent of substance but an identity or continuity of essence/substance (*ousia*).[13] The sea is "beyond" the water of the cup in its extent; at the same time it contains and intimately identifies with the water of the cup so that they are not other than each other or, better to say, there is only the Sea.

The Absolute is transcendent Unity.[14] It is that in which all possibilities are equal by virtue of essential identification. In this context one can say that Being and Non-Being are identical, if not the same. At the same time Non-Being is identified with Beyond-Being. In this connection Titus Burckhardt mentions the Islamic term *al-udum*, which expresses on the one hand "the positive sense of non-manifestation, of a principial state beyond existence or even beyond Being, and on the other hand a negative sense of privation, of relative nothingness."[15] "If I say: 'God is a being,'" says Meister Eckhart, "it is not true; he is a being transcending being and a transcending nothingness."[16]

It is the relativity born of Being that allows for the possibility of Non-Being. The illusion of the Relative represents the possibility for Being of not being. Schuon: "It is in order not to be, that Being

---

[13] As Titus Burckhardt observes, the Greek term *ousia* connotes both substance and essence (*Alchemy* [Baltimore: Penguin, 1974], p. 36, n. 3); this is likewise the case with the Arabic term *'ayn* (T. Burckhardt, *An Introduction to Sufi Doctrine* [Wellingborough: The Aquarian Press, 1976], p. 62, n. 1).

[14] "Hear, O Israel: the Lord our God is one Lord" (*Shema: Deuteronomy* 6:4 [5]). This is the supreme and transcendent Unity and not simply the immanent uniqueness of Being. As Clement of Alexandria says, "God is one, and beyond the one and above the Monad itself" (*Paedagogus*, 71, 1). The distinction in the Islamic tradition is that between *al-Wahidiyah* (the Divine Uniqueness) and *al-Ahadiyah* (the Transcendent Unity).

[15] T. Burckhardt, *An Introduction to Sufi Doctrine*, p. 126

[16] Meister Eckhart, Sermon 83 in *Meister Eckhart: The Essential Sermons*, p. 100.

incarnates in the multitude of souls; it is in order not to be, that the ocean squanders itself in myriad flecks of foam."[17] This is to regard manifestation as a tendency to nothingness, an idea alluded to by Meister Eckhart when he speaks of all creatures as "nothing."[18] On the one hand, creatures are "nothing" in that they have no reality in comparison with the ultimate Reality of the Absolute. On the other hand, creatures have as their substance principial potentiality, that is, by symbolic transposition, the "Divine Nothingness," analogous, at the appropriate level, to the Waters of Genesis.[19] In the Hindu tradition the identification of Being and Non-Being is expressed by the saying: "Form (*rupa*) is emptiness (*sunyata*), and emptiness is not different from form, nor is form different from emptiness: indeed emptiness is form."[20] Again, this is to say with Nagarjuna that, "There is nothing that distinguishes *samsara* from *nirvana*."[21]

Being is both transcendent principle and immanent creation. It is the isthmus, the Islamic *barzakh*, between the Unmanifest and the manifest.[22] Schuon refers to the *barzakh* as "a dividing line between two domains [which] line appears, from the standpoint of each side, to belong to the other side."[23] He adds, "The archetype of the *barzakh* is the half-divine, half-cosmic frontier separating, and in another sense uniting, Manifestation and the Principle; it is the 'Divine Spirit' (*Ruh*) which, seen 'from above' is manifestation, and seen 'from below' is Principle. Consequently, it is *Maya* in both its aspects; the same thing appears, in a certain manner, in the Christian expression 'true man and true God.'"[24] Similarly,

---

[17] F. Schuon, *Language of the Self* (Bloomington, IN: World Wisdom Books, 1999), p. 27.

[18] Meister Eckhart, Sermon 4 in *Meister Eckhart: Sermons & Treatises*, trans. M.O.'C Walshe (Dorset: Element Books, 1987), Vol. 1.

[19] On the notion of "Divine Nothingness" see F. Schuon, *Survey of Metaphysics and Esoterism*, p. 53.

[20] *Maha-Prajnaparamita-Hrdaya*, cited in A. Govinda, *Foundations of Tibetan Mysticism* (Maine: Samuel Weiser, 1969), p. 84.

[21] *Madhyamakakarika*, xxv.19-20.

[22] Surah 25, *Al-Furqan*; Surah 55, *Al-Rahman*. On the *barzakh* see T. Burckhardt, *Mirror of the Intellect* (Cambridge, U.K.: Quinta Essentia, 1987), Ch. 19.

[23] F. Schuon, *In the Face of the Absolute* (Bloomington, IN: World Wisdom Books, 1988), p. 187.

[24] F. Schuon, *In the Face of the Absolute*, p. 187, n. 1.

Burckhardt remarks that when seen "from the outside" the *barzakh* must necessarily have the definite meaning of "partition" or "separative element" ("an insurmountable barrier") but, that it cannot be merely this for a perspective which applies to it the principle of non-otherness. He continues: "Looking at it in regard to its ontological situation, if one may so put it, it appears as a simple partition only from the point of view of lesser reality, whereas seen 'from above,' it is the very mediator between the two seas ... The *barzakh* is thus separation only in that it is itself the starting point of a separative perspective, in the eyes of which it appears to be a limit."[25] This echoes the Christian doctrine of the *Logos*, both created and uncreated.

The paradox of Being is that of relativity. It is however a paradox that satisfies the logic of the All-Possibility. As Schuon says, "If the relative did not exist, the Absolute would not be the Absolute."[26] This is necessary, which is simply to say that God cannot not be God.[27] Again: "the All-Possibility must by definition and on pain of contradiction include its own impossibility."[28] This is logical but non-rational, for it pertains to a level of Reality that is beyond the rational domain. Being non-rational it allows of no discursive communication; the nature of Being is inexpressible or, if it may be expressed, it is through silence, which is the root meaning of the term mystery.[29] Here is the place of mystery in the logical framework of Reality: it is the inexpressible meeting of the manifest and the Unmanifest. This is not some "uncertainty" shrouded in "fuzziness," but a precise and clear certainty upon which the argument of existence rests.

[25] T. Burckhardt, *Mirror of the Intellect*, pp. 193-94.

[26] F. Schuon, *Language of the Self*, p. 28.

[27] Necessity in no way places a limit on the Absolute. As Schuon says, "Necessity—not constraint—is a complementary quality of Freedom"; he adds, "Liberty is related to the Infinite, and Necessity to the Absolute" (*In the Face of the Absolute*, p. 57). The Absolute is Necessary by definition; the Infinite expresses Freedom by virtue of its Totality, which is to say, by virtue of being Absolute.

[28] F. Schuon, *Spiritual Perspectives and Human Facts* (London: Perennial Books, 1987), p. 102.

[29] "The word 'mystical' ... must be given its root meaning of 'silent,' of a knowledge inexpressible because escaping the limits of form." (M. Pallis, *A Buddhist Spectrum* [London: George Allen & Unwin, 1980], p. 36).

To say Being is to say Relative. To say Relativity is to say relationship (*ratio*) and it is here that the rational faculty comes into play as the means of distinguishing between relativities. Ironically, it is the "fall" into relativity that allows the All-Possibility the opportunity for perfection. Thus Ibn Arabi says, "It is part of the perfection of Being that there is imperfection in it."[30] Being is the possibility of God knowing Himself as "other." In the words of the famous *hadith qudsi*: "I was a hidden treasure and I loved to be known, so I created the creation in order that I might be known." Meister Eckhart: "God cannot know himself without me"; "He hath brought me forth in the image of His eternal fatherhood, that I should also be a father and bring forth Him."[31] "God," says Schuon, "unfolds His possibilities in differentiated mode and He creates man in order to have a witness to this unfolding; in other words, He projects Himself into relativity in order to perceive Himself in relative mode."[32]

The Relative fundamentally comprises something of the Absolute, and this is necessarily so for Relativity to be. As Ibn Arabi says, "Were it not that the Reality permeates all beings as form [in His qualitative form], and were it not for the intelligible realities, no [essential] determination would be made in individual beings. Thus, the dependence of the Cosmos on Reality for existence is an essential factor."[33] Similarly, Schuon says, "if the relative did not comprise something of the absolute, relativities could not be distinguished qualitatively from one another."[34] This "something of the absolute" is Meister Eckhart's "something in the soul that is uncreated and not capable of creation."[35] At the same time the distinguishing qualifications or limitations that allow relativities to be, cannot be themselves absolute: "The Infinite is that which is absolutely without limits, but the finite cannot be that which is

---

[30] Ibn Arabi, *Al-Futuhat al-Makkiyyah* (*Meccan Revelations*), cited in R.W.J. Austin's introduction to his translation of Ibn Arabi's *The Bezels of Wisdom* (*Fusus al-Hikam*) (New Jersey: Paulist Press, 1980), p. 40.

[31] Meister Eckhart, both citations from W. Perry, *A Treasury of Traditional Wisdom* (Louisville: Fons Vitae, 2000), p. 50.

[32] F. Schuon, *Islam and the Perennial Philosophy* (London: World of Islam Festival Trust, 1976), p. 185.

[33] Ibn Arabi, *The Bezels of Wisdom*, p. 57.

[34] Schuon, *Language of the Self*, p. 28.

[35] See Sermons 13 & 48, among others.

'absolutely limited,' for there is no absolute limitation. The world is not an inverted God: God is without a second."[36]

Between the Absolute and the Relative there is at once discontinuity and continuity: discontinuity, for there can be no common measure between God and man; continuity, for nothing can be other than God. Schuon: "it might be said that this separation is absolute as from man to God and relative from God to man."[37] The separation between God and man is in fact relative, dissolved by man's realization that he is not other than God. The separation between man and God is absolute inasmuch as man must "die" absolutely to himself to achieve this realization. This is to say that the very individuality that defines a human subject—the point of reference from which the rational faculty measures the world— must be relinquished on the path back to God inasmuch, precisely, as it constitutes the illusion of the "insurmountable barrier" between man and God.

The "path back to God." From the perspective here being considered the Absolute gives rise to the Relative to maintain logical consistency; but this is not enough, for the Relative must also realize its absoluteness to satisfy a logically sound whole. God must know Himself as both Ipseity and other. God created the world in which to know Himself and created man to know this world in its full potential. Thus the meaning of our existence is to "Know thyself"—our final entelechy, the return to our true self in God. In the words of the Fathers, "God became man so that man could become God."

Man is asked to step into the mystery of "unknowing" so as to know in the fullness of identification, a knowledge so utterly without objectification as to imply absence of knowing. Thus, in the Hindu tradition it is said, "*Brahman* is known to him to whom It is unknown, while It is unknown to him to whom It is known. It is unknown to those who know and known to those who do not know."[38] Again: "Although he does not know, nevertheless he knows; he does not know but there is no loss on the knower's part, since he is indestructible; it is just that there is no second thing

---

[36] F. Schuon, *Spiritual Perspectives and Human Facts*, p. 168.

[37] F. Schuon, *Spiritual Perspectives and Human Facts*, p. 167.

[38] *Kena Upanisad* 2.3.

other than and distinct from himself that he might know."[39] "God," says Erigena, "does not know what He himself is, because He is not any what; this ignorance surpasses all knowledge."[40] This is Nicolas of Cusa's *docta ignorantia*, a term that exactly indicates the "location" of this unknowing as being the *coincidentia oppositorum*, which has its root in the coincidence of Being and Non-Being, the manifest and the Unmanifest.

The human subject must sacrifice itself in an act of faith, which, from the point of view of Creation, will inevitably appear irrational. The human begins, and necessarily so, from the position of illusion. This is the illusion of Creation, of otherness and relationship, comprehended by the rational faculty. To have faith is to know, intellectually or intuitively (and in the final analysis these are one and the same), the Reality. This is to know that there is that which is beyond the rational domain. However this knowledge remains latent or potential until it is fully actualized by the sacrifice of the individualizing and rational self. Thus the rational self must sacrifice itself to something it cannot by definition know. One must step into the void, the place of silence or mystery, without any rational justification for doing so, but in perfect accord with logic.

There can be no dialectical description of mystery, just as there is no rational argument that can bring about faith. The illusion of a purely empirical "answer" can be penetrated but not necessarily removed. For the person afraid of the darkness of the void the illusion of "objective verification" remains a crutch, regardless of its validity. Faith remains its own argument and justification. It need not apologize but remains patiently, to accept those with courage enough to go beyond their limits, to step into the darkness of mystery.

---

[39] *Brhadaranyaka Upanisad* 4.3.30.

[40] Erigena, cited in A. Snodgrass, *Architecture, Time, and Eternity* (New Delhi: Sata-Pitaka Series, 1990), Vol. 1, p. 17, n. 48.

"Fundamentalism":

A Metaphysical Perspective[*]

M. Ali Lakhani

> ... In religion,
> What damned error, but some sober brow
> Will bless it and approve it with a text,
> Hiding the grossness with fair ornament?
> (William Shakespeare, *The Merchant of Venice*, III.ii.77)

History is replete with examples of those who have desecrated and degraded religion, sadly and ironically in the name of religion itself. Wars, massacres, persecutions, and the destruction of sacred works of art, have all been sanctioned by religious authorities throughout recorded history, fueling skepticism about the legitimacy, and claims to moral authority, of traditional religion. The infamy in history of the Crusades or the Inquisition, or more contemporary examples such as the demolition of Babri Masjid or the Bamiyan Buddha, and countless political wars rooted in religious differences—including the more recent turmoils in the Middle East, the Balkans, Northern Ireland, and Sri Lanka—all add to the evidence of the skeptics. But these actions, many of which are forced to wear the badge of religion, are in fact defamatory of authentic religion. We must be careful not to reject an authentic tradition on account of those abuses and violations perpetrated by its counterfeit in its name. Not every act done in the name of religion is in fact true to its spirit. As Gai Eaton states:

> Religion is one thing, decadent human nature quite another, and the truths inherent in a particular Faith are not effaced by the misbehavior of its adherents.

It is therefore necessary to distinguish between genuine religion and its counterfeit, between the "fundamentals" of a religion and the "fundamentalist" offences committed in its name.

---

[*] Editor's Note: Editorial in *Sacred Web* 7 (July 2001).

The term "fundamentalism," however, is anomalous and its usage fraught with difficulty. Though one can speak of many types of "fundamentalism" (for example, political, economic, or scientific), the term is primarily associated with religion. In the context of religion, the term was originally applied to an early twentieth century Christian revivalist group known as the "Fundamentalist Movement," whose views were characterized by religious rigidity and evangelism, but in recent years, particularly dating to the time of the Iranian Revolution in the late 1970s, the term has come to be extended to other religions, so that one now speaks, for example, of Sikh, Hindu, Buddhist, Christian, or Muslim "fundamentalists." The term has come to be laden with connotations of political and religious extremism or militancy, which the media frequently labels as "terrorism" (one is reminded here of the comment by Robert Fisk that terrorism is in fact "a political contrivance. 'Terrorists' are those who use violence against the side that is using the word."). This is particularly true in the case of Islam, which has been demonized in the aftermath of the Cold War and the fall of the Soviet Union, by being depicted as a threat to modern American civilization by writers within the dominant media, such as the influential Samuel P. Huntington for whom this portrayal was an important component to his thesis of the "clash of civilizations." The deconstruction of the media's portrayal of religious (particularly so-called Islamic) "fundamentalism" in the West by writers such as Edward Said has yielded important insights. The language employed by the dominant media reveals its own biases. It is selective to brand, for instance, a veiled Muslim woman as an "Islamic fundamentalist," falsely implying that she would condone violence carried out in the name of her religion, while avoiding the term altogether in the case of the Jewish settler who guns down worshipers in a mosque in Hebron, or a Catholic car-bomber in Belfast, or a Protestant extremist who detonates a bomb killing innocent civilians in Oklahoma. "Fundamentalism" is a term that disguises a host of complexities. It reflects the dominant culture's modernist bias towards secularism and individualism, which are largely rejected by the traditional cultures that it labels as "fundamentalist." And it ignores the nuances that reflect the complexities underlying what it labels as "fundamentalism." What, for instance, does the term reveal when applied equally to the Taliban's desecration of Buddhist artifacts and to the Iranian government who opposed that desecration? It is far too simplistic to understand the term to refer merely to the monolithic culture of religious violence that is commonly denoted by its use within the dominant media. One has to seek a deeper understanding of the term.

This editorial proposes a definition of religious "fundamentalism" from the perspective of traditional metaphysics. There are two features that distinguish "fundamentalism" in this definition: in its inward aspect, though not synonymous with the formal, it is formalistic to the point where the "spirit" of religion is sacrificed to its "letter"; and in its outward aspect, though not synonymous with the exclusive, it is exclusivist to the point where it denies any religious pluralism premised on transcendent unity. Each of these aspects needs elaboration.

To understand how the inward aspect of authentic religion differs from that of "fundamentalism" as defined here, a starting point is perhaps to consider the object of religion. Faced with the mysteries of existence and death, humanity has sought throughout history to understand the nature of reality and existential meaning. All authentic religion, premised on the transcendental origin and end of reality, holds that human beings may, by the grace of revelation and intellection, discern the underlying unity and integrity of reality which is embedded within our very selves, and that such knowledge, where it permeates our being, is transformative, unitive, and salvific. It is the spiritual ground of reality, realized in us, that imbues us with a sense of the sacred, transforming our perception of manifest reality into a theophany in which we participate, not as separate creatures but as the Divine Self, the Eternal Witness, the only Existent. This is the inward aspect of religion, its heart or core. Considered from this standpoint, the object of religion is an alchemical transformation that corresponds in all religious lexicons to an intrinsic beauty or virtue that radiates as compassionate piety. This piety expresses itself in a sacred relationship between humanity, as Trustee, and the theophanic creation, as Beneficiary, whose spiritual radiance we, as transcendent beings, are privileged to both witness and express. This notion of piety and its concomitant obligation of stewardship—in Quranic terminology, *Amanah* or the Divine Trust—are in fact far removed from the dry formalism of "fundamentalism." It is important to note, however, that this definition does not reduce fundamentalism to exoterism. In all authentic religions, form is a necessary component of tradition, celebrated in its scriptures, rituals, and liturgies. It is not the adherence to these forms, but the loss of their kardial significance, that is indicative of fundamentalism. Formalism, in the sense of deracinated religion, is the inward gaze of fundamentalism.

To understand how the outward aspect of authentic religion differs from that of "fundamentalism" as defined here, we note that religion as such admits of two approaches to the Divine: as Truth and as Presence. The first stresses the transcendence of Absolute reality, the Supreme Principle, and approaches the Divine through Knowledge. The second stresses the immanence of Infinite reality, the manifest Self, and approaches the Divine through Love. Outwardly, these approaches may sometimes appear to clash, but inwardly they are perfectly compatible. Truth is the transcendent aspect of Presence, and Presence is the immanent aspect of Truth. These polarities are in fact complements of each other, and no religious conception of the Divine is complete without including both. In Islam, for example, this is one of the central meanings of the principle of *tawhid*. While an authentic religious tradition may emphasize one approach to the Divine over another (for example, Judaism and Islam will generally favor Truth over Presence and are therefore iconoclastic in matters of artistic expression, while Hinduism, Buddhism, and Christianity will generally favor Presence over Truth, and are therefore iconodulic), it will not do so at the expense of religious pluralism. The commitment to a particular religious tradition, while entailing subscription to its creed and submission to its forms of worship, does not mandate the rejection of other genuine religious approaches. The infinity of Divine expression, and the consequent diversity of religious typologies, are dictated by the very structure of reality itself, whose transcendent and esoteric unity are the underlying foundations of its pluralism. The rejection of such pluralism is the outward gaze of fundamentalism.

From this it can be seen that "fundamentalism," as the term is defined here, is a form of reductionism—the "spirit" reduced to the "letter," multiple expressions of Truth reduced to one. But, it may be objected, surely all orthodox doctrines are reductionist by virtue of their very orthodoxy. And here it becomes important to distinguish between "orthodoxy"—or "right thinking" according to the doctrines and principles of traditional metaphysics—and "fundamentalism." Where fundamentalism isolates or ignores aspects of reality, mistaking the part for the whole, orthodoxy, by contrast—

though it may emphasize a particular part—views reality as a whole, embracing all its aspects. These aspects, though they may appear to be opposed, are reconciled and accommodated within the traditional "principle of complementarity," which regards reality as a synthesis of polarities, a *coincidentia oppositorum.* To claim that orthodoxy amounts to reductionism is to fail to perceive any distinction between dogma (the necessary component of doctrine— necessary as a corollary of transcendence) and dogmatism (the fallacy of doctrine, deriving from its reductionist tendency). This is one of the errors of post-modernist deconstructionism.

But traditional orthodoxy is not itself immune from a tendency to reductionism. There are many diverse expressions of Truth, which are potentially salvific or redemptive in content, though these may sometimes appear to be orthodoxly unsound from the point of view of a particular tradition, or even from within the same tradition. Thus, it is as erroneous to claim that "Pure Consciousness cannot say 'I'" (Sri Ramana Maharshi) as to claim "I am the Truth" (al-Hallaj). Either both these statements are true, or neither is. Not only "I am in the Father" but also "the Father is in me." Or again, not only *La ilaha* but also *illa'llah.* God cannot be reduced to an aspect of reality, though every aspect of reality is an aspect of God— because God is absolute reality. Similarly, orthodoxy cannot be reduced to a "zero-sum" view of reality. Truth, in the end, must embrace all gradations within reality, though these may be ordered hierarchically. Any expression of reality that falls short of the Absolute, Unconditioned, Supreme Principle is nonetheless an aspect of reality, on pain of denying that the Absolute is also Infinite. Yet it is not Reality itself, on pain of denying that Reality is hierarchically transcendent. Orthodoxy cannot be so rigorous as to deny, in the name of Truth, the humanity of man—notwithstanding his spiritual potential; just as it cannot reject that potential in the face of the imperfections of man. This then is the challenge of traditional orthodoxy: to avoid the tendency to reduce a particular doctrine—which may be an aspect of Truth—to Truth itself; or to reduce Truth to an abstraction that devalues or denies the experiential reality of Presence.

RUDOLF STEINER, ANTHROPOSOPHY, AND TRADITION

Rodney Blackhirst

René Guénon and others have detailed the fundamental objections integral tradition has to the syncretisms of the Theosophy movement, so prominent among Westerners attracted to Eastern traditions in the late nineteenth and early twentieth centuries. Less well documented are the shortcomings of other, related, movements that have developed out of Theosophy and that have been at the apogee of their influence in more recent decades. The most important of these is undoubtedly Anthroposophy, a peculiarly European and Germanic offshoot of mainstream Theosophy, centered on the writings and teachings of Rudolf Steiner.

The Anthroposophical Society has been described by its critics, who characterize it as a type of "cult," as the world's "largest occult organization." Based in Switzerland where it is housed in strange, "organic" architecture, the design of Steiner himself, the Society describes its work as "Spiritual Science" and perpetuates its founder's distinctive amalgam of German esotericism and eastern Theosophy, as well as coordinating the many practical endeavors initiated by Steiner and by which he is increasingly well known, such as the Steiner (or Waldorf) education system. Throughout middle-class life in European countries, South Africa, Australia, New Zealand, and the United States one is likely to encounter some aspect of the Anthroposophical Society's activities. Health food stores sell a range of products made according to Steiner's recommendations and carrying Steiner-endorsed labels; Steiner schools are in most major cities; a Steiner-inspired Church prospers; gardeners use Steiner's system of organic composting and many other Steiner-connected ideas and products turn up in surprising places. In Australia, Walter Burley Griffin, the architect who designed the national capital, Canberra, was influenced by Steiner's ideas, using his social and political theory of a "Threefold Commonwealth" as the guiding principle of the city's organization. Although it is not numerically large, the Anthroposophical movement has been remarkably successful in establishing its presence and influence in some sections of contemporary Western society.

It is somewhat alarming to many ordinary suburbanites to discover beneath a respectable, middle-class, and ostensibly Christian veneer, the movement's roots in European occultism and its highly unusual, if not bizarre, interpretations of traditional Eastern wisdom. It is now well-documented that Steiner had, early in his career, an unfortunate association with the magical (left-hand) organization, the O.T.O. (Ordo Templi Orientis), with the English satanist Aleister Crowley, and with several unsavory German species of freemasonry that are usually associated in the popular mind with "Black Magic." Steiner himself had recourse to terms like "occult" in describing his ideas and more than once hinted that he himself had some relation of destiny to Christian Rosencruz, the legendary founder of the Rosicrucians. These are not aspects of the movement that its adherents readily make known to the general public; instead, they foster the image of a productive, practical movement of ordinary citizens inspired to good works by Steiner's humane and insightful teachings.

Guénon, of course, was briefly taken in by Theosophy, and it is common enough to meet sincere seekers of the truth of tradition who, knowing no better, first seek for a lost spirituality in the various forms of occultism that are abroad and that prey upon exactly such seekers. Steiner cannot be blamed altogether for the misadventures of his early career but, unlike Guénon, there never came a point in his life where he sought to attach himself to a living branch of the *philosophia perennis*, where he saw the coherence and accepted the unshakeable authority of the unanimous testimony of the great sages and saints, the true spiritual representatives of mankind. Instead, though he broke away from Masonic-inspired ritual magic, and later saw through the pretensions of the leadership of the Theosophical Society, he forged his own syncretic system of "occultism" that was intended, at length, to blaze a new path in the spiritual destiny of man.

Steiner at no point embraced or surrendered to an orthodox religion or to any legitimate representatives of the world's integral spiritual traditions nor did he receive any orthodox initiation. Instead, he believed the era of the orthodox religions was fading and that he and Anthroposophy had a world-mission to point the way to a more spiritual order in a new era. At first Steiner saw this as the role of the Theosophical movement. In a short period of time he became the head of its German section and one of its most brilliant advocates. However, disputes with the leadership of the Society especially over the recruitment of a young Hindu boy named Jiddu Krishnamurti as "World-Teacher"—arguably the lowest ebb of Theosophical folly—led Steiner to strike out on his own, taking a good number of German and other European Theosophists with him. After this he lectured widely and wrote voluminous works describing his own permutation of Theosophy and, in effect, declaring himself the prophet of a new "spiritual science" to replace the outmoded spiritualities of the old order. He crafted a worldview that explained why the old spirituality no longer satisfied the soul of modern man and how his "spiritual science" was the next vital link in humanity's spiritual destiny. In this Steiner was in the company of many other syncretists, from Crowley to Gurdjieff. Characteristically, these "occultists"—confronted, it must be said, by truly world-shattering events such as the First World War—could find nothing in Christian orthodoxy, and had not the patience and perseverance needed to seek out the authentic roots of other traditions, in the midst of the confusion of the modern malaise; they dispensed with tradition, declared it irrelevant to the crisis of the times, and offered their own "systems" instead.

Guénon and other modern exponents of traditional wisdom, such as Coomaraswamy, were contemporaries of these "occultists"; in contrast to them, they found the answers to the modern crisis in the universal and ageless wisdom of mankind, preserved and sanctified by the great, orthodox religions and their Scriptures. While they may have been tempted by syncretisms like Theosophy, they saw through them and shunned them thereafter. Steiner saw through Theosophy, but—like others of that generation—then went no further than the creation of his own syncretic parallel movement. It is perhaps unfair to group him with Crowley and Gurdjieff for he was, it seems, a sincere and modest man of good character and noble motive and of undoubted intellectual power. Despite being a type of self-proclaimed prophet, there was nothing of the charlatan about him. It is probably one of the more significant but unacknowledged tragedies of early twentieth century European intellectual life that Rudolf Steiner chose to concoct Anthroposophy from Theosophy rather than finding in Theosophy a bridge into Vedanta or some other expression of authentic metaphysic that might have given his thinking sure foundations.

The other feature that Steiner's syncretism has in common with pseudo-spiritual "systems" devised in his time, and since, is the claim to bridge the gulf separating modern science from spiritual understandings of the world. Guénon, Coomaraswamy, and such writers as Titus Burckhardt, were devastating in their critique of modern scientific paradigms, exposing the failings of the scientific worldview from the position of first principles. Burckhardt composed what is arguably the most comprehensive and penetrating analysis of the Darwinian fallacy ever written.[1] But Steiner, like Crowley and Gurdjieff, and many others besides, saw modern science in a more positive light and felt the need to create some mixture of old spirituality and new science supposedly befitting these modern times. In Steiner's case, he was not a mere pretender to scientific qualifications. He was recognized as a gifted student of the natural sciences and when still a young man was honored by an invitation to edit the scientific papers of Goethe. His doctoral thesis was a work on epistemology, later published under the title *The Philosophy of Freedom*, and it is recognized as a work of some enduring philosophical merit. Steiner was particularly impressed by the studies of Haeckel and other German pioneers of the modern, profane life-sciences and by an evolutionary approach to nature in general. He was critical of the modern sciences for what he recognized as a narrow, materialist perspective, and felt that pioneers like Haeckel could not see the full significance of their discoveries because their vision was confined to the material realm. Steiner, however, through "spiritual vision" or "clairvoyance" and "the methods of spiritual science," could see the broader, indeed cosmic, implications of these "breakthroughs" in the natural sciences. Many twentieth century syncretisms attempt to marry profane psychology or even quantum physics with spirituality. Steiner's "system" is distinctive for its emphasis on the biological sciences. The Anthroposophical enterprise, in a way, may be summed up in this manner: Steiner sought to marry the new biological sciences with a spiritual view of the world.

"Spiritual Science"—Anthroposophy—is a hybrid of Steiner's occultism, Theosophy and nineteenth century German natural science. Typically, Steiner related such things as the geological history

---

[1] Editor's Note: See Titus Burckhardt, "The Theory of Evolution," in this volume.

of the Earth as revealed by the modern earth sciences to ancient Hindu cycles or *yugas* of time. Madame Blavatsky and others had attempted to do the same, always claiming that the data of modern science only serve to confirm the ancient doctrines, but Steiner's grasp of what modern geology had to say was far more formidable and his explanations far more convincing. Some of Steiner's university teachers bemoaned his lapse into "occultism" and felt that a potentially great German scientific mind had been squandered on nonsense. However, Steiner developed a considerable following and his lectures had considerable appeal on the fringes of German intellectual life. His teachings catered to the cherished delusion—still abroad—that the modern sciences can in some way be turned to spiritual ends, that the monster of materialism can be tamed. He taught that the modern scientific mentality is, in fact, a breakthrough in human spiritual evolution—a new "ego-consciousness" has arisen in the world—and though it takes, necessarily, a destructively materialist form in its "early development" (the language of Haeckel's embryology), it will—with the help of Anthroposophy—grow into a new, spiritual faculty to guide man in the next phase of his "cosmic evolution." Steiner referred to the present age as the *Kali Yuga*, but in his estimation the *Kali Yuga*—the Dark Age in traditional Hindu understandings—is an age of unparalleled opportunities for man, and the advent of the modern sciences is the germ of his future spiritual being. We need only contrast this type of teaching with Guénon's account of the *Kali Yuga* and the place of the modern sciences within it to see again how Steiner chose a path of syncretic fancy instead of submitting to the testimony of tradition.

As a religious teacher Steiner must also be counted as eccentric and syncretistic. The occultists and Theosophists of his early acquaintance had, all of them, a profound aversion for Christianity. People in revolt against their Christian heritage turn to such pseudo-spiritual movements precisely because they are "Eastern" and exotic. Steiner, however, always insisted on the centrality of Christ among the "Masters" acknowledged by Theosophy and his own breakaway movement took an even more explicitly Christian form. The "Christ-event," he began to teach—along similar lines to thinkers such as Teilhard de Chardin—was the pivotal moment in human spiritual evolution. But unlike de Chardin, Steiner was not seeking to marry evolutionism with Catholic orthodoxy; rather, the

Christianity to which he wedded this evolutionism was a reinvention of many old Christian heresies of a dualistic character. There are, Steiner taught, two mutually opposed forces at work in the universe, and he named these by their Zoroastrian titles, *Ahriman* and *Amazda*. "The Christ," a highly evolved solar being (*Sonnenwesen*), he taught, is a reconciling force whose "Golgotha event" brought into the stream of history mysteries previously only known to a select few. Steiner's heritage of inspiration for this hotchpotch has been well described in Yuri Stoyanov's recent book *The Hidden Tradition in Europe* where he documents the persistence of Manichean and other forms of dualism in medieval Christian heresy. Assembling a new version of' these dualist creeds, analogizing *Ahriman* and *Amazda* with other polarities, and reading the whole in the context of Biblical contortions of Hindu concepts such as "the *Akasha*," Steiner devised a new Christian sect. He gave lectures on the "secret" meaning of the gospels—meanings only apparent to "spiritual scientists"—and on the sacraments and liturgy. He was careful not to demand that Anthroposophists practice Christianity as he described it—he insisted he was not seeking to create a new faith or amend an existing one, because "faith" is a feature of the consciousness of the old age, not the new—but he helped create an organized Church among wayward Lutheran clergy, with its own Anthroposophical theology and Rudolf Steiner's sacraments.

The Roman Catholic Church investigated Anthroposophy and its various Christian branches and condemned them as heretical on numerous points of dogma in 1919. More comprehensively, Steiner's Christianity seems to be lacking any higher theological dimension or any metaphysical foundations. The foundations of *all* Steiner's work seem to be epistemological, stemming ultimately, as he said, from *The Philosophy of Freedom*. The authority for his radical revision of the Christian faith, and his pronouncements on a whole range of matters, from ancient Atlantis to modern pharmacology, was his own "seership." The sacraments, he explained, and various exercises he had developed, and food grown according to his methods, and an education according to his indications, would all help others to evolve organs of spiritual perception apparently highly evolved in himself. Again, it must be stressed that Steiner received no formal initiation in any integral initiatic tradition. He had a fair knowledge, no doubt, of certain undercurrents in German

Protestantism, some of which may have a place in the fullness of the Christian mythos, but from even the broadest definition of the authentic Christian tradition his religious teachings must be counted as outside the bosom of sanctity.

In must be conceded, nevertheless, that there is, on the face of it at least, something very impressive about Steiner's work and that even from a strictly traditional point of view it deserves some consideration. Roger Lipsey reports, somewhat surprisingly, that Ananda Coomaraswamy had a brief interest in Steiner and was evidently approving of things he had heard about Steiner's activities. As Lipsey notes, no doubt Coomaraswamy would have recognized the fatal errors in Anthroposophy had he investigated it further, but he nevertheless heard favorable reports and evidently thought of Steiner in a category above the likes of Annie Besant, for instance.

We have so far stressed the failure of Steiner to place his work within the guiding framework of an integral tradition, and emphasized his marriage of the sacred with the profane; but there are also aspects of Steiner that conceivably serve to perpetuate fragments of living traditions, especially European traditions, and that should be given some cautious applause. Like many syncretisms, the standard works of Anthroposophy, the numerous books and transcriptions of lecture series, are—for all but insiders—tortuously garbled with a vocabulary of Anthroposophical terms that it takes many years of devoted Anthroposophical study to master. But, now and then, as in his extraordinary lectures on bees or his challenging lectures on childhood cognition, one can recognize in Steiner an extraordinary capacity to *think out of phase*, a quality not unlike that found, if we may dare make the comparison, in Guénon too. Such minds can set aside the characteristic modes of thought of modernity and speak directly from age-old, perhaps primordial, patterns of association and identity. Evidently, Steiner could not see the metaphysical absurdity of the modern physical sciences as could a pneumatic mind like that of Guénon, but he could, all the same, speak as if from another time. This side of Rudolf Steiner comes through sources other than masonic "occultism," Theosophy, and evolutionary biology; it comes through Goethe, firstly, and then through alchemy, and, more importantly, through direct acquaintance with vestiges of authentic folk traditions in central Europe. Not a great deal is known of Steiner's early life, but he grew up in the mountains of the German-Austrian border and on several occasions is reported as speaking of certain "herb gatherers" he would meet on trains when young, representatives of the old "folk consciousness" now giving way to new forms of consciousness, he explained. In his lectures on agriculture, delivered in 1924 to a select group of Anthroposophist farmers—lectures quite as remarkable as his lectures on bees—he prescribes methods for the enhancement of natural farming that are almost certainly adaptations of "secrets" of traditional agriculture learned from peasants and such "herb gatherers" in his youth. Steiner seems not only to have acquired many practical "tips" from these early experiences, but an ability to see something of the symbols of nature. There are more than a few places in Steiner's work where one feels that one is confronted by a genuine acquaintance with a traditional mentality. This virtue, however, never extends beyond the cosmological. As soon as he ventures into matters with more direct metaphysical implications, Steiner is lost. On the one hand, several of his lecture transcripts reveal a striking restatement of a traditional cosmological mind—a cosmological mind that might, for example, converse with that of a character like Plato's Timaeus of Locri—but, on the other hand, we find Steiner explaining to his audiences—in a work like the *Cosmic Memory* series—how the great sages of Islam had all reincarnated as nineteenth century German scientists, now that Islam was no longer needed (its world-historical role being over), and the world was henceforth being prepared, through science, for the New Age! Coomaraswamy was probably right to suspect something of value in Steiner, but on other counts he is easily dismissed. A "spiritual evolutionism" and a complex of misconstructions of sacred doctrines of the Eastern traditions, such as reincarnation, mar his work throughout.

It would be petty to belittle the practical achievements of various Anthroposophical enterprises. This must be conceded too. Steiner, it must be said, has, in a small measure at least, contributed something to the survival and rediscovery of traditional ideas. When one examines the decay of modern education and considers the utter soullessness of the modern curriculum, Steiner schools emerge as, in some ways, the only glimmer of hope for those who want to inculcate in their children a knowledge of mythology, skill in traditional crafts, and such features of tradition as it is still possible to foster. It was refreshing for the present writer to witness the principal of a

Steiner school field questions about the Steiner education methods from inquiring parents several years ago.

"What about religious education?" one of the parents wanted to know. The principal explained that, in the Steiner system, everything is religious. "We teach religious mathematics," he said. "And religious chemistry. And religious arts and crafts. But no, not 'Religious Education.'" He explained that the Steiner philosophy did not accept a breach between the spiritual and the secular. This is closer to a traditional point of view than will be found in any other school system. But against these positive points is the fact that Steiner-trained teachers consider children "incarnating spirits" on an "evolutionary journey" and, conspicuously, God figures nowhere in their philosophy, except perhaps as an antiquated idea from the "old age" that, at best, prepared the way for the "spiritual scientific" understandings of today.

It is clear that, from a traditional viewpoint, Rudolf Steiner and Anthroposophy deviate in significant ways from the canons of perennial wisdom. There is, throughout Steiner's works, a tendency to dismiss and relegate to the past even the most profound expressions of the human spirit. The *Bhagavad Gita*, for instance, seems to be regarded as a work that was important to the development of man in his spiritual adolescence, rather than as a timeless treasure that speaks with equal relevance to the human predicament in all ages. The spiritual heritage of mankind is diminished in the ideas of Rudolf Steiner by being made subject to a progressive evolutionism. We cannot say that Steiner was altogether ignorant of tradition; but he described it as a thing of the past and on that point alone must be counted as ignorant of what tradition truly is—the unanimous witness to Truth by the best of men in all times and places. Steiner supposed that the scientific revolution made this heritage obsolete, though the "spiritual scientist," he said, should not overlook the early embryonic stages of man's "development." The wisdom of Lao Tzu may have nourished the soul in former times, but now "scientists of the spirit" are needed to explain its "spiritual scientific" meanings which alone will nourish the new consciousness of modern man. This is a modern mentality in itself, no better than Newton standing upon the shoulders of giants.

On the other hand, one gets a sense of wasted genius from Steiner's works. It is similar to the sense of waste one gets from reading Nietzsche—a "volcanic genius," as Schuon described him, who might have been a great sage of the *via negativa*, had he been born in another time. Steiner is another flowering of a related German philosophic genius who, in another time, might have been an inspired polymath, an Avicenna (since he has Muslim sages reincarnating in modern Germany!). His complete works—lecture transcripts included—run into hundreds of volumes on an extraordinary range of topics. A reluctant admirer of Steiner once declared that he had read over fifty of his works without encountering anything that was pedestrian, consistently meeting with material that was remarkable for the flashes of insight that seemed to come from another era. Steiner has had an impact in fields as diverse as agriculture, architecture, the visual arts, education, and the treatment of retardation and cancer. He asked to be judged by his works not his words. But as Guénon points out in his critique of the Theosophical movement and its impact on the intellectual and spiritual life of the West—and as could equally be said of its Anthroposophical sister—the anti-traditional forces of modernity operate precisely by offering novelties and false syntheses, labyrinths of half-truths, and vigorous but barren hybrids of East and West, old and new, to deflect systematically the best of men from the unanimous witness of the Truth. Steiner was so deflected, and Anthroposophy, as much as Theosophy, is a trap for those seeking an authentic spiritual path.

References

S.C. Easton. *Man and World in the Light of Anthroposophy.* New York: Anthroposophic Press, 1975.

J. Godwin. *The Theosophical Enlightenment.* Albany, NY: SUNY Press, 1994.

R.A. McDermott. "Rudolf Steiner and Anthroposophy." In *Modern Esoteric Spirituality.* Edited by A. Faivre and J. Needleman. New York: Crossroads, 1995, pp. 288-310.

R. Steiner. *The Anthroposophic Movement.* 8 lectures (Dornach, June 10-17, 1923). New York: Anthroposophic Press, 1998.

——. *Occult Science: An Outline.* Translated by A. & M. Adams. London: Rudolf Steiner Press, 1969.

3

The Social Order

Riches and piety will diminish daily, until the world
will be completely corrupted. In those days it will be
wealth that confers distinction, passion will be the sole
reason for union between the sexes, lies will be the
only method of success in business, and women will be
the objects merely of sensual gratification. The earth
will be valued only for its mineral treasures, dishonesty
will be the universal means of subsistence, a simple
ablution will be regarded as sufficient purification ...
The observances of castes, laws, and institutions will
no longer be in force in the Dark Age, and the ceremonies prescribed by the Vedas will be neglected.
Women will obey only their whims and will be infatu-
ated with pleasure ... men of all kinds will presumptu-
ously regard themselves as equals of *brahmans* ... The
vaishyas will abandon agriculture and commerce and
will earn their living by servitude or by the exercise of
mechanical professions ... The dominant caste will be
that of the *shudras* ...

THE VISHNU PURANA

THE BUGBEAR OF DEMOCRACY, FREEDOM, AND EQUALITY*

Ananda K. Coomaraswamy

Of all the forces that stand in the way of a cultural synthesis, or as I would rather say, in the way of a mutual understanding indispensable for cooperation, the greatest are those of ignorance and prejudice. Ignorance and prejudice underlie the naïve presumption of a "civilizing mission," which to the "backward" peoples against whom it is directed and whose cultures it proposes to destroy, appears a simple impertinence and a proof of the provincialism of the modern West, which regards all imitation as sincerest flattery, even when it amounts to caricature, at the same time that it is ready to take up arms in self-defense if the imitation becomes so real as to involve a rivalry in the economic sphere. Actually, if there is to be any growth of good will on earth, the white man will have to realize that he must live in a world predominantly colored (and "colored" for him usually means "backward," i.e., unlike himself); and the Christian will have to realize that he is living in a world predominantly non-Christian. These things will have to be realized and accepted, without indignation or regret. Before a world government can even be dreamed of, we must have citizens of the world, who can meet their fellow citizens without embarrassment, as gentlemen meet gentlemen, and not as would-be schoolmasters meeting pupils who are to be "compulsorily," even if also "freely" educated. There is no more place in the world for the frog in a well who can judge others only by his own experience and mores. We have got to realize, for example, that as El Glaoui, the Pasha of Marrakesh lately said, "the Moslem world does not want the wondrous American world or the incredible American way of life. We (Moslems) want the world of the Koran," and that, *mutatis mutandis*, the like holds good for the majority of Orientals, a majority that includes not only all those who are still "cultured and illiterate," but also a far larger number of those who have spent years of life and study in the West than might

---

* Editor's Note: An essay unpublished during Ananda Coomaraswamy's lifetime, appearing in *The Bugbear of Literacy*.

be supposed, for it is among these that many of the most convinced "reactionaries" are to be found.[1] Sometimes, "the more we see of democracy, the more we value monarchy"; the more we see of "equality," the less we admire "that monster of modern growth, the financial-commercial state" in which the majority lives by its "jobs," and the dignity of a vocation or profession is reserved for the very few, and where, in the words of Eric Gill, "on the one hand we have the artist concerned solely to express himself; on the other is the workman deprived of any self to express."

I have long had in mind to write a series of essays on "bugbears." "Am I My Brother's Keeper?" (which appeared in *Asia and the Americas*, March, 1943) may be regarded as the Preface. "The Bugbear of Literacy" appears in the February 1944 issue of the same journal.[2] Others projected include "The Bugbear of Scholarship," "The Bugbear of Woman's Emancipation" (by my wife), "The Bugbear of World Trade," and "The Bugbear of Spiritual Pride," the last with special reference to the improper use of such pejorative terms as "natural religion" and "idolatry." Perhaps these will never be written, for I, too, have a vocation, which is much rather one of research in the field of the significance of the universal symbols of the *Philosophia Perennis* than one of apology for or polemic on

---

[1] Cf. Demetra Vaka, *Haremlik* (1909), p. 139, where the speaker is a young Turkish woman of high birth, well acquainted with the masters of Western literature. She says: "From what I read in your (American) papers, I do not like your world, and I am glad that I am a Mahometan girl." On another page the author asks a Turkish friend, "Don't you really sometimes wish you were a free European woman," and receives the baffling answer, "I have never seen a European man to whom I should like to belong." Again, p. 259, she is told, "When, as a girl, I had read about European life it had seemed to me so attractive, so wonderful. But when I came to taste it, it was empty and bitter." Speaking for herself, Demetra Vaka (p. 221) says: "Among the Orientals I am always overwhelmed by a curious feeling of resigned happiness, such as the West can hardly conceive of." Because you cannot conceive of it, it angers you to think that men and women can be happy under conditions that would be irksome to you, as you now are, you whose ambition is to be "somebody." You do not understand that there can be a higher ambition, to become a "nobody." Resignation to the will of God, that is the very meaning of Islam; contentment, *cultiver son jardin*; these are our ambitions. It is not against our pattern of life that we Orientals "protest and rebel," but against your interference. It is your way of life that we repudiate, wherever it has not already corrupted us.

[2] Editor's Note: These articles also appear in Ananda Coomaraswamy's *The Bugbear of Literacy* (Pates Manor, Bedfont: Perennial Books, 1979), as Chapters 1 and 2.

behalf of doctrines that must be believed if they are to be understood, and must be understood if they are to be believed.

In the present article I propose to discuss the prejudices that are
aroused in every hundred per cent progressive and democratic-
egalitarian mind by the (Portuguese) word "caste." Dr. Niebuhr, for
example, calls the Indian caste system "the most rigid form of class
snobbishness in history"; he means of course, "class *arrogance*," since
he must have intended to criticize the supposed attitude of the
higher castes (comparable to that of Englishmen in India, and to
that of those who maintain the Mason-Dixon line in America), while
it is, by dictionary definition, only an inferior that can be a "snob."
But how can there be either arrogance or snobbishness where there
is no social ambition? It is in a society whose members aspire to
"white collar" jobs, and must "keep up with the Joneses" that these
vices prevail. If you ask a man in India what he is, he will not say
either that "I am a *brahman*" or that "I am a *shudra*" but that "I am a
devotee of Krishna," or "I am a Shaivite"; and that is not because he
is either "proud" or "ashamed" of his caste, whatever it may be, but
because he mentions first what seems to him more important than
any social distinction.

For H.N. Brailsford (whose sincerity and courage I respect),
author of *Subject India*, caste is indeed a "bugbear." It offends him
that men's lives, should be "hedged round from infancy by a network of prohibitions and commandments" and that "an Indian can
become a Protestant or a rebel only by an effort of which none but
the strongest natures are capable." He scarcely reflects that it may
take a stronger nature to obey than to rebel; or that a strict pattern
of "good form" is no more necessarily deplorable than is the fact
that no one can compose a sonnet in free verse. Caste, he says,
"makes of the individual a unit submissive in mind and body to a
degree which startles and shocks the European observer," who is
himself, of course, an "untouchable," and possibly a little "startled"
by the implied disparagement. And yet, what admissions Mr.
Brailsford makes when he comes to speak of caste in practice! One
of the religious "prohibitions" or taboos ("save among the more
degraded castes") is of drink. (The late Sister Nivedita once
observed that Christianity "carries drunkenness in its wake"). But
Mr. Brailsford tells us that "the Congress had Indian morality
behind it when it organized a boycott of the government's toddy-
shops ... no Indian dare brave the condemnation of his fellows by

entering them. In some places the all-powerful caste organization re-enforced the prohibition of Congress." You see that when it suits his argument, "prohibitions and commandments" become a "morality." There are other prohibitions and commandments that also pertain to our morality, and against which we do not feel called upon to "rebel or protest" against; and if there are some that he does not understand, has Mr. Brailsford ever thought of investigating their significance for us? Similarly in the case of the boycott of English manufactured goods he states, "its general success was an amazing proof of the solidarity of Indian society." How does he make that square with his statement that in India "by far the most serious obstacle to social unity comes from caste and its rule of endogamy"?[3]

Let us remember that in India men of different castes are divided neither by religion, culture, or language, but only by rules against intermarriage and interdining;[4] for example, no king could aspire to marry his own *brahman* cook's daughter. That different castes have never found it difficult to work together for common ends is amply demonstrated by the almost universal institution of the *Pancayat,* or village council, a committee of men of different castes. Again, it may be observed that caste is not, in Hindu law, a legal disability; men of any caste may act as witnesses in suits, the only qualifications having to do with character and impartiality and being the same for all (*Manu* VIII.61-63).

The Imperial Gazetteer remarks that the inhabitants of the typical Indian village "are welded together in a little community with its own organization and government ..., its customary rules, and its little staff of functionaries, artisans, and trades." Mr. Brailsford objects that "the only obstacles to the growth of internal trade on a

---

[3] The cultural unity of India is emphasized even by Mr. Brailsford (p. 122). I should say that a much higher degree of "social unity" is realized in India than in the United States of America.

[4] It may be observed (1) that a Hindu does not "interdine" even with his own wife, or his own caste, and that this has nothing whatever to do with "social prejudice" of any kind, but reflects a functional differentiation; and (2) that the "prohibitions and commandments" of the caste system are not always so inconvenient as the superficial student supposes—for example, "From one's own ploughman, an old friend of the family, one's own cowherd, one's own servant, one's own barber, and from whomsoever else may come for refuge and offer service—from the hands of all such *shudra*s food may be taken" (*Manu* VI.253).

gigantic scale is the poverty of the villages and the self-sufficiency that belongs to its oldest traditions ... there is still many a village in which the hereditary craftsmen, who serve it for an allowance of grain, or some acres of free land, will weave all the cloth it needs, hammer its hoes for it and turn its pots." Unfortunately, "the growth of internal trade on a gigantic scale" is by no means one of our primary ambitions; we still hold (with Philo, *De Decalogo* 69) that it is an obvious truth that the craftsman is of higher value than the product of his craft, and perceive that it is chiefly in industrial societies that this truth is ignored; nor from what we know of factory conditions already existing in Bombay and elsewhere do we see the slightest prospect that the condition of even the lowest outcastes will ever be improved by a gigantic development of internal trade. Again, "we do not want the incredible American way of life."

What we do see very clearly is that, in the words of A.M. Hocart, perhaps the only unprejudiced European sociologist who has written on caste, "hereditary service has been painted in such dark colors only because it is incompatible with the existing industrial system" (*Les castes*, p. 238).[5] Incompatible, because caste involves human relationships and mutual responsibilities for which there is no room in a world of capital and labor and manufacture for profit on the one hand or in the Soviet types of collective organization on the other. No type of civilization can be accepted that does not provide for the worker's happiness: and no man can be happy who is forced to earn a living otherwise than by the labors for which he is naturally fitted and to which therefore he can literally devote himself with enthusiasm. I say that no man can be happy but in "that sta-

---

[5] Similarly Mr. Brailsford (p. 160): "The caste line will have to be broken, *if* industrial work is to be provided for the superfluous cultivators" (italics mine).

On the other hand, in his excellent book *Dharma and Society* (London, 1935), G. H. Mees remarks that "no serious student of caste will propagate the abolishment of the caste system" (p. 192). It will not be overlooked that Mahatma Gandhi himself, so well known as a champion of the "untouchables," does not wish to do away with caste.

See also Bhavan Das, *The Science of Social Organization* ([Madras, 1910], pp. 226 and 335). "Manu's scheme is the nearest and only approach to a workable socialism that has been tried in our race, and that succeeded for thousands of years." [Editor's Note: The interested reader is also referred to Frithjof Schuon's "The Meaning of Caste" in his book *Language of the Self* (Bloomington, IN: World Wisdom, 1997).]

tion of life to which it has pleased God to call him"; that man is literally unfortunate (deprived of his due inheritance) if either the state or his own ambition bring it about that his fortune and his nature are incongruous—"*d'un vrai travail on ne peut pas se débarrasser, c'est la vie même*" ["you can't get away from real work, that's how life is"].

What we said above on village organization ought to have made it clear that the traditional government of India is far less centralized and far less bureaucratic than any form of government known to the modern democracies. One might, indeed, say that the castes are the stronghold of a self-government far more real than could be achieved by any counting of the noses of all the millions of a proletariat. To a very large extent the caste group coincides with the trade guild; and before the impact of industrialism and *laissez faire*, and especially in the great cities, these trade guilds exercised very many of the functions that the bureaucracies now undertake with far less efficiency, and some that the bureaucracies scarcely attempt to fulfill. Thus, apart from their function of maintaining standards of quality both as to materials and workmanship, and providing for education through apprenticeship (or, rather, the master-and-disciple relationship), they covered the whole field of charity and what is now known as that of "social security." One might say that if India was not in the Chinese or Islamic sense a democratic country, it was nevertheless a land of many democracies, i.e. self-governing groups in full control of all matters really falling within their competence; and that perhaps no other country in the world has been better trained in self-government. But, as Sir George Birdwood said, "under British rule in India, the authority of the trade guilds has necessarily been relaxed"; the nature of such a "necessity" will hardly bear analysis.

There are types of society that are by no means "above," but on the contrary "below" caste; societies in which there prevails what the traditional sociologies term a "confusion of castes"; societies in which men are regarded primarily if not, indeed, exclusively as economic animals, and the expression "standard of living," dear to the advertising manufacturer, has only quantitative connotations. Such societies as these have, indeed, "progressed" toward, and perhaps attained to "the pure and 'inorganic' multiplicity of a kind of social atomism, and to the exercise of a purely mechanical activity in which nothing properly human subsists so that a man can adopt any

126

profession or even change it at will as if this profession were something purely exterior to himself" (René Guénon).[6] The mere existence of these great proletarian aggregates, whose members, exploited by one another, pullulate in "capitals" that have no longer any organic connection with the bodies on which they grew, but depend on world markets that must be opened by "wars of pacification" and continually stimulated by the "creation of new wants" by suggestive advertisement, is destructive of the more highly differentiated traditional societies in which the individual has a status determined by his function and in no sense merely by wealth or poverty; their existence is automatically destructive of the individual whom its "efficiency" reduces to the level of a producer of raw materials, destined to be worked up in the victor's factories, and again unloaded upon the "backward" peoples who must accept their annual quota of gadgets, if business is to prosper.[7] Even such a good "progressive" as Mr. Brailsford is forced to ask whether man "is not too wicked to be trusted with powerful machines!"

The economic results of commercial exploitation ("world trade") are typically summarized in Albert Schweitzer's words, "whenever the timber trade is good, permanent famine reigns in the Ogowe region." When thus "commerce settles on every tree," the spiritual consequences are even more devastating; "civilization" can destroy the souls as well as the bodies of those whom it infects. Of course, I am aware that there are plenty of Westernized Orientals who are perfectly willing and even anxious to welcome the *dona ferentes* of industry without for a moment hesitating to examine these gift horses; but strange as it may appear to the Wallaces who would like to "get (us) started on the path of industrialism," it is precisely from the standpoint of the caste system that an Indian can most confidently and effectively criticize modern Western civilization.

Among the most severe of these critics are to be found some of those deceptively Westernized Orientals who have themselves lived

---

[6] For René Guénon and his work, which is of so much significance from the standpoint of "Synthesis," see my "Eastern Wisdom and Western Knowledge" in *Isis* 34 (1943):359-363. [Editor's Note: This article is also available in *The Bugbear of Literacy*, Chapter 4.]

[7] "After this war, England must increase her exports 50 per cent over 1938" (from a speech by Lord Keynes, 1942). Commentary: "The American Revolution was in main a revolt against mercantilism" (R.L. Buell, editor of *Fortune*).

and studied longest in Europe and America. To such people it is clear that, in the undifferentiated social antheaps of the Western world, the "common man" finds his labors so detestable that he is always hankering after a "leisure state"; that this "common man" is in fact a mass product in a world of uniform mass productions and universal compulsory "education"; that the "collective wisdom of a literate (Western) people" is little better than a collective ignorance; and that there can be no comparison between the proletarian "common man" of the West with the cultured but illiterate peasant of the traditional "community whose intellectual interests are the same from the top of the social structure to the bottom" (G.L. Kittredge). He sees that it is precisely in the most "individualistic" societies that the fewest individuals are to be found.[8] It certainly does not surprise him to find native observers saying that in the West "there remains the show of civilization, without any of its realities" (A.N. Whitehead), or admitting that "while inventions and mechanical devices have been developed to a tremendous extent, there has been no moral or spiritual development among men to equal that process" (J.C. Hambro); describing modern society as a "murderous machine, with no conscience, and no ideals" (G. La Piana), or recognizing that "civilization, as we now have it, can only end in disaster" (G.H. Estabrooks). Just what is it that you, who are so conscious of your "civilizing mission," have to offer us? Can you wonder that, as Rabindranath Tagore said, "there is no people in the whole of Asia which does not look upon Europe with fear and suspicion" or that we dread the prospect of an alliance of the imperialistic powers whose "Atlantic Charter" was not meant to apply to India, and will not be applied to China if it can be avoided? An aphorism several times repeated in Buddhist scripture runs, "war breeds hatred, because the conquered are unhappy"; and that is even more true of economic than of military wars, for in the former no holds whatever are barred, and there are no truces of any intention to make peace.

In any discussion of the caste system, just as would be the case if it were a matter of kingship,[9] we have always to deal with a host of

---

[8] "Ce que l'État moderne craint le plus, c'est l'individu" ["The modern State fears the individual more than anything else"] (Jean Giono, *Lettre aux Paysans* [1938], p. 64).

[9] References to the "absolute monarchies" of the Orient are continually repeated,

errors that are constantly repeated even by otherwise well-informed Western writers. One of the chief of these is a view that is stated as a fact by the authors of *Twentieth Century India* (Institute of Pacific Relations, 1944, p. 17), viz., that: "The caste system is peculiar to Hinduism." On this subject let me quote Hocart again: He says in his Preface that something at least will have been accomplished "if the reader can be persuaded that the Indian caste system is not, as is generally believed, an isolated phenomenon, but belongs to a widely diffused social-category (*genre*). And since it is not an isolated phenomenon, it cannot be understood if we isolate it." Rather less than half of his book has to do with India; the remainder deals with Persia, the Hebrews, South Sea Islands, Greece, and Egypt, and one may add that considerable space might have been given to Japan and to the feudal system in Europe.[10] All we can say is that in India the vocational structure of society has been more strongly emphasized, and has longer survived intact than elsewhere. Another error is that of the scholars who attribute the caste system in India to the enslavement of the darker indigenous races by

as if these monarchies could be compared to that of France immediately before the revolution. There have been, of course, good and bad kings there, as everywhere else. The normal Oriental monarchy is really a theocracy, in which the king's position is that of an executive who may do only what ought to be done and is a servant of justice (*dharma*) of which he is not himself the author. The whole prosperity of the state depends upon the king's virtue; and just as for Aristotle, the monarch who rules in his own interest is not a king but a tyrant, and may be removed "like a mad dog," According to the old Hindu law, a king is to be fined a thousand times as much as a *shudra* for the same offence. It is in a very different way that one observes in the democracies "one law for the rich and another for the poor." What we see in a democracy governed by "representatives" is not a government "for the people" but an organized conflict of *interests* that only results in the setting up of unstable balances of power; and that "while the tyranny of one is cruel, that of many cannot but be most harsh and intolerable" (Philo, *Spec.* IV.113). So just as an Oriental criticizes the industrial system by his own vocational standards, so he criticizes democracy by his ideal of kingship. See further my *Spiritual Authority and Temporal Power in the Indian Theory of Government* (1942), for India especially, p. 86; for Persia, note 60.

[10] Similarly T.W. Rhys Davids in *Sacred Books of the Buddhists*, II.96ff: "Evidence has been yearly accumulating on the existence of restrictions as to intermarriage, and as to the right of eating together, among other Aryan tribes—Greeks, Germans, Russians and so on. Both the spirit, and to a large degree, the actual details of modern Indian caste usages, are identical with these ancient, and no doubt universal customs."

blonde conquerors. It suffices to point out, as Hocart has, that the four castes are connected with the four quarters and are of four "colors"—white, red, yellow, and black—and that to be consistent, the ethnic theory ought to have presupposed invaders of three separate colors, a white race becoming the priests, a red race the rulers, and a yellow race the merchants of the invaded territory! The only real color distinction is between the three and the one, the colors in question being respectively those of day and night, or "gold" and "iron"; in the divine operation the Supreme Identity assumes now the one, now the other, at will. The distinction is only partially reflected in the sensible world; the actual color of Indian peoples varies from blonde to black, and it is by no means the case that all *brahman*s are blonde or that all *shudra*s are black.

The word *brahmana* is a patronymic from Brahma (God); the "true" *brahman*, as distinguished from the "*brahman*-by-birth," is the "knower of Brahma." In the sacrificial myth we are told that the *brahman* is "born from the mouth" of the Divine Person; and that this implies a second birth (members of the three upper castes are all *dvija*, "twice-born") is clear from the fact that even the child of a *brahman* family receives only an existence from his parents, and is no better than a *shudra* before his birth of the Veda (*Manu* II.147, 172); he only becomes a *brahman* properly to be so called when he has been initiated by *brahman* teacher, who represents the Progenitor *in divinis*, and of whom he is reborn "from his mouth" (*Satapatha Brahmana* XI. 5.4.1).[11] So we find a man who has studied the scriptures at the feet of a competent teacher described in the *Chandogya Upanishad* as "shining like a Brahma-knower," and that is what it really means to be of the "*brahmana* complexion" (*varna*). The two Indian words for "caste" are *varna* (color) and *jati* (birth).[12] Of these two, *varna*, from a root meaning to "cover" or "conceal" means a good deal more than just "color" or "complexion"; it means an appearance, individuality, or character that a given

---

[11] The distinctions cited above make the Buddhist polemic of *Mujjhima Nikaya* II.148 ridiculous. The modern Western reader to whom the notion of a ritual second birth may be strange should study the second chapter of Dionysius' *Ecclesiastical Hierarchy*.

[12] "The word *jati* literally means 'birth,' but one must not understand it, or at least not exclusively, nor on principle, in the sense of 'heredity'; it designates the individual nature of the being, inasmuch as it is necessarily determined from birth

essence may assume; *varna* and *jati* are not synonymous but normally concomitant. In a Buddhist context we find a *brahmana* explaining that a *brahman* is such who is of pure descent (*jati*), knowledge of scripture, flowerlike complexion (*varna-pushkarata*), virtuous (*silavat*) and cultured (*pandita*); but of these five qualifications, only the two last are indispensable.

It will be necessary now to consider the origin, nature, and implications of the caste system, mainly in India. This we shall attempt entirely from an Indian point of view, and quite independently of the conflicting, changeable, and often prejudiced theories of the Western sociologists. In the first place, it must be understood that the terms of the hierarchical classifications are applicable not merely to human beings but *in divinis* and throughout the universe.[13] We must begin with the great distinction of the gods (*Devas*, *Aryas*) and Titans (*Asuras*, *Anaryas*) who are nevertheless brothers, and children of a common father. The distinction is as of day from night, or light from darkness, and in this sense, one of color (*varna*); the opposition is due to the fact that the Titans are the original possessors of the Source of Life and of the Light and of the world itself, all of which must be wrested from them if there is to be a world in which gods and men shall be enabled to fulfill their destiny.

The power of exercising all function whatever inheres in the unity of the primordial World-Man or Divine Person, the *Purusha*, who is so called because in every political body, whether collective or individual, he is the essential citizen,[14] just as for Philo the deity is μόνος πολιτικός [*monos politicos*]. From the sacrificial division of his functions, at the same time that having been one he becomes a

---

itself, as a gathering of possibilities that will develop in the course of his existence" (René Guénon, *Studies in Hinduism* [Éditions Traditionnelles, 1966], Chapter 6 ["Varna"]). Heredity, that is to say, is normally the largest factor in determining an individual's possibilities; but even where a character arises as it were spontaneously, it is still, in the sense that we speak of, "a born poet," a "birth" that defines the individual's possibilities.

[13] See especially *Taittiriya Samhita* VII.1.1-3 and *Aitareya Brahmana* VIII.4 where the four castes originating from the mouth, arms, thighs, and feet of the Sacrifice correspond to the four lauds of the Agnistoma and the qualities of brilliance, strength, fertility, and support.

[14] *Pur* = πόλις *polis*, the root appearing also in *plures*, *plebs*, people, fill, etc; *sha* = κεῖμαι [*Keimai*], *cubare*.

plurality of citizens, arise the two groups of the four castes, *brahmana*, *kshatriya*, *vaishya*, and *shudra*, by a distribution of qualities and functions (*Rgveda* X.90, *Bhagavad Gita* IV.13, etc). The classes of the gods are those of the Sacerdotium (Regnum and Commons corresponding to the three first of the castes just mentioned), while the *Asura*s are the *shudra*s.[15]

Humanly speaking, the hierarchy of the castes is the same. It is not a hierarchy of races, but of functions and of standards and ways of living. Very many things are allowed a *shudra* which a *brahman* may not do. In law, for the same offence, a *brahman*'s punishment is to be sixty-four times that of a *shudra*. We are not for a moment pretending that the untouchability of the lower and (out-)castes, which is so offensive to modern minds, is in any sense an excrescence upon the caste system; neither shall we defend it by a citation of English or American parallels, since two wrongs would not make a right, and in any case we are not apologizing for, but rather explaining the caste system. Nor, indeed, would such a comparison be really valid; for the caste taboos are not based upon racial or color prejudice as such (a fallen *brahman*, however well-born or fair, is under the same disabilities as an outcaste by birth, *Manu* XI.245, 98, etc), but are for the sake of the preservation of a ritual purity at once physical and psychic. I wonder, sometimes, if foreign reformers ever realize that if we should admit the Indian outcastes to our temple sanctuaries, we might as well admit Europeans? Actually, just as the Titans are by all means excluded from the sacrifices offered by the Gods, so are *shudra*s from participation in the cults of the higher castes (*Taittiriya Samhita* VII.1.1.6). At least as early as the eighth century B.C. (*Satapatha Brahmana* XI.1.1.31), we find that the teacher of an esoteric doctrine, which may not be taught to anyone and everyone, but only to the qualified,[16] may neither touch nor even look at a *shudra*. But this does not mean that the lower castes, or even the outcaste, is in any way deprived of a religion. In

---

[15] It has been maintained by many Western scholars that apart from the "late" hymn (*Rgveda* X.90) the *Rgveda* knows only of three castes. But the equation *shudra* = *Asura* (explicit in *Taittiriya Brahmana* 1.2.6.7) would need no demonstration to an Indian. It is, indeed, precisely because *Asura* = *shudra* that the Soma from which the ritual "ambrosia" is prepared must be "purchased" from a *shudra*.

[16] Cf. Matthew 7:6, Luke 8:10; Dionysius, *Ecclesiastical Hierarchy* VI.2; St. Thomas Aquinas, *Exp. s. Boetium De Trinitate* II.4.

the first place, he has cults of his own, intimately connected with his own *metier,* and these are by no means extraneous to, but only a phase of, Hinduism as a whole; distinctions of cult in India are not a matter of "other gods," but of convenience; the way of works and of devotion is open to all, and actually not a few of India's greatest saints have been of *shudra* or even *chandala* birth. Nor can we ignore the case of the "mother-son" who comes, as is told in the *Chandogya Upanishad,* to a *brahmana* teacher, to be his disciple. He is asked of what family he is, and can only answer that he is the son of his mother, and cannot possibly say who his father may have been: the *brahmana* accepts him, on the ground that such candor is tantamount to *brahman* lineage, and withholds nothing of his doctrine, so that he in turn becomes a "knower of God" and a teacher of disciples of his own.

However, we are not so much concerned here with the secular history of caste as a social institution as with its spiritual significance. At the back of all Indian metaphysics lies the conception that the existent world in all its variety originates in a primordial differentiation of one into many;[17] and that it can only be preserved in a state of well-being by an "extension of the thread of the sacrifice," i.e., by its ritual perpetuation, whereby the process of creation is continued:[18] just as a human "line" can only be extended by a perpetuation of father-mother relationships which are also to be regarded as ritual acts. Now the archetypal sacrificer is often called the "All-worker" (*visva-karman*), and its human mimesis in fact demands a cooperation of all the skills that men possess, or in other words that of all kinds of men (since, in vocational societies, the artist is not a special kind of man, but every man a special kind of artist).

Hence, if the sacrifice (i.e., in Christian terms, the Mass) is to be correctly, that is, perfectly performed—which is essential to the success of its purpose, which are those of present well-being and future

---

[17] The deity is one transcendentally "there," but many as he is immanent in his children "here" (*Satapatha Brahmana* X.5.2.16).

[18] On the "circulation of the shower of wealth" for which the sacrificial order provides, see *Satapatha Brahmana* IX.3.3.15-19 and my *Spiritual Authority and Temporal Power,* p. 68 and note 50.

beatitude—the sacrificial society must include all kinds of artists.[19] In this sense it is literally true that, as the Indian phrase would run, the vocations are "born of the sacrifice." Conversely, the vocations themselves are "sanctified"; and even when the craftsman is working for the benefit of other men and not obviously to provide the essentials of a divine service, his operation (*karman*) is a rite, as in *Rgveda* IX.11d, I where the works of priests, physicians, and carpenters are all alike *vratani*. One might add with reference to the "free" *actus primus* in which the idea of the thing to be made is conceived in an imitable form, before the "servile" *actus secundus* of manual operation is undertaken, that the artist may be called, like any other contemplative *dhira, yogi,* or *sadhaka,* and that the iconographic prescriptions of the technical books are referred to as *dhyana mantrams*, i.e., contemplative formulas.

Illustrations of the sacred quality of the traditional arts could be cited from India and many other cultures; for example, Japan, where a "carpenter still builds according to Shinto tradition: he dons a priestly costume at a certain stage of his work, performs rites, and chants invocations, and places the new house under the protection of the gods. But the occupation of the swordsmith was in old days the most sacred of the crafts: he worked in priestly garb, and practiced Shinto rites of purification while engaged in the making of a good blade. Before his smithy was then suspended the rope of rice straw, which is the oldest symbol of Shinto; none even of his family might enter there, or speak to him; and he ate only of food cooked with holy fire" (Lafcadio Hearn, *Japan*, 1905, p. 169). Similarly, in the Marquesas Islands, when a new canoe was to be built, liturgical service is first performed in which the whole of the work is referred to the archetypal process of creation; and while the work itself is being carried on, the craftsmen and their assistants live and work together in a sacred precinct protected by *tabus*, observing a strict continence and cooking their own food (W.C. Handy, *L'Art des Îles Marquises*, 1938). It will be self-evident that while, from the missionary point of view, all such "superstitious practices" must

---

[19] In the traditional and legitimate, rather than the current sense of the word, "the concept of the artist, and the related concept of the fine arts are both special bad accidents of our own local European tradition" (Margaret Mead).

be suppressed in the interests of their own "true religion" (and, in fact, the French, in the course of their *oeuvre civilisatrice*, have forbidden them), they are quite "incompatible with the existing industrial system," and must be abandoned if the Marquesas Islanders are to "progress." It might be no exaggeration to say that modern civilization is fundamentally a "racket"; needless to name the gangsters.

The traditional arts and crafts are, in fact, "mysteries," with "secrets" that are not merely "tricks of the trade" of economic value (like the so-much-abused European "patents"), but pertain to the worldwide and immemorial symbolism of the techniques, all of which are analogies or imitations of the creative nature in operation:[20] the universe itself, for example, being a "tissue" of which the warp threads are formal rays of the uncreated image-bearing light, the woof the primary matter in contact with which the aforesaid illumination becomes a color, and the pattern their progeny. The knowledge of these analogies is that of the "lesser mysteries," and these are a property of the *métier* into which an apprentice is not simply admitted, but "initiated."[21]

Let us now turn for a moment to the word *karman* which has been cited above. The meanings of the verbal root *kar*, present also in the Latin *creare* and the Greek κραίνω [*kraino*], are to make, do, and effect. And significantly, just as the Latin *facere* is originally *sacra facere*, literally "make sacred," and as the Greek ποιέω = ἱεροποιέω [*poieo = hieropoieo*], so *karman* is originally and very often not merely "work" or "making," but synonymous with *yajna*, "sacrifice" and

---

[20] With this scholastic formula, cf. *Aitareya Brahmana* V.27, where we are told that human works of art are made in imitation of celestial paradigms and the artist is described as "visiting heaven" (a reference to the primary act of contemplation) in order to observe the forms that he will, upon his return, embody in the material. "Wisdom" σοφία [*sophia*], cf., the Sanskrit *kausalyam* was originally the maker's "skill." Analogies from the constructive arts are notably absent from the writings of modern philosophers, but abound in those of ancient, medieval and oriental philosophers, who are still masters of "le symbolisme qui sait." It is of these analogies that St. Bonaventura remarks, "Behold, how the light of a mechanical art is the path to the illumination of Holy Scripture! There is nothing therein that does not bespeak a true wisdom (*sapientia = scientia cum amore*), and it is for this reason that Holy Scripture very properly makes frequent use of such similes" (*De reductione artium ad theologiam* 14). It is just that sort of "wisdom" that cannot be found where manufacture is only for profit, and not primarily for use.

[21] Cf. René Guénon, "Initiation and the Crafts," *Journal of the Indian Society of Oriental Art* 6 (1938).

also with *vrata*, "sacred operation," "obedience," "sphere of activity," "function," and especially as in the *Bhagavad Gita*, with *dharma*, "justice" or "natural law." In other words, the idea is deeply rooted in our humanity that there is no real distinction of work from holy works, and no necessary opposition of profane to sacred activities. And it is precisely this idea that finds such vivid expression in the well-known Indian philosophy of action, the "Way of Works" (*karma-marga*) of the *Bhagavad Gita*.

In the following citations from the *Bhagavad Gita*, it must be understood that while we render *karma* by "action," it is actually impossible to make any essential distinction of the meaning "sacrificial operation" for that of "operation" or "duty." This is, indeed, in full agreement with several texts of the Upanishads in which all the activities of life are sacrificially interpreted. It is precisely such an "interpretation," by which activities are referred to their paradigms *in divinis*, that marks the difference between the Comprehensor (*evamvit*) and the mere behaviorist. *Siddhi*, rendered by "perfection," is a hard word to translate; the root implies the achievement of whatever ends one has in view, also to be set right, to be healed or matured; the sense in our contexts is as nearly as possible that of the Greek τελείωσις [*teleiosis*]. With these premises, we cite from this Indian sermon as follows:[22]

> The "four colors" arise from Me, who am the distributor of qualities and actions. The activities proper to each have been distributed according to the qualities that predominate in the nature (*sva-bhava*) of each. There is nothing whatever in this whole universe that I needs must do, naught that I lack or might obtain that is not already mine; and yet I participate in action. Else would these worlds upset, and I should be the author of "confusion of colors" and a destroyer of my children. So even as the ignorant act, because of their attachment to activity, so should the Comprehensor act, but without attachment for the holding together of the world.[23] "Skill" in actions is what is meant by "yoking"

[22] The verses cited are II.50; III.22, 24, 25, 35; IV.12; XVIII.41, 45-48, but in a different order.

[23] Just as in the *Republic* 519G ff., where those who have seen the light, and would not willingly partake in the activities of the "cave," are nevertheless expected to "go down again" καταβαίνειν [*katabainein* = *avatartum*] and to participate in them, for the sake of the other cave-dwellers, but unlike them in having no ends of their own to be attained, no personal motives. "Holding together" (*samgrahana*) corresponds exactly to Plato's *Republic* 519E.

(*yoga*).[24] Better is one's own duty (*sva-dharma*), however mean, than that of others, however highly praised. Better to die in the doing of one's own duty (than to desert); another's duty is a fearsome thing! He who is a doer of actions determined by his own nature (*sva-bhava*) incurs no sin. One should never abandon the work to which one is born (*sahajam karma*). For man reaches perfection when each is in love with (*abhi-ratah*) his own work. It finds perfection in that in his own work he is praising Him from whom is the sending forth of all beings and by whom all this universe has been extended—*Laborare est orare.*

In other words, everyman's Way to become what he is—what he has it in him to become—is one of perfectionism in that station of life to which his own nature (i.e., nativity) imperiously summons him. The pursuit of perfection is everyman's "equality of opportunity"; and the goal is the same for all, for the miner and the professor alike, because there are no degrees of perfection. This whole point of view is already implicit in the old equation *karma = yajna*, i.e., *facere = sacra facere.* For it is again and again insisted upon in the ritual texts that the Sacrifice must be perfectly performed—nothing too little or too much—if the sacrificer's purpose is to be attained; and this of course implies that whatever is done in or made for the Sacrifice must be perfectly done or made. It is a striking illustration of this perfectionism (and one that vividly reminds us of the Shaker philosophy of work) that in a Buddhist context (*Anguttara Nikaya* 111, 363) in which the entelechies of the monk, ruler, and householder, etc., are defined, the "fulfillment" (*pariyosana*) of the householder, whose means of livelihood is the practice of an art, is "perfected workmanship." In the words of St. Thomas Aquinas, "the craftsman is naturally inclined by justice to do his work faithfully" (*Summa Theologica* I-II, 57, 3 *ad* 2).

---

[24] "Yoga" here in its primary sense, with reference to the control of the sense powers by the governing mind (in the Indian and Platonic-Philonic symbolism of the chariot, i.e., bodily vehicle of the spirit, the sense-powers being the team of horses). If we are also told in the *Bhagavad Gita* that "the renunciation of actions" is what is meant by "yoking," there is no contradiction, because this is explicitly *not* a repudiation of activity but implies the reference of all activities not to oneself but to the veritable Agent whose *instruments* we only are. The work will be done the more easily and the more "skillfully" the less it is referred to our self, and the more we let Him act through us. It is not an idleness, but a facility that the "action without activity" of the *Bhagavad Gita*, and the corresponding Taoist *wu wei* intend.

The modern mind, it may be observed, is not opposed to the concept of vocation *per se*, in the absence of an established heredity of functions, it sets up, on the contrary, "vocational tests" and seeks to provide for a guidance in the "choice of a vocation." What it most of all resents is the hereditary principle, which seems to set an arbitrary limit to the individual's equality of opportunity. This resentment is natural enough in the case of a proletarian society in which a confusion of castes has already taken place, and where the constitution of traditional civilization based on first principles and "in which all is ordered and in a hierarchy consistent with these principles" (René Guénon) can hardly be imagined.

As to this, let us say in the first place that while such principles are immutable in themselves, their application to circumstances of time and place is contingent, or, rather, a matter of convenience (using this excellent term in its strict sense).[25] Accordingly, if one were to imagine a caste system imposed upon the existing American scene, it would not necessarily have to be a hereditary system, if it were really provided for that even a majority of men could earn their living by doing what they would rather be doing than anything else in the world;[26] if the workman's unions were at once ready and able to insist upon the workman's human responsibility both for the production of the necessaries of life, and for their quality. Even supposing that the traditional caste systems in practice fall short, or for the sake of argument very far short of their theory, would it not be better if the social reformer, instead of attacking a theory (of which he very rarely has any real understanding) were to ask himself whether the traditional systems were not in fact designed to realize a kind of social justice that *cannot* be realized in any competitive industrial system where all production is primarily for profit, where the consumer is a "guinea pig," and where for all but a fortunate few, occupation is *not* a matter of free choice, but economically, and in that sense arbitrarily, determined?[27] It is not, then, to apologize

[25] Editor's Note: "convenience"—from the Latin *convenientia*, meaning "harmony," "agreement."

[26] In even more popular terms, if men could live by what are now only their hobbies.

[27] "We live as if economic forces determined the growth and decay of institutions and settled the fate of individuals. Liberty becomes a well-nigh obsolete term; we start, go, and stop at the signal of a vast industrial machine" (J. Dewey, *The Individualism Old and New* [1931], p. 12).

for the caste system, but to explain it, that we write, in the hope that the reader will put such questions as these to himself.

Let us, then, explain the significance of the hereditary principle in a society in which the castes are not yet confused. The inheritance of functions is a matter of re-birth—*not* in the current misinterpretation of the word, but as rebirth is defined in Indian scriptures and in accordance with the traditional assumption that *the father himself is reborn in his son.* We have seen that the function is "born of the sacrifice," and this means that if the needs of the theocentric society are to be met, the ministerial functions by which the dual purposes of the sacrifice (well-being here and beatitude hereafter) are to be secured must be perpetuated from generation to generation; the function is at once an estate and an incumbency and, as such, entailed. Just as for Plato and in Scholastic philosophy, so for the Vedanta, *duo sunt in homine*, and of these two, one is the mortal personality or character of this man, so-and-so, the other, the immortal part and very person of the man himself.[28] It is only to the former, individual nature that the category of "color" can be applied; the word *varna* itself could, indeed, be rendered not inaccurately by "individuality," inasmuch as color arisen from the contact of light with a material, which then exhibits a color that is determined not by the light, but by its own nature.

"My" individuality or psychophysical constitution is not, from this point of view, an end in itself either for me or for others, but always a means, garment, vehicle, or tool to be made good use of for as and for so long as it is "mine"; it is not an absolute, but only a relative value, personal insofar as it can be utilized as means to the attainment of man's last end of liberation (*Bhagavad Gita* V.11), and social in its adaptation to the fulfillment of this, that, or the other specialized function. It is the individuality, and not the person, that is bequeathed by the father to his son, in part by heredity, in part by example, and in part by formal rites of transmission: when the father becomes *emeritus*, or at his death, the son inherits his position, and, in the widest sense of the word, his debts, i.e., social

---

[28] This is a discrimination that may be more familiar to the reader in the Christian terms of the distinction of our outer from our inner man, or "sundering of soul from spirit." For a further analysis see my "*Akimcanna, self-naughting,*" *New Indian Antiquary* 3 (1940). [Editor's Note: Also in *Coomaraswamy 2: Selected Papers, Metaphysics*, ed. Roger Lipsey (Princeton, NJ: Princeton University Press, 1977).]

responsibilities. This acceptance of the paternal inheritance sets the father free from the burden of social responsibility that attached to him as an individual; "having done what there was for him to do," the very man departs in peace. It is not, then, for our mere pleasure or pride that children are to be begotten; indeed, they will be "no children of ours" if they do not in their turn assume our burden of responsibilities—"Children are begotten in order that there may be a succession of sacrificial functionaries"—"for the perpetuation of these worlds" (*Satapatha Brahmana* I, 8.1.31; *Aitareya Upanishad* IV.4), and just as in India, so for Plato, "Concerning marriage, it is decreed that we should adhere to the ever-productive nature by providing servants of God in our own stead; and this we do by always leaving behind us children's children" (*Laws* 774 A).

It is only in the light of the doctrine of the two selves and the no less universal imperative to "Know thyself" (to know, that is, which of these two selves is our very Self), that we can really understand the resentment of "prohibitions and commandments" and of "inequality" and the corresponding advocacy of "protest and rebellion" that we spoke of above. That resentment has far deeper roots than are to be found in the mere fact of an existing confusion of castes, which should be regarded much rather as a symptom than as a primary cause of disorder.

An impatience of restraints is not in itself reprehensible, but natural to every prisoner. The traditional concept of liberty goes far beyond, in fact, the demand of any anarchist; it is the concept of an absolute, unfettered freedom to be as, when, and where we will. All other and contingent liberties, however desirable and right, are derivative and to be valued only in relation to this last end. But this conception of an absolute liberty is coupled with the assured conviction that of all possible restraints upon it by far the strictest is that of a subjection to whatever-is-not-ourself, and most notably within this category, that of a subjection to the desires and passions of our outer man, the "individual." When, now, like Boethius, we have "forgotten who we are" and, identifying ourselves with our outer man, have become "lovers of our own selves," then we transfer to him all our longing to be free, and imagine that our whole happiness will be contained in his freedom to go his own way and find pasture where he will. There, in ignorance and in desire, lie the roots of "individualism" and of what we call in India "the law of the sharks," and in America "free enterprise." Whoever proposes to discontent the members of a traditional society (whose present "submissive-ness" annoys him) with what is rightly called their "lot" must realize that he will only be able to do so to the extent that he is able to impose on them his own conviction of the identity of his ego with himself.

In the same way, when it is asserted that "all men are born equal," of what "men" are we speaking? The statement is evidently untrue of all "outer men," for we see that they are both physically and mentally differently endowed and that natural aptitudes have to be considered even in nominally egalitarian societies. A predica-tion of equality is only absolutely true of *all inner men*; true of the men themselves, but not of their personalities. Accordingly, in the *Bhagavad Gita* itself (V.18) where, as we have already seen, the valid-ity of caste distinction is strongly emphasized, and a confusion of castes is tantamount to the death of a society, it is also taught that "the true philosopher (*pandit*) is *same-sighted* towards a *brahman* per-fected in wisdom and conduct, towards a cow, or an elephant, or even a dog or an eater of dogs," i.e., a *chandala*, or "outcaste." Same-sighted, untouched by likes or dislikes: this does not mean that he is unaware of inequalities among the "outer men" to whom the cat-egories of the social system really apply, and who are still burdened with rights and duties; it means that as a perfected seer, one who has himself risen above all distinctions established by natural qualities (as all men may), and is no longer of the world, he is color-blind, and sees nothing but the ultimate and colorless essence, immortal and divine, and "equal" because unmodified and undivided, not only in every man, but in every living creature "down to the ants."

Our object in bringing forward these considerations (which it would hardly occur to a modern sociologist to deal with in any social analysis) is to make it perfectly clear that, just as in criticizing a work of art we cannot isolate the object of our study from its total environment without "killing" it, so in the case of any given custom, we cannot expect to understand its significance for those whose cus-tom it is, if we vivisect the society in which it flourishes, and so extract a "formula" which we then proceed to criticize as if it were to be forthwith imposed upon ourselves by *force majeure*. The parts of a traditional society are not merely aggregated in it, but coordi-nated; its elements are fitted together like the parts of a jigsaw puz-zle; and it is only when and where the whole picture can be seen that we can know what we are talking about. Wholes are immanent in all their parts; and the parts are intelligible only in the context of the whole.

The reader may have noticed above that the *Bhagavad Gita* in commending the caste system also speaks of the worker's "delight" in his work; the word employed, *abhi-rata* (*ram* with an intensifying prefix), might as well have been rendered by "being in love with," as if with a bride; a fundamental sense of the root is to "come to rest in," as desire comes to rest in its object, when this has been attained. The craftsman, under normal conditions, likes nothing better than to talk about his work. We cannot but regard as abnormal the condition of the chain-belt worker who would rather talk about anything but his work; his deep interest is not in the work, in the doing of which he is little more than an irresponsible instrument of the "manufacturer" for profit, but in racing, baseball, films, or other means of entertainment or diversion.[29] It could not be said of such as these that their work is their "rest," or that an Eros or Muse inspires them. In a vocational society, on the other hand, it is taken for granted that "everyone is very proud of his hereditary science" (*kula-vidya*, Kalidasa, *Malavikagnim mitra* 1.4). So, Philo, pointing out that when the king asks, "What is your work?" he receives the answer, "We are shepherds, as were our fathers" (Genesis 47:3), comments: "Aye, indeed! Does it not seem that they were more proud of being shepherds than is the king, who is talking to them, of his sovereign power?" (*Agr.* 59, 60). In one of Dekker's plays, he makes his grocer express the fervent wish, May no son of mine ever be anything but a grocer![30] As Jean Giono says, apropos of overtime,

---

[29] "These workers look on labor as a necessary evil, as an opportunity to earn money which will enable them not only to supply their essential needs but also to treat themselves to luxuries and give free rein to their passions" (A.J. Krzesinski, *Is Modern Culture Doomed?* [1942]. p. 54). "It matters not whether the present-day factory worker is, as regards the duration and intensity of his exertion, in a better or worse condition than the savage hunter or the artisan of the Middle Ages. The point that does matter is that his mind has no share in determining the aims of his work and that his body, as an instrument of independent creative power, has lost most of its significance ... and now (work) interests him almost exclusively *as a source of pleasure and discomfort*" (*ibid.*, p. 54, note 8). Pleasure and discomfort—the very "pairs" from the domination of which the Indian and Platonic philosophers would liberate us! It would be absurd, indeed, to pretend that modern society is not based upon and supported by slave labor; it is only the name of slavery and not its reality that is repudiated.

[30] Synonymous with the *sahajam karma* of *Bhagavad Gita*, cited above, and with the householder's *sippa* in *Anguttara Nikaya*, III.363, where we are told that this man's

that as things are *"les ouvriers font quarante heures de travail par semaine. Je voudrais bien qu'ils ne fassent point d'heure du tout, quitte à leur gré à faire cent heures d'un travail qui leur passionnerait"* (*Lettre aux Paysans*, p. 37). *Moi, je le veux aussi! Cela me passionnerait* ["the workers work for forty hours a week. I would rather that they did not have to work for one hour at all, but be able to work a hundred hours doing something that interests them" (*Letters to the Peasants*, p. 37). I want that too! It would be great]: I have known hereditary craftsmen in Ceylon, carpenters and painters who regarded themselves as descendants of the archetypal All-worker (whose image they drew for me). At one time they were working for me at my own house, chiefly at the making of a painted chest for my own use.[31] They were to be paid at a day rate when the work was done; but far from trying to spin out the time, they were so much interested, so much involved in their work, that they insisted on being supplied with adequate light, so that they could go on working after dark.[32] There is your answer to the problem of overtime.[33] It is under these conditions, as Plato says, that *"more* will be done, and *better* done, and *more easily* than in any other way."

We adopted above a widely accepted rendering of Sanskrit *dharma* as "law" or "justice." Absolutely, *dharma* is the eternal substance on which all being rests, and as such a property and appellation of the deity who is "the sustainer" (*dhartr*) of every operation" (*karma*, as in *Rgveda* 1.11.4), i.e., in his royal nature as King of kings and accordingly *Dharma = Raja eminenter*. So what is natural and right is that which happens *dharmanas pari* or *dharmatas*, "normally"; it is, for example, thus "in order" that a father is begotten in his descendants (*Rgveda* VI.70.3). Relatively, one's *sva-dharma* (*sua justitia*) is the natural law of one's own being, and so at the same time one's

---

concern is for wealth, his domain an art (*sippadhitthana*), his interest in work, and his entelechy one of work accomplished (*nitthita-kammanta*), and it may not be overlooked that these expressions are of more than exclusively secular significance, the last, for example, corresponding to the *kata-karaniya* of the Arhat formula.

[31] Now in the Colombo Museum.

[32] I once cited these facts in the course of a lecture given at one of our larger woman's colleges. I was informed that most of my audience found it almost incredible that men could thus ignore their own best economic interests; they could not imagine a willingness to work, unless for money.

[33] For those whose means of livelihood is also their natural vocation, the word has no meaning; their work is never done.

"lot" and one's "duty," which is also one's own task or vocation (*sva-karma*). Unquestionably then, a correspondence of functions to varieties of natural (natal) endowment in a human society is, from the Indian point of view, nothing arbitrary, but a reflection on earth of the immutable Justice by which all things are governed. Whoever may maintain that the caste system is in fact unjust must nevertheless allow that its primary purposes are just.

In this matter, as in so many others, there is a fundamental agreement of the Indian and Greek theories. For Plato, the cosmic, civic, and individual orders or "cities" are naturally governed by one and the same law of justice δικαιοσύνη [*dikaiosyné*]; and among the accepted senses of "just" is that of "civilized." What "justice" means is discussed at some length in the second and fourth books of the *Republic*. For Plato it is, of course, obvious that the same kinds (γένος [*genos*], etymologically the Sanskrit *jati*) equal in number are to be found in that state and in the soul and that a city and a man are to be called just or unjust by the same standards, and he says that justice is realized "when each of the several parts of the community of powers performs its own task" (τὰ ἑαυτοῦ πράττει). Justice, he says, is the principle of doing what it is ours to do (τὸ τὰ ἑαυτοῦ πράττειν [*to ta eautou prattein*] = *sva-karma*). Nothing will be more ruinous to the state than for the cobbler to attempt to do the carpenter's work, or for an artisan or money maker "led on by wealth or by command of votes or by his own strength to take upon himself the soldier's 'form' (εἶδος [*eidos*] = *varna*), or for a soldier to take upon himself that of a counselor or warden, for which he is not fitted, or for one man to be a jack-of-all-trades"; and he says that wherever such perversions occur there is injustice. He points out that "our several natures (ἑκάστου φύσις [*physis*] = *sva-bhava*) are not all alike, but different," and maintains that "everyone is bound to perform for the state one social service, that for which his nature is best adapted." And in this way "more will be produced, and of a better sort (or, more beautiful), and more easily, when each one does one work, according to his own nature, at the right time and being at leisure from other tasks." In other words, the operation of justice provides automatically for the satisfaction of all the real needs of a society.

In the light of this conception of justice we can better understand Matthew 6:31, 33 where when men ask, What shall we eat and drink, and wherewith shall we be clothed? they are told: "Seek first the kingdom of God and his righteousness, and all these things shall be added unto you." For the word that here is rendered by "righteousness" the *Atharva Veda* employs the equivalent of that very εικαιοσύνη [*eikaiosyne*] about which Plato has been talking; and it is evident that if we understand by God's righteousness, His justice as defined by Plato, to seek it first will mean that all other necessaries will be provided for—"for the administration διακονία [*diaconia*] of this service λειτουργία [*leitourgia*] not only supplies the wants of the Saints, but is abundant also by many thanksgivings unto God" (2 Corinthians 9:12). That such are the real meanings of the texts is borne out by St. Paul's recommendation elsewhere to remain in that station of life in which we are, even when the higher call to the service of God has been heard. In the following quotation the italics are mine: "But as God hath distributed μεμέρικεν [*memeriken*] to every man, as the Lord hath called every one, so let him walk ... Let *every man abide in the same calling wherein he was called* ...[34] For he that is called in the Lord, being a slave δοῦλος [*doulos*], is the Lord's freeman; likewise also he that is called, being free, is Christ's slave ... Brethren, let every man wherein he is called, therein abide with God" (1 Corinthians 7:17-24). There is no incompatibility of human with divine service.

Plato's functional order takes account not only of the three "kinds" of free men in the state, which correspond to the three upper castes of the Indian system, but of another kind to which he refers as that of the "servants" διάκονος [*diakonos*] comparable to the Indian *shudra*s and men without caste. These are those "who in the things of the mind are not altogether worthy of our fellowship, but whose strength of body is sufficient for toil; so they, selling the use of this strength and calling the price 'wages,' are called 'wage-earners'" (*Republic* 371E). These are, of course, the "wage-slaves" of an industrial society, where they form a majority; those whose bodies are all they have to offer can only be described as slaves, if not, indeed, as prostitutes (cf. Aristotle, *Politics* 1254b18). Conversely,

---

[34] Like the corresponding Skr. *vi-bhaj* (*Bhagavad Gita* IV.13), implies the allotment of a due share or inheritance or "fate," the individuality that is born "like a garden already planted and sown." That distribution or dispensation is "a wondrous easy task," because it is not an arbitrary appointment, but rather the operation of an infallible justice by which we receive what our nature demands (cf. *Laws* 904 and Heracleitos fr. 79). It must always be remembered that "all is offered, but each takes only what it can receive."

one who is legally a slave, but has far more than his mere physical strength to offer, is in no sense a prostitute, but a responsible individual with only political disadvantages: a good example of what I mean can be cited in Chrétien de Troyes' *Cligés,* where the faithful John is a master builder, who holds that he "ought to be burnt or hanged, were I to betray my lord or refuse to do his will." Or in Homer, where Odysseus' faithful swineherd and porter is anything but an irresponsible slave (*Odyssey* XVI.1, XVII.385).

In the Orient, where human relations count for more than money, the consensus of feeling rates slavery above wage-earning. For, as Aristotle says, "the slave is a partner in his master's life ... there is a certain community of interest and friendship between slave and master in cases when they have been qualified by nature for these positions, although when they do not hold them in that way, but (only) by law and constraint of force, the reverse is true" (*Politics* 1255 b 21; 1260 a 10); while where men, however nominally free, are merely hired until their services are no longer needed, there may be no community of interest or friendship at all.[35] We could develop this point at great length, but can only indicate here that modern conceptions of slavery (and in like manner of serfdom) are too exclusively based on our imagination of the lot of galley slaves in the Roman Empire and upon what has been seen of slavery in America where (not to mention the iniquities of the trade itself) the condition of the slave was that of a man not merely suffering legal disabilities but also of one exploited economically in the same way that the wage-slave is now exploited, although actually "free" to work or starve. From evidences such as these alone we cannot judge of any institution. In Persia, a colleague of mine

---

[35] "On peut chasser un mercenaire mais non un serviteur héréditaire. Donc pour récolter la tranquillité et un bon service, il faut user de tact et de bonnes manières. L'hérédité, loin de les mettre à la merci de leur maître, place celui-ci entre leurs mains. Sparta conserva le servage sous un forme qui paraissait très rude aux Athéniens, mais leurs opinions ont à peu près autant de valeur que les opinions de nos libéraux sur la caste indienne et l'esclavage africain" ["You can dismiss hired help, but not a family servant. So if you want peace and good service, you must have tact and good manners. The family servant system, far from putting them at their masters' mercy, puts the latter in their hands. Sparta had a system of slavery the Athenians thought was very harsh, but their opinions have about as much value as our tolerance of the Indian caste system and African slavery"] (A.M. Hocart, *loc. cit.*, pp. 237-238).

engaged in excavation often received from the local Sheikh gifts of fruits and sweetmeats: one day he said to the messenger, "I suppose you are the Sheikh's servant?" and received the indignant answer, "No, sir! I am his *slave*." My reason for mentioning these things is to remind the student of institutions, and indeed all those who have to live in the modern world of enforced intimacy with people of all nations, that we must not be misled by the mere names of things, but ask ourselves whether, for example, "liberty" and "serfdom" are actually exactly what we had supposed them to be; what we are really concerned about is the human reality of the institutions, and that depends far more upon the people whose institutions they are than upon the looks of the institutions themselves. That is also the rea-son why we have to take so much account, not merely of the form themselves, but of the ideological background in which they ar worked. It must be impossible to judge of the propriety of any soc formula unless we have a knowledge of what is regarded as the m purpose of life in the society that we are examining. We are defending slavery, or even the caste system as such, but m pointing out that under normal circumstances slavery may be less oppressive institution than wage-slavery must always b that the caste system cannot be judged by concepts of succ govern life in a society organized for overproduction and any price, and where it is everyone's ambition to rise on t ladder, rather than to realize his own perfection.

In one respect the vocational organization of Gre seems at first sight to differ from that of India, viz., in th time and later, the vocation is not necessarily hereditar tion in this respect being different in different comr Aristotle, *Politics* 1278 5). What this really mear Hellenistic Greece an older system in which vocatio been hereditary and divinely sanctioned was breakin Hocart says, "Nous avons ici un excellente exemp appelé communément, sans qu'on sache exacteme siste, secularization" ["This is an excellent exa commonly call progress, without anyone clearly u it involves secularization."] (p. 235). Secularizati meaning from form, a "sundering of soul fro scriptural sense but *à l'envers*, a materialization what factually takes place whenever a tradit whelmed by those who believe that "progre

36 "
tom
beso
["Th
have
robbe
quanti

manufacturing enterprise of civilization must be allowed free course" whatever the human consequences may be;[36] whenever those who maintain that "such knowledge as is not empirical is meaningless" assume the control of education; whenever hereditary services and loyalties are "commuted" for money payments, and become "rents," and classes of *rentiers* or shareholders are created whose only interest is in their "interest." I am well aware, of course, that the "scientific humanist," rationalist, economic determinist, and village atheist are agreed that religion, designed by cunning aristocrats and interested priests in order to secure their own privileged positions, has been "the people's poison"; we shall not argue here that religion has either a supernatural basis or is not a religion, but will say that in societies organized for moneymaking, *advertisement*, designed by cunning manufacturers to secure their own privileged status, is *really* the people's poison, and that that is only one of the many ways in which what is called a civilization has become "a curse to humanity." Has it ever occurred to those who attack the caste systems, which they regard as unjust, that there are also values, or that the liberal destroyer of institutions, the protestant and rebel, *ipso facto* makes himself responsible for the preservation of their *val ues*?

Let us conclude with a reference to only one of these values. We have seen that in India it is taken for granted that a man is in love with the work to which he is born and for which he is by nature fitted. It is even said that a man should rather die at his post than adopt another's vocation. That may have seemed extreme. But let us see what Plato thinks. He tells us that Asclepius knew that for all well-governed peoples there is a work assigned to each man in the ty which he must needs perform, and no one has leisure to be sick d doctor himself all his days. And this we see, absurdly enough in e craftsman's case, but not in that of the wealthy, and so-called ssed man. He points out that "a carpenter, if he falls sick, will

a été également possible d'avilir les artisans grâce à la machine ... On a fait er de leurs mains la possibilité du chef d'oeuvre. On a effacé de leur âme le n de la qualité; on leur a donné le désir de la quantité et de la vitesse" nks to the machine, it has been just as possible to degrade craftsmen ... We aken away from them the possibility of being a master craftsman. We have l their soul/heart of the need for quality; we have given them the desire for ty and speed"] (Jean Giono, *loc. cit.*, p. 67).

indeed consult a doctor, and follow his advice. But if anyone prescribes for him a long course of treatment with swathings about the head and other paraphernalia, he hastily says that he has no leisure to be sick, and that such a life of pre-occupation with sickness and neglect of the work that lies before him is not worth living. And is not the reason for this that the carpenter has a task and that life is not worth living upon condition of *not* doing his work? But the rich man has no such appointed task, the necessity of abstaining from which renders life intolerable" (*Republic* 406C-407A).

Suppose that in Western societies a rectification of existing economic injustices has taken place in the natural course of the progress of manufacturing enterprise, that poverty is no more, that all men are really "free," and everyone is provided with his television, radio, car (or autogyro), and icebox, and is always sure of good wages (or a dole). Under these circumstances, what is to make him work, even for all the shorter hours that will still be necessary if the necessaries of life are to be provided for everyone? In the absence of the "work or starve" imperative, will he not be inclined to take long holidays, or, it may be, to live on his wife's earnings? We know how difficult it is at the present day to adequately "regiment" the "lazy natives" of the savage lands that have not yet been so completely industrialized that a man must work for wages, or die. Suppose that men were really free to choose their work, and refused to undertake any such uncongenial tasks as, for example, mining, or refused to assume the burdens of public office? Might not a conscription of manpower be needed even in times of peace? That might be worse than the caste system looks even to be. I can see no other alternative to this situation but for a man to be so in love with the work for which he is naturally qualified that he would rather be doing this work than idling; no other alternative than for the workman to be able to feel that in doing of what is his to do he is not only performing a social service and thereby earning a livelihood, but also serving God.

ONE FOR ALL, ALL FOR ONE:[1]
THE INDIVIDUAL AND THE COMMUNITY
IN TRADITIONAL AND MODERN CONTEXTS

Patrick Laude

As Aristotle argued, man is a social or political animal.[2] On the other hand, any authentic spiritual point of view presupposes that man does not exclusively nor primarily realize his highest destiny in the realm of the collectivity, since his ultimate end lies in the One that dwells in the deepest heart of each and every human person. These basic remarks already suggest that the relationship between the individual and the collectivity is a complex matter that deserves to be pondered in its several dimensions and on its various levels. The present essay is an attempt to clarify some aspects of this relationship by aiming at three fundamental goals: firstly, to briefly rehearse the basics of the traditional metaphysics of the subject, thereby defining the ontological status of the individual in relationship to the Absolute, God, and on the basis of this relationship, other human beings; secondly, on the basis of these principles, the development of a brief critique of both modern individualism and the aberrant contemporary emphasis upon social and collective realities; thirdly, in contradistinction to modern misunderstandings of the matter at stake, to conclude with a few remarks concerning the traditional and spiritual notion of community.

*

The Advaitin doctrine teaches that the absolute Reality is situated beyond any duality and polarity, including that of a subject and an

---

[1] Editor's Note: A deliberate reversal of the famous battle cry of Alexandre Dumas' three musketeers: "tous pour un, un pour tous!" ("all for one, one for all!").

[2] "Political" is to be understood here as referring to the *polis*, the "city," society. "We have already said, in the first part of this treatise, when discussing household management and the rule of a master, that man is by nature a political animal. And therefore, men, even when they do not require one another's help, desire to live together; not but that they are also brought together by their common interests in proportion as they severally attain to any measure of well-being" (Aristotle, *Politics* III.vi, trans. Benjamin Jowett).

object.[3] This transcendent position, however, does not preclude a consideration of the Absolute as supreme Object, nor *a fortiori* a recognition of *Atman* as the only Subject. Considered from the standpoint of mankind *qua* relative reality, the Absolute appears as Supreme Being and is, as such, both the interlocutor *par excellence* of human beings and the ultimate Object of human worship. This is the point of view of Semitic scriptures, as well as that of monotheistic theologies and bhaktic paths. The "relativity" of this standpoint does not in the least negate that there is something "absolute" in the gap separating the Creator from the creature. And this, precisely, is the reason why any spiritual path, as centered as it may be on the knowledge of the fundamental Unity of Being, includes a devotional element[4] that testifies to the fact that the human individual is a relative being and as such distinct from the Absolute. That is as true in Advaita Vedanta as it is in Taoism and Zen.[5] Still, the Supreme Reality is more fundamentally Subject than Object, if one may say so, because its objectification as Being is already situated by definition within the realm of Relativity. Therefore, the Oneness of Being can only be considered and experienced from the standpoint of the Absolute Subject, which is properly speaking the Supreme Reality as such. This Reality is immanent, in an essential and mysterious way, through the entire field of universal reality. Human existence, however, enjoys a privileged situation in this respect.[6] Notwithstanding exceptional occurrences of spiritual liberation from other terrestrial states, such as that of the animals, Hindus assert that the human state is a center from which the

---

[3] "Brahman, the One, is a state of being. It is not a 'He,' a personal being; nor is it an 'It,' an impersonal concept. Brahman is that state which *is* when all subject/object distinctions are obliterated" (Eliot Deutsch, *Advaita Vedanta: A Philosophical Reconstruction* [Hawii: University Press of Hawaii, 1969], p. 9).

[4] This devotional element might be implicit or minimally emphasized, as in the case of Zen, but there is always a way in which the soul must "worship" what transcends her.

[5] The first duty of the Zen abbot when entering the *zazen* hall is to bow before Manjushri, a Bodhisattva who represents wisdom. "When it is time for *zazen*, the abbot enters the hall from the north side of the front entrance, and goes in front of Manjushri, bowing and offering incense" (*Dogen's Pure Standards for the Zen Community: A Translation of Eihei Shingi*, trans. Taigen Daniel Leighton and Shohaku Okumura [Albany, New York: SUNY Press, 1996], p. 64).

[6] At least in our world.

Supreme *Atman* may be realized in this life. The Self is immanent with regard to all individuals. It is not fragmented and divided among *jivas* or individual souls, but It is the one and only Substance immanent to all subjects. The unicity of a given subject is nothing but a projection or a manifestation on the relative level of the unicity of the Self. This is the paradoxical mystery of the unicity of the Subject, which already appears, as Frithjof Schuon has indicated, in the fact that "the phenomenon of an 'I' that is unique, yet multiple in fact, is so contradictory—why is it that 'I' am 'I,' why is the 'other' an other?—that, for whoever is sensitive to the essence of things, it necessarily opens onto the dazzling intuition of the absolute Subject, whose unicity, at once transcendent and immanent, is unambiguous."[7] In a sense, the individual is the "locus" of the Self and it is from this individual "point of departure" that the Self may be realized.[8] From this stems a relative spiritual eminence of the individual over any group or collectivity, since no collective entity as such can realize the Self. In this essential sense, and in this sense only, there is no access to Truth through the collectivity. However, as we have indicated above, the multiplicity of individual souls reflects the one and only Subject on the level of relativity. Each individual as such is but a fragmented reflection of the Self, whence the spiritual need for other subjects who function as a kind of reminder that "I am not the real I" since any other "I" can claim "I-ness" for himself/herself as well. That corrective function of others, and of collectivities and communities as embodiments of "the neighbor"— and in a more profound way as representatives of the Divine "Other" since the neighbor can and must play the "role of God" vis-à-vis the individual subject to the extent that the latter is in itself nothing other than a "distorted vision needing to be corrected"[9]—

[7] Frithjof Schuon, *Roots of the Human Condition* (Bloomington, IN: World Wisdom, 2002), p. 56.

[8] This is in another sense a most ill-sounding, but more or less unavoidable, way of expressing oneself since there is literally no "way" to pass from the individual to the universal Self.

[9] "Modern man believes himself adult, complete, having no more to do, until death, than to gain and spend goods (money, vital forces, learning), without these transactions affecting that which calls itself 'I.' The Hindu regards himself as an entity to complete, a false vision to rectify, a composite of substances to transform, a multiplicity to unify" (René Daumal, *Rasa or Knowledge of the Self: Essays on Indian Aesthetics and Selected Sanskrit Studies*, trans. Louise Landes Levi [New York, 1982], p. 9).

accounts for a relative superiority of the collectivity over the individual. It goes without saying that this collective body must be "sacralized" or "sanctified" by its ultimate end in order to enjoy and exercise the prerogatives entailed by this superiority. Societies and communities have rights over individuals only to the extent that they show the way and provide the means toward a transcending of both the individual and society. No society *qua* society has ultimate rights over the individual, but it enjoys such rights only as a collective repository of the sacred—directly or indirectly. It therefore bears stressing that the eminence of the collectivity over the individual is of a more relative nature than the eminence of the individual over the collectivity. One of the most cogent arguments for this lies in the fact that no group or society can "conceive of a relation"—or a standpoint, or perspective,[10] to use Simone Weil's elliptical expression, which amounts to saying that no collectivity can gain access to the Truth: all it can do, at best, is to be a passive reflection and means of transmission of the Truth. Another irrefutable evidence of the spiritual limits of social and collective prerogatives appears when one considers that no saint is in need of society, whereas all societies are in need of saints.

*

The modern world is characterized by a paradoxical dual emphasis on the "rights of the individual" and the "need for communities" and "collective" and "social consciousness." On the one hand the "individual" seems to have become a substitute for the sacred. The freedom of individual opinions and choices seem to be the cornerstone of the modern outlook, since they correspond to relativistic claims and a sense of unconstrained possibility. On the other hand, the pressure of collective conformity and the global homogenization of the masses through the media has never before been so advanced, so that it could easily be demonstrated that there have never been so few "individuals"—in the sense of persons who would

---

[10] "La relation appartient à l'esprit solitaire. Nulle foule ne conçoit la relation …. Ceci est bien ou mal à l'égard de … dans la mesure où … cela échappe à la foule" ["The relation belongs to the solitary spirit. No crowd can conceive a relation …. This is good or evil with respect to … in so far as … such relations elude a crowd"] (*La pesanteur et la grâce* [Paris, 1948], p.161). In that sense, any collective consciousness is "planimetric."

base their identity on something other than the exterior pressures of collective "trends" and "imperatives." Modern man is as if torn between these two tendencies. Still he cannot totally embrace either. For one thing, the solitude of the individual is unbearable to him since he needs to find his substance and sustenance outside of himself, in other individuals or in groups. But at the same time, he cannot be a real "communitarian" since a community cannot simply be based on a collection of individuals. A genuine community finds its unity in something other than the mere aggregation of individuals. In fact, a real collectivity is more than the sum of its individual members; this is as much true of a monastery, on a spiritual level, as of an army or a battalion on a physical and animic level. Now the relativistic and fragmented outlook that prevails today is plainly incompatible with such a meaningful unity.

In a sense, contemporary mainstream concepts of the collectivity can be considered as parodies of universality, or parodies of spiritual identity. Some commentators have argued that the fight between these two forms of parody, in the form of "globalism" versus "ethnic and religious particularisms," could very well be understood as the reign of Antichrist.[11] Modern industrial and democratic societies, representatives of "globalism," appear to subordinate their principles to the idea of the primacy of the individual as a locus of inalienable rights and the pursuit of happiness. This concept emerged with the Enlightenment, when the organicist and holistic concept of society was replaced by the universal reference to man *qua* individual.[12] But in fact, universal globalism, while claiming to treat the individual as a supreme value and as an ideal of reason, opens onto an atomization of society that leaves the individual with no real identity, since he has become a mere mechanical element within the grids of industrial society. The individual is deprived of a spiritual center, and he is even deprived—at the

---

[11] See Charles Upton, *The System of Antichrist*: "Globalism and One World Government, in my opinion, are not the system of Antichrist, though they are among the factors which will make that regime possible. I believe the system of Antichrist will emerge—is in fact emerging—out of the conflict between the New World Order and the spectrum of militant reactions against it" (Ghent, NY: Sophia Perennis, 2001, p. 41).

[12] For a remarkable study of the emergence of individualism and its opposition to holism, see Louis Dumont's *Homo Hierarchicus* and *Essais sur l'Individualisme*.

extreme point of this atomization—of the sustenance of natural and social groups such as the family and the nation. At the opposite end of the spectrum, as a reaction to globalism, we see more and more individuals making an apparent "self-sacrifice" through "religious" and nationalist engagements that may even lead to "terrorism" in its most pathological form. In one way or another, these individuals become "martyrs" for a cause that is larger than their own individual existence. In fact, however, the "absolutization" of "religious" or national identities that is entailed by such engagements also fosters an "identification" of the individual to the absolutized cause: the "martyr" makes a god out of his own "ideological" passion, thereby making a god out of himself. Such an identification amounts to what Saint Augustine profoundly described as the paradoxical phenomenon of a "martyrdom" for the sake of oneself or, what amounts to the same thing, for the sake of the ideological "idol" with which the ego has identified. So, as globalist "individualism" ultimately results in a suppression of the individual, the particularist "submission" to the group opens onto the most perverse form of individualism. By contrast with these ideological parodies, traditional universalism is never adverse to authentic particularities, while true identity is never totally closed to universality. Universal creeds such as Buddhism, Christianity, and Islam have not been exclusive of specific national and ethnic crystallizations of their message. Sri Lankan (or Singhalese) Buddhism is not Japanese Zen, and a Chinese mosque does not look like a Moroccan one.[13]

The two parodies that we have briefly sketched may also be situated within the context of the processes of "solidification" and "dissolution" which René Guénon identifies as fundamental keys to an understanding of the modern world. Guénon understands "solidification" as being representative of materialism in its scientistic or ideological form, whereas "dissolution,"[14] corresponding to a subsequent phase, is primarily highlighted, in his view, by the various forms of "neo-spiritualism" to which the New Age movement is by and large an heir. Now today's situation presents, in a sense, a far

---

[13] Let us note, by contrast, that a skyscraper does not look any different in New York or Shanghai.

[14] See *The Reign of Quantity and the Signs of the Times* (Ghent, NY: Sophia Perennis, 2001), Chapters 17 and 24.

more complex picture because of the intricate association of these two subversive tendencies. On the one hand, "dissolution" is akin to the relativistic and liberal ideals of democratic capitalism that are only "solidified," so to speak, by the smallest common denominator of production and consumption, as expressed by the free market. So, while "globalism" is a principle of dissolution, it is also, on a lower level, a principle of "solidification" that keeps the modern world running with a minimally necessary level of law and order. It thereby helps consolidate, at least temporarily, the world of dream—or the dream of a world—that constitutes "reality" for most modern men. On the other hand, "particularism"—"religious" or otherwise—is characterized by a "solidifying" effect, since it tends to "freeze", so to speak, the most deleterious aspects of contemporary "freedom"; it also contributes in a powerful way—through "balkanization" and criminal destruction—to the process of "dissolution" in its fanatical fight to the death with the forces that it opposes, or rather thinks that it opposes. In addition, by providing a caricatured distortion of religious and national identities that serves as a "bogeyman" for liberal globalism, it also leads to the relativistic dissolution of the modern world. As for globalism, it also conveys some "religious" undertones through its appeal to a kind of abstract and universal moralism and its reliance upon a non-metaphysical brand of humanitarian "theology."[15] In other words, the "prince of this world" has never displayed such virtuosity in confusing the world picture and in dividing in order to reign.

*

As was suggested in the first part of our essay, a spiritual person is "alone" because his or her personal subjectivity has something unique about it, by virtue of being a reflection of the one and only Self. On the other hand, a person is "limited" by definition and therefore cannot claim to be the only self, or to exhaust the Self. A prideful and egocentric individual, or even man in his unreformed and congenitally "innocent" self-centeredness, is a murderer of the Self, to use a most suggestive Vedantic phrase. That is why the real-

[15] The "theological" and "apostolic" tone of a Woodrow Wilson is echoed by the discourses of the current apostles of a New World Order.

ization of the Self is also, by the same token–but on an infinitely lower level—a realization of the personal archetype, or the "individual" as willed by God. Such a realization is only possible when individuality as such is no longer taken as a reference or a principle of action. The difference that we have just sketched is fundamentally implied by the distinction that was drawn in some seventeenth century French schools of Christian spirituality between "self-love" (*amour-propre*) and "love of oneself" (*amour de soi*),[16] the latter referring to a legitimate attitude resulting from a consideration of oneself as "willed by God," whereas the former amounts to the error of perspective that is brought about by the Fall and manifests itself in the ego's usurpation of God's central position. In other words, one should not stand in the Divine Light; one should simply become a ray from that Light by letting it be the only Light.

We find an analogous ambiguity in the realm of the collectivity. There is a "feminine" aspect to the social dimension of the community, that is both "nurturing" and "limiting." The nurturing dimension pertains to a conservative function of transmission and, more profoundly, to a spiritual function of remembrance of the Divine through contact with other human beings. It is important to remember, in this connection, that from a Hindu standpoint, and analogically for any perspective that is centered upon the primacy of the spiritual, the primary *raison d'être* and justification for the frequentation of human beings is *satsanga*.[17] In one of his interviews Ramana Maharshi reminds his audience that the word *satsanga* literally means "community (*sanga*) of being (*sat*)."[18] *Sat* is the first essential identification of *Brahman*, the Absolute. This indicates very

---

[16] Roughly speaking, there is a Christianity that emphasizes the first perspective (it often seeks its sources in St. Augustine), and there is another (lesser known, by and large) that stresses the second. This is, for example, what would distinguish a Blaise Pascal from a St. Francis of Sales.

[17] *Satsanga* is not limited to frequenting human beings however, since sacred phenomena, nature, animals, or any being—inasmuch as it manifests God—can be experienced as *satsanga*.

[18] "*Satsanga* means *sanga* (association) with *Sat. Sat* is only the Self. Since the Self is not now understood to be *Sat*, the company of the sage who has thus understood it is sought. That is *Satsanga*. Introversion results. Then *Sat* is revealed" (*Talks with Ramana Maharshi*, [Inner Directions, 2001], p. 200). The "introversion" that Ramana Maharshi is referring to in this passage is obviously not a psychological or character-type tendency, but an attitude of spiritual inwardness.

clearly that any normative association of human beings should be in view of the Absolute, and should find its foundation in *being* and not primarily in any other secondary modes of relationship or communication. As Frithjof Schuon has indicated, the spiritual master conveys first to his disciples a reality of "being"; in an analogous way human interactions that rely on a spiritual basis communicate first and foremost a reality and a sense of being.[19] As we have indicated earlier, *satsanga* may function as a reminder of the limitations of the individuality and, as such, correct the congenital habits of the ego and its tendency to think of itself as a center and as being essentially different from others. In that sense, monastic and communitarian disciplines are designed to teach a way of being that conforms to the collective norm, thereby chiding any form of individualistic ostentation, vanity, or pride. Master Dogen thus describes the proper attitude of a Zen monk in relation to his community:

> When the assembly is sitting, sit together with them; as the assembly (gradually) lies down, lie down also. In activity and stillness at one with the community, throughout deaths and rebirths do not separate from the monastery. Standing out has no benefit; being different from others is not our conduct.[20]

Since the ultimate goal of the spiritual path consists of transcending, not destroying, the egoic consciousness, anything that favors the affirmation of the ego must be kept in check. In this respect, inasmuch as they tend to crush the individual in the name of collective and traditional imperatives and priorities, the rules, restrictions, and even more or less unavoidable "injustices" imposed upon the individual by the group—inasmuch as they are understood as coming from God, through men, so to speak—are part and parcel of any spiritual life and growth.

The previous remarks indicate that a spiritual community functions as a "collective embodiment" of the human and spiritual norm that is, so to speak, the door separating the individual from the Self.

---

[19] "Representing *a priori* a 'substance' or a 'being,' Sat, the spiritual master is *a posteriori*, and on this very basis, the vehicle of an 'intellection' or 'consciousness' ... " (Frithjof Schuon, *Logic and Transcendence* [Bedfont, Pates Manor: Perennial Books, 1984], p. 218).

[20] *Dogen's Pure Standards for the Zen Community: A Translation of Eihei Shingi*, p. 63.

In that sense, a spiritual community is what George Vallin has called a "collective individuality"; as such it is, as it were, the very "body" of the Founder. In Christianity, for example, we find the idea that the faithful are "members of Christ."[21]

Notwithstanding this fundamental and necessary normativeness of the collectivity, the function of community or society as basis for *satsanga* does not exclude some limitations inherent to human collectivities as such—whether or not they be spiritually focused—as well as those of human individuals in relation to the latter. Spiritual instructors have not been oblivious to these limitations and to the deviations to which they may give rise. In fact, the liberation from one's ego that is normatively fostered by communitarian imperatives must also be a liberation from the egos of others. In the words of Archimandrite Sophrony (1896-1993), the sign of spiritual liberty lies both in "a disinclination to impose one's will on others" and "an inner release from the hold of others on oneself."[22] There is in any human society a tendency to "fixate" or "identify" its individual members at the level of their relatively exterior identity, the external shell of their being.[23] There is no doubt that such a tendency always lurks in the consciousness of the individual human being as well, in his dealings with others, but the very nature of community predisposes it to this sort of reduction because of the principle of "gravity" that is inherent to quantity.[24]

---

[21] Cf., for example, St. Symeon the New Theologian's *Hymns of Divine Love* and Pascal's *Pensées*.

[22] Quoted by John Chryssavgis, "Paths of Continuity: Contemporary Witnesses of the Hesychast Experience," in *Paths to the Heart: Sufism and the Christian East*, ed. James Cutsinger (Bloomington, IN: World Wisdom, 2002), p. 120.

[23] Even though the highest form of *satsanga* is undoubtedly to be found in frequenting sages and saints, there have been voices, in Hinduism as elsewhere, to caution disciples against the unintended dangers of relying too much on this spiritual support. Such *satsanga* may produce the opposite effects of what is intended, either through a diminution of aspiration through over-familiarity, or stifled development and passivity. This point of view, which is not normative but preventive or corrective, is well expressed by the following analogy: "A young plant growing beneath the shade of a full-grown giant tree does not develop strength and stature. Its growth will be dwarfed, shriveled, and diseased. Whereas if the same plant were put into the open ground directly exposed to the storms, heat, cold, and other rigors of changing weather, it is bound to grow into a mighty tree drawing sustenance from both above and below" (*Talks with Ramana Maharshi*, pp. 356-357).

Any community, like any society, is a protective collective entity that aims at the liberation of its members while paradoxically manifesting a bent to imprison them within its limitations; this is analogous to the general relationship between "form" and "essence." This is why a healthy society, or human collectivity, must always integrate within its fold the means of its transcendence. If it does not, it runs the risk of petrifaction, or at least of limiting its spiritual prospects. In India, the social structure, though it is based on a strict definition of the four *varnas* and the four "stages of life," or *ashramas*, includes within itself, so to speak, its very negation in the form of the wandering ascetic, the *sannyasin*. Despite the abrupt changes of social status that they entail, these four stages present a sort of genetic continuity that symbolizes spiritual development as a whole.[25] *Brahmacharya* corresponds to an early stage of formation that is characterized by a student's exclusive concentration on studies and rigorous virtues like chastity. *Garhasthya*, or married life, emphasizes inclusion and generosity. *Vanaprastha* is a kind of spiritual retirement that is, at it were, perfected in the final stage of *sannyasa* or renunciation. This final stage of *sannyasa* transcends all others in the sense that it takes us outside of the social order as such, whether the *sannyasin* live in physical isolation or not. At this stage, the individual no longer has any social identity because he contains the entelechy of society within himself. As exemplified by

[24] This principle of "collective gravity" has been highlighted by Simone Weil in *Waiting for God*: "Everybody knows that really intimate conversation is only possible between two or three. As soon as there are six or seven, collective language begins to dominate. That is why it is a complete misinterpretation to apply to the Church the words 'Wheresoever two or three are gathered together in my name, there am I in the midst of them.' Christ did not say two hundred, or fifty, or ten. He said two or three. He said precisely that he always forms the third in the intimacy of the tête-à-tête" (New York, 2000, p. 35).

[25] "According to Vedic teachings, man's life is divided into four stages. First is *brahmacharya*, or student life, when a boy lives with his teacher and receives both religious and secular instruction. The youth is trained in self-control and acquires such virtues as chastity, truthfulness, faith, and self-surrender. The next stage is *garhasthya*, or married life. The chief injunction for this stage is to practice the ritualistic sacrifices as explained in the *Brahmanas*. At the stage of *vanaprastha*, or retirement, a man is no longer required to adhere to ritualism, but is instructed to follow the *Aranyakas* and engage in symbolic meditation. Finally he enters upon the life of renunciation, in which he is bound neither by work, nor by desire, but is dedicated wholly to acquiring knowledge of Brahman" (Swami Prabhavananda, *Spiritual Heritage of India* [Madras, 1981], p. 37).

the Hindu system, a genuine traditional order does not absolutize its structure; a spiritual community does not absolutize the means that it provides, even though they be binding for its members and, as such, somewhat "absolute." Moreover, collective life is never an end in itself, by the simple fact that death, and rebirth into the Self, remain an individual matter, notwithstanding the precious support and spiritual intercessions that the sacred community may provide for its individual members.

Even a traditional civilization like China, attuned as it was to apprehensions of the Divine within the strictures of social reality, could not but offer spiritual avenues of inner liberation that transcended the providentially formative boundaries of the Confucian order. The Taoist sage, whose eremitic life was—and still is—a spiritual height and a norm, is the best embodiment of this principle.[26] By contrast with Hinduism, which is characterized by an integration of all points of view on social reality within its genetic system of *ashramas*, the traditional Chinese view could be defined as dialectical since it is based on a sort of complementary tension—which sometimes borders on opposition—between the Confucian ideal of spiritual realization within the exclusive confines of social bonds and the Taoist transcending of all social shackles and limitations. Although the Hindu and Chinese models are sharply different in this respect, both points of view are possible and legitimate since there is indeed both continuity and discontinuity between society and the individual. On the one hand the person is part of society; on the other hand he or she is not. A philosophical perspective as intent on stressing the former point of view as Aristotle's—defining man as a "political animal"—is itself constrained to recognize, even if sometimes reluctantly, the possibility of an asocial realization of the Good. In his *Nicomachean Ethics*, Aristotle acknowledges that contemplative wisdom is the only virtue that does not have need of others (i.e., society), being entirely self-sufficient[27] (*autarkestatos*)

---

[26] Taoism does not exclude communities, as indicated by the existence of Taoist monasteries in China, but it definitely places an emphasis on natural freedom, as expressed in the inner relationship between master and disciple, rather than on external structures.

[27] Aristotle extols the supreme eminence of the contemplative life while qualifying it with restrictions that demonstrate his own tendencies, so to speak. The reference to "fellow-workers" and the adjective "too high" are quite revealing in this respect. "The philosopher, even when by himself, can contemplate truth, and the better the

and quasi-divine. The sage is both a model for society and a negation of the social sphere by his integration of its essence.

Less central but still of vital significance is the fact that virtually
all traditional structures integrate institutions or figures that allow
some room for the "subversion" of collective "stupidity" and opaci-
ty inasmuch as they hinder spiritual growth and the liberty of the
"spirit that bloweth where it listeth." These institutions and figures
are marginal by definition, and they may often be characterized by
a kind of "oddity" or "monstrosity" that sets them apart from the
ordinary and regular order of things. "Madness," in this respect, is
the most accurate symbolic approximation of this function:

> Folly alone can allow itself to enunciate cruel truths and to touch
> idols, precisely because it stands apart from certain human rela-
> tionships (*engrenage*), and this proves that, in this world of theatri-
> cal artificiality (*coulisses*) which is society, the pure and simple truth
> is madness. This is no doubt why the function of the court jester
> succumbed in the end to the world of formalism and hypocrisy ...[28]

As cracks in the wall of tradition and society, such phenomena
may allow for the light to shine from beyond the confines of protective boundaries, thereby reminding those "who have eyes to see"
that no formal structure is to be equated with the Ultimate, albeit
the least imperfect approximation of the latter on a relative level.
Collective institutions bear the eroding influence of time,[29] and

---

wiser he is; he can perhaps do so better if he has fellow-workers, but still he is the
most self-sufficient ... But such a life would be too high for man; for it is not in so
far as he is man that he will live so, but in so far as something divine is present in
him" (*Nicomachean Ethics* X.vii, trans. W.D. Ross).

[28] Frithjof Schuon, *Light on the Ancient Worlds* (Bloomington, IN: World Wisdom
Books, 1984), p. 25 note 4.

[29] A major sign of collective spiritual sclerosis lies in a tendency to focus almost exclusively on the past. As George Vallin has judiciously noted: "*La présence passive des
valeurs*, c'est l'aspect négatif de la tradition (culturelle, spirituelle, politique, etc.).
C'est l'enkystement des valeurs qui sont comme figées dans leur aspect statique et
formel, et privées de leur dynamisme interne. Cet enkystement axiologique se
traduit en langage 'temporel' par la présence dominatrice du passé ... Le passé est
vécu ici par la collectivité non pas comme ce dont les individus seraient tragique-
ment séparés, mais il est 'conservé' et maintenu comme l'âme de la collectivité,
comme la structure intime de ses coutumes, de ses réactions et de tous ses com-
portements essentiels" ["*The passive presence of values* is the negative aspect of tradition

they no better reveal their fragility and contingency—notwithstanding the "relatively absolute" nature of their sacred core—than when considered at the alpha and omega points of sacred history. The relative informality of apostolic communities bears witness to that contingent dimension of collective structures. In early times spiritual communities are more "fluid" and "informal" in their external form, in proportion to the profundity of the bonds that tie their members. The "solidifying" of sacred collectivities is a lesser evil that is indeed demanded by a lesser spiritual good. Let us recall, for example, the hyperbolic but profoundly revealing sentence by Abu'l Hasan Fushanji according to which "today [the tenth century C.E.] Sufism is a name without a reality. It was once a reality without a name."[30] Analogously, by virtue of the principle that "extremes meet," there are clear indications that, at the end of times, or toward the end of a spiritual cycle, outer structures tend to erode and even collapse, most often destroyed from within. Consequently, authentic spiritual communities become more interiorized, as it were, and are "exiled" to the inward dimension, thereby becoming relatively "absent" from the external plane of manifestation. The principles of an "invisible Church" or that of an "Islam in exile" undoubtedly correspond to such a situation. The very notion of the "Hidden Imam" in Shi'ite eschatology is a symbolic pointer to that reality. Let us add that the hypothetical return of prophets and the eschatological return of Christ, or similar redeeming figures, is often envisaged by traditional sources as taking place in a context that emphasizes their "shockingness" or their "marginality" in the world of collective norms. Thus, Sulami quotes Abu'l Hasan al-Husri as commenting that "if it were possible that there be a

---

(cultural, spiritual, political, etc.). It is the sclerosis of values that are as if immobilized in their static and formal aspect, and deprived of their internal dynamics. This axiological sclerosis is translated into 'temporal' language by the domineering presence of the past ... In such cases, the past is not experienced by the collective body as that from which individuals would be tragically separated, but it is 'conserved' and maintained as the soul of the collective body, as the intimate structure of its customs, reactions and all of its essential ways of being"] (*Être et individualité*, [Paris, 1959], p. 163).

[30] Quoted by Martin Lings, *What is Sufism?* (Cambridge, UK: Islamic Texts Society, 1993), p. 45. Lings adds Hujwiri's commentary: "In the time of the Companions of the Prophet and their immediate successors this name did not exist, but its reality was in everyone."

prophet (after Muhammad) in our days, he would be one of them (the *malamatiyyah,* or 'people of blame')." A prophet could only be hidden or scandalous in a time when the world has become a spiritual wasteland. He would be totally inconspicuous and unassuming or else so "different" and "marginal" that he would disconcert and unsettle even those—perhaps particularly those—who claim to be religious.[31]

The complexity of the spiritual relationship between the individual and the collectivity is reflected in the diverse forms in which the principle of spiritual community has manifested itself throughout the ages and within various traditional contexts. There appear to be at least five normative forms of a spiritual community. First, at the most basic level—that which is situated in an intermediary zone where the animic and spiritual realms meet—one must first mention a collective psyche, which is informed by specific spiritual archetypes that define a whole religious universe or a given segment of it. In this sense, to be part of a religion, or even of a given community within this religion, amounts to sharing in this psycho-spiritual entity. Given the relatively exterior nature of this collective entity, one will find within its domain the most fundamental psychic sustenance necessary for the integration of the individual, but also,

---

[31] One finds in Lieh Tzu's classic an analogous description of the ill-fitting nature of the sage in times of spiritual forgetfulness: "When Lung Shu asked Wen Chih: 'Your art is subtle and I am sick. Could you cure me?' Wen Chih said: 'I am at your service, but I want you to describe the symptoms of your sickness.' Lung Shu explained: 'Praise from my fellow citizens does not make me feel honored, and I do not feel shame because of their blame. Profits do not rejoice me and losses do not afflict me either. I consider life as death and wealth as poverty. As for humans they seem to me to be as good as pigs, and I consider myself to be no different. I live among my family like a traveler at an inn. My native land is like a foreign country to me. Dignities and rewards are useless against these ill tendencies; blames and chastisements do not frighten me; grandeur and decadence, gains and losses would be ineffective, and no less so mourning or joys. I therefore have no aptitude to serve the prince nor to engage in normal relationships with my relatives and friends, my wife and my children, and I do not govern my servants well. What is the nature of my sickness and how can I be cured?' Wen Chih asked Lung Shu to turn his back to the light and he positioned himself behind his patient to examine his figure the lines of which appeared now in full light. He said: 'I see your heart quite clearly: it is a square inch of void! You are not far from being a saint. Six openings in your heart are perfectly free, and only one is still obstructed. These days holy wisdom is taken for sickness. It is probably your kind of illness. I do not know of any cure against it'" (*Lieh Tzu* IV.8).

the most limitative—not to say stifling—dimension of the collectivity with respect to any full flowering of spiritual possibilities. This is also the domain of what can be called "spiritual heredity"—with all the blessings, and occasional hindrances, that such a genealogical identity carries in its wake.[32]

Second, on a more directly spiritual and institutional level, the principle of a spiritual integration and methodical use of the collectivity manifests itself in its purest form in the various forms of monasticism. Monasticism is designed to foster a collective solitude before the Divine, a maximal reduction of the complexity of existence to the simplicity of contemplation. Frithjof Schuon expresses this in terms that synthesize this whole perspective:

> Man was created alone and he dies alone; monasticism aspires to preserve this solitude in its metaphysically irreplaceable aspects: it aims to restore to man his primordial solitude before God, or again, it wants to bring man back to his spiritual integrity and to his totality.[33]

Whether it be in a Christian or Buddhist context, monasticism is entirely centered upon contemplative duties and daily work. Consequently there is a kind of impersonality inherent in the relationship between monks and nuns. They meet either in the golden silence of their concentration, or in the words of light of their collective prayers and chanting. They also meet, secondarily, in the practical goals that they share in preparing food, attending to work demands, and so on. This means that social interactions are limited to a strict minimum. Conversations are rare and rigorously regulated. In fact, silence is conceived as a perfection, one epitomized in a Christian context by the Trappists.[34] This sense of solitude and

---

[32] The "cult of ancestors" and its correlative emphasis on the family as a psychic center, as expressed in Confucianism, is probably the most perfect expression of this psycho-spiritual reality.

[33] Frithjof Schuon, *Light on the Ancient Worlds*, p. 119.

[34] "... the time between Compline and Lauds is a special time for silence. During the rest of the day the monk speaks only to the extent necessary for work and for the good ordering of the house. Recreation is exceptional. Private conversations between monks is subject to special permission or approval by the abbot. Conversations in small groups or with the whole community take place more frequently but in general not more often than once a week" (André Louf, *The Cistercian Way* [Kalamazoo, 1983], p. 92).

silence allows for a profound relationship to develop with the communitarian life of the monastery, since the solitary and collective function together in a kind of interconnected complementarity. Monasticism is a form of collective solitude, just as, conversely, vocations of eremitic solitude may "find their fulfillment, their development and their flowering in an intensely common life where strict silence guarantees solitude."[35] In addition to silence, a sedentary attachment to a particular place is conceived as a spatial analogy of silence, whereas daily discipline and holy monotony reflect the same principle of simplicity in the temporal realm. Fundamentally, monasticism opens onto eremitism, whether it be in the literal sense of a life in physical isolation, or the more general and inner sense of a retreat into the heart.

Third, traditions such as Hinduism, Judaism, and Islam, which do not emphasize "otherworldliness" to the same extent as do Buddhism and Christianity, tend to present forms and institutions of collective spiritual life that are generally less formalized and rigorous than monasticism. Whether it be a matter of the Hindu *ashram*, the existence of which is generally predicated upon the presence or the spiritual radiance of a sage, or the Hassidic or Sufi community, the ties that unite the various members of the group are less binding, at least on an external level, than those of a monastery. In keeping with the social dimension of their religion, Hassidim and Sufi are involved in family and professional life, and they are not bound to a particular place or to a collective daily liturgy, although they may be so at particular times in their life, and for relatively short periods. All this means that, in such contexts, the concept of spiritual community takes on more definitely social connotations. Normatively, this relatively more exteriorized aspect of communal life can be compensated by a deeper participation in the interior dimension of the spiritual path as a principle of collective identity. However, it is also unavoidable that the "mixed" nature of these collective modalities carries in its wake a relative exteriorization that is the price to be paid for the horizontal balance and social and economic sustenance that such institutions provide.

Fourth, and in a deeper way that may in fact be the inner dimension of monastic and communitarian structures as described above,

---

[35] *Ibid.*, p. 125.

a spiritual community can also, and above all, be defined in terms of spiritual love and friendship through the affinities woven between its individual members. These inner correspondences are like an expression, or at least a prefiguration or a symbol, of the "mystical body" that is the most essential reality of any spiritual community. In a way, this modality draws the collectivity toward the individual in its most positive sense since it rests upon relationships that are relatively free from the principle of gravity inherent within collective entities. In fact, it could be argued that such an understanding and practice of spiritual community opens onto eremitism,[36] which is itself the synthesis and perfection of collective life since, as Frithjof Schuon expresses it, "a perfect society would be a society of hermits ... "[37] Eremitism can be conceived, in this sense, as a fifth kind of spiritual community. This society would at the same time be a primordial society. And it is certainly not by mere chance that societies like those of American Indians of the Plains were still providing, until the coming of the white man, an approximation of this primordial realization of "social eremitism."[38] The social discipline of the community, conceived as a spiritual and psychic entity in its own right, exercised extremely rigorous demands upon indi-

---

[36] "Strictly speaking, the hermit alone is absolutely legitimate, for man was created alone and dies alone" (Frithjof Schuon, *Light on the Ancient Worlds*, p. 21).

[37] *Ibid.*, p. 119.

[38] Georges Vallin has analyzed this phenomenon in his *Etre et individualité* (pp. 208-209): "... on sera tenté d'identifier l'intégration de l'homme contemporain dans la structure d'un État totalitaire avec celle de l'homme primitif dans son clan ... Le clan est ouvert par en haut, si l'on peut dire ... Si le primitif n'est pas comme cristallisé en individu, c'est qu'il est sans doute infiniment plus qu'un individu, et même qu'une Personne ... Chacun des membres individuels du clan—par exemple dans les tribus des Sioux qui nous offrent peut-être le modèle parfait de peuples vraiment 'primitifs' et non pas 'dégénérés'—possède une 'autonomie spirituelle' en quelque sorte ontologique et non pas institutionalisée, et sans doute infiniment plus profonde que celle du citoyen conscient et organisé de nos cités modernes, bardé de 'droits' et de 'libertés,' mais constamment projeté hors de lui-même par les innombrables relations qu'il doit assumer avec le monde objectif" ["... one will be tempted to identify the integration of contemporary man within the structure of a totalitarian State with that of primitive men in their clans ... The clan is open from above, if one may say so ... If the primitive is not crystallized as an individual, it is no doubt because he is infinitely more than an individual, and even more than a Person ... Each of the individual members of the clan—for example in the Sioux tribes that arguably presents us with a perfect model of a truly 'prim-

viduals, requiring sacrifice and selflessness for the benefit of the group. At the same time, in a seemingly paradoxical way, it encouraged the individual to reach a kind of "prophetic" autonomy based on his direct relationship with the Great Mystery,[39] thereby enriching and serving the group by being himself, and being himself by giving himself to the One.[40]

and not simply 'degenerated'—possesses a so to speak ontological and not institutionalized 'spiritual autonomy' which is probably infinitely more profound than that of the conscious and organized citizen of our modern cities, shielded with 'rights' and 'liberties,' but constantly projected out of himself by the innumerable relationships that he must entertain with the objective world"].

[39] "That solitary communion with the Unseen which was the highest expression of our religious life is partly described in the word *hambeday* ... It may better be interpreted as 'consciousness of the divine' ... The American Indian was an individualist in religion as in war ... There was no priest to assume responsibility for another's soul" (*Light on the Indian World: The Essential Writings of Charles Eastman (Ohiyesa)*, ed. Michael Fitzgerald [Bloomington, IN: World Wisdom, 2002], pp. 7-9).

[40] In a sense, the adept of *karma-yoga* is himself by serving others, whereas the *jnanin* serves others by being himself.

Islamic Cosmological Concepts of Femininity and the Modern Feminist Movement

Fatima Jane Casewit[*]

One of the most important innovations of Islamic legislation was to restore the dignity and rights of women as responsible human beings, as individual souls standing before God. Whilst Islam emphasizes the rights and duties of all human beings towards God the Creator, woman is honored in Islam as the bearer of life and the pivot of the family unit. Her God-given function as spouse, mother, nurturer, and teacher of her children is vital for a stable society. The value of this essential function has been called into question in our times within a social movement, which is one of the many "isms" that has arisen in the modern era.

Feminism is one of the "isms" of our times. It is a movement that has re-shaped the attitudes and changed the lives of countless numbers of people, mostly born in the Western world, in the second half of the twentieth century. It is a way of thinking of the modern age, which has also profoundly influenced many who, although not born Westerners, have followed in the wake of the modern Western value system. Like the other "isms" of our age (atheism, nazism, communism, fundamentalism, etc.) feminism is a "collectivism." Its strength lies in numbers, from the masses of its followers, rather than in its ideology. Like other collectivisms, its power of persuasion is culled from quantity; and quantity necessarily constrains quality. The Feminist movement has called upon millions of women to ignore their primary responsibilities as human beings and to put their God-given roles in life into question. It has been the motive for many to rebel against their femininity, their identity, their destinies. Many women have spent their lives fighting for social and economic equality with men in the world and have forgotten the real significance of both the human state and their femininity.

* The author wishes to express sincere thanks to her colleague M'hammed Abderebbi for his critical reading and helpful comments about this article.

Rather than attempt to justify Islamic legislation as regards the rights and duties of women, this article aims to examine the deeper significance of the male/female complementarity from the Islamic perspective and to attempt to explain how the very source of masculinity and femininity is in God most High. The precepts and demands of the modern feminist movement will be examined within the Islamic cosmological viewpoint of femininity.

The Supreme Polarity

God is One. He[1] is the Supreme Real, and as such He is the Absolute.[2] Because He is Absolute, God is also Infinite.[3] The masculine-feminine principles in the cosmos have their origin in God Himself. The first supreme polarity begins here, at the level of God, in His Absoluteness and in His Infinity, because He has no bounds. We could also say that, at the same level, God is at once all-Exclusive and all-Inclusive. That is, nothing exists or is truly real except Him, but at the same time all of manifestation is included in Him. From one point of view, nothing can exist outside of God, or from another point of view, only God truly exists. Absolute or Exclusive—Infinite or Inclusive. This is the highest level of duality or polarization. Absoluteness and Infinity are the archetypes or the celestial pattern of the male-female complementarity in manifestation. The Absolute aspect of God is the masculine or "active" pole, and the Infinite aspect of God is the feminine or "passive" pole.

Now, by definition, Infinity has no bounds. It is what engenders All Possibility or All Potentiality. Infinity is the total of all the possibilities latent in manifestation. All of creation unfolds out of the

---

[1] The third person masculine personal pronoun is used to refer to God in this article, following common usage. Although God most High encompasses the Absolute and the Infinite, or the active and passive poles (Yin and Yang)—and this is reflected at every level of manifestation—the masculine gender dominates in languages which encompass gender as a part of their grammatical structure. The metaphysical reason for this may be due to the hierarchical relationship between the masculine and feminine. In referring to God, the masculine pronoun does not exclude the infinite, merciful, or "feminine" nature of the Divine.

[2] Martin Lings, *Symbol and Archetype* (Cambridge, UK: Quinta Essentia, 1991), Chapter 1.

[3] *Ibid.*

172

infinite aspect of God. However, the Infinite cannot "be" without the Absolute. "The Infinite is so to speak the intrinsic dimension of plenitude proper to the Absolute; to say Absolute is to say Infinite, the one being inconceivable without the other."[4] The polarization of Being into Absolute and Infinite is the first duality, the active and passive principles which are the basis of creation. The supreme polarity of Being is the *archetypal pattern* of masculinity and femininity.

The pervading presence of this fundamental "supreme polarity" reveals itself to us most evidently in the miracle of the human state. Every human being is created "in the image of God." However, human beings are of two types: man and woman, and since we are all created "in the image of God," our souls must be like mirrors reflecting the light of God. The supreme polarity of the cosmos, or the macrocosm, is reflected in the human soul, the microcosm. As human beings our souls reflect God's oneness. As men and women we reflect the supreme polarity: the Absolute and the Infinite, and we combine these two divine aspects in the human state.

> Man stabilizes woman, woman vivifies man; furthermore, and quite obviously, man contains woman within himself, and vice versa, given that both are *homo sapiens* ... If we define the human being as *pontifex*, it goes without saying that this function includes woman.[5]

The Supreme Polarity from the Islamic Perspective: From Unity to Duality

As the final revelation in this cycle of humanity, Islam reaffirms the Oneness of God through the Quran, which in itself is a miraculous reflection of *tawhid* or unity. The words of God are woven into a miraculous tapestry which threads together the divine message but continually draws us back to the central doctrine of Unity. The Creator is One, but His Creation begins with multiplicity and multiplicity necessarily begins with duality. This duality in manifestation is a reflection of the supreme polarity inherent in God most High.

---

[4] Frithjof Schuon, *Survey of Metaphysics and Esoterism* (Bloomington, IN: World Wisdom, 2000), p. 15.

[5] Frithjof Schuon, *Esoterism as Principle and as Way* (Pates Manor, Bedfont: Perennial Books, 1981), p. 139.

And of everything We created a pair ... (51:49)

The most commonly mentioned pair in the Quran refers to the total universe as we know it: the *Heavens* and *Earth*. The phrase "Heavens and Earth" (*samawati wal ard*) occurs over 200 times in the Quran. Because this was the first "pair" in creation, the Quran usually mentions one with the other. The Heavens and Earth refer to the whole of the universe and the phrase, which often follows it, is *ma baynahuma* which includes all the rest of creation. The Quran's description of God's creation of the Heavens and Earth recalls a primordial act that brings duality into existence from Unity and establishes the "pairs" as the fundamental components of existence. The Quran also teaches us that the Heavens and Earth existed together in an undifferentiated state before creation, just as the state of the original single soul:

> Have those who disbelieved known that the Heavens and the Earth were of one piece, then We parted them, and We made every living thing of water? Will they not then believe? (21:30)

This first great pair is miraculously repeated at every level of creation: in animals, plants, the sun and moon, gold and silver, lightness and darkness and in all of existence: affirmation and negation, motion and rest, cause and effect, origin and return.

As spiritual principles of created duality in the universe, mention must be made of the creation of the Pen and the Tablet as symbols of principles of Creation. Although the Quran mentions both Pen and Tablet in rather ambiguous verses, the Hadith literature provides a number of suggestive explanations for these verses. Most of these explanations have to do with the idea of "measuring out" (*qadar*) of good and evil, that is, "predestination," which is an article of faith for all Muslims. Ibn Abbas reported that the Prophet said, "The first thing God created was the Pen. Then He (God) said, 'Write what will be until the Day of Resurrection.'"

The Heavens and Earth and the Pen and the Tablet thus symbolize the passage from Unity in God to duality at the origin of existence.

The *Ikhwan al-Safa*, or the "Brethren of Purity" were Muslim sages of the tenth century C.E. who were influenced by Greek philosophical texts translated into Arabic. They expounded on numerical symbolism and have left us with many writings, which aptly portray the Muslim cosmological view. The following extract explicitly illustrates the male and female principles on which creation exists:

> When God originated the existent things and devised the creatures, He arranged them in existence and put them into a hierarchy like the levels of the numbers emerging from one. Thereby their manyness provides evidence for His Unity, while their hierarchy and arrangement provide evidence for the sound order of His wisdom in His handiwork. And thereby their relationship to Him who is their creator and originator will be like the relationship of the numbers to the one which is before two and which is the root and origin of number, as we explained in the treatise on arithmetic.
>
> The explanation of this is as follows: God is truly one in every respect and meaning, so it is not permissible that any created and originated thing be truly one. On the contrary, it is necessary that it be a one that is multiple, dual, and paired. For God first began through a single act with a single object of that act, united in its own activity. This was the cause of causes. It was not one in reality. No, within it there was a certain duality. Hence it has been said that He brought into existence and originated dual and paired things, and He made them the principles of the existent things, the roots of the engendered things.
>
> That is why philosophers and sages spoke about matter and form. Some of them spoke about light and darkness, while others spoke about substance and accident, good and evil, affirmation and negation, confirmation and deprivation, spiritual and corporeal, Tablet and Pen, effusion and intellect, motion and rest, existence and non-existence, soul and spirit, generation and corruption, this world and the next world, cause and effect, origin and return, or seizure and extension ... And know, my brother, that all existent things are of two kinds, no less and no more: the universal and the particular, nothing else.[6]

Unity and Duality in the Human Microcosm

The universe and all of existence is what is metaphysically referred to as the macrocosm.

[6] Sachiko Murata, *The Tao of Islam* (Albany, NY: SUNY Press, 1992).

> The creation of the Heavens and the Earth is greater than the creation of mankind. (40:57)

But the quintessence, or summit of all creation is the human being.

> We created the human being in the most beautiful stature. (95:4)

In the above passage, as in many others, the Quran testifies to the oneness of the human soul by using the Arabic word *insan*, which has no equivalent in English or other European languages. *Insan* refers to all human beings, humankind, and does not differentiate between male and female.

Whereas the macrocosm refers to the entire universe, the soul of the human being is often referred to as the microcosm or smaller universe. Islamic cosmology teaches us that everything that exists in the universe also exists in a mysterious way in the human soul. A well-known *hadith qudsi* confirms this:

> My heavens and My earth embrace Me not, but the heart of My gentle and meek servant with faith does encompass Me.

Now the Pen and Tablet correlate to intellect and soul in every human being (*aql* and *nafs*). The word Pen in Arabic, *qalam*, is masculine in gender and the word *loha*, Tablet, is feminine in gender. *Aql* is grammatically masculine in gender and *nafs* is feminine in gender. The human soul is one and therefore is a reflection of the unity and oneness of God. The first separation at the beginning of creation, the division into Heaven and Earth in the macrocosm, and the creation of the Pen and Tablet, have their equivalence in the creation of two souls from a single soul in the microcosm. These two souls, derived from the primordial single soul, became the first human pair, Adam and Eve.

> Fear your Lord, Who created you from a single soul, and from her (it) He created her spouse, and from the two of them scattered forth many men and women. (4:1)

It is significant that, from the point of view of Arabic grammar, it is ambiguous as to who was created first, man or woman, since the word *nafs* is feminine, and the first "her" in the quotation refers to the single soul.

Femininity and masculinity therefore exist already in the universe and correspond to the primordial duality at the origin of creation. The "pairs" (*zaoujain*) at every level of creation are part of the divine Plan. Divine duality thus exists in every human being, the level of the microcosm, and also pervades the universe, the macrocosm.

Cosmological Relationships

Heaven and Earth as the beginning of creation are the first duality, and duality is reflected in complementary relationships, which pervade all of manifestation. At the same time there is a relationship of subordination between God and the universe, because the Heavens and the Earth are totally submitted to God.

> To Him belongs all that is in the Heavens and the Earth. All are obedient to Him. (2:116)

This relationship between God and the universe is repeated in the relationship between the Heavens and Earth. Cosmologically, the universe is submitted to God just as Earth is submitted to Heaven.

> And we sent down out of Heaven water blessed, and caused to grow thereby gardens and grains of harvest and tall palm trees laden with clusters of dates, a provision for the servants, and thereby we brought to life a land that was dead. (50:9-11)

The Earth gives forth life, a providential mercy and gift, from which we nourish ourselves. In Arabic, the word for Earth, *ard*, is feminine. The Earth is a Great Mother who gives us life, nourishes us, and cares for us. All other traditional civilizations have also honored the Earth and revered her and they knew that their very lives depended on her. The unprecedented environmental problems that we are experiencing today are a result of modern man's lack of respect for the sanctity of Mother Earth.

On the human plane, the Earth's obvious correspondent is woman in her function as a mother who mercifully gives forth and nourishes new life. There is an evident parallel here between the

177

destruction of our Earth and our God-given environment and the growing lack of respect for motherhood on the part of Western feminists who look with disdain upon women, both in the Muslim world and in the West, who do not desire to join the work force but choose to stay home and take care of their families.

This brings us to the centrality of the womb as a supreme symbol of femininity. God said in a *hadith qudsi*, "I am God and I am the All-merciful. I created the womb and I gave it a name derived from My own name. Hence if someone cuts off the womb, I will cut him off, but if someone joins the womb, I will join him to Me."

The connection in Arabic between mercy and the womb is clear in both the form and meaning of the words. The relationship between the All-Merciful and Compassionate attribute of God is reflected in the mercy which a mother shows to her children before their birth and after they are in the world. The elevated station of the mother in the Islamic tradition is reflected in the importance that is placed on observing the rights of "womb relatives." It is also reflected in the natural care given by a mother to the child that is born from her womb. The essence of this attribute is mercy, and mercy is inherent in God. Affectionately carrying out the duties of motherhood is incumbent upon woman *a priori*. The love and care of a mother towards her children is a reflection of the loving mercy of God towards all His creatures. This is confirmed in the following well known *hadith*: Salman, one of the companions of the Prophet, reported that God's Messenger said:

> Verily, on the same day that God created the Heavens and the Earth He created one hundred parts of loving mercy (*rahma*). Every part of loving mercy is analogous to the space between the Heavens and the Earth; and out of this loving mercy He sent one part to the world, and it is from this that a Mother shows affection to her child. (Sahih Muslim)

The Modern Feminist Movement

The underlying humanistic philosophy of the feminist movement has its origins in the liberal, egalitarian, and reformist ideas of that period in European history known as the "Enlightenment." During this period, individualism and self-worth became the basis of

Western philosophy, replacing the consciousness of one's duties to God and the life in the next world.

With the onset of the Industrial Revolution and the accompanying mechanization of labor, particularly of the textile industries, an increased work force was needed to keep up the demand for goods in expanding, greedy markets. Women joined men in accomplishing mindless, meaningless, dehumanizing work in factories. Under such conditions, women certainly did deserve equal pay, shorter hours, and the right to vote. But the question lies with the justification of the entire capitalistic system based on a greed for material goods and a new social outlook where values were no longer spiritual but more and more materialistic and individualistic. Women were dragged into this arguably male-instigated process, but, on a collective level, are also to be blamed for losing sight of the essential in life and for the pursuit of happiness based on worldly gain. Within Western society at that time there was also a rapid degeneration of mores. With the downgrading of religion, women's roles were re-evaluated and the whole crucial area of religion and values in the home and family as traditionally preserved by women lost much of its meaning. As women moved out of the home, not only was the family unit gradually broken up, but the stable refuge that the home had been became less and less a place of divine-human meeting. In our times, the urge to acquire and to achieve in life has led us so far away from God, from our Center, and from our families, that the lives of both men and women have become empty.

History books tell us that the real agitation for women's rights in the modern world began in the wake of the Industrial Revolution in England. The new industrial society put new demands on women without offering them the compensation that they obviously deserved. Moreover, it was normal that women would want to participate in the functioning of this evolving society and benefit from the unprecedented material prosperity. At the same time, urbanization and industrialization were causing a rapid erosion of family life and values. The family, the basis of a stable society, was being stripped of many of its traditional roles. Schools and child labor were taking over the upbringing of children. Religious faith had been on a steady decline since the Renaissance and the Age of Reason, and hit rock bottom with the widespread acceptance of Darwin's theory of evolution. The role of woman was changing very quickly, mainly in the urban centers. Small, peaceful towns grew into noisy, dirty cities as people migrated into them from the countryside. On the land in Europe social stability based on the Christian tradition had at least been maintained to a certain extent and had permitted men and women to lead lives which, although physically strenuous and often filled with suffering, led to salvation at the moment of death. The migration off the land into the cities disrupted all of this. Physical struggles in the mushrooming urban areas were not usually less strenuous and the stability of the family unit was at stake. Thus, the *raison d'être* of the roles of both men and women came into question.

The precepts of the modern feminist movement are, as we mentioned above, based on the modern mentality of the collectivity. Although a collective movement, it is a zealous concern for individual rights. The concerns of feminists are, like those of other "minority" movements, focused on the rights of the individual rather than on the greater good of society. Individual achievement and the securing of equal rights with men are priorities for the feminist movement. As an offshoot of a decline in faith and resultant social upheaval in Christian and Jewish Europe, the feminist movement, although on a certain plane comprehensible within the context of the dehumanization of both men and women, inevitably locks horns with cosmology and traditional values.

Muslims need to understand this "civilizational" context of the modern feminist movement, and understand that the situation of women in the Islamic civilization has always been very different. Muslims were blessed with a God-given social structure, which is outlined in the Quran and elaborated upon by the Sunna (words and deeds) of the Prophet. It provides guidance for every aspect of life including a framework for marriage and sexuality which has been a great blessing for these times and has helped to preserve the family unit in Muslim societies. The feminist movement in the West is centered on woman in this world and rights which she is able to obtain here and now. A woman's relationship with God and eternity are not taken into consideration.

As we have pointed out above, femininity is not only a miracle of creation, but is also, metaphysically speaking, an inherent part of God. The feminist movement, on the contrary, sees femininity as an obstacle to being a successful human being. Modern feminists disregard the function of the human being as at once slave and vice-regent (*khalifa*) upon Earth. They also ignore the complementary relationships that exist between God and His servants, God and the Universe, and Heaven and Earth. These relationships are repeated at every level of creation and between man and woman, the divine purpose being harmony in the family unit and maximum social equilibrium. In essence, the feminist movement seeks justice in this lower world (*ad-dunya*) and ignores the common destiny of all of us: death, the meeting with God, and eternity.

Both men and women in our age need to be reminded that the complementarities of noble masculinity and merciful femininity are of divine origin. Man's revolt against God and woman's revolt against man are leading to complex disequilibria in human souls and irresolvable social problems within the family and our communities.

In formulating our complaints in the world, we should not forget this ultimate destiny of every human being, and we should all, men and women, ask ourselves: "What does God really want of me?" From this perspective, we may better situate the rights and duties of both men and women in Islam.

THE DESACRALIZATION OF WORK*

Roger Sworder

And if a man takes upon himself in all its fullness the proper office of his own vocation, it comes about that he and the world are the means of right order to each other ... For since the world is God's handwork, he who maintains and heightens its beauty by his tendance is cooperating with the will of God, when by the aid of his bodily strength, and by his work and his administration, he makes things assume that shape and aspect which God's purpose has designed. What is the reward? ... That when our term of service is ended, when we are divested of our guardianship of the material world and freed from the bonds of mortality, God will restore us, cleansed and sanctified, to the primal condition of that higher part of us which is divine.

—Hermes[1]

The Traditional Work Ethic

In the West, as we have seen, the earliest theorist of work at any length or in any detail was the Greek philosopher Plato. His account of work has remained one of the standard accounts. An almost identical theory to Plato's is to be found in other cultures and particularly in India where it underlies the practice of Karma Yoga, the yoga of action. This theory, wherever it is found, may be called the traditional or perennial theory of work, and most of what has been said in the last four chapters derives from it. A brief outline of its major tenets should therefore be enough to establish it clearly and firmly in the mind of anyone who has read this far. But we should take care from the beginning not to confuse this traditional theory of work with a theory which superficially resembles it,

---

* Editor's Note: Chapter 6 of *Mining, Metallurgy, and the Meaning of Life*.

[1] Hermes Trismegistus, *Asclepius* I ("The Virgin of the World"), trans. A. Kingsford and E. Maitland (1885; reprint, Wizard Bookshelf, 1977).

the theory of work which is usually called the Protestant work ethic. Though both of these theories suppose a relationship between work and the life of the spirit, they do so in quite different ways.[2] Any understanding of the traditional theory of work must also be an understanding of how it differs from the Protestant work ethic which largely displaced it.

According to Plato everyone born into this world has an innate predisposition for a particular kind of work. Only by the finding and doing of this work can a person become who he or she truly is. This predisposition is the single determining factor of the human personality, in comparison to which all other traits of character, accidents of birth, environmental conditionings are negligible. Each of us is born to carry out a particular task and only when that task is completed have we done what we came for. In some people this predisposition is very clear, as in the case of child prodigies who evince at an early age a degree of competence in a particular art or science which is inexplicable in the light of their actual experience. According to the Hindus this is one of the strongest reasons for a belief in some form of metempsychosis or transmigration of souls from one body to another. So natural and unforced is the facility which a predisposition confers that the person so gifted is hardly aware of it. It is only with difficulty that a child who can draw can be made to understand that others cannot. There is some evidence to suggest that these predispositions run in families, but both Plato and the Indian philosophers are careful to point out that there is no guarantee of this, and that in a well organized society people are free to pursue other vocations than those of their parents. Nonetheless there is an expectation in traditional societies that children will follow their parents in this regard, and this expectation, taken together with the central importance of these predispositions to the personality, explains why families are often named after vocations. In northwestern Europe the names of Bergman and Smith are particularly common and derive from the professions of mining and metallurgy. Sworder is another such name but much less common.

To a society like ours which has largely done away with the traditional arts and crafts, it may appear that they are the products of

---

[2] *Bhagavad Gita*, Bks 3, 4, trans. Swami Chinmayananda (Bombay: Chinmaya Mission Trust, n. d.). Plato, *Republic*, Bk 2, from *Collected Dialogues*, ed. E. Hamilton & H. Cairns (Princeton, 1963).

convention rather than of nature, and that they can be dispensed with when cheaper and more efficient means of production are discovered. This assumption is debatable. One of the most remarkable developments of the two centuries since the Industrial Revolution is the hobby. After working in the factory or the office people return home to practice in their periods of leisure what previously they would have done as work. This is the significance of gardening in a society which has mostly dispensed with agricultural labor, and of the millions of workshops in the backyards of suburban houses. Nothing could show more clearly than this that the old predispositions continue to exercise their sway over the personality, and they do so regardless of the fact that the work for which they fit us is no longer paid, nor otherwise rewarded than by the intrinsic satisfaction which it provides. When Plato starts to talk about work in the *Republic* this is the very first point he makes.[3] He asks whether people would be better off if each did or made everything, or whether each should do or make one kind of thing only and then share the fruits of this labor with everyone else. In deciding that it is better to divide labor than have each person do everything, Plato argues that each person is naturally fitted for one kind of work only and is better served by doing just that. For Plato the prime reason for dividing labor is not that it is more efficient, but that it conforms to our innate predispositions. Acting in accordance with one's innate predisposition is the basis of Plato's theory of justice.

In the Indian philosophy this same theory or law of justice is called the Dharma and it is one of the major themes in the best known of all Indian scriptures, the *Bhagavad Gita*.[4] As the Indians understand it, we are impelled into action by the mere fact of our bodies. We cannot do other than act, given our equipment of arms and legs. Actions are constantly flowing from us, and what is required if we are to be happy is a way of organizing and directing this ceaseless flow of actions to some worthy end. This will finally enable us to free ourselves from the otherwise unending chain of causes and effects by which our actions bind us. This release is achieved by the selfless performance of our proper work, without any regard for the fruits of it, until we become capable at last of a

---

[3] Plato, *Republic* 2.368ff.

[4] *Bhagavad Gita*, 3.1ff.

kind of desireless, actionless action which is liberation. This way of thinking has something in common with the story of the Fall from the Garden of Eden. Before the Fall Adam tended the garden, cooperating in the work of God. But after eating the fruit of the Tree of the Knowledge of Good and Evil, he was expelled from the Garden and forced to provide for himself by the sweat of his brow. This concern with good and evil is precisely what transforms the selfless work of the one who is liberated into the anxious toil of the fallen. As the *Bhagavad Gita* puts it:

> Without hope, with the mind and self controlled, having abandoned all possessions, doing mere bodily action, he incurs no sin. Content with what comes to him without effort, free from the pairs of opposites and envy, even minded in success and failure, though acting he is not bound.[5]

This is how the *Bhagavad Gita* describes the man liberated through work. This selflessness in action is characteristic of the work ethic in traditional societies. The work is done anonymously and workers do not seek to arrogate to themselves the credit for having done it. This is why much of the greatest work done in the Middle Ages, or in the archaic period of ancient Greece, is unsigned and unattributed. The practice of claiming work as one's own is an index of the extent to which the traditional work ethic is in decline, and on this score both the classical period of Greek art and the Renaissance are in the process of falling away from the selfless ideal of the periods which immediately preceded them. In the ancient world this falling away was merely a matter of degree, since in the Greek and Roman traditions as we have seen, credit for the work had always finally to be given to the patron god or goddess. It was always believed that a divine power was responsible for the miracle of skillful action or creation.

These ways of thinking about work made it clear that workers were not to use their work to aggrandize themselves, at whatever level in the society they might be. Nor was work, even of the most artistic kind, a medium of self-expression, in which the personality of the artist as an individual was exposed. The personalities of artists

[5] *Bhagavad Gita*, 4.21.

were of no more interest to those who made use of their work than the personalities of their tailors or cobblers. At best they had nothing at all to do with the work. In such a society each kind of work was done by people who sought through the doing of their work to escape the limitations of the egoic self. Instead of thinking of themselves as individuals who were as far as possible separate and independent of each other, they thought of themselves as belonging to parts of a single organism. These parts were the classes and professions, each of which was different from the others, but necessary to the survival and success of the whole. Just as the same food produces and maintains the different organs of the human body, all of which are necessary to its fulfillment, so in the one society all those innate predispositions were to be found which were needed to complete it. Acting in accordance with one's innate predisposition was justice which was at once the source of the deepest satisfaction to oneself and the means of maintaining the society.

In many different ways the social order was continuous with the natural order. The innate predispositions which equipped people for particular kinds of work were in nature in much the same way that we now consider, say, the home building instincts of animals to be. The idea of whatever was to be done or made stood in the divine mind in exactly the same way as did the ideas of the natural species or those of the elements. The contemplation of the idea was the superior part of the different kinds of work, while the material realization of the idea in the world of time and space was regarded as derivative and secondary. Since every such idea came from God, it could hardly be regarded as the creation of an individual craftworker or artist, and therefore the notion of originality counted for very little. This is not to say that research, experiment, and innovation were suppressed. Plato was emphatic that enquiry is essential to the proper development and maintenance of any art or science. Instead there was a tendency to attribute the latest finding to some earlier, often legendary exponent of the art, as a token of veneration and as a way of ensuring the continuity of the tradition. In some places the same way of doing or making things persisted for many centuries, as was the case, for example, with Gregorian chant. But it would be wrong to suppose that the artists at the end of one of these periods were less capable than those at its beginning. For traditional workers, originality consisted in the recreation within themselves of that understanding which the centuries had inherited from the founder of their art, who had received it from God.

Another respect in which human work was continuous with the natural order was in the relation between the worker and the material on which the work was done. Of almost all kinds of work there was an assumption that between the worker and the material a bond existed, a deep affinity. The carpenter had a feel for the wood, the smith for the gold or iron, the gardener had green fingers. This affinity, which underlay the activity of most working lives, established a connection between the deepest element in the personality of the worker and the universe beyond, between the microcosm and the macrocosm. This was no abstract speculation but an immediate recognition that by working through the creations of the outer world of nature, a vocation could be answered and a life fulfilled. This connection between the innermost and the outermost dimensions of experience has much more to do with human happiness than is now realized. It is the only means to the thorough integration of the human being, and the loss of it produces an alienation far more pervasive and acute than that described by Marx. Between the idea which is known through contemplation, and the material through which that idea is realized in the world of time and space, there may be a union which is the marriage of heaven and earth.

Just as the worker required the material on which the work was done in order to achieve fulfillment, so the material required the worker if it too was to be fulfilled. It seems strange to us to suppose that wood can only be fulfilled, come fully into its own, through the intervention of the carpenter. On this view the wood's fulfillment consists not in its living out its full span in the forest, but in being axed and sawn, sanded and polished. Only then are its beauties revealed. A cathedral mason who ruined the block of stone he was dressing was required to follow the cart which disposed of it as chief mourner. As stone the block would not be affected much by whatever the mason did to it. But by being turned into a block it became, as it were, alive, and then died again through the incompetence of the mason. For many traditions the metals in the ground were embryonic and the processes of mining and smelting were obstetric, bringing them to birth. According to some scholars this is the primordial view of mining, the oldest and most profound.[6] But what

---

[6] Mircea Eliade, *The Forge and the Crucible* (Chicago: Chicago University Press, 1978).

all these examples have in common is the notion that nature longs for human intervention in order to become most fully itself. Intervention by humans in the natural order is not a rape but nature's glory, the only means by which the greatest treasures can be brought to light. As William Blake put it:

> Where man is not, nature is barren.[7]

The alchemists put the same thought even more abruptly:

> Nature unaided fails.

It is hard for us now, two hundred years on from Wordsworth, to realize that for by far the greater part of recorded history, wilderness was not regarded as beautiful but as ugly and frightening. Very often it was believed demonic, in the bad sense, a natural condition quite different from that of Eden which was a deliberately planted and tended garden. For the greater part of Christian history, wilderness was precisely the natural correlative of Adam's Fall, a place of no virtue except for what could be won from it by human effort. There was normally only one class of people attracted to it for its own sake, the anchorites and hermits, for whom it was at once a solitude and a test, a retreat from the world and an arena for spiritual combat. Even so, this use of the wilderness is far from universal, appearing most often at times when the social order is markedly decadent. At those times the most extreme luxury and the most extreme asceticism are found side by side, and from the point of view of several religious traditions the luxury and the asceticism are equally suspect. It is one thing to retreat to an ashram in the forest and quite another to endure the terrible privations of the desert. The place presently occupied by the notion of wilderness in our range of emotions and attitudes was in early times taken by pasturage and the pastoral tradition. This probably means that we can no longer quite grasp what the idea of wilderness was for our ancestors. For us there are no longer wild and dangerous places on the earth as once there were. For us a wilderness may also be a park, a confusion of categories impossible before.

---

[7] William Blake, *The Marriage of Heaven and Hell*, in *Blake: Complete Writings with Variant Readings*, ed. Geoffrey Keynes (Oxford: Clarendon Press, 1978), pl. 10, 1.8.

But if the wilderness was almost entirely bad from the point of view of earlier times, so also were those who did nothing to transform the raw materials of nature, of whatever kind. People who failed to respond to their vocations, who did nothing to develop themselves in accordance with their innate predispositions, were despised and condemned. On this view everyone is born to be an artist in some field; there is nothing finally to distinguish the work of the person whom we now call an artist from the work of anyone else. The artist, as one scholar has put it, is not a special kind of person, but everyone who is not an artist in some field, everyone who does not respond to their vocation, is an idler.[8] The traditional theory of work cannot, I think, conceive even of the possibility of a person without an inborn vocation, since the vocation is the single greatest determinant of personality. There is only one person who has the right to abstain from all constructive activities, the contemplative monk or nun. But these people not only make nothing, they do not use anything either. In a strict sense they are no longer members of human society. But even these people may be said to engage in the work of transforming the raw materials of nature, since they are wholly intent on correcting and improving their own fallen natures as human beings. And, of course, it is the activity of these people which we still think to be the most truly vocational of all.

For all these reasons sloth was one of the seven deadly sins in the medieval understanding. But the traditional doctrine of work entailed much more than the mere banning of idleness. Other activities were regarded with the deepest suspicion. Merchants, for example, were typically unproductive. Engaging in no constructive activity of their own, merchants bought cheap and sold dear, and it was not easy to find a justification for this within the limits of the doctrine just outlined.[9] This problem was, however, peculiar to the West; in India the merchant class was always highly respected. Still harder to accommodate, but also apparently indispensable, were the money lenders, around whose operations the later Middle Ages built an enormous scaffolding of casuistical argument and counter argument. The traditional argument was that metal, the metal of

[8] A.K. Coomaraswamy, *Christian and Oriental Philosophy of Art* (New York: Dover, 1956), p. 24.

[9] R.H. Tawney, *Religion and the Rise of Capitalism* (Harmondsworth: Penguin, 1938), p. 97.

the coinage or the precious metals, was essentially barren and could not in the normal course of nature propagate itself. But this is precisely what it did when lent out at interest, and therefore the lending of money at interest was unnatural, a sin against nature. Though not a deadly sin in itself, it was very closely connected in the medieval mind with sloth and avarice, so that throughout this period the merchant and money lender alike were thought to stand in imminent danger of hell.

These consequences of the traditional doctrine of work were brought out very clearly in a passage of Dante's *Inferno* in which Virgil explained to Dante the reason why usurers were condemned by divine justice to suffer the torments of hell:

> "Would you go back a little way," I said;
> "To where you said that usury offends
> Divine goodness, and untie that knot for me?"
> "Philosophy," he said, "to him who heeds
> Indicates in more than a single place
> How Nature derives the course she follows
> From the divine intelligence and skill,
> And if you study the 'Physics' carefully,
> You will find, after not too many pages,
> That your human skill, as far as possible,
> Follows her, as pupil follows teacher,
> So that your skill is like a grandchild of God.
> From these two, if you recollect
> The opening part of Genesis, mankind
> Must draw its sustenance and move ahead.
> And because the usurer pursues another course,
> He scorns Nature for herself and for her
> Follower, and sets his hopes on something else."[10]

Virgil's source for some of this is the *Physics* of Aristotle, though he goes far beyond what Aristotle says there. All human activity, on this view, should model itself on nature, which models itself on the divine intellect. In this way, by depending on art and nature, humankind should gain its livelihood and develop. Human art repeats and imitates the creative powers of nature on the one hand,

[10] Dante, *Inferno*, trans. J. Ciardi & A. MacAllister (New York: New American Library, 1954), 11.94ff.

and the creator of nature itself, the divine intellect, on the other. As for Plato, so for Dante there is something divine about human work. On Dante's account the usurers' sin is one of omission. They produce nothing and in that failure are guilty of despising God and nature. They are guilty of violence towards God, and their punishment is to be condemned to the burning sands of a desert plain where fiery embers fall on them like flakes of snow.

Virgil explains to Dante that human work is an imitation or repetition of the divine intellect. It is just here that we see the significance of Homer's accounts of Hephaestus and of the revelation to Moses on Mount Sinai. These stories are exemplary. They do not apply merely to the making of Achilles' shield or the vessels of the tabernacle. They show that the work of the smith is always a repetition of the divine act of creation. Every craftworker realizes in human form the creative power of God, just as every contemplative realizes the divine inactivity and inwardness of God. The whole world of human work is a bodying forth at many levels of the different aspects of the divine nature. By a splendid anachronism Dante's Virgil makes his point about God, nature, and art by referring both to Aristotle and to Genesis.

The Protestant Work Ethic

Dante composed the *Inferno* about 1300 C.E. From that time to the time of William Blake was a period of five hundred years, during which the traditional doctrine of work was successively forsaken until it was almost forgotten. If that should seem a very extended period for the demise of a single theory, we must remember that this theory was the basis for much of the psychology, sociology, economics, and politics of the traditional order, and that it had persisted in the West from at least the time of Homer. There are reasons for believing that the theory played a central part in Egyptian civilization from early times, which would date it back another two millennia. It is not surprising therefore that a theory of this age and importance took a long time to disappear. We must now study its decay in some detail since it is precisely from this decay and its consequences for our understanding of work and nature that the terms of the present debates about mining have emerged.

At some points it is easy enough to trace the slow decline of the traditional doctrine of work, especially in the later stages. This is because the decline corresponded to the emergence of a new doctrine of work which has been of the greatest interest to historians and sociologists. This new doctrine is usually called the Protestant work ethic, though this name is not entirely satisfactory. This new ethic is generally thought to be the religious and psychological basis for the rise of capitalism in the Western world from the sixteenth century onwards. It has been minutely studied in an attempt to isolate those factors which created the capitalist order. Of all the questions and issues raised by historians and social scientists since the beginning of the nineteenth century, this is one of the most vital.

Unfortunately, from our point of view, this great question has been discussed almost entirely the wrong way round. The task has not been to explain how the older theory of work declined but how the new one emerged. There has been a presumption, at least from the time of Marx, that the formation of capitalism is a positive development, a social and economic order into which Europe grew, a stage on its journey towards full maturation. Accordingly, very little attention has been given to the virtues and values of the order which preceded capitalism and the new ethic of work. The best known historian of the new ethic was Max Weber who claimed that Luther originated the notion of vocation, for which there had been no historical precedent![11] This perhaps is an exceptional case, but there can be no doubt that students of this period have given very little weight to the theory of work which the Puritan and capitalist revolutions deposed. To trace, therefore, the demise of the older doctrine is to take on a task that has been little attempted.

The decline of the traditional theory of work was bound up with the decline of the Middle Ages. The feudal order of the Middle Ages was irreparably damaged by the Black Death, which created so great a shortage of agricultural laborers that the manors could no longer enforce the service of their serfs. Their labor was at a premium and could be sold to the highest bidder. The weakening of the manorial system encouraged an increasing lawlessness in the countryside and a shift to the towns. To sustain the towns, new manufacturing industries had to be developed which produced goods for export and not merely for local consumption. The most impor-

[11] Max Weber, *The Protestant Ethic and the Spirit of Capitalism* (London: George Allen & Unwin, 1930).

tant of these in the early period were woolen goods and the towns which produced the best woolen products were in the Lowlands. These towns developed their woolen manufactures to the point where they needed to import raw wool from further and further afield, and so there began the conversion of agricultural land into pasturage in many parts of Europe.[12] This in turn led to a still greater exodus from the land, so that by the early sixteenth century Thomas More could describe the sheep as a man eating animal since it deprived agricultural workers of their livelihood.[13]

As the power of the towns increased, the power of the landed nobility declined, and money as well as land became a standard of wealth. This transference of power was a serious, if invisible, blow to the Church which had come to mirror the world of the peasantry and the countryside in its calendar and rituals. The rich townsfolk did not owe their wealth and power to a long established order, and from the beginning of the Renaissance a new emphasis on the individual appeared. The patronage of the arts was also in part transferred, as the new wealth gave the direction of the crafts into the hands of the merchant princes. This was particularly true of Florence, the greatest woolen manufacturing city in Italy, but it can be seen also in the paintings of the Lowlands. Personal portraiture re-emerged on a large scale after its eclipse during the Middle Ages, as the merchants redirected the arts to the task of immortalizing themselves rather than of glorifying God. The artists, too, forsook their personal anonymity and quickly developed a remarkable bravado and braggadocio, as can be seen, for example, in the autobiography of Benvenuto Cellini.[14]

This increase in trade between cities and nations required a corresponding development in the mechanisms of international finance. The first great private bankers had acted as agents for the Church in Rome, to which they facilitated the payment of tithes and taxes by means of letters of credit. The fact that such methods were used by the Church itself made it much more difficult to maintain the religious strictures on merchants and usury. One great histori-

[12] R.H. Tawney, *Religion and the Rise of Capitalism*; Max Weber, *The Protestant Ethic and the Spirit of Capitalism*.

[13] Thomas More, *Utopia*, trans. R. Adams (New York: Norton, 1992), 1.24.

[14] Benvenuto Cellini, *The Life of Benvenuto Cellini* (London: Phaidon, 1949).

an of usury during this period, R.H. Tawney, traces in detail the slow relaxing of the rules concerning usury under the pressure of the new economic order. According to Tawney, the accumulation of wealth during the late Middle Ages reached a critical point in the fourteenth and fifteenth centuries. At this point it burst the narrow limits within which it had grown to that time, and then reconstituted the social and religious orders to accommodate itself.[15]

The development of trade and international finance weakened the nexus between people and the locale in which they lived. The idea of self-sufficiency as a desirable goal for a society gave way to an increasing appetite for the exotic. The limited aims of medieval government yielded to quite new ways of calculating political and economic success, of which the possibilities were continually being enlarged. As more and more people encountered products from abroad, the connection between the immediate environment and the amenities and utensils of daily life was lost, and this brought about a revision of attitudes to the natural world. To this change the discoveries of the New World were soon to make a massive contribution, not only in the natural sciences but because the wealth which flowed into Europe from the other side of the world had no immediate relation to the places which it enriched. The marriage between heaven and earth which the crafts had achieved through their transformation of natural resources immediately to hand, became less and less central to the economic arrangements of society.

It is an old belief that social institutions can be destroyed only by the corruption of those who govern them. In 1510 Martin Luther went to Rome and was appalled by the decadence which he saw there, particularly the sale of papal pardons for mortal sins. The same reforming anger which inspired Luther to attack the system of indulgences drove him on to attack other traditional accretions to the word of God in the Bible. According to Luther pilgrimages and saints' days were an excuse for idleness and should be done away with. He had a profound distrust of mendicant friars and the contemplative orders. He was a strong believer in the value of work and vocation, but these beliefs had much more to do with their moral than their spiritual value. Work had to be done because it was given

---

[15] R.H. Tawney, *Religion and the Rise of Capitalism*; Max Weber, *The Protestant Ethic and the Spirit of Capitalism*.

by God and because it served the community. But it was not itself a spiritual path. At best for Luther it was a means of keeping the soul from the temptations of leisure and wealth. Hard work was good for the soul as a duty and a discipline, but finally it had nothing to do with salvation. Luther's hatred for the papal traffic in salvation led, from the traditional point of view, to a dangerous overreaction. Anxious as he was to ensure that salvation ceased to be a marketable commodity, he detached it from the social world altogether and made it entirely a matter of faith.

At the first level Luther's distrust of idleness made him emphasize the value of work more than had his predecessors. We can already see in Luther that tendency to think of work as a mechanical discipline which was to play a central part in the Industrial Revolution. But from the traditional point of view Luther's notion of work was very limited. He was exclusively concerned with the physical act of labor in this world, the slavish element of work. We do not hear from Luther, nor indeed from any of the reformers, about the contemplative or free act, which must precede and accompany the realization of the idea so contemplated, in the world of time and space. We may put it simply by saying that they had not fully understood the exemplary nature of those metallurgical revelations which Moses had been shown on Mount Sinai. They underestimated or ignored the element of contemplation in the practice of the arts and crafts, paying little attention to the question of where those ideas originated of which every work of art or craft is an embodiment. Of a piece with this oversight was their destruction of the mendicant and contemplative orders, on the ground that these people did no productive work. Far from believing that contemplatives were the highest class of humanity, they refused to acknowledge them at all. They supposed instead that everyone should commune with God in the same way, without intermediaries, in the solitude of prayer. It is as though suddenly everyone was required to be a monk or a nun while still living in society. It may be claimed of this as of other forms of inflation, that it brought an apparent increase in wealth, followed by a long impoverishment.

Luther's view of work, with different emphases and some important modifications, was the view shared by almost all the reformers of the next two centuries.[16] For Calvin, for example, work had even

---

[16] Max Weber, *The Protestant Ethic and the Spirit of Capitalism*, Ch. 3.

less to do with salvation than it had for Luther. Calvin's doctrine of predestination made salvation a gift of God, given irrevocably and without any consideration of the virtue or otherwise of the soul to which it was given. By just so much did Calvin suppose the gift of salvation to be above the human capacity to earn or deserve it. The moral life for Calvin was not a means to this immeasurable grace but a sign of it. The soul which was saved had only one goal in the world, to glorify God in every word and deed. This theory of the moral life and of work is not unlike the traditional doctrine in one respect, since there too the worker works for no advantage extrinsic to the work, but achieves a divine selflessness through his commitment to the work for its own sake. In the traditional view the fully realized worker is concerned only for the good of the work to be done. But in the traditional view the doing of the work is itself the means of achieving this selflessness, which is not predestined but won. And this selflessness is found at the very heart of the work, where the innate predisposition of the worker for that particular kind of work turns out to be a divine genius which transcends the limits of the human, but is at the same time peculiar to that kind of work and no other.

Calvin's theory of work was more like the traditional doctrine than was Luther's in this respect but it was less like it in others. In social theory Luther was conservative, with a medieval belief in the life of the peasant and a medieval distrust of trade. For Luther the vocation to a traditional kind of work was of vital significance, especially in his later writings, because it was the principal means of service to the community. The smith's work was priestly because it served the community. Luther was himself the son of a miner. In Calvin's thought the traditional vocations were by no means central. His social theory was less peasant than urban, and applied as well if not better to the life of trade as to the lives of craft and field. He was concerned with questions of fair exchange and fair profit and was prepared to engage in the complex economic considerations that these issues demanded. Though his religious vision enabled him to create a social organization at every level and on a grand scale, that organization was in theory if not in fact very different from the social system of the Middle Ages. Gone is that governing ideal of integration in which all the different functions of the social organism were predisposed by divine providence to meet the needs of the whole and to fulfill the differing talents of each. In its place was a social order derived from and consistent with the doctrine of individual predestination, a city of the elect marked off from the rest of humanity and held together by a communal sense of this unbridgeable gulf.

In their own lifetimes the teachings of Calvin and Luther profoundly altered the societies in which they lived. They were men whose time had come, and continental Europe was instantly changed by them. Their effect on England was less immediate but when it came it was even more profound. In the meanwhile, throughout the fourteenth, fifteenth, and early sixteenth centuries, there were other tendencies in English life which ran counter to the general movement from the feudal to the mercantilist order, or at least counter to the desacralization of work. During these centuries there was an increase in the number and power of the craft guilds. These guilds conferred upon their members a strong sense of how their work was valuable of itself. Each guild was proud of the peculiar nature of its work, the special knowledge which its members shared to the exclusion of outsiders. Quite new occupations quickly developed this sense of their own mystique so that very soon after their invention printing and gun making were organized on the basis of guilds.[17]

Each of the crafts had its patron saint and its own shrine, the maintenance of which was the responsibility of the guild. The members of the guild prided themselves on their exclusive privilege of worshiping at that shrine. Each craft had its own holy days in honor of its patron saint and took part as a guild in other festivals of the Church. In many parts of England the guilds were charged with the responsibility for putting on the miracle plays, the great cycle of plays which the Church mounted annually for the edification and education of the townspeople. In the city of Chester each of twenty five such companies put on a play. Each of the guilds had its own uniform or livery, to be worn by its members on special occasions.

This practice and others are still preserved by the livery companies of the City of London. There were also the apprenticeship rituals which further developed the craftworkers' pride in the mystique of their work. We know from many sources that the

---

[17] E. Lipson, *Economic History of England* (London: A.C. Black, 1960-64); *Cambridge Economic History of England* (Cambridge: Cambridge University Press, 1952).

apprentices of each craft formed a very tightly knit body which often made riot in the streets with cudgels and barricades against its rivals. Each group had its own oaths and boasts. The good natured rowdiness of the shoemakers is dramatized in Thomas Dekker's play "The Shoemakers' Holiday" which was published in 1600. The play pictures the city life of Elizabethan England though it is nominally set in the reign of Henry V. It tells the story of how the yearly feast of apprentices was established by Simon Eyre, shoemaker and lord mayor of London. It was a matter of the greatest pride to shoemakers that they should be the hosts on this occasion to all the apprentices of London. Dekker's play was the most popular comedy in London in Elizabethan times and it reveals a side of English life not found in Shakespeare.[18]

In the very nature of the case it is extremely difficult to determine how far the lore and rituals of these guilds were truly initiatic. We do not know their secrets but we cannot be sure whether this is because there were no secrets or because their secrets were jealously guarded. No doubt the "rites of passage" from the condition of layman to apprentice, from apprentice to journeyman, from journeyman to master, marked vital stages in the careers of craftworkers, in parallel to the sacraments of the Church. We have already considered the kissing of St. Barbara and the ritual leap over the leather apron of the German miners and mining engineers. But whether these rites realized for those who underwent them any substantial connections between the nature of their daily work, the cosmic creation, and the final redemption or release of the spirit, is not easily discoverable. The one case in which it is claimed that a genuine initiatic tradition has been preserved, masonry, is hotly contested. It is enough to say here that some of the claims made by masons are quite consistent with traditional understandings, for example that the human act of building is a repetition of the universal creation by the great Architect of the universe. Given the layer upon layer of symbolism concerning the crafts in scripture, myth, and folklore, it is highly probable that craftworkers made use of these symbols in their daily occupations, and developed practices to deepen their insight into them. The guild system inculcated in craftworkers a strong sense of pride in their crafts. This pride would have urged

---

[18] Thomas Dekker, *The Shoemaker's Holiday* (London: J.M. Dent, 1926).

them to an understanding of their crafts at the deepest level. To think of one's craft as a symbol of the divine creation or of spiritual redemption is to see it in its most glorious aspect. Many guilds accompanied their members to their burial, covering their coffins in elaborate palls on which the instruments and symbols of their craft were embroidered.

We cannot know for certain how things stood in this regard in sixteenth century England. We do know that from the middle of this century the religious affiliations of the guilds were attacked and progressively destroyed by the reformers.[19] The miracle plays were suppressed, not because they had lost their popular following but by reformist zeal, reinforced by state opposition to their alleged idolatry and superstition. We have already noted Luther's opposition to the saints' days and holy days which craftworkers regarded as important privileges, since on the days dedicated to the patron saints of each of the crafts, those craftworkers celebrated at the expense of their employers. Calvin likewise attacked the practice in his *Institutes*. In England the attempt to suppress these festivals was justified in the name of industry, just as Luther had criticized them for encouraging idleness. But it is hard to resist the feeling that the reformers had more positive objections to them, that they encouraged merry making, pranks, and high spirits, and that they were superstitious. The behavior of the apprentices in London and the various attempts to control them are matters of the greatest interest throughout this period.

In the seventeenth century reformist attacks on the religious practices of the craft guilds continued. According to the Puritans there was no authority in scripture for their worship of the saints, nor for the elaborate rituals, ornaments, and vessels of the high Church. These remnants from the time before the Reformation were banned or destroyed, and with them went some of the most powerful and enduring links between religion and the crafts. At this point a distinction may be drawn between southern Germany and Puritan England, since in Germany the Lutherans retained much of the medieval decoration in their churches and have preserved it to our own time. The Lutheran mining communities in southern Germany still keep paired wooden statues of miners and angels in

---

[19] R.H. Tawney, *Religion and the Rise of Capitalism*, pp. 101–102, 107.

their churches, together with screens illustrating the miners' work.[20] They have also preserved the practice of dedicating their work to the patron saints of mining.[21] Mathesius, an immediate disciple of Luther gave sixteen sermons to miners about mining, on the basis of St. Paul's Epistle to the Philippians who were the first Christian mining community. In short, this part of Germany did not suffer from the iconoclasm which in the name of a purer religion smashed much of the finest craftwork in England. In this way we can distinguish between the Protestant and Puritan work ethics and acknowledge that the Lutherans' emphasis on traditional vocations, however much they diminished the notion, did something to preserve the connections between craft and religion. In England, however, the inspiration of the Puritan divines was Calvin, not Luther. By the time the high Church party was finally successful in 1660, the damage had been done.

There is some evidence that the Puritans themselves felt the vacuum that their iconoclasm had created, and their attempts to fill that vacuum demonstrate better than anything else the distance between the doctrines of their reformed Church and the traditional doctrine of work. Towards the end of the seventeenth century there were books published with titles such as *Navigation Spiritualized, Husbandry Spiritualized,* and *The Religious Weaver.*[22] But such works were hardly at all concerned with what we might expect from their titles, the exposition of how each of these crafts is symbolic of the divine creation or of spiritual redemption. They are concerned with saving their readers from the social vices attendant upon those forms of work: in the case of sailors, for example, from drunkenness, swearing, and whoring. Nonetheless their titles promise much more, a promise which would attract readers who had some understanding of what these forms of work had meant before they came under the new dispensation.

The desacralization of the crafts, on the ground that their religious practices were superstitious and idolatrous, was carried through by the reformers at the same time as they desacralized the

---

[20] W. Paul, *Mining Lore* (Portland, Or.: Morris Printing Co, 1970), pp. 140–141.

[21] W. Paul, *Mining Lore*, pp. 124–126.

[22] R.H. Tawney, *Religion and the Rise of Capitalism*, pp. 242–243.

land. The conversion of Christianity into a religion of the book, and the stripping away of Catholic tradition, entailed that many of the practices which sanctified the land also had to be suppressed. Once again there was no authority for them in Christ's teaching. Almost from the beginning of the Reformation in England the procession-al beating of the bounds of the parish was severely modified. Up to this time the tradition had been that just before Ascension Day the priest and others would ceremonially walk all the way round the boundaries of his parish. The old ritual with banners and crosses and a large crowd of followers had thanked God for the gifts of the earth, had strengthened the parish against the incursion of evil spir-its, and had reinforced the people's sense of the inviolability of titles and legal boundaries. But from the middle of the sixteenth century processions were banned and the beating of the bounds became instead a perambulation. The wayside crosses and the ritual drawing of crosses on the earth were done away with. Richard Corbet, who was Bishop of Oxford in the early seventeenth century, when Oxford was the center of high Church opposition to the Puritan movement, described the effects of such reforms in a famous poem.

> Farewell, rewards and fairies,
> Good housewives now may say,
> For now foul sluts in dairies
> Do fare as well as they.
> And though they sweep their hearths no less
> Than maids were wont to do,
> Yet who of late for cleanliness
> Finds sixpence in her shoe?
>
> At morning and at evening both
> You merry were and glad,
> So little care of sleep or sloth
> These pretty ladies had;
> When Tom came home from labor,
> Or Cis to milking rose,
> Then merrily went their tabor,
> And nimbly went their toes.
>
> Witness those rings and roundelays
> Of theirs, which yet remain,
> Were footed in Queen Mary's days

On many a grassy plain;
But since of late, Elizabeth,
And, later, James came in,
They never danced on any heath
As when the time hath been.

By which we note the fairies
Were of the old Profession.
Their songs were "Ave Mary's,"
Their dances were Procession.
But now, alas, they all are dead;
Or gone beyond the seas;
Or farther for Religion fled;
Or else they take their ease.[23]

Corbet was a sharp observer of his times and particularly of the effects of the Puritan revolution. He described in another poem how the old wooden crucifixes were used by Puritans as splints for horses' legs. This story of the fairies' departure reflected a common and widespread belief of the time, which often credited the West Country and then Ireland with being the last refuges of these dispossessed spirits of the land. As spirits of the land they had enabled the human inhabitants of a place to imagine the occult intelligence of the natural world around them, as though it were an extension of themselves or they an extension of it, all members finally of a single species. In another poem written nearly two centuries later, Wordsworth was to mourn the loss of the pagan gods of nature for just this reason.

We have already considered the dwarfs of mining folklore, the help they gave miners, and the connections which such beliefs established between miners and the ground they worked. Similarly Corbet's poem makes very clear how the fairies played a part in domestic work and the work of the farm. These spirits of place were powerful agencies in the traditional beliefs about work. They not only rewarded the scrupulous housekeeper but celebrated the industry of the laborer and the milkmaid. Being themselves very active and alert, the fairies introduced an element of playfulness into the workaday world, the same element we have seen in the feast

---

[23] Richard Corbet, *The Fairies' Farewell.*

days, festivals, and pageants of the craftworkers' year. Their departure typifies the novelty of the Puritan attitude to work. For the Puritan, work was not an occasion for making merry, any more than it was in itself a means of spiritual development.

Blake and Wordsworth on Work and Nature

Despite the defeat of the Puritans and the restoration of the monarchy in 1660, the damage which had been done to the traditional understandings of work and nature was not repaired. On these issues there seems to have been a compromise or a standoff between the forces of Cromwell's commonwealth and those of the restoration. It is fascinating to speculate on how far the loss of these traditional understandings contributed to the Scientific and Industrial Revolutions which now transformed Britain and later the world. Could the chemists of the eighteenth century have done what they did if they had supposed their material to be charged with those occult powers in which their alchemical predecessors had believed? How much more difficult would it have been to establish production line processes in English factories on such a scale if manufacture had retained the aura of the sacred? Would the English Midlands have become the black country if the fairies had remained? Might it not have been the removal of these restraints rather than capital accumulation, technological advances, or political freedom which enabled Britain to create an entirely new human order? The old doctrines of work and nature were discarded, but was this because they were no longer in step with the new economic and political circumstances? Or were these circumstances themselves the outcome of a new spiritual order? It is just on this issue that Weber and Tawney diverge, as Marx diverged from Hegel on what governs the dialectic of history.

To these issues we cannot attend here, except to point out that the decay of the traditional doctrines of work and nature played a much greater part than is generally acknowledged. The easiest way of tracing the decay of these traditional doctrines from this point to the present time is to examine the ideas of two representative authors at the turn of the nineteenth century. One of them, William Blake, made an heroic attempt to re-enact the traditional doctrine of work in his own life, but despite his personal triumph was ignored. The other, William Wordsworth, helped to establish in the

English understanding an entirely new way of regarding nature, the spirit, and the moral life. It is this way, devastatingly criticized by Blake, which has become a twentieth century norm and the source of many of the disputes about mining.

William Blake regarded himself as a prophet in the Old Testament manner and he remains, two centuries later, one of the most acute commentators on contemporary life. He matters here because he is the clearest exponent of the traditional doctrine of work since the Puritan revolution, both in his writing and in the way he lived. He is also the greatest poet of the metals and of metallurgy in the English language, as well as being an engraver on metal by profession and the inventor of an entirely original method of printing from metal plates. His poetry is characteristically complex and difficult; it is also a treasury of traditional doctrine or, as Blake called it, the wisdom of ages. One of his last and greatest works was called *Jerusalem*, that visionary city which he believed would be the final apotheosis of London where he lived.

Blake's *Jerusalem* is in four chapters, each of which begins with a sermon addressed to a particular group in the society of his time. The sermon at the beginning of the fourth and final chapter is addressed to the Christians:

> We are told to abstain from fleshly desires that we may lose no time from the Work of the Lord: Every moment lost is a moment that cannot be redeemed; every pleasure that intermingles with the duty of our station is a folly unredeemable, and is planted like the seed of a wild flower among our wheat: All the tortures of repentance are tortures of self-reproach on account of our leaving the Divine Harvest to the Enemy, the struggles of entanglement with incoherent roots. I know of no other Christianity and of no other Gospel than the liberty both of body and mind to exercise the Divine Arts of Imagination, Imagination, the real and eternal World of which this Vegetable Universe is but a faint shadow, and in which we shall live in our Eternal or Imaginative Bodies when these Vegetable Mortal Bodies are no more. The Apostles knew of no other Gospel. What were all their spiritual gifts? What is the Divine Spirit? is the Holy Ghost any other than an Intellectual Fountain? What is the Harvest of the Gospel and its Labors? What is that Talent which it is a curse to hide? What are the Treasures of Heaven which we are to lay up for ourselves, are they any other than Mental Studies and Performances? What are all the Gifts of

the Gospel, are they not all Mental Gifts? Is God a spirit who must be worshiped in Spirit and in Truth, and are not the Gifts of the Spirit Everything to man? O ye Religious, discountenance every one among you who shall pretend to despise Art and Science! I call upon you in the Name of Jesus! What is the Life of Man but Art & Science? is it Meat and Drink? is not the Body more than Raiment? What is Mortality but the things relating to the Body which Dies? What is Immortality but the things relating to the Spirit which Lives Eternally? What is the Joy of Heaven but Improvement in the things of the Spirit? What are the Pains of Hell but Ignorance, Bodily Lust, Idleness and devastation of the things of the Spirit? Answer to yourselves and expel from among you those who pretend to despise the labors of Art and Science, which alone are the labors of the Gospel. Is not this plain and manifest to the thought? Can you think at all and not pronounce heartily That to Labor in Knowledge is to Build up Jerusalem, and to Despise Knowledge is to Despise Jerusalem and her Builders. And remember: He who despises and mocks a Mental Gift in another, calling it pride and selfishness and sin, mocks Jesus the giver of every Mental Gift, which always appear to the ignorance-loving Hypocrite as sins; but that which is a Sin in the sight of cruel Man is not so in the sight of our kind God. Let every Christian, as much as in him lies, engage himself openly and publicly before all the World in some Mental pursuit for the Building up of Jerusalem.[24]

Elsewhere Blake wrote:

A Poet, a Painter, a Musician, an Architect, the Man or Woman who is not one of these is no Christian.[25]

These statements set out the major tenets of the traditional doctrine of work in a way which perhaps only became possible at a time when this doctrine was obsolescent. Blake can say what he says here because the position which he expounds is already only one view among others of what work is or should be. To an extent Blake is recapitulating teachings which he had inherited. He mentions the duty of our station in a way which is reminiscent of Luther, and his talk of the real and eternal world of which this vegetable world is

[24] Blake, *Jerusalem*, pl. 77, lines 1-50.
[25] Blake, *Laocoon*, k. 776.

but a shadow is Platonic. The emphasis on mental studies and performances in connection with liberty recalls the free act of contemplation. In the traditional doctrine, but not in this passage of Blake, this is contrasted with the servile act of manufacture. In the opening lines of the sermon Blake sets out the ancient doctrine that the greatest moral evil is dissipation, the wasting of one's time and talents on idle pleasures and pursuits. This evil, it seems for Blake, is not usually a deliberate turning away from one's proper work, but an incapacity to make clear to oneself what exactly that work is. He describes this in a wonderful phrase as "the struggles of entanglement with incoherent roots."

But what of Blake's claim that according to the Gospel, art and science are the real work of the spirit? Blake feels the need to argue for this and he leads up to it carefully by referring to those passages in the New Testament which he takes to support his case, but without making it immediately clear how he intends to use them. Leaving aside the apostles for a moment, we may ask what justifies his claim that the Holy Ghost is the origin of the ideas which artists contemplate. We remember in this context the spirit of God which moved on the face of the waters in the first verses of Genesis and that same spirit with which God filled Bezaleel, Aholiab and the other craftworkers who made the tabernacle, its altars, and its vessels. But is this the spirit which descended on the disciples at Pentecost and gave them the gift of tongues? Blake believed that it was, on the ground that this divine visitation conferred the art and science of poetry on those who received it. For Blake, Jesus too was essentially a poet.

In the case of the hidden talent, there is no reason to suppose that Jesus meant what Blake and we mean by this word.[26] For Jesus it meant simply a certain weight of precious metal. But this word has come to mean what we mean by it because Jesus uses it as he does in the parable, even though it is impossible to tell what Jesus himself intended by the metaphor. As for the treasures in heaven, we would normally take these to be the moral virtues. But Blake distrusted the moral virtues, seeing in them little more than an occasion for accusing others of sin. He was always working to restore what he thought to be the intellectual power of Christianity, as

[26] Matthew 25:14-30.

opposed to its morality and its devotional practice. He writes later in *Jerusalem*:

> I care not whether a Man is Good or Evil; all that I care is
> Whether he is a Wise man or a Fool. Go, put off Holiness
> And put on Intellect.[27]

Blake lived what he wrote. Overwhelmed by the delights of the intellect and imagination he neglected all other considerations. Not for him the outward prosperity and reputation of the Puritan as the sure signs of God's grace. For Blake poverty and the stigma of madness were as nothing compared to the happiness of doing his own work for its own sake. If other people failed to appreciate that work, Blake knew that the angels in heaven were delighted by it just as he was. His output was prodigious: from childhood to the songs he sang on his deathbed he lived his seventy years in an unremitting fury of creation. There was never any money. In his later years he owned a single rusty black jacket which he never wore indoors but preserved for when he had to go out. Having no servant, he embarrassed his friends by greeting them in the street as he carried his own jug of porter back from the public house. If his poor wife Catherine told him they were penniless he would fly into a rage, so she learnt to present him with an empty plate at dinner to show him he would have to earn a commission by engraving someone else's designs.[28] His disciple, the great painter Samuel Palmer, wrote of him that he ennobled poverty and made two little rooms off the Strand more attractive than the threshold of princes.

For Blake as for the Greeks and Jews the paradigm of creative activity was metallurgy. In his poem *Milton* he represented the creation of the physical universe as the making of the mundane egg by means of anvils and furnaces.[29] We may see in this some recollection of Ptah's creating the world as an egg. In his famous poem "The Tyger" Blake wrote:

---

[27] Blake, *Jerusalem*, pl. 91, lines 54-56.

[28] Alexander Gilchrist, *Life of William Blake* (1880; reprint, New Jersey: Rowman & Littlefield, 1973), p. 356.

[29] Blake, *Milton*.

And what shoulder and what art,
Could twist the sinews of thy heart?
And when thy heart began to beat
What dread hand? and what dread feet?

What the hammer, what the chain?
In what furnace was thy brain?
What the anvil, what dread grasp
Dare its deadly terrors clasp?[30]

But though the imagery of the smithy abounded in the early work as symbolic of universal creation, it was not much elaborated. According to some scholars, a great change came over Blake's work about halfway through his career, after which the metallurgical imagery was far more potent.[31] They suggest that Blake must actually have seen a casting mill in operation, since from this point the imagery of smelting was both more specific and more widely applied. Now we hear of the glare and roar of the fire, the clatter of hammers and blowing of bellows, the clinkers, the rattling chains, the ladles carrying molten ore, the dark gleam of the ashes still burning before the iron doors of the furnace. These are the tremendous images which Blake now used to illuminate the processes of the imagination and of the human body.

The protagonist in Blake's highly original mythology of creation is Los, whose name is probably an anagram of the Latin word for the sun, and who represents the divine imagination. He is the intellectual sun who creates the worlds of space and time and also the worlds of the imagination. Almost always he accomplishes this work by forge and furnace, and we must ask why Blake conceived of his own creative work as a poet and painter in these images. Partly it has to do with energy, which Blake often compared to the fires of hell and which he always imagined as burning. He may also have thought of his poems and designs as unbreakable, so well composed that the bonds which bound each of them in its integrity were as strong or stronger than iron or steel. Certainly they have endured. Then again, despite what has just been said, Blake was a tireless

[30] Blake, "The Tyger," *The Songs of Experience.*
[31] S. Foster Damon, *A Blake Dictionary* (London: Thames & Hudson, 1973).

reviser of his longer works, recasting the patterns and contexts of the various passages which comprised them. Though many of the same passages appear again and again in these works, their relations to each other are changed. This process Blake seems to have thought of as a refinement, as Los throws back the earlier work into the furnace that it may emerge purified and be formed anew.

But the work of Los does not end with the creations of the poet and the painter. His metallurgical labors are also the processes of the human body.

> In Bowlahoola Los' Anvils stand and his Furnaces rage;
> Thundering the Hammers beat and the Bellows blow loud,
> Living, self moving, mourning, lamenting, and howling incessantly.
> Bowlahoola thro'all its porches feels, tho' too fast founded
> Its pillars and porticoes to tremble at the force
> Of mortal or immortal arm; and softly lulling flutes,
> Accordant with the horrid labors, make sweet melody.
> The Bellows are the Animal Lungs; the Hammers the Animal Heart:
> The Furnaces the Stomach for digestion: terrible their fury.
> Thousands and thousands labor, thousands play on instruments
> Stringed or fluted to ameliorate the sorrows of slavery.
> Loud sport the dancers in the dance of death, rejoicing in carnage.
> The hard dentant Hammers are lull'd by the flutes' lula lula,
> The bellowing Furnaces blare by the long sounding clarion,
> The double drum drowns, howls and groans, the shrill fife shrieks
>   and cries.
> The crooked horn mellows the hoarse raving serpent, terrible but
>   harmonious:
> Bowlahoola is the Stomach in every individual man.[32]

This fantastic evocation of the animal organism shows how Blake conceived of the natural world. It is a continuous and infinite miracle in which the tiniest particles, the minute particulars, are organized in accordance with the will of divine powers. More than anyone else, Blake seems to have found his way to the threshold of creation where he could observe the making of thoughts and things in the realm of the invisible. In the ameliorating of the painful processes of the body by music, there is perhaps a prevision of the

---

[32] Blake, *Milton*, pl. 24, lines 51-67.

physiological theory that the pain occasioned by these organic processes is moderated by anesthetic secretions of the glands.

It is always a shock to turn from the fury of Blake to the passivity of Wordsworth. The two men were contemporary for nearly sixty years, each knew the other's poems, they are both regarded as Romantics, and yet in their understandings of work and nature it would be hard to find two thinkers less alike. Blake at least was aware of the gulf which separated them. For Blake the natural world, the world of space and time, was the arena of the earthly struggles which he fought against himself and against others till he died. Through the work of his hands he engaged with that world as thoroughly as anyone could, and he believed in his work as the proper means to his salvation according to the way he interpreted the teachings of Christ and the Bible. And yet at the deepest level he abhorred the material world as a constant hindrance to his vision. In his own words, it was no more than the dirt on his feet; he looked through the eye, not with it. Wordsworth, on the other hand, regarded the world of the countryside as his teacher and moral guardian. A man of the middle classes and sustained throughout his life by sinecures and bequests, he worshiped the natural world with a fervor which Blake considered idolatrous.[33]

For all the achievement of his early years Wordsworth seems to have known little of work, even of his own. He had doubts about whether his art would earn him a livelihood and he was uncomfortably aware that such a career might begin happily enough but often ended in disaster. He does not appear to have considered himself a poet born, with a destiny to fulfill. He was on occasion very doubtful of the value of books compared to the direct influence of nature. He lacked a sense of himself as a poet and this probably helped his readers to identify themselves with him. He was a man speaking to men, one who had divested himself of all the poetic artifice of the past in order to speak everyone's language. Wordsworth claimed nothing special for himself, no peculiar gift or talent, only that heightened sensibility which elevates anyone who has it in whatever walk of life. He presented himself as a person in no way distinguishable from his fellows by any predisposition for a particular kind of work. But if the moral life did not consist for Wordsworth in

[33] Blake, *Annotations to Poems by William Wordsworth.*

the doing of one's own work to the best of one's ability, in what did it consist? Instead he wrote of,

> that best portion of a good man's life,
> His little, nameless, unremembered acts
> Of kindness and of love.[34]

There is nothing to be said against little acts of kindness and love. But to claim that these constitute the best portion of a moral life is, in my view, staggeringly wrong. When we attempt to measure the distance between this claim and the spiritual ideal of work which Blake sets out in his sermon to the Christians, we realize that we are in two different worlds.

Wordsworth believed that merely to have lived among the works of nature in the country had called forth and strengthened his powers of imagination in boyhood and youth. In this way, according to Wordsworth, the external world sustained inward vision. That his inward vision was very powerful in his early years we cannot doubt.[35] He described later in life how he had found it almost impossible to believe in the external reality of the world, and many times on his way to school had had to grasp hold of things to convince himself that they were not the projections of his own mind. He called the vertigo which this feeling induced in him "the abyss of idealism." In one of his poems he described how a visitor to a waterfall had to distract his own mind by mathematical calculations, so deeply was he affected by what he was seeing. In this visitor we may catch a glimpse of Wordsworth himself. At the first level, then, Wordsworth had visionary capacities quite as great as those of Blake, but where Blake gladly committed himself to them, even at the cost of seeming mad to those around him, Wordsworth feared them.

As a result there is little in Wordsworth's poetry which is truly visionary, nor did he investigate the source of his ideas in the way that Blake did. Instead he created for himself a dependency upon the forms of the natural world, which at once evoked and curbed his visionary powers. He remained aware that much of what he had seen in his early years he had himself envisioned, and his greatest

---

[34] Wordsworth, "Tintern Abbey," line 34.

[35] Thomas de Quincey, *Recollections of the Lakes and the Lake Poets* (Harmondsworth: Penguin, 1970).

poems detail the gradual closing of these visionary springs which had transformed, as he believed, the world of his childhood. But he was incapable of creating entirely from within himself as Blake could. His poems were typically the product of meditations in which he recollected past experiences in tranquility. The daffodils which he once saw are brought to life in his mind as he lies upon his couch, but they are those daffodils by that shore.[36] Blake's tiger, on the other hand, is all tigers and none of them, the veritable first tiger which God himself made. When Blake read in a copy of Wordsworth's poems Wordsworth's claim that natural objects strengthened his imagination, he wrote in the margin that natural objects always had and still did weaken, deaden, and obliterate his own imagination. Wordsworth, he adds, must know that what he writes valuable is not to be found in nature.[37]

Wordsworth's belief that natural objects strengthened the imagination is the simplest and most plausible explanation of his failure as a poet in middle age. Where Blake continued to design and write with genius to the end of his long life, Wordsworth lost his gift. He died at the age of eighty, having produced little of note during the latter half of his life. The source of Wordsworth's power as a visionary poet lay in his capacity to remember the inner events and experiences of his childhood. This was a finite stock and in any case further and further from him as he grew older. For Blake, on the other hand, the source of creation was imagination, not memory, and the ideas upon which he drew were infinite and inexhaustible. Wordsworth alone among the Romantic poets did not know his way to these waters of life in which the poetic genius is continually renewed. And so he could have no understanding of the traditional doctrine of work, in which the invisible ideas of what is to be done or made are central. Wordsworth's flight into nature and away from vision disabled him morally and in the spirit to an unusual degree. This same flight into nature is one of the great spiritual problems of our own time.

For there can be no doubt that the Wordsworthian view has triumphed. His is the moral order in which we now live, where the doing of one's work is of little or no moral significance, while kind-

---

[36] Wordsworth, "Daffodils."

[37] Blake, *Annotations to Poems by William Wordsworth.*

ness is all. This is the victory of niceness, for which all other moral values have been discarded and the high spiritual aspirations of previous generations forgotten. It is hard not to believe that Blake was thinking of Wordsworth when he wrote:

> He smiles with condescension, he talks of Benevolence and Virtue,
> And those who act with Benevolence and Virtue they murder time
>   on time.
> These are the destroyers of Jerusalem, these are the murderers
> Of Jesus, who deny the Faith and mock at Eternal Life,
> Who pretend to Poetry that they may destroy Imagination
> By imitation of Nature's Images drawn from Remembrance.[38]

Such people are the destroyers of Jerusalem because Jerusalem, as Blake explained in his sermon, is the spiritual city which is built by the labors of inspired artists. We can appreciate why Blake should consider benevolent people to be murderers only when we set this new morality against the traditional doctrine of work. In Blake's view benevolence had usurped the place of art.

The shift in attitudes to which these lines of Blake point is, of all historical changes, the one most relevant to the place of mining in contemporary society. This shift is the culmination of those departures from the traditional doctrine of work which we have traced through the Renaissance, the Reformation, and the Puritan revolution of the sixteenth and seventeenth centuries. But what distinguishes the Wordsworthian morality from those which preceded it, is that it was almost entirely secular. For Wordsworth the most important part of the moral life was not the realization of the divine within us, as the traditional doctrine of work proposed, nor even the glorification of God as the Puritans believed. At best there was the possibility of perceiving the divine through the contemplation of natural objects. But this was idolatrous, as Blake saw, when it turned into the worship of nature as divine in itself. Nonetheless there can be no question but that the time for this new morality had come. The Wordsworthian view was already the standard view or became so very quickly, and was to be found in the other most widely read moralist in the English language in the nineteenth century, Charles Dickens. For Dickens, too, kindness was all, and work had almost no part in the moral order.

[38] Blake, *Milton*, pl. 41, lines 19-24.

We are now in a position to see all the way around the Wordsworthian conception of nature, and to appreciate it fully. This conception of nature is so deeply a part of our thinking that it takes an act of violence to that thinking to free us from it long enough to look at it. Essentially, the Wordsworthian nature is pure spectacle: it is perceived by the eye and the ear but it is not touched. We are cut off from it as by a screen, and even the peasants who stand on the other side of the screen, though they may sing, hardly ever work. The rustic is superior to the citizen, but not because he is engaged in work which employs his intellect as well as his body, while his counterpart in the city has been transformed by the factory system into a mere hand. The rustic is superior because his passions are incorporated with the great and permanent forms of nature and because he is, like the poet, more sensitive to the simple beauties around him. He too is a spectator, and the irony is that he should have seemed so to a poet and a nation which inhabited one of the most highly cultivated landscapes in the world.

Wordsworth's views of nature and of the moral life were sentimental. They were the views of a class which had already forgotten how the wealth on which it lived had been produced, and how traditional forms of work had sustained the spirit of those who engaged in them. This is not to say that anyone who respects nature is soft in the head. Blake, too, passionately denounced cruelty to animals and the wanton destruction of the natural world. But Blake also wrote:

> The cut worm forgives the plough.[39]

More particularly Blake did what he could to resist the new productive processes which displaced the traditional forms of work. This for Blake was where the evil lay. For Wordsworth it was the city which was evil because it was noisy, dirty, and crowded, and because it was cut off from the great and permanent forms of nature. The city grated on Wordsworth's sensibility which had been most delicately attuned to the beauties of natural objects. On the one occasion in which he was tricked out of his fear by the city's beauty at dawn, his very amazement shows how settled was his conviction of

---

[39] Blake, *The Marriage of Heaven and Hell*, pl. 7, line 6.

its evil. Blake lived in the middle of London almost all his life, sustained entirely by the beauties of his own imagination and by his belief in the value of his work, despite his own stark vision of the city's horror.

But Blake was a man unknown. In his later years as he composed his prophetic books, he was far outside the intellectual world of his time. These were the years of deepening neglect as his first biographer called them. Meanwhile Wordsworth's star was in the ascendant. Common enough before he wrote, his view of nature was more and more widely accepted during these years. It is no coincidence that the English came to believe in the value of untouched nature at the very same time as new means of production were being introduced which ravaged the natural world to an unprecedented degree. In one important respect these events were complementary, not antithetical. As the traditional views of work and nature were lost, so the new modes of production and the Wordsworthian view of nature appeared. From then on, it looked as though the belief in untouched nature was a reaction to the devastation, but in fact, historically and psychologically, it was just another aspect of the same loss. To think of untouched nature as perfect is, from the traditional point of view, as mistaken as to think of it as an expendable resource. Nature is neither a goddess to be worshiped from a distance, nor a whore to be used up and dismissed. Nature is the wife of the human genius: together they are to produce their manifold creations to the simultaneous fulfillment of both.

Neither the love of nature nor the pastoral tradition began with Wordsworth. Poets have been idealizing country life and ignoring the work of the peasant since the times of Theocritus and Virgil. But they were very different from Wordsworth. It is instructive in this connection to juxtapose how Queen Marie Antoinette played at being a shepherdess and the high moral tone of the Wordsworthian pastoral just a few years later. Before Wordsworth the pastoral tradition had existed side by side with deeper moral and spiritual codes, with the transcendent God of theology and with the traditional doctrine of work. But at this time, as Blake saw, the new morality of nature and kindness began to displace these older teachings entirely. It replaced them with a divinized, untouchable nature and an unfocussed benevolence.

WHY WORK?[*]

Dorothy Sayers

I have already, on a previous occasion, spoken at some length on the subject of Work and Vocation. What I urged then was a thorough-going revolution in our whole attitude to work. I asked that it should be looked upon—not as a necessary drudgery to be undergone for the purpose of making money, but as a way of life in which the nature of man should find its proper exercise and delight and so fulfill itself to the glory of God. That it should, in fact, be thought of as a creative activity undertaken for the love of the work itself; and that man, made in God's image, should make things, as God makes them, for the sake of doing well a thing that is well worth doing.

It may well seem to you—as it does to some of my acquaintances—that I have a sort of obsession about this business of the right attitude to work. But I do insist upon it, because it seems to me that what becomes of civilization after this war is going to depend enormously on our being able to effect this revolution in our ideas about work. Unless we do change our whole way of thought about work, I do not think we shall ever escape from the appalling squirrel-cage of economic confusion in which we have been madly turning for the last three centuries or so, the cage in which we landed ourselves by acquiescing in a social system based upon Envy and Avarice. A society in which consumption has to be artificially stimulated in order to keep production going is a society founded on trash and waste, and such a society is a house built upon sand.

The question that I will ask you to consider today is this: When the war is over, are we likely, and do we want to keep this attitude to work and the results of work? Or are we preparing and do we want to go back to our old habits of thought? Because I believe that on our answer to this question the whole economic future of society will depend. Sooner or later the moment will come when we have to make a decision about this. At the moment, we are not making

[*] Editor's Note: A lecture given in Eastbourne, April 1942. The lecture has been edited to remove topical material which is less pertinent to our present themes.

it—don't let us flatter ourselves that we are. It is being made for us. And don't let us imagine that a war-time economy has stopped waste. It has not. It has only transferred it elsewhere. The glut and waste that used to clutter our own dustbins have been removed to the field of battle. That is where all the surplus consumption is going to. The factories are roaring more loudly than ever, turning out night and day goods that are of no conceivable value for the maintenance of life; on the contrary, their sole object is to destroy life, and instead of being thrown away they are being blown away— in Russia, in North Africa, over Occupied France, in Burma and China, and the Spice Islands, and on the Seven Seas. What is going to happen when the factories stop turning out armaments? No nation has yet found a way to keep the machines running and whole nations employed under modern industrial conditions without wasteful consumption. For a time, a few nations could contrive to keep going by securing a monopoly of production and forcing their waste products onto new and untapped markets. When there are no new markets and all nations are industrial producers, the only choice we have been able to envisage so far has been that between armaments and unemployment. This is the problem that some time or other will stare us in the face again, and this time we must have our minds ready to tackle it. It may not come at once—for it is quite likely that after the war we shall have to go through a further peri- od of managed consumption while the shortages caused by the war are being made good. But sooner or later we shall have to grapple with this difficulty, and everything will depend on our attitude of mind about it. Shall we be prepared to take the same attitude to the arts of peace as to the arts of war? I see no reason why we should not sacrifice our convenience and our individual standard of living just as readily for the building of great public works as for the building of ships and tanks—but when the stimulus of fear and anger is removed, shall we be prepared to do any such thing? Or shall we *want* to go back to that civilization of greed and waste which we dig- nify by the name of a "high standard of living"? I am getting very much afraid of that phrase about the standard of living. And I am also frightened by the phrase "after the war"—it is so often pro- nounced in a tone that suggests: "after the war, we want to relax, and go back, and live as we did before." And that means going back to the time when labor was valued in terms of its cash returns, and not in terms of the work.

Now the answer to this question, if we are resolute to know what we are about, will not be left to rich men—to manufacturers and financiers. If these people have governed the world of late years it is only because we ourselves put the power into their hands. The question can and should be answered by the worker and the consumer. It is extremely important that the worker should really understand where the problem lies. It is a matter of brutal fact that in these days labor, more than any other section of the community, has a vested interest in war. Some rich employers make profit out of war—that is true; but what is infinitely more important is that for all working people war means full employment and high wages. When war ceases, then the problem of employing labor at the machines begins again. The relentless pressure of hungry labor is behind the drive towards wasteful consumption, whether in the destruction of war or in the trumpery of peace. The problem is far too much simplified when it is presented as a mere conflict between labor and capital, between employed and employer. The basic difficulty remains, even when you make the State the sole employer, even when, you make Labor into the employer. It is not simply a question of profits and wages or living conditions—but of what is to be done with the work of the machines, and what work the machines are to do. If we do not deal with this question now, while we have time to think about it, then the whirligig of wasteful production and wasteful consumption will start again and will again end in war. And the driving-power of labor will be thrusting to turn the wheels, because it is to the financial interest of labor to keep the whirligig going faster and faster till the inevitable catastrophe comes.

And, so that the wheels may turn, the consumer, that is, you and I, including the workers, who are consumers also—will again be urged to consume and waste; and unless we change our attitude—or rather unless we keep hold of the new attitude forced upon us by the logic of war—we shall again be bamboozled by our vanity, indolence, and greed into keeping the squirrel-cage of wasteful economy turning. We could—you and I—bring the whole fantastic economy of profitable waste down to the ground overnight, without legislation and without revolution, merely by refusing to cooperate with it. I say, we could—as a matter of fact, we have; or rather, it has been done for us. If we do not want it to rise up again after the war, we can prevent it simply by preserving the war-time habit of valuing work instead of money. The point is: do we want to? Whatever we do, we shall be faced with grave difficulties. That cannot be disguised. But it will make a great difference to the result if we are genuinely aiming at a real change in economic thinking. And by that I mean a radical change from top to bottom—a new system; not a mere adjustment of the old system to favor a different set of people. The habit of thinking about work as something one does to make money is so ingrained in us that we can scarcely imagine what a revolutionary change it would be to think about it instead in terms of the work done. It would mean taking the attitude of mind we reserve for our unpaid work—our hobbies, our leisure interests, the things we make and do for pleasure—and making *that* the standard of all our judgments about things and people. We should ask of an enterprise, not "will it pay?" but, "is it good?"; of a man, not "what does he make?" but "what is his work worth?"; of goods, not "can we induce people to buy them?" but "are they useful things well made?"; of employment, not "how much a week?" but "will it exercise my faculties to the utmost?" And shareholders in—let us say—brewing companies, would astonish the directorate by arising at shareholders' meetings and demanding to know, not merely where the profits go or what dividends are to be paid, not even merely whether the workers' wages are sufficient and the conditions of labor satisfactory, but loudly, and with a proper sense of personal responsibility: What goes into the beer?

You will probably ask at once: How is this altered attitude going to make any difference to the question of employment? Because it sounds as though it would result in not more employment, but less. I am not an economist, and I can only point to a peculiarity of war economy that usually goes without notice in economic textbooks. In war, production for wasteful consumption still goes on: but there is one great difference in the goods produced. None of them is valued for what it will fetch, but only for what it is worth in itself. The gun and the tank, the airplane and the warship have to be the best of their kind. A war consumer does not buy shoddy. He does not buy to sell again. He buys the thing that is good for its purpose, asking nothing of it but that it shall do the job it has to do. Once again, war forces the consumer into a right attitude to the work. And, whether by strange coincidence, or whether because of some universal law, so soon as nothing is demanded of the thing made but its own integral perfection, its own absolute value, the skill and labor of the worker are fully employed and likewise acquire an absolute value.

This is probably not the kind of answer that you will find in any theory of economics. But the professional economist is not really trained to answer, or even to ask himself questions about absolute values. The economist is inside the squirrel-cage and turning with it. Any question about absolute values belongs to the sphere, not of economics, but of religion. And it is very possible that we cannot deal with economics at all, unless we can see economy from outside the cage; that we cannot begin to settle the relative values without considering absolute values. And if so, this may give a very precise and practical meaning to the words: "Seek first the kingdom of God and His righteousness, and all these things shall be added to you" ... I am persuaded that the reason why the Churches are in so much difficulty about giving a lead in the economic sphere is because they are trying to fit a Christian standard of economics to a wholly false and pagan understanding of work.

What is the Christian understanding of work? ... I should like to put before you two or three propositions arising out of the doctrinal position which I stated at the beginning: namely, that work is the natural exercise and function of man—the creature who is made in the image of his Creator. You will find that any one of them, if given in effect everyday practice, is so revolutionary (as compared with the habits of thinking into which we have fallen), as to make all political revolutions look like conformity.

The first, stated quite briefly, is that work is not, primarily, a thing one does to live, but the thing one lives to do. It is, or it should be, the full expression of the worker's faculties, the thing in which he finds spiritual, mental, and bodily satisfaction, and the medium in which he offers himself to God.

Now the consequences of this are not merely that the work should be performed under decent living and working conditions. That is a point we have begun to grasp, and it is a perfectly sound point. But we have tended to concentrate on it to the exclusion of other considerations far more revolutionary.

(a) There is, for instance, the question of profits and remuneration. We have all got it fixed in our heads that the proper end of work is to be paid for—to produce a return in profits or payment to the worker which fully or more than compensates the effort he puts into it. But if our first proposition is true, this does not follow at all. So long as society provides the worker with a sufficient return in real wealth to enable him to carry on the work properly, then he has his reward. For his work is the measure of his life, and his satisfaction is found in the fulfillment of his own nature, and in contemplation of the perfection of his work. That, in practice, there is this satisfaction, is shown by the mere fact that a man will put loving labor into some hobby which can never bring him in any economically adequate return. His satisfaction comes, in the godlike manner, from looking upon what he has made and finding it very good. He is no longer bargaining with his work, but serving it. It is only when work has to be looked on as a means to gain that it becomes hateful; for then, instead of a friend, it becomes an enemy from whom tolls and contributions have to be exacted. What most of us demand from society is that we should always get out of it a little *more* than the value of the labor we give to it. By this process, we persuade ourselves that society is always in our debt—a conviction that not only piles up actual financial burdens, but leaves us with a grudge against society.

(b) Here is the second consequence. At present we have no clear grasp of the principle that every man should do the work for which he is fitted by nature. The employer is obsessed by the notion that he must find cheap labor, and the worker by the notion that the best-paid job is the job for him. Only feebly, inadequately, and spasmodically do we ever attempt to tackle the problem from the other end, and inquire: What type of worker is suited to this type of work? People engaged in education see clearly that this is the right end to start from; but they are frustrated by economic pressure, and by the failure of parents on the one hand and employers on the other to grasp the fundamental importance of this approach. And that the trouble results far more from a failure of intelligence than from economic necessity is seen clearly under war conditions, when, though competitive economics are no longer a governing factor, the right men and women are still persistently thrust into the wrong jobs, through sheer inability on everybody's part to imagine a purely vocational approach to the business of fitting together the worker and his work.

(c) A third consequence is that, if we really believed this proposition and arranged our work and our standard of values accordingly, we should no longer think of work as something that we hastened to get through in order to enjoy our leisure; we should look on our leisure as the period of changed rhythm that refreshed us for the delightful purpose of getting on with our work. And, this being so, we should tolerate no regulations of any sort that prevented us from working as long and as well as our enjoyment of work demanded. We should resent any such restrictions as a monstrous interference with the liberty of the subject. How great an upheaval of our ideas that would mean I leave you to imagine. It would turn topsy-turvy all our notions about hours of work, rates of work, unfair competition, and all the rest of it. We should all find ourselves fighting, as now only artists and the members of certain professions fight, for precious time in which to get on with the job—instead of fighting for precious hours saved from the job.

(d) A fourth consequence is that we should fight tooth and nail, not for mere employment, but for the quality of the work that we had to do. We should clamor to be engaged on work that was worth doing, and in which we could take a pride. The worker would demand that the stuff he helped to turn out should be good stuff; he would no longer be content to take the cash and let the credit go. Like the shareholders in the brewery, he would feel a sense of personal responsibility, and clamor to know, and to control, what went into the beer he brewed. There would be protests and strikes—not only about pay and conditions, but about the quality of the work demanded and the honesty, beauty, and usefulness of the goods produced. The greatest insult which a commercial age has offered to the worker has been to rob him of all interest in the end-product of the work and to force him to dedicate his life to making badly things which were not worth making.

This first proposition chiefly concerns the worker as such. My second proposition directly concerns Christians as such, and it is this: It is the business of the Church to recognize that the secular vocation, as such, is sacred. Christian people, and particularly perhaps the Christian clergy, must get it firmly into their heads that when a man or woman is called to a particular job of secular work, that is as true a vocation as though he or she were called to specifically religious work. The Church must concern herself, not only with such questions as the just price and proper working conditions: she must concern herself with seeing that the work itself is such as a human being can perform without degradation—that no one is required by economic or any other considerations to devote himself to work that is contemptible, soul-destroying, or harmful. It is not right for her to acquiesce in the notion that a man's life is divided into the time he spends on his work and the time he spends in serving God. He must be able to serve God in his work, and the work itself must be accepted and respected as the medium of divine creation.

In nothing has the Church so lost her hold on reality as in her failure to understand and respect the secular vocation. She has allowed work and religion to become separate departments, and is astonished to find that, as a result, the secular work of the world is turned to purely selfish and destructive ends, and that the greater part of the world's intelligent workers have become irreligious, or at least, uninterested in religion. But is it astonishing? How can anyone remain interested in a religion which seems to have no concern with nine-tenths of his life? The Church's approach to an intelligent carpenter is usually confined to exhorting him not to be drunk and disorderly in his leisure hours, and to come to church on Sundays. What the Church *should* be telling him is this: that the very first demand that his religion makes upon him is that he should make good tables. Church by all means, and decent forms of amusement, certainly—but what use is all that if in the very center of his life and occupation he is insulting God with bad carpentry? No crooked table-legs or ill-fitting drawers ever, I dare swear, came out of the carpenter's shop at Nazareth. Nor, if they did, could anyone believe that they were made by the same hand that made heaven and earth. No piety in the worker will compensate for work that is not true to itself; for any work that is untrue to its own technique is a living lie. Yet in her own buildings, in her own ecclesiastical art and music, in her hymns and prayers, in her sermons and in her little books of devotion, the Church will tolerate, or permit a pious intention to excuse, work so ugly, so pretentious, so tawdry and twaddling, so insincere and insipid, so *bad* as to shock and horrify any decent draftsman. And why? Simply because she has lost all sense of the fact that the living and eternal truth is expressed in work only so far as that work is true in itself, to itself, to the standards of its own technique. She has forgotten that the secular vocation is sacred. Forgotten that a building must be good architecture before it can be a good church; that a painting must be well painted before it can be a good sacred picture; that work must be good work before it can call itself God's work.

Let the Church remember this: that every maker and worker is called to serve God in his profession or trade—not outside it. The Apostles complained rightly when they said it was not meet they should leave the word of God and serve tables; their vocation was to preach the word. But the person whose vocation it is to prepare the meals beautifully might with equal justice protest: It is not meet for us to leave the service of our tables to preach the word. The official Church wastes time and energy, and moreover commits sacrilege, in demanding that secular workers should neglect their proper vocation in order to do Christian work—by which she means ecclesiastical work. The only Christian work is good work well done. Let the Church see to it that the workers are Christian people and do their work well, as to God: then all the work will be Christian work, whether it is Church embroidery or sewage-farming. As Jacques Maritain says: "If you want to produce Christian work, be a Christian, and try to make a work of beauty into which you have put your heart; do not adopt a Christian pose." He is right. And let the Church remember that the beauty of the work will be judged by its own, and not by ecclesiastical standards. Let me give you an illustration of what I mean. When my play "The Zeal of Thy House" was produced in London, a dear old pious lady was much struck by the beauty of the four great archangels who stood throughout the play in their heavy gold robes, eleven feet high from wing-tip to sandal-tip. She asked with great innocence "whether I selected the actors who played the angels for the excellence of their moral character?" I replied that the angels were selected, to begin with, not by me but by the producer, who had the technical qualifications for selecting suitable actors—for that was part of his vocation. And that he selected, in the first place, young men who were six feet tall, so that they would match properly together. Secondly, angels had to be of good physique, so as to be able to stand stiff on the stage for two and a half hours, carrying the weight of their wings and costumes, without wobbling, or fidgeting, or fainting. Thirdly, they must be able to speak verse well, in an agreeable voice and audibly. Fourthly, they must be reasonably good actors. When all these technical conditions were fulfilled, we might come to the moral qualities, of which the first would be the ability to arrive on the stage punctually and in a sober condition, since the curtain must go up on time, and a drunken angel would be indecorous. After that, and only after that, one might take character into consideration, but that—provided his behavior was not so scandalous as to cause dissension among the company—the right kind of actor with no morals would give a far more reverent and seemly performance than a saintly actor with the wrong technical qualifications. The worst religious films I ever saw were produced by a company which chose its staff exclusively for their piety. Bad photography, bad acting, and bad dialogue produced a result so grotesquely irreverent that the pictures could not have been shown in churches without bringing Christianity into contempt. God is not served by technical incompetence; and incompetence and untruth always result when the secular vocation is treated as a thing alien to religion ... And conversely: when you find a man who is a Christian praising God by the excellence of his work—do not distract him and take him away from his proper vocation to address religious meetings and open church bazaars. Let him serve God in the way to which God has called him. "If you take him away from that, he will exhaust himself in an alien technique and lose his capacity to do his dedicated work. It is your business, you churchmen, to get what good you can from observing his work—not to take him away from it, so that he may do ecclesiastical work for you. But, if you have any power, see that he is set free to do his own work as well as it may be done. He is not there to serve you; he is there to serve God by serving his work.

This brings me to my third proposition; and this may sound to you the most revolutionary of all. It is this: the worker's first duty is to *serve the work*. The popular "catch" phrase of today is that it is everybody's duty to serve the community. It is a well-sounding phrase, but there is a catch in it. It is the old catch about the two great commandments. "Love God and your neighbor; on those two commandments hang all the Law and the Prophets." The catch in it, which nowadays the world has largely forgotten, is that the second commandment depends upon the first, and that without the first, it is a delusion and a snare. Much of our present trouble and disillusionment have come from putting the second commandment before the first. If we put our neighbor first, we are putting man above God, and that is what we have been doing ever since we began to worship humanity and make man the measure of all things. Whenever man is made the center of things, he becomes the storm-center of trouble—and that is precisely the catch about serving the community. It ought perhaps to make us suspicious of that phrase when we consider that it is the slogan of every commercial scoundrel and swindler who wants to make sharp business practice pass muster as social improvement. "Service" is the motto of the advertiser, of big business, and of fraudulent finance. And of others, too—Listen to this: "I expect the judicature to understand that the nation does not exist for their convenience, but that justice exists to serve the nation"—that was Hitler yesterday—and that is what becomes of "service," when the community, and not the work, becomes its idol. There is in fact a paradox about working to serve the community, and it is this: that to aim directly at serving the community is to falsify the work; the only way to serve the community is to forget the community and serve the work. There are three very good reasons for this: The first is, that you cannot do good work if you take your mind off the work to see how the community is taking it—any more than you can make a good drive from the tee if you take your eye off the ball. "Blessed are the singlehearted" (for that is the real meaning of the word we translate "the pure in heart"). If your heart is not wholly in the work, the work will not be good—and work that is not good serves neither God nor the community; it only serves Mammon.

The second reason is that the moment you think of serving other people, you begin to have a notion that other people owe you something for your pains; you begin to think that you have a claim on the community. You will begin to bargain for reward, to angle for applause, and to harbor a grievance if you are not appreciated. But if your mind is set upon serving the work, then you know you have nothing to look for; the only reward the work can give you is the satisfaction of beholding its perfection. The work takes all and gives nothing but itself; and to serve the work is a labor of pure love.

And thirdly, if you set out to serve the community, you will probably end by merely fulfilling a public demand—and you may not even do that. A public demand is a changeable thing. Nine-tenths of the bad plays put on in theaters owe their badness to the fact that the playwright has aimed at pleasing the audience, instead of at producing a good and satisfactory play. Instead of doing the work as its own integrity demands that it should be done, he has falsified the play by putting in this or that which he thinks will appeal to the groundlings (who by that time have probably come to want something else), and the play fails by its insincerity. The work has been falsified to please the public and in the end even the public is not pleased. As it is with works of art, so it is with all work. We are coming to the end of an era of civilization which began by pandering to public demand, and ended by frantically trying to create public demand for an output so false and meaningless that even a doped public revolted from the trash offered to it and plunged into war rather than swallow any more of it. The danger of "serving the community" is that one is part of the community, and that in serving it one may only be serving a kind of communal egotism. The only true way of serving the community is to be truly in sympathy with the community—to be oneself part of the community—and then to serve the work, without giving the community another thought. Then the work will endure, because it will be true to itself. It is the work that serves the community; the business of the worker is to serve the work.

Where we have become confused is in mixing up the *ends* to which our work is put with the *way* in which the work is done. The end of the work will be decided by our religious outlook: as we *are* so we *make*. It is the business of religion to make us Christian people, and then our work will naturally be turned to Christian ends, because our work is the expression of ourselves. But the *way* in which the work is done is governed by no sanction except the good of the work itself and religion has no direct connection with that, except to insist that the workman should be free to do his work well according to its own integrity. Jacques Maritain—one of the very few religious writers of our time who really understand the nature of creative work—has summed the matter up in a sentence:

> What is required is the perfect practical discrimination between the end pursued by the workman (*finis operantis*) and the end to be served by the work (*finis operis*), so that the workman may work for his wages but the work be controlled and set in being only in relation to its proper good and nowise in relation to the wages earned; so that the artist may work for any and every human intention he likes, but the work taken by itself be performed and constructed for its proper beauty alone.

Or perhaps we may put it more shortly still: If work is to find its right place in the world, it is the duty of the Church to see to it that the work serves God, and that the worker serves the work.

Envisioning the Future[*]

Robert Aitken

"Small is beautiful," E.F. Schumacher said, but it was not merely size that concerned him. "Buddhist economics must be very different from the economics of modern materialism," he said. "The Buddhist sees the essence of civilization not in a multiplication of wants but in the purification of human character."[1]

Schumacher evokes the etymology of "civilization" as the process of civilizing, of becoming and making civil. Many neglect this ancient wisdom of words in their pursuit of acquisition and consumption, and those with some civility of mind find themselves caught in the dominant order by requirements of time and energy to feed their families. As the acquisitive system burgeons, its collapse is foreshadowed by epidemics, famine, war, and the despoliation of the earth and its forests, waters, and air.

I envision a growing crisis across the world as managers and their multinational systems continue to deplete finite human and natural resources. Great corporations, underwritten by equally great financial institutions, flush away the human habitat and the habitat of thousands of other species far more ruthlessly and on a far greater scale than the gold miners who once hosed down mountains in California. International consortia rule sovereign over all other political authority. Presidents and parliaments and the United Nations itself are delegated decision-making powers that simply carry out previously established agreements.

Citizens of goodwill everywhere despair of the political process. The old enthusiasm to turn out on election day has drastically waned. In the United States, commonly fewer than 50 percent of those eligible cast a ballot. It has become clear that political parties are ineffectual—whether Republican or Democrat, Conservative or Labor—and that practical alternatives must be found.

[*] Editor's Note: A revised paper from a conference of the International Network of Engaged Buddhists, Thailand, February 1995, published in *Original Dwelling Place*.

[1] E.F. Schumacher, *Small is Beautiful: Economics As If People Mattered* (New York: Harper & Row, 1975), p. 55.

We can begin our task of developing such alternatives by meeting in informal groups within our larger *sangha*s to examine politics and economics from a Buddhist perspective. It will be apparent that traditional teachings of interdependence bring into direct question the rationale of accumulating wealth and of governing by hierarchical authority. What, then, is to be done?

Something, certainly. Our practice of the Brahma Viharas—kindliness, compassion, goodwill, and equanimity—would be meaningless if it excluded people, animals, and plants outside our formal *sangha*. Nothing in the teachings justifies us as a cult that ignores the world. We are not survivalists. On the contrary, it is clear that we're in it together with all beings.

The time has surely come when we must speak out as Buddhists, with firm views of harmony as the Tao. I suggest that it is also time for us to take ourselves in hand. We ourselves can establish and engage in the very policies and programs of social and ecological protection and respect that we have heretofore so futilely demanded from authorities. This would be engaged Buddhism, where the *sangha* is not merely parallel to the forms of conventional society and not merely metaphysical in its universality.

This greater *sangha* is, moreover, not merely Buddhist. It is possible to identify an eclectic religious evolution that is already under way, one to which we can lend our energies. It can be traced to the beginning of this century, when Tolstoy, Ruskin, Thoreau, and the New Testament fertilized the *Bhagavad Gita* and other Indian texts in the mind and life of M.K. Gandhi. The Southern Buddhist leaders A. T. Ariyaratne and Sulak Sivaraksa and their followers in Sri Lanka and Thailand have adapted Gandhi's "Independence for the Masses" to their own national needs and established programs of self-help and community self-reliance that offer regenerative cells of fulfilling life within their materialist societies.[2]

Mahayana has lagged behind these developments in South and Southeast Asia. In the past, a few Far Eastern monks like Gyogi Bosatsu devoted themselves to good works, another few like Hakuin Zenji raised their voices to the lords of their provinces about the poverty of common people, and still others in Korea and China

---

[2] A.T. Ariyaratne, *Collected Works*, vol. 1 (Dehiwala, Sri Lanka: Sarvodia Research Institute, n.d.); Sulak Sivaraksa, *A Buddhist Vision for Renewing Society: Collected Articles by a Concerned Thai Intellectual* (Bangkok: Thai Watana Panich, 1981).

organized peasant rebellions, but today we do not see widespread movements in traditional Mahayana countries akin to the village self-help programs of Ariyaratne in Sri Lanka, or empowerment networks similar to those established by Sulak in Thailand.

"Self-help" is an inadequate translation of *swaraj*, the term Gandhi used to designate his program of personal and village independence. He was a great social thinker who identified profound human imperatives and natural social potentials. He discerned how significant changes arise from people themselves, rather than from efforts on the part of governments to fine-tune the system.

South Africa and Eastern Europe are two modern examples of change from the bottom up. Perceptions shift, the old notions cannot hold—and down come the state and its ideology. Similar changes are brewing, despite repressions, in Central America. In the United States, the economy appears to be holding up by force of habit and inertia in the face of unimaginable debt, while city governments break down and thousands of families sleep in makeshift shelters.

Not without protest. In the United States, the tireless voices of Ralph Nader, Noam Chomsky, Jerry Brown, and other cogent dissidents remind us and our legislators and judges that our so-called civilization is using up the world. Such spokespeople for conservation, social justice, and peace help to organize opposition to benighted powers and their policies and thus divert the most outrageous programs to less flagrant alternatives.

Like Ariyaratne and Sulak in their social contexts, we as Western Buddhists would also modify the activist role to reflect our culture as well as our spiritual heritage. But surely the Dharmic fundamentals would remain.[3] Right Action is part of the Eightfold Path that begins and ends with Right Meditation. Formal practice could also involve study, reciting the ancient texts together, Dharma discussion, religious festivals, and sharing for mutual support.

In our workaday lives, practice would be less formal and could include farming and protecting forests. In the United States, some of our leading intellectuals cultivate the ground. The distinguished poet W.S. Merwin has through his own labor created an arboretum

---

[3] I originally used "Dhamma," the Pali orthography, rather than "Dharma," out of deference to my Theravada listeners.

of native Hawaiian plants at his home on Maui. He is thus restoring an important aspect of Hawaiian culture, in gentle opposition to the monocultures of pineapple, sugar, and macadamia nut trees around him. Another progressive intellectual, Wendell Berry, author of some thirty books of poetry, essays, and fiction, is also a small farmer. Still another reformative intellectual and prominent essayist, Wes Jackson, conducts a successful institute for small farmers. Networking is an important feature of Jackson's teaching. He follows the Amish adage that at least seven cooperating families must live near each other in order for their small individual farms to succeed.[4]

All such enterprise takes hard work and character practice. The two go together. Character, Schumacher says, "is formed primarily by a man's work. And work, properly conducted in conditions of human dignity and freedom, blesses ourselves and equally our products."[5] With dignity and freedom we can collaborate, labor together, on small farms and in cooperatives of all kinds—savings and loan societies, social agencies, clinics, galleries, theaters, markets, and schools—forming networks of decent and dignified modes of life alongside and even within the frames of conventional power. I visualize our humane network having more and more appeal as the power structure continues to fall apart.

This collaboration in networks of mutual aid would follow from our experience of *paticca-samuppada*, interdependent co-arising. All beings arise in systems of biological affinity, whether or not they are even "alive" in a narrow sense. We are born in a world in which all things nurture us. As we mature in our understanding of the Dharma, we take responsibility for *paticca-samuppada* and continually divert our infantile expectations of being nurtured to an adult responsibility for nurturing others.

Buddhadasa Bhikkhu says:

> The entire cosmos is a cooperative. The sun, the moon, and the stars live together as a cooperative. The same is true for humans

[4] Wes Jackson, *Altars of Unhewn Stone: Science and the Earth* (San Francisco: North Point Press, 1987), p. 126.

[5] Schumacher, *Small is Beautiful*, p. 55. A woman's work blesses us and equally our products as well! Schumacher wrote his words before male writers finally learned that the term "man" is not inclusive.

and animals, trees and soil. Our bodily parts function as a cooperative. When we realize that the world is a mutual, interdependent,
cooperative enterprise, that human beings are all mutual friends
in the process of birth, old age, suffering, and death, then we can
build a noble, even heavenly environment. If our lives are not
based in this truth, then we shall all perish.[6]

Returning to this original track is the path of individuation that
transforms childish self-centeredness to mature views and conduct.
With careful, constant discipline on the Eightfold Noble Path of the
Dharma, greed becomes *dana*, exploitation becomes networking.
The root-brain of the newborn becomes the compassionate, religious mind of the elder. Outwardly the elder does not differ from
other members; her or his needs for food, clothing, shelter, medicine, sleep, and affection are the same as anyone else's. But the
elder's smile is startlingly generous.

It is a smile that rises from the Buddha's own experience.
Paticca-samuppada is not just a theory but the profound realization
that I arise with all beings and all beings arise with me. I suffer with
all beings; all beings suffer with me. The path to this fulfillment is
long and sometimes hard; it involves restraint and disengagement
from ordinary concerns. It is a path that advances over plateaus on
its way, and it is important not to camp too long on any one plateau.
That plateau is not yet your true home.

Dharmic society begins and prevails with individuals walking this
path of compassionate understanding, discerning the noble option
at each moment and allowing the other options to drop away. It is a
society that looks familiar, with cash registers and merchandise, fire-
fighters and police, theaters and festivals, but the inner flavor is
completely different. Like a Chinese restaurant in Madras: the
decor is familiar, but the curry is surprising.

In the United States of America, the notion of compassion as the
touchstone of conduct and livelihood is discouraged by the culture.
Yet here and there one can find Catholic Workers feeding the poor,
religious builders creating housing for the homeless, traditional
people returning to their old ways of agriculture.

---

[6] Donald K. Swearer, "Three Legacies of Bhikkhu Buddhadasa," in *The Quest for a
New Society*, ed. Sulak Sivaraksa (Thai Interreligious Commission for Development;
Santi Pracha Dhamma Institute, 1994), p. 17. Cited from Buddhadasa Bhikkhu,
Buddhasasanik Kap Kan Anurak Thamachat [Buddhists and the Conservation of
Nature] (Bangkok: Komol Keemthong Foundation, 1990), p. 34.

Small is the watchword. Huge is ugly, as James Hillman has pointed out.[7] Huge welfare goes awry, huge housing projects become slums worse than the ones they replace, huge environmental organizations compromise their own principles in order to survive, huge sovereignty movements fall apart with internal dissension. The point is that huge *anything* collapses, including governments, banks, multinational corporations, and the global economy itself—because all things collapse. Small can be fluid, ready to change.

The problem is that the huge might not collapse until it brings everything else down with it. Time may not be on the side of the small. Our awareness of this unprecedented danger impels us to take stock and do what we can with our vision of a Dharmic society.

The traditional *sangha* serves as a model for enterprise in this vision. A like-minded group of five can be a *sangha*. It can grow to a modest size, split into autonomous groups, and then network. As autonomous lay Buddhist associations, these little communities will not be *sangha*s in the traditional sense but will be inheritors of the name and of many of the original intentions. They will also be inheritors of the Base Community movements in Latin America and the Philippines-Catholic networks that are inspired by traditional religion and also by nineteenth-century anarchism.[8] Catholic Base Communities serve primarily as worship groups, study groups, moral support societies, and nuclei for social action. They can also form the staff and support structure of small enterprises.

The Catholic Base Community is grounded in Bible study and discussions. In these meetings, one realizes for oneself that God is an ally of those who would liberate the poor and oppressed. This is liberation theology of the heart and gut. It is an internal transformation that releases one's power to labor intimately with others to do God's work.[9]

---

[7] James Hillman, "And Huge Is Ugly." Tenth Annual E.F. Schumacher Memorial Lecture, Bristol, England, November 1988.

[8] Charles B. Maurer, *Call to Revolution: The Mystical Anarchism of Gustav Landauer* (Detroit: Wayne State University Press, 1972), pp. 58-66. For Spanish origins and developments of the Grupo de Afinidad, see *The Anarchist Collectives: Workers' Self-Management in the Spanish Revolution 1936-1939*, ed. Sam Dolgof (New York: Free Life Editions, 1974).

[9] Mev Puleo, *The Struggle Is One: Voices and Visions of Liberation* (Albany: SUNY Press, 1994), pp. 14, 22, 25, 29.

The Buddhist counterpart of Bible study would be the contemplation and realization of *paticca-samuppada,* of the unity of such intellectual opposites as the one and the many found in Zen practice, and the interdependence presented in the sacred texts, such as the *Hua-yen ching.*[10] Without a literal God as an ally, one is thrown back on one's own resources to find the original track, and there one finds the ever-shifting universe with its recurrent metaphors of interbeing to be the constant ally.

There are other lessons from liberation theology. We learn that we need not quit our jobs to form autonomous lay *sangha*s. Most Base Communities in Latin America and the Philippines are simply groups that have weekly meetings. In Buddhist countries, coworkers in the same institution can come together for mutual aid and religious practice. In the largest American corporations, such as IBM, there will surely be a number of Buddhists who could form similar groups. Or we can organize co-housing arrangements that provide for the sharing of home maintenance, child care, and transportation and thus free up individuals for their turns at meditation, study, and social action. Buddhist Peace Fellowship chapters might consider how the Base Community design and ideal could help to define and enhance their purposes and programs.[11]

Thus it wouldn't be necessary for the people who work in corporations or government agencies to resign when they start to meet in Buddhist Base Communities. They can remain within their corporation or government agency and encourage the evolution and networking of communities, not necessarily Buddhist, among other corporations and agencies. Of course, the future is obscure, but I find myself relating to the mythology of the Industrial Workers of the World—that as the old forms collapse, the new networks can flourish.

[10] Thomas Cleary, *Entry into the Inconceivable: An Introduction to Hua-yen Buddhism* (Honolulu: University of Hawaii Press, 1983), p. 7.

[11] William Foote Whyte and Kathleen King Whyte, *Making Mondragon: The Growth and Dynamics of the Worker Cooperative Complex* (Ithaca, NY: ILR Press, Cornell University, 1988), pp. 3, 30. Other cooperatives worthy of study include the Transnational Information Exchange, which brings together trade unionists in the same industry across the world; the Innovation Centers, designed in Germany to help workers who must deal with new technologies; and Emilia Romagna in northern Italy, networks of independent industries that research and market products jointly. Jeremy Brecher, "Affairs of State," *The Nation* 260, no. 9 (6 March 1995): 321.

Of course, the collapse, if any, is not going to happen tomorrow. We must not underestimate the staying power of capitalism. Moreover, the complex, dynamic process of networking cannot be put abruptly into place. In studying Mondragon, the prototype of large, dynamic cooperative enterprise in the three Basque counties of northern Spain, William and Kathleen Whyte counted more than a hundred worker cooperatives and supporting organizations with 19,500 workers in 1988. These are small—even tiny—enterprises, linked by very little more than simple goodwill and a profound sense of the common good. Together they form a vast complex of banking, industry, and education that evolved slowly, if steadily, from a single class for technical training set up in 1943.[12]

We must begin with our own training classes. Mondragon is worth our study, as are the worker-owned industries closer to home—for example, the plywood companies in the Pacific Northwest. In 1972 Carl Bellas studied twenty-one such companies whose inner structures consisted of motivated committees devoted to the many aspects of production and whose managers were responsible to a general assembly.[13]

In the course of our training classes, it is also essential that we examine the mechanism of the dominant economy. Usury and its engines have built our civilization. The word "usury" has an old meaning and a modern one. In the spirit of the old meaning of usury—lending money at interest—the banks of the world, large and small, have provided a way for masses of people for many generations across the world to own homes and to operate farms and businesses. In the spirit of the modern meaning of usury, however—the lending of money at *excessive* interest—a number of these banks have become gigantic, ultimately enabling corporations almost as huge to squeeze small farmers from their lands, small shopkeepers from their stores, and to burden homeowners with car and appliance payments and lifetime mortgages.

---

[12] After presenting this paper, I learned about Tavivat Puntarigvivat's Ph.D. dissertation at Temple University, 1994: *Bhikkhu Buddhadasa's Dhammic Socialism in Dialogue with Latin American Liberation Theology* (Ann Arbor, University Microfilms, 1995).

[13] Carl J. Bellas, *Industrial Democracy and the Worker-Owned Firm: A Study of Twenty-one Plywood Companies in the Pacific Northwest* (New York: Praeger Publishers, 1972).

For over 1,800 years, the Catholic church had a clear and consistent doctrine on the sin of usury in the old sense of simply lending money at interest. Nearly thirty official church documents were published over the centuries to condemn it.

Out of the other side of the Vatican, however, came an unspoken tolerance for usury so long as it was practiced by Jews. The church blossomed as the Medici family of bankers underwrote the Renaissance, but at the same time, pogroms were all but sanctioned. The moral integrity of the church was compromised. Finally, early in the nineteenth century, this kind of hypocrisy was abandoned— too late in some ways, for the seeds of the Holocaust had already been planted. Today the pope apologizes to the Jews, and even the Vatican has its bank.[14] Usury in both old and modern implications is standard operating procedure in contemporary world culture.

Like the Medicis, however, modern bankers can be philanthropic. In almost every city in the United States, bankers and their institutions are active in support of museums, symphony orchestras, clinics, and schools. Banks have almost the same social function as traditional Asian temples: looking after the poor and promoting cultural activities. This is genuine beneficence, and it is also very good public relations.

In the subdivisions of some American cities, such as the Westwood suburb of Los Angeles, the banks even look like temples. They are indeed the temples of our socioeconomic system. The banker's manner is friendly yet his interest in us is, on the bottom line, limited to the interest he extracts from us.

One of the banks in Hawaii has the motto: "We say 'Yes' to you," meaning, "We are eager for your money." Their motto is sung interminably on the radio and TV, and when it appears in newspapers and magazines we find ourselves humming the tune. Similar lightweight yet insidious persuasions are used with Third World governments for the construction of freeways and hydroelectric dams and administrative skyscrapers.

Governments and developers in the Third World are, in fact, the dupes of the World Bank and the International Monetary Fund (IMF):

---

[14] Peter Stiehler, "The Greed of Usury Oppresses," *The Catholic Agitator* 24, no. 7 (November 1994): 5.

It is important to note that IMF programs are not designed to increase the welfare of the population. They are designed to bring the external payments account into balance ... The IMF is the ultimate guardian of the interests of capitalists and bankers doing international business.[15]

These are observations of the economist Kari Polyani Levitt, quoted as the epigraph of a study entitled *Banking on Poverty*. The editor of this work concludes that policies of the IMF and the World Bank "make severe intrusions upon the sovereign responsibilities of many governments of the Third World. These policies not only often entail major additional cuts in the living standards of the poorest sectors of Third World societies but are also unlikely to produce the economic results claimed on their behalf."[16]

Grand apartment buildings along the Bay of Bombay show that the First World with its wealth and leisure is alive and well among the prosperous classes of the old Third World. The Third World with its poverty and disease flares up in cities and farms of the old First World. In *The Prosperous Few and the Restless Many*, Noam Chomsky writes:

In 1971, Nixon dismantled the Bretton Woods system, thereby deregulating currencies.[17] That, and a number of other changes, tremendously expanded the amount of unregulated capital in the world and accelerated what's called the globalization of the economy.

That's a fancy way of saying that you can export jobs to high-repression, low-wage areas.[18]

[15] Jill Torrie, ed., *Banking on Poverty: The Global Impact of the IMF and World Bank* (Toronto: Between the Lines, 1983), n.p.

[16] Torrie, *Banking on Poverty*, 14. See also Doug Bandow and Ian Vasquez, eds., *Perpetuating Poverty: The World Bank, the IMF, and the Developing World* (Washington, DC: Cato Institute, 1994), and Kevin Danafer, *Fifty Years Is Enough: The Case Against the World Bank and the IMF* (Boston: South End Press, 1994).

[17] The Bretton Woods system of international currency regulation was established at the United Nations Monetary and Financial Conference, representing forty-five countries, held at Bretton Woods, New Hampshire, in July 1944. The United States dollar was fixed to the price of gold and became the standard of value for all currencies.

[18] Noam Chomsky, *The Prosperous Few and the Restless Many* (Berkeley: Odonian Press, 1993), p. 6.

Factories in South Central Los Angeles moved to Eastern Europe, Mexico, and Indonesia, attracting workers from farms. Meantime, victims in South Central Los Angeles and other depressed areas of the United States, including desolate rural towns, turn in large numbers to crime and drugs to relieve their seemingly hopeless poverty. One million American citizens are currently in prison, with another two million or so on parole or probation. More than half of these have been convicted of drug-related offences.[19] It's going to get worse. Just as the citizens of Germany elected Hitler chancellor in 1932, opening the door to fascism quite voluntarily, so the citizens of the United States have elected a Congress that seems bent on creating a permanent underclass, with prison expansion to provide much of its housing.

Is there no hope? If big banks, multinational corporations, and cooperating governments maintain their strategy to keep the few prosperous and the many in poverty, then where can small farmers and shopkeepers and managers of clinics and social agencies turn for the money they need to start up their enterprises and to meet emergencies? In the United States, government aid to small businesses and farms, like grants to clinics and social agencies, is being cut back. Such aid is meager or nonexistent in other parts of the world, with notable exceptions in northern Europe.

Revolving credit associations called *hui* in China, *kye* in Korea, and *tanamoshi* in Japan have for generations down to the present provided start-up money for farmers and owners of small businesses, as well as short-term loans for weddings, funerals, and tuition. In Siam there are rice banks and buffalo banks designed for sharing resources and production among the working poor.[20] The Grameen banks of Bangladesh are established for the poor by the poor. Shares are very tiny amounts, amounting to the equivalent of just a few dollars, but in quantity they are adequate for loans at very low interest to farmers and shopkeepers.[21]

---

[19] Gore Vidal, "The Union of the State," *The Nation* 259, no. 22 (26 December 1994): 789.

[20] I use "Siam" rather than "Thailand" to honor the position taken by progressive Buddhists in that country, who point out that the Thais are only one of their many ethnic peoples and that the new name was imposed by a Thai autocrat.

[21] Abu N.M. Wahid, *The Grameen Bank: Poverty Relief in Bangladesh* (Boulder, Colo.: Westview Press, 1993).

Similar traditional cooperatives exist in most other cultures. Such associations are made up of like-minded relatives, friends, neighbors, coworkers, or alumni. Arrangements for borrowing and repayment among these associations differ, even within the particular cultures.[22] In the United States, cooperatives have been set up outside the system, using scrip and labor credits—most notably, Ithaca Hours, involving 1,200 enterprises. The basic currency in the latter arrangement is equal to ten dollars, considered to be the hourly wage. It is guaranteed by the promise of work by members of the system.[23]

We can utilize such models and develop our own projects to fit our particular requirements and circumstances. We can stand on our own feet and help one another in systems that are designed to serve the many, rather than to aggrandize the wealth of the few.

Again, small is beautiful. Whereas large can be beautiful too, if it is a network of autonomous units, monolithic structures are problematic even when fuelled by religious idealism. Islamic economists theorize about a national banking system that functions by investment rather than by a system of interest. However, they point out that such a structure can only work in a country where laws forbid lending at interest and where administrators follow up violations with prosecution.[24] So for those of us who do not dwell in certain Islamic countries that seek to take the Koran literally, such as Pakistan and some of the Gulf states, the macrocosmic concept of interest-free banking is probably not practical.

Of course, revolving credit associations have problems, as do all societies of human beings. There are defaults, but peer pressure among friends and relatives keep these to a minimum. The discipline of Dharma practice would further minimize such problems in a Buddhist loan society. The meetings could be structured with rit-

[22] See, for example, Ivan Light and Edna Bonacich, *Immigrant Entrepreneurs: Koreans in Los Angeles, 1965-1982* (Berkeley, Los Angeles, London: University of California Press, 1988), p. 244.

[23] Paul Glover, "Creating Economic Democracy with Locally Owned Currency," *Terrain* (December 1994): 10-11. See also "An Alternative to Cash: Beyond Banks or Barter," *New York Times*, 31 May 1993, p. 8, and "The Potential of Local Currency," by Susan Meeker Lowrey, *Z Magazine*, July-August 1995, pp. 16-23.

[24] Nejatullah Siddiqui, *Banking Without Interest* (Delhi: Markazi Maktaba Islami, 1979), pp. x-xii.

ual and Dharma talks to remind the members that they are practicing the virtues of the Buddha Dharma and bringing *paticca-samuppada* into play in their workaday lives. They are practicing trust, for all beings are the Buddha, as Hakuin Zenji and countless other teachers remind us.[25] Surely only serious emergencies would occasion a delinquency, and contingency planning could allow for such situations.

Dharma practice could also play a role in the small Buddhist farm or business enterprise. In the 1970s, under the influence of Buddhists, the Honest Business movement arose in San Francisco. This was a network of small shops whose proprietors and assistants met from time to time to encourage one another. Their policy was to serve the public and to accept enough in return from their sales to support themselves, sustain their enterprises, and pay the rent. Their account books were on the sales counters, open to their customers.[26]

The movement itself did not survive, though progressive businesses here and there continue the practice of opening their account books to customers.[27] Apparently the Honest Business network was not well enough established to endure the change in culture from the New Age of the 1970s to the pervasive greed of the 1980s. I suspect there was not a critical mass in the total number of shops involved, and many of them might have been only marginal in their commercial appeal. Perhaps religious commitment was not particularly well rooted. Perhaps also there was not the urgency for alternatives that might be felt in the Third World—an urgency that will surely be felt in all worlds as the dominant system continues to use up natural resources.[28] In any case, we can probably learn from the Honest Business movement and avoid its mistakes.

[25] Robert Aitken, *Encouraging Words: Zen Buddhist Teachings for Western Students* (San Francisco: Pantheon Books, 1993), p. 179.

[26] Michael Phillips and Sallie Rashberry, *Honest Business: A Superior Strategy for Starting and Conducting Your Own Business* (New York: Random House, 1981).

[27] Real Goods, for example, retailers of merchandise that helps to sustain the habitat. Address: 966 Mazzoni Street, Ukiah, CA 95482-0214. Catalog for March 1995, p. 37.

[28] One does feel this urgency in the literature of Real Goods. Let us hope this remarkable company is a forerunner of others.

In establishing small enterprises—including clinics and social agencies and their networks—it is again important not to be content with a plateau. The ordinary entrepreneur, motivated by the need to support a family and plan for tuition and retirement, scrutinizes every option and searches out every niche for possible gain. The manager of an Honest Business must be equally diligent, albeit motivated by service to the community as well as by the family's needs.

Those organizing to lobby for political and economic reforms must also be diligent in following through. The Base Communities throughout the archipelago that forms the Philippines brought down the despot Ferdinand Marcos, but the new society wasn't ready to fly and was put down at once. The plateau was not the peak, and euphoria gave way to feelings of betrayal. However, you can be sure that many of those little communities are still intact. Their members have learned from their immediate history and continue to struggle for justice.

A.J. Muste, the great Quaker organizer of the mid twentieth century, is said to have remarked, "There is no way to peace; peace is the way." For our purposes, I would reword his pronouncement: "There is no way to a just society; our just societies are the way." Moreover, there is no plateau to rest on, only the inner rest we feel in our work and in our formal practice.

This inner rest is so important. In the short history of the United States, there are many accounts of utopian societies. Almost all of them are gone—some of them lasted only a few weeks. Looking closely, I think we can find that many of them fell apart because they were never firmly established as religious communities. They were content to organize before they were truly organized.

Families fall apart almost as readily as intentional communities these days, and Dharma practice can play a role in the household as well as in the *sangha*. As Sulak Sivaraksa has said, "When even one member of the household meditates, the entire family benefits."[29] Competition is channeled into the development of talents and skills; greed is channeled into the satisfaction of fulfillment in work. New things and new technology are used appropriately and are not

---

[29] Sulak, *A Buddhist Vision for Renewing Society*, p. 108.

allowed to divert time and energy from the path of individuation and compassion.

New things and new technology are very seductive. When I was a little boy, I lived for a time with my grandparents. These were the days before refrigerators, and we were too far from the city to obtain ice. So under an oak tree outside the kitchen door we had a cooler—a kind of cupboard made mostly of screen, covered with burlap that trailed into a pan of water. The burlap soaked up the water, and evaporation kept the contents of the cupboard cool, the milk fresh, and the butter firm. We didn't need a refrigerator. I can only assume that the reason my grandparents ultimately purchased one in later years was because they were persuaded by advertisements and by their friends.

We too can have coolers just outside the kitchen door or on the apartment veranda, saving the money the refrigerator would cost to help pay for the education of our children. Like our ancestors, we too can walk or take public transportation. We can come together like the Amish and build houses for one another. We can join with our friends and offer rites of passage to sons and daughters in their phase of experimenting and testing the limits of convention.

Our ancestors planned for their descendants; otherwise we might not be here. Our small lay Buddhist societies can provide a structure for Dharma practice, as well as precedent and flexible structures for our descendants to practice the Dharma in turn, for the next ten thousand years.

In formally sustaining the Dharma, we can also practice sustainable agriculture, sustainable tree farming, sustainable enterprise of all kinds. Our ancestors sustain us; we sustain our descendants. Our family members and fellow workers nurture us, and we nurture them—even as *dana* was circulated in ancient times.

Circulating the gift, the Buddhist monk traditionally offers the Dharma, as we offer him food, clothing, shelter, and medicine. But he also is a bachelor. Most of us cannot be itinerant mendicants. Yet as one who has left home, the monk challenges us to leave home as well—without leaving home. There are two meanings of "home" here. One could be the home of the family, but with the distractions that obscure the Dharma. The other may involve the family but is also the inner place of peace and rest, where devotion to the Buddha Way of selflessness and affection is paramount. The monks and their system of *dana* are, in fact, excellent metaphorical models for us. The gift is circulated, enhancing character and dignity with each round. Festivals to celebrate the rounds bring joy to the children and satisfaction to the elders.

I don't suggest that the practice of circulating the gift will be all sweetness and light. The practice would also involve dealing with mean-spirited imperatives, in oneself and in others. The Buddha and his elder leaders made entries in their code of *vinaya* (moral teachings) after instances of conduct that were viewed as inappropriate. Whether the Buddhist Base Community is simply a gathering of like-minded followers of the Dharma that meets for mutual support and study, whether it has organized to lobby for justice, or whether it conducts a business, manages a small farm, or operates a clinic, the guidelines must be clear. General agreements about what constitutes generous conduct and procedure will be valuable as references. Then, as seems appropriate, compassionate kinds of censure for departing from those standards could gradually be set into place. Guidelines should be set for conducting meetings, for carrying out the work, and for networking. There must be teaching, ritual, and sharing. All this comes with trial and error, with precedent as a guide but not a dictator.

Goodwill and perseverance can prevail. The rounds of circulating the gift are as long as ten thousand years, as brief as a moment. Each meeting of the little *sangha* can be a renewal of practice, each workday a renewal of practice, each encounter, each thought-flash. At each step of the way we remember that people and indeed the many beings of the world are more important than goods.

4

The "Single Vision" of Scientism

Mock on, mock on, Voltaire, Rousseau;
Mock on, mock on; 'Tis all in vain!
You throw the sand against the wind,
And the wind blows it back again.

And every sand becomes a Gem
Reflected in the beams divine;
Blown back they blind the mocking eye,
But still in Israel's paths they shine.

The Atoms of Democritus
And Newton's Particles of light
Are sands upon the Red Sea shore,
Where Israel's tents do shine so bright.

WILLIAM BLAKE

"PROGRESS" IN RETROSPECT*

Wolfgang Smith

Every age, every civilization, has a spirit of its own. It is this that determines the habitual outlook, the typical way of looking at things, the values, norms, and interdictions—in short, the essentials of the culture. It is quite certain, moreover, that most individuals will conform to the prevailing tendencies of the civilization into which they have been born, and this applies also no doubt to the majority of those who consider themselves to be non-conformists. On the other hand, it must also be possible to transcend cultural boundaries: there can really be no such thing as a rigid cultural determinism. But yet this crossing of boundaries turns out to be a rather rare occurrence; it happens much less frequently than we are led to suppose. We must not let ourselves be fooled. It is true, for example, that in modern times there has been an unprecedented interest in the study of history; and yet one finds that it is almost invariably a case of history truncated by the mental horizon of our age and colored by the humanistic sentiments of our civilization. The Zeitgeist is indeed a force to be reckoned with, and it is never easy to swim against the stream.

Yet this is precisely what must be done if we are to gain an unbiased perspective on the modern world. To put it rather bluntly, we need to break out of the intellectual smugness and provincialism of the typically modern man, the individual who has become thoroughly persuaded that our civilization represents the apex of a presumed "human evolution," and that mankind had been groping in darkness until Newton and his scientific successors arrived upon the scene to bring light into the world. Now, this is not to deny that bygone ages have known their share of ignorance and other ills, and that in certain respects the human condition may have been improved. Our point, rather, is that these supposedly positive developments which figure so prominently in the contemporary perception of history represent only a part of the story: the lesser part, in

---

* Editor's Note: Chapter 7 of *Cosmos and Transcendence*.

fact. We see the things that we have gained and are blind—almost by definition—to all that has been lost. And what is it that has been lost? Everything, one could say, that transcends the physical and psychological planes, the twin realms of a mathematicized objectivity and an illusory subjectivity. In other words, as intellectual heirs to the Cartesian philosophy we have become denizens of an impoverished universe, a world whose stark contours have been traced for us by the renowned French rationalist. At bottom there is physics and there is psychology—answering to the two sides of the great Cartesian divide—and together the two disciplines have in effect swallowed up the entire locus of reality: *our* reality, that is. Beyond this we see nothing; we cannot—our premises do not permit it.

But what then is out there that could possibly be seen? And by what means? The answer is surprisingly simple: what is to be seen is the God-made world, and this seeing—this prodigy—is to be accomplished through the God-given instruments consisting of the five senses and the mind. In this way we actually come into contact with the real, objective cosmos, which turns out to be a live universe full of color, sound, and fragrance, a world in which things speak to us and everything has meaning. But we must learn to listen and to discern. And that is a task which involves the whole man: body, soul, and above all, "heart." Everyone has seen a bird or a cloud, but not everyone is wise, not everyone is an artist in the true sense. This is of course what an education worthy of the name should help us to achieve: it should make us wise, it should open the eye of the soul.

But then: what is it that Nature has to tell—if only one has "ears to hear"? Now, to begin with, it speaks of subtle things, of invisible causes, and of cosmic harmonies. There is a science to be learned, a "natural philosophy" that is not contrived. But that is not all; it is only the merest beginning. For at last—when "the heart is pure"—we discover that Nature speaks, not of herself, but of her Maker: "Heaven and earth are full of Thy glory." Or in the words of the Apostle, "the invisible things of Him from the creation of the world have been clearly seen, being understood by the things that are made, even His eternal power and Godhead."

But as we are well aware, the very recollection of this exalted knowledge began to wane long ago, and by the time of the Renaissance had grown exceedingly dim, except in the case of a few outstanding souls. When it comes to Galileo and Descartes, moreover, it would appear that the light had gone out entirely: their philosophy of Nature leaves little room for doubt on that score. And from here on one encounters a prevailing intellectual milieu that is truly benighted, whatever the history books may say. To be sure, there have been some notable voices crying in the wilderness, and yet it is plain to see that "Bacon and Newton, sheath'd in dismal steel" have carried the day, and that their "Reasonings like vast Serpents" have infolded "the Schools and Universities of Europe," as Blake laments to his everlasting glory. It was the victory of "single vision": a kind of knowing which paradoxically hinges upon a scission, a profound alienation between the knower and the known. Now this is the decisive event that has paved the way to modern culture. From that point onwards we find ourselves (intellectually) in a contrived cosmos, a world cut down to size by the profane intelligence—a man-made universe designed to be comprehensible to physicists, and for its very lack of objective meaning, to psychologists as well.

Or this is where we would find ourselves, better said, if the great modern movement had fully succeeded in converting us to its preconceived notions. But that is not really possible; on closer examination we are bound to discover that there is in fact no one on earth who fully believes—with all his heart—what science has to say: such a Weltanschauung can speak only to a part of us, to a single faculty as it were, and so it is in principle unacceptable to the total man. Still, there is no denying that collectively we have become converts to a high degree. And if the vision does not fit the whole man, he can learn to live piecemeal, by compartments so to speak. Having become alienated from Nature—the object of knowledge—he becomes in the end estranged from himself.

We are beginning to see that the cosmological train of thought which started idyllically enough with the garden meditations of Descartes has had cultural reverberations. Roszak is unquestionably right when he insists that "cosmology implicates values," and that "there are never two cultures; only one—though that one culture may be schizoid."[1] He may also be right when he speaks of the outward consequences of this cultural neurosis in the following terms:

> We can now recognize that the fate of the soul is the fate of the social order; that if the spirit within us withers, so too will all the

[1] T. Roszak, *Where the Wasteland Ends* (New York: Doubleday, 1973), p. 200.

world we build about us. Literally so. What, after all, is the ecological crisis that now captures so much belated attention but the inevitable extroversion of a blighted psyche? Like inside, like outside. In the eleventh hour, the very physical environment suddenly looms up before us as the outward mirror of our inner condition, for many the first discernible symptom of advanced disease within.[2]

*

Following upon these summary observations, it may be well to reflect on the first major achievement of modern science, which is no doubt the Copernican astronomy. One generally takes it for granted that the displacement of the Ptolemaic by the Copernican world-view amounts to a victory of truth over error, the triumph of science over superstition. There are even those who perceive the Copernican position as a kind of holy doctrine having Giordano Bruno as its martyr and Galileo as its saintly confessor. But strangely enough it is forgotten that twentieth-century physics is in fact neutral on the entire issue. There was first of all the question whether the sun moves while the Earth remains fixed, or whether it is really the Earth that moves, and not the sun. Now, what modern physics insists upon—ever since Einstein recognized the full implication of the Michelson-Morley experiment—is that the concepts of rest and motion are purely relative: it all depends on what we take to be our frame of reference. Thus, given two bodies in space, it makes no sense whatever to ask which of the two is moving and which is at rest. So much for the first point of contention. The second issue, moreover, related to the position of the two orbs, each side claiming that the body which they took to be at rest occupies the center of space. And here again contemporary physics sees a pseudo-problem arising from fallacious assumptions. The question is in fact senseless on two counts: first, because (as we have seen) one cannot say that a body is at rest in an absolute sense; and secondly, because there is actually no such thing as a center of space. Thus, whether one conceives of cosmic space as unbounded (like the Euclidean plane) or as bounded (like the surface of a sphere), there exists in either case no special point that is marked out from

[2] *Ibid.*, p. xvii.

the rest, and so also no point which could be taken as the center of space. But in the absence of a center the Copernican debate loses its meaning; from this perspective the entire controversy appears indeed as the classic example of "much ado about nothing."

Yet this way of looking at the matter—which equalizes the two contesting sides—turns out to be no less deceptive than the popular view which bestows the palm of victory on the Copernicans. If the popular verdict is based on little more than prejudice and propaganda, the scientific appraisal for its part rests on the no less gratuitous assumption that cosmology is to be formulated in purely quantitative and "operationally definable" terms. One tacitly assumes, in other words, that quantity is the only thing that has objective reality, and that the *modus operandi* of empirical science constitute the only valid means for the acquisition of knowledge. Now, historically this is just the position to which Western civilization has been brought through a series of intellectual upheavals and reductions in which the Copernican revolution has played a major role. In fact, the new outlook stems directly from the later Copernicans, individuals like Galileo, whose thought was already modern in that regard. One should also remember that these (and not Copernicus) are the men who ran afoul of the ecclesiastical authorities and precipitated the famous debates. It was in the year 1530, let us recall, that Copernicus communicated his ideas to Pope Clement VII and was encouraged by the Pontiff to publish his inquiries; and it was a century later (in the year 1632) that Galileo was summoned before the Inquisition. The point is that there was more to the celebrated controversy than first meets the eye; and while overtly the debate raged over such seemingly harmless issues as whether it is the Earth or the sun that moves, one can see in retrospect that what was actually at stake was nothing less than an entire Weltanschauung.

We tend to forget that the Ptolemaic world-view was incomparably more than simply an astronomical theory in the contemporary sense; we forget that it was a *bona fide* cosmology as distinguished from a mere cosmography of the solar system. Now to appreciate the point of this difference, it must be recalled that the ancient Weltanschauung conceives of the cosmos as an hierarchic order consisting of many "planes," an order in which the corporeal world—made up of physical bodies, or of "matter" in the sense of modern physics—occupies precisely the bottom rank. This implies, in particular, that whatever can be investigated by the methods of physics—everything that shows up on its instruments—belongs *ipso facto* to the lowest fringe of the created world. Newton was right: we *are* only gathering pebbles by the seashore; for indeed, the physical sciences, by their very nature, are geared to the corporeal order of existence. Now, basically this is just the world that is perceptible to our external senses; only we must remember that even this lowest tier of the cosmic hierarchy is incomparably richer than the so-called physical universe—the ideal or imagined cosmos of contemporary science—because the corporeal world comprises a good deal more than simply mathematical attributes. Thus, if we wanted to locate the universe of modern physics on the ancient maps, we would have to say that it constitutes an abstract and exceedingly partial view of the outermost fringe, the "shell" of the cosmos. A *bona fide* cosmology, on the other hand, in the traditional sense, is a doctrine that bears reference—not just to a single plane—but to the cosmos in its entirety.

The question arises, of course, how the Ptolemaic theory, which after all does speak of the sun and its planets, could "bear reference to the cosmos in its entirety," seeing that the corporeal order as such constitutes no more than the smallest part of that total cosmos. And the answer is simple enough, at least in principle: the things of Nature point beyond themselves; though they be corporeal, they speak of incorporeal realms—they are symbols. In fact, there is an analogic correspondence between the different planes: "as above, so below" says the Hermetic axiom. We must not forget that despite its hierarchic structure the cosmos constitutes an organic unity, much like the organic unity of mind, soul, and body which we can glimpse within ourselves. Does not the face mirror the emotions or thoughts, and even the very spirit of the man? We have become oblivious of the fact that the cosmos, too, is an "animal," as the ancient philosophers had observed.

This, then—the miracle of cosmic symbolism—is what stands behind the Ptolemaic world-view and elevates it from a somewhat crude cosmography to a full-fledged cosmology. There was a time, moreover, when men could read the symbol, when they sensed that the solid Earth as such represents the corporeal realm, which stands at the very bottom of the cosmic scale; and that beyond this Earth there are spheres upon spheres, each larger and higher than the one before, until one arrives at last at the Empyrean, the ultimate limit or bound of the created world. They sensed too that there is an axis extending from Heaven to Earth, by which all these spheres are held together as it were, and around which they revolve; and they realized intuitively that the relation of containment is expressive of preeminence: it is the higher, the more excellent, that contains the lower, even as the cause contains the effect or the whole contains the part.

Let us add that in attempting to appraise these ancient beliefs we must not be put off by the fact that their erstwhile proponents—men who supposedly had some intuitive apprehension of higher realms—were evidently ignorant of things that are nowadays known to every schoolboy. We need not be unduly astonished, for example, that Ptolemy took our globe to be fixed in space because "if there were motion, it would be proportional to the great mass of the Earth and would leave behind animals and objects thrown into the air."[3] Childish, yes; but we should remember that the Book of Nature can be read in various ways and on different levels, and that no one knows it all. To be sure, "There are more things in heaven and earth, Horatio, than are dreamt of in your philosophy."

Getting back to the Copernican debate, it has now become apparent that the change from a geocentric to a heliocentric astronomy is not after all such a small or harmless step as one might have imagined. The fact is that for all but a discerning few it has undermined and discredited a cosmic symbolism which had nurtured mankind throughout the ages. Gone was the visible exemplification of higher realms and the vivid sense of verticality which spoke of transcendence and of the spiritual quest. Gone was the world that had inspired Dante to compose his masterpiece. With the demise of the Ptolemaic world-view the universe was in effect reduced to a single horizontal cross-section—the lowest, no less. It has become for us this narrow world, which remains so for all the myriad galaxies with which we are currently being regaled. Nature has become "a dull affair," as Whitehead says, "merely the hurrying of material, endlessly, meaninglessly."

One might object to this assessment of what was actually at stake in the Copernican issue on the grounds that a heliocentric astron-

---

[3] Quoted in E.A. Burtt, *The Metaphysical Foundations of Modern Physical Science* (New York: Macmillan, 1951), p. 35.

omy too admits of a symbolic interpretation, since it identifies the sun—a natural symbol of the Logos—as the center of the cosmos. But yet the fact remains that its rediscovery by Copernicus has not been propitious to a spiritual vision of the world; "rather was it comparable to the dangerous popularization of an esoteric truth," as Titus Burckhardt observes.[4] One must remember that our normal experience of the cosmos is obviously geocentric, a fact which in itself implies that the Ptolemaic symbolism is apt to be far more accessible. Moreover, the Copernican victory came at a time when the religious and metaphysical traditions of Christianity had already fallen into a state of partial decay, so that there was no longer any viable framework within which the symbolic content of heliocentrism could have been brought to light. As Hossein Nasr has pointed out, "the Copernican revolution brought about all the spiritual and religious upheavals that its opponents had forecasted would happen precisely because it came at a time when philosophical doubt reigned everywhere ... "[5] It was a time when European man was no longer especially attuned to the reading of transcendental symbols and had already to a large extent lost contact with the higher dimensions of existence. And this is what lends a certain air of unreality to the Copernican dispute, and what from the start assured the eventual triumph of the new orientation. By now the wisdom of bygone ages—like every truth that is no longer understood—had become a superstition, to be cast aside and replaced by new insights, new discoveries.[6]

*

With the disappearance of the Ptolemaic world-view Western man lost his sense of verticality, his sense of transcendence. Or rather these finer perceptions had now become confined to the purely religious sphere, which thus became isolated and estranged from the rest of the culture. So far as cosmology—Weltanschauung in the lit-

---

[4] T. Burckhardt, "Cosmology and Modern Science," in *The Sword of Gnosis*, ed. J. Needleman (Baltimore: Penguin, 1974), p. 127.

[5] S.H. Nasr, *Man and Nature* (London: Allen & Unwin, 1976), p. 66.

[6] Editor's Note: For an in-depth treatment of these topics see Wolfgang Smith, *The Wisdom of Ancient Cosmology* (Oakton, VA: The Foundation for Traditional Studies, 2004).

eral sense—was concerned, European civilization became de-Christianized.

At the same time a radical change in man's perception of himself was taking place. We need to recall in this connection that according to ancient belief there is a symbolic correspondence between the cosmos in its entirety and man, the theomorphic creature who recapitulates the macrocosm within himself. Thus man is indeed a "microcosm," a universe in miniature; and that is the reason why, symbolically speaking, man is situated at the very center of the cosmos. In him all radii converge; or better said, from him they radiate outwards in every direction to the extremities of cosmic space—a mystical fact which we find graphically depicted in many an ancient diagram. No doubt the reason for this centrality is that man, having been made "in the image of God," carries within himself the center from which all things have sprung. And that too is why he can understand the world, and why in fact the cosmos is intelligible to the human intellect. He is able to know the universe because in a way it pre-exists in him.

But of course all this means absolutely nothing from the modern point of view. To be sure, once the cosmos has been reduced to the corporeal plane, and that in turn has been cut down to its purely quantitative parameters, there is little left of the aforementioned analogy. Admittedly our physical anatomy does *not* resemble the solar system or a spiral nebula. It is first and foremost in the qualitative aspects of creation, as revealed to us through the God-given instruments of perception, that cosmic symbolism comes into play. We need not be surprised, therefore, that a science which peers upon Nature through lifeless instruments fashioned by technology should have little to say on that score.

In any case, along with the Ptolemaic theory the ancient anthropology fell likewise into oblivion. Man ceased in effect to be a microcosm, a theomorphic being standing at the center of the universe, and became instead a purely contingent creature, to be accounted for by some sequence of terrestrial accidents. Like the cosmos he was flattened out, shorn of the higher dimensions of his being. Only in his case it happens that "mind" refuses to be altogether exorcised. It remains behind as an incomprehensible concomitant of brain-function, a kind of ghost in the machine, a thing that causes untold embarrassment to the philosophers. The fact is that man does not fit into the confines of the physical universe. There is another side to his nature—be it ever so subjective!—which cannot be described or accounted for in physical terms. And so, in keeping with the new outlook, man finds himself a stranger in a bleak and inhospitable universe; he has become a precarious anomaly—one could almost say, a freak. There is something pathetic in the spectacle of this "precocious simian"; and behind all the noise and bluster one senses an incredible loneliness and a pervading *Angst*. Our harmony and kinship with Nature has been compromised, the inner bond broken; our entire culture has become dissonant. Moreover, despite our boast of knowledge, Nature has become unintelligible to us, a closed book; and even the act of sense perception—the very act upon which all our knowledge is supposed to be based—has become incomprehensible.

What then are we to say concerning the stupendous knowledge of science? It is evidently a knowledge that has been filtered through external instruments and that partakes of the artificiality of these man-made devices. Strictly speaking, what we know is not Nature but certain methodically monitored effects of Nature upon that mysterious entity termed "the scientific observer." It is thus a positivistic knowledge geared to the prediction and control of phenomena, and ultimately—as we know—to the exploitation of natural resources and the practice of terrestrial rapine. All euphemisms aside, science—like most else that modern man busies himself with—is well on the way to becoming simply an instance of "technique" in the sense of the sociologist Jacques Ellul.

Meanwhile all the ideal aspects of human culture, including all values and norms, have become relegated to the subjective sphere, and truth itself has become in effect subsumed under the category of utility. Transcendence and symbolism out of the way, there remains only the useful and the useless, the pleasurable and the disagreeable. There are no more absolutes and no more certainties; only a positivistic knowledge and feelings, a veritable glut of feelings. All that pertains to the higher side of life—to art, to morality, or to religion—is now held to be subjective, relative, contingent—in a word, "psychological." One is no longer capable of understanding that values and norms could have a basis in truth; how could this be in a world of "hurrying material"? And so man has become the great sophist: he has set himself up as "the measure of all things." Having but recently learned to walk on his hind legs (as he staunchly believes), he now fancies himself a god! "Once Heaven was closed," writes Schuon, "and man was in effect installed in God's place, the objective measurements of things were, virtually or actually, lost. They were replaced by subjective measurements, purely human and conjectural pseudo-values ..."[7] Thus, too, all the elements of culture, having once been subjectivized, have become fair game to the agents of change. Nothing is sacrosanct any more, and at last everyone is at liberty to do as he will. Or so it may seem; for in reality the manipulation of culture has become a serious enterprise, a business to be attended to by governments and other interest groups.

We find thus that cosmology does indeed "implicate values"; one could even say that eventually it turns into politics. So too a pseudo-cosmology necessarily implicates false values, and a politics destructive of good. It is by no means a harmless thing to be cut off from the higher spheres or from the mandates of God. Our civilization has forgotten what man is and what human life is for; as Nasr notes, "there has never been as little knowledge of man, of the *anthropos*."[8] To which one might add that apparently no previous culture has managed to violate so many natural and God-given norms to any comparable extent.

*

Some reflections on the subject of art may not be inappropriate at this point. The first thing to be noted is that the very conception of art has changed: the word has actually acquired a new meaning. Thus art has become "fine art," something to be enjoyed in leisure moments and generally by the well-to-do. It has become a luxury, almost a kind of toy. In ancient times, on the other hand, "art" meant simply the skill or wisdom for making things, and the things made by art were then called "artefacts." Strictly speaking everything that answered a legitimate need and that had to be produced by human industry was an artefact. Thus an agricultural implement or a sword was an artefact, a piece of furniture or a house was an artefact, and so too was a cathedral or an icon or an ode. The arte-

[7] F. Schuon, *Light on the Ancient Worlds* (London: Perennial Books, 1965), p. 30.
[8] S.H. Nasr, "Contemporary Man, between the Rim and the Axis," *Studies in Comparative Religion* 7 (1963): 116.

fact, moreover, was there for the whole man, the trichotomous being made up of body, soul, and spirit; and so even the humblest tool or utensil had to possess more than simply "utility," in the contemporary sense. That "more," of course, derives from symbolism, from the language of forms. It is the reason why a water-pot can be a thing of immense beauty and meaning. Not that this beauty had to be somehow superimposed upon the object, like an ornament. It was there as a natural concomitant of utility, of the "correctness," one could say, of the work. And that is the reason why in ancient times there was an intimate link between art and science, and why Jean Mignot (the builder of the cathedral at Milan) could say that "art without science is nothing" (*ars sine scientia nihil*). In a word, both beauty and utility were conceived to spring from truth.

It was understood, moreover, that authentic art can never be profane. For let us remember that according to Christian teaching the eternal Word or Wisdom of God is indeed the supreme Artist: "All things were made by Him, and without Him was not anything made." Now it follows from the profound sense of this text that whatever is *truly* made, or made rightly, *is made by Him.* And this implies that the human artist—every authentic artist—must participate to some degree in the eternal Wisdom. "So, too, the soul can perform no living works," writes St. Bonaventure, "unless it receive from the sun, that is, from Christ, the aid of His gratuitous light."[9] Man, therefore, the human artist, is but an agent; to achieve perfection in his art he must make himself an instrument in the hands of God. And so the production of the artefact is to be ascribed to the divine Artificer in proportion as it is beneficent and well made; for indeed "every good gift and every perfect gift is from above, and cometh down from the Father of lights" (James 1:17).

To some extent this constitutes a universal doctrine that has guided and enlightened the arts of mankind right up to the advent of the modern age. Thus even in the so-called primitive societies all art, all "making," was a matter of "doing as the gods did in the beginning." And that "beginning," moreover, is to be understood in a mythical, that is to say, in a metaphysical sense. Basically it is the ever-present "now," that elusive point of contact between time and eternity which is also the center of the universe, the "pivot around

---

[9] St Bonaventure, *De Reductione Artium ad Theologiam*, 21.

which the primordial wheel revolves." As Mircea Eliade has amply demonstrated, the traditional cultures have been cognizant of that universal center and have sought by ritual or other symbolic means to effect a return to that point of origin, that "beginning." That is where man was able to renew himself; from thence he derived strength and wisdom. And from thence too, needless to say, he derived his artistic inspiration. Thus, strange as it may sound, the traditional artist works not so much in time as in eternity. His art partakes somehow of the instantaneous "now"; and this explains its freshness, the conspicuous unity and animation of its productions. No matter how long it may take to fashion the external artefact, the work has been consummated internally in a trice, at a single stroke.

The Scholastics were no doubt heirs to this immemorial conception of art. It is evidently what St. Thomas has in mind when he defines art as "the imitation of Nature in her manner of operation,"[10] for we must understand that here the term "Nature" is employed not in the current sense—not in the sense of *natura naturata*, a nature that has been made—but in the sense of *natura naturans*, the creative agent which is none other than God. The human artist thus imitates the divine Artificer; for in imitation of the Holy Trinity he works "through a word conceived in his intellect" (*per verbum in intellectu conceptum*),[11] which is to say, through a word or "concept" which mirrors the eternal Word. Man too "begets a word" in his intellect; and this constitutes the *actus primus* of artistic creation.

It follows from these considerations that there is a profound spiritual significance both in the enjoyment and in the practice of authentic art. On the one hand, a *bona fide* artefact will possess a certain charisma, a beauty and significance which no profane or merely human art could effect—not to speak of mechanized production. Such an artefact will exert an invisible influence upon the user; it will benefit the patron in unsuspected ways. But what is still more important, the exercise of his art will bring not only material remuneration but also spiritual benefit to the artist. "Manufacture, the practice of an art," writes Coomaraswamy, "is thus not only the production of utilities but in the highest possible sense the educa-

---

[10] St Thomas Aquinas, *Summa Theologiae*, 1.117.1.
[11] *Ibid.*, 1.45.6.

tion of men."[12] It is a spiritual way, a means to perfection. And one could even say that the practice of an art should be a normal and integral part of the Christian life: everyone should be an artist of some kind, each in accordance with his vocation. As William Blake has expressed it, "The Whole Business of Man is the Arts ... the unproductive Man is not a Christian."

One also knows, however, that as Blake was writing these lines the Industrial Revolution was gathering momentum and the Arts were on their way out. The machine age was upon us, and that kind of manufacture which had been so much more than the mere "production of utilities" was fast being replaced by the assembly line. We know that efficiency has been increased a hundredfold and that the "standard of living" has never been so high. And we know too that the promised utopia has not arrived, and that unforeseen difficulties are cropping up at an accelerating pace. What we generally don't know, however, is that our civilization has become culturally impoverished to an alarming degree. We are beginning to become cognizant of the ecological crisis and shudder at the reports of acid rain, but still fail to behold the spiritual wasteland that has been forming around us for centuries. We speak of "the dignity of labor" and forget that there was a time when manufacture was more than a tedium, a meaningless drudgery which men endure only for the sake of pecuniary reward. We speak of "the abundant life" and forget that happiness is not simply play, entertainment, or "getting away from it all," but the spontaneous concomitant of a life well lived. We forget that pleasure does not come in pills or via an electronic tube but through what the Scholastics termed "proper operation," the very thing that authentic art is about. In short, what we have totally forgotten is that "The Whole Business of Man is the Arts."

Besides industry, of course, our culture comprises also "the fine arts," which are there presumably to supply "the higher things of life." Now, whatever else might be said in behalf of these productions, it is clear that for the most part they are bereft of any metaphysical content. Our art ceased long ago to be a "rhetoric" and became an "aesthetic," as Coomaraswamy has pointed out; which is

[12] A.K. Coomaraswamy, *Christian and Oriental Philosophy of Art* (New York: Dover, 1956), p. 27.

to say that it is no longer intended to enlighten but only to please. It is not the function of our fine arts "to make the primordial truth intelligible, to make the unheard audible, to enunciate the primordial word, to represent the archetype," which from a traditional point of view is indeed "the task of art, or it is not art," as Walter Andrae[13] observes. And however sublime this "fine art" may be, it does not in fact bear reference to "the invisible things of Him" because the artist who made it was simply a man—a genius, perhaps, but a man nonetheless. Unlike ancient art it does not derive "from above," nor does it refer to spiritual realities, or to God "whom we never mention in polite society." As a matter of fact, in keeping with the overall subjectivist trend of modern culture, art has become more and more a matter of "self-expression," right up to the point where the contingent, the trivial, and the base have all but monopolized the scene. A stage has been reached where much of art is plainly subversive—one needs but to recall those bizarre paintings of patently Freudian inspiration which could very well have originated within the walls of a lunatic asylum. The history of modern art teaches us that the merely human, cut off from spiritual tradition and the touch of transcendence, is unstable: It degenerates before long into the infrahuman and the absurd.

*

There is an intimate connection between the machine metaphor as a cosmological conception and the creation of a technological society. Let us not forget that a machine has no other *raison d'être* than to be used. When Nature, therefore, is viewed as being nothing more than a machine, it will as a matter of course come to be regarded simply as a potential object of exploitation, a thing to be used in all possible ways for the profit of men. The two attitudes, moreover, go hand in hand; for as Roszak points out, "only those who experience the world as dead, stupid, or alien and therefore without a claim to reverence, could ever turn upon their environment ... with the cool and meticulously calculated rapacity of industrial civilization."[14] It is therefore not surprising that no sooner had

[13] Quoted in A.K. Coomaraswamy, *Christian and Oriental Philosophy of Art*, p. 55.
[14] T. Roszak, *Where the Wasteland Ends*, pp. 154-155.

the postulate of cosmic mechanism gained official recognition than men began on an unprecedented scale to build their own machines with which to harness the forces of Nature; in the wake of the Enlightenment came the Industrial Revolution.

But the story does not end there; for it was inevitable within the perspective of the new cosmology that man, too, should come to be viewed as a kind of machine. What else could he be in a Newtonian universe? And if man is a machine, society too is a machine and human behavior is deterministic: Newton, Lamettrie, Hobbes, and Pavlov clearly lie on a single trajectory. And these recognitions—or better said, these new premises—open up incalculable possibilities! Whether we realize it or not, the cold and rigorous dialectic of science in its concrete actuality leads step by step to the formation of a technological society in the full frightening sense of that term.

Let us consider the matter a little more carefully. To understand the scientific process we need to recall an essential idea which goes back not so much to Newton as to Descartes, and is especially associated with the name of Francis Bacon (the first of the two "arch villains" in Blake's vision of Victorious Science). Now Bacon's contribution resides in his perception of a universal and all-encompassing method for the systematic acquisition of knowledge. In the first place, this process is envisaged as collective and cumulative; it is an enterprise that keeps on gathering momentum. Thus "the business" of knowing should not be left in the hands of the individual but is to be carried out by teams of experts, as we would say; and significantly enough (this is its second notable characteristic), it is to be done "as if by machinery." Here it is again: the all-conquering omnivorous machine metaphor! But this time in an entirely new key: as a methodological principle. With telling effect Bacon goes on to observe how very small would be the accomplishments of "mechanical men" if they worked only with their bare hands, unaided by tools and instruments contrived through human ingenuity. In like manner very little can be accomplished when men seek to acquire knowledge through "the naked forces of understanding." In the mental domain, too, we need a tool, an instrument of thought; and that is just what his *"novum organum"*—Bacon's famed method of science—is intended to supply. "A new machine for the mind," he calls it. And like every machine, it is there to be used for profit; truth and utility, he assures us, "are here one and the same thing."

One can say in retrospect that whereas Bacon's specific recipes for scientific discovery have proved to be relatively useless (as many have pointed out), his dream of a systematic and collective science in which "human knowledge and human power meet in one" has no doubt been realized beyond his wildest expectations. What has triumphed is not so much any specific "machine for the mind" but the idea of method or technique as something formal and impersonal that interposes itself between the knower and the known. And whereas, on the one hand, this artificial intermediary has isolated the knower—impeded his direct access to reality—it has also made possible the development of a formal and depersonalized knowledge, based upon the systematic labors of countless investigators. First came the development of classical physics and what might be termed "hard" technology. Later the modern biological sciences began to emerge, and later still the so-called behavioral and social sciences. Meanwhile the process of scientization began to extend itself beyond the boundaries of every formally recognized science and proceeded to exert a dominant influence in other domains. "Scientific knowledge becomes, within the artificial environment, the orthodox mode of knowing," writes Roszak; "all else defers to it. Soon enough the style of mind that began with the natural scientist is taken up by imitators throughout the culture."[15] And as the matter stands, this "style of mind" is to be encountered everywhere; it has entered into cloisters and convents. It has become a mark of enlightenment, the respected thing; "all else defers to it." As Bacon had shrewdly seen, there are in principle no limits to the scientization of culture: given free reign, the process is bound to insinuate itself into virtually every sphere of human thought and every activity.

It is obvious to all that our outer lifestyles are being drastically altered as a direct consequence of the scientific advance. What we generally fail to realize, on the other hand, is that the impact of this same development on our inner lives—yes, on the condition of our soul—is no less pronounced. To begin with, the mechanization of our work-environment, the phenomenon of urban sprawl, the rising congestion and perpetual noise, the proliferation of concrete, steel, and plastic, the loss of contact with Nature and with natural

---

[15] *Ibid.*, p. 31.

things, the invasion of our homes by the mass media—all this in itself is bound to have its effect on our mental and emotional condition. Add to this the uprooting of people from their ancestral environment, an unprecedented mobility which shuffles populations like a deck of cards. Add also the other innumerable mechanisms within the technological society which tend to break down every natural division and all cultural ties. Let us add up (if we are able!) all the factors which homogenize and level out. For it must not be forgotten that people too have to be standardized, like interchangeable parts of a machine, so that the wheels of the mechanized civilization may run smoothly and efficiently.

It is to be noted, moreover, that in the course of the present century this leveling, which began with the Industrial Revolution, has entered upon a new phase due to the rise of the behavioral and social sciences. Now from a purely academic point of view it may well appear that these disciplines are of little consequence; for apart from the factual information which they have accumulated (much of it in the form of statistical data) it would seem that one can hardly speak of "science" at all. The trappings of science (fancy terms and reams of computer print-out) are there no doubt, but very little of its substance—so long, at least, as one insists that the objective verification of hypotheses, without obfuscation and fudging, constitutes a *sine qua non* of the scientific process. And this deficiency is occasionally admitted even by members of the profession. There is the case of Stanislav Andreski, for example, who has offered[16] insightful observations on such subjects as "The Smoke Screen of Jargon," "Quantification as Camouflage," "Ideology Underneath Terminology," and most important of all, "Techno-Totemism and Creeping Crypto-Totalitarianism." There it is! This is just the point: if we take a closer look at these seeming pseudo-sciences, we find that they too fit perfectly into the integral framework of the technological society. Here too one encounters a kind of "knowledge" which begets power. As we have already seen in the case of Freudian and Jungian psychology, a pseudo-science may not be without its "utility," its technical efficacy. And if Voltaire could say that even lying becomes "virtuous" when it is practiced for the right end, then why (in a pragmatic civilization) should not these human techniques be deemed a science and their dogmas "truth"?

---

[16] S. Andreski, *Social Sciences as Sorcery* (London: Deutsch, 1972).

Be that as it may, the fact remains that our century has witnessed a dramatic increase in the utilization on the part of governments, industries, and other powerful interest groups of methods based upon the so-called behavioral and social sciences. A well-known story about Pavlov may be recalled in this connection: it is reported that shortly after the Bolshevik Revolution the famed scientist was virtually imprisoned in the Kremlin and ordered to write a book describing in detail how behavioral methods based upon his theory of conditioned reflexes may be applied to the indoctrination and control of human beings. Whether it be true that Lenin, upon reading the book, exclaimed to Pavlov, "you have saved the Revolution!"—one does know with certainty that Pavlovian methods have been used extensively in the Soviet Union, and that similar techniques have also been developed and applied in the Western democracies.[17]

However, this does not preclude the fact that the vast majority of people, be it in Russia or in the United States, are almost entirely unaware of this process and could not even imagine the extent to which it has already influenced their own beliefs and psychic make-up. As Jacques Ellul has pointed out with reference to propaganda as a specific area of human technique:

> Propaganda must become as natural as air or food. It must proceed by psychological inhibition and the least possible shock. The individual is then able to declare in all honesty that no such thing as propaganda exists. In fact, however, he has been so absorbed by it that he is literally no longer able to see the truth. The natures of man and propaganda have become so inextricably mixed that everything depends not on choice or on free will, but on reflex and myth. The prolonged and hypnotic repetition of the same complex of ideas, the same images, and the same rumors condition man for the assimilation of his nature to propaganda.[18]

Much the same could be affirmed, moreover, with regard to many other areas of human technique which are not simply "propaganda" in the strict sense. Thus it is only to be expected that in our

[17] See William Sargent, *Battle for the Mind* (Westwood, CT: Greenwood, 1957).
[18] J. Ellul, *The Technological Society* (New York: Knopf, 1965), p. 366.

kind of civilization almost every organized "encounter"—from kindergarten to post-graduate seminars—will entail an element of concealed indoctrination. As Ellul has shown, virtually all education—on both sides of the Iron Curtain—involves mechanisms of conditioning and control designed to fit the individual into the projects of the society.[19] Even our leisure is "literally stuffed with technical mechanisms of compensation and integration" which, though different from those of the work environment, are "as invasive and exacting, and leave man no more free than labor itself."[20] Within the last decade even religious and priestly retreats have become fair game to the scientific methods of "sensitivity training"! It is the greatest mistake to think that the technological society can be "culturally neutral," or that the celebrated "pluralism" about which one hears so much in Western countries can be anything more than a passing phase or an outright fake. "Cosmology implicates values"—to say it once more—and without any doubt the manipulation of man, the most vital "resource" of all, constitutes the ultimate technology.

*

While it is sociologically certain that science begets technology, it also cannot be denied that in its purest form science is simply the pursuit of knowledge for its own sake. Like philosophy, it begins in wonder, or in a certain curiosity about Nature; and especially when it comes to the great scientists—an Einstein or a Schrödinger—one finds that the driving force behind their scientific inquiries is indeed worlds removed from any thought of application. One needs but to recall with how much diffidence and anguish Einstein offered his fateful formula to the service of the Free World when the hard exigencies of the time seemed to demand this step. It is one of the great ironies of fate that the most terrible instruments of destruction have been pioneered by men who above all others loved peace, and that the most powerful means of enslavement owe their existence to some of the greatest champions of human liberty.

[19] *Ibid.*, p. 347.
[20] *Ibid.*, p. 401.

But let us pause to reflect a little on the idea of "knowledge for its own sake"; our sentiments notwithstanding, might there not be an intrinsic connection between this noble quest and such bitter fruit? Preposterous, the humanist will say; and admittedly it has become an almost universally accepted premise that the unbridled pursuit of knowledge constitutes one of the most beneficial and praiseworthy of human occupations. No one seems to question that "research" of just about any description is a wonderful thing which in some mysterious way is bound to enhance "the dignity of man" or "the quality of life." Not infrequently one finds individuals of even the most prosaic type waxing eloquent in praise of those who are said to have "pushed back the frontiers of the unknown." Our libraries are already filled to bursting with the products of this great passion, and yet the cry is always for more. And even when it is recognized that the fruits of this knowledge—the consequences of its applications—have proved to be equivocal or to threaten the very survival of man—even then it is thought that science as such is in no wise at fault. The blame must always be placed at the door of the avaricious entrepreneur or the unscrupulous politician, or it must lie with the short-sighted members of Congress held responsible for the under-funding of research. For indeed all ills resulting from "research and development" are thought to be curable, homeopathic style, with yet another dose of R & D; no one seems prepared to weigh the possibility that the malaise may actually be due, not to an insufficiency, but to an excess of this factor.

Come what may, pure science—science with a capital S—can do no wrong. It is astounding that in an age of unprecedented skepticism, when immemorial beliefs are being tossed aside like worn toys or blithely held up to public ridicule, one should encounter this virtually limitless faith in the unfailing beneficence of scientific research.

What lies behind this passion for more and more science, more and more technology—this mania, one is tempted to say, which has taken hold of our civilization? Is it indoctrination? Yes, no doubt; but then, who first indoctrinated the educators and the technocrats? It is not really quite so simple. Nor can one expect to understand the phenomenon in depth from the typical perspectives of humanist thought. Has not humanism been closely allied with the scientific mentality from the start? Is not the one as well as the other a characteristic manifestation of the contemporary Zeitgeist?

Do they not share a common anti-traditional thrust? Were not both equally implicated, for example, in the French Revolution, when "the Goddess of Reason" was installed on the high altar of Notre Dame? And have not the two—despite the interlude of Romanticism—stood together on almost every issue? It would appear, then, that there can be no searching critique of science which is not also at the same time a critique of humanism. To go beyond superficial appearances and banalities we must be prepared to step out of the charmed circle of contemporary presuppositions and avail ourselves of the only viable alternative to modern thought: and that is traditional thought.

What, then, does traditional teaching have to say on the subject of science? We propose to look at the matter from a specifically Christian point of vantage; and even at the risk of speaking what can only be "foolishness to the Greeks," we shall attempt to place ourselves in an authentically Biblical perspective. This means in particular that we need to reflect anew on the familiar account in Genesis concerning the "forbidden fruit" and the fall of Adam, his expulsion from "the garden of paradise." Now, in the first place we must go beyond the customary explanation of this event, which is based upon an essentially moral as opposed to a metaphysical point of view. It is all well and good to attribute Adam's fall to "the sin of disobedience," and this no doubt expresses a profound and vital truth. But we must also realize that this line of interpretation, valid though it be, cannot possibly cover the entire ground. For one thing it leaves open the question as to why Adam had been commanded to abstain from this particular fruit in preference to all others, and why the tree which brought forth this forbidden harvest is referred to as "the tree of the knowledge of good and evil." It is reasonable to suppose, moreover, that "the apple of knowledge" was indeed fatal not simply because it was forbidden, but that it was forbidden precisely because it would prove fatal to man. Furthermore, we must not think that the "good" which was to be known through the eating of this fruit is that true or absolute good which religion always associates with the knowledge of God; and neither must we assume that the "evil" which comes to be revealed through the same act is something objectively real, something which has been created by God. For indeed the opening chapter of Genesis has already informed us many times over that God had surveyed the entire creation and found it to be "good." The knowledge, therefore, that is symbolized by the forbidden fruit is a partial and fragmentary knowledge, a knowledge which fails to grasp the absolute dependence of all things upon their Creator. It is a reduced knowledge which perceives the world not as a theophany but as a sequence of contingencies: not *sub specie aeternitatis* but under the aspect of temporality. And it is only in this fragmented world wherein all things are in a state of perpetual flux that evil and death enter upon the scene. They enter thus, on the one hand, as the inescapable concomitant of a fragmentary knowledge, a knowledge of things as divorced from God; and at the same time they enter as the dire consequences of "disobedience"—the misuse of man's God-given freedom—and so as "the wages of sin."

Thus Adam fell. "The link with the divine Source was broken and became invisible," writes Schuon; "the world became suddenly external to Adam, things became opaque and heavy, they became like unintelligible and hostile fragments."[21] In other words, the world as we know it came into existence: history began. But that is not the whole story. The Biblical narrative has in fact an extreme relevance to what is happening here and now; for as Schuon points out, "this drama is always repeating itself anew, in collective history as in the life of individuals." The fall of Adam, then, is not only a primordial act which antedates history as such, but it is also something which comes to pass again and again in the course of human events. It is re-enacted on a smaller or larger scale wherever men opt for what is contingent and ephemeral in place of the eternal truth.

It appears that a "fall" of major proportions has in fact taken place roughly between the fourteenth and eighteenth centuries. Even the most casual reading of European history reveals the contours of a gigantic transformation: the old order has crumbled and a new world has come to birth. To be sure, this is the cultural metamorphosis which we normally behold under the colors of Evolution and Progress; what we do not perceive, on the other hand, is that we have forfeited our sense of transcendence in the bargain. In other words, we have become sophisticated, skeptical, and profane. Much as we might wish to be enlightened, the wisdom of the ages has become for us a superstition, a mere vestige of a supposedly primitive past; or at best it is seen as literature and poetry in the exclu-

---

[21] F. Schuon, *Light on the Ancient Worlds*, p. 44.

sively horizontal sense which we currently attach to these terms. Like it or not, we find ourselves in a desacralized and flattened-out cosmos, a meaningless universe which caters mainly to our animal needs and to our scientific curiosity.

Admittedly there are compensations. Energy has been diverted, so to speak, from higher to lower planes, and this accounts undoubtedly for the incredible vigor with which the modernization of our world has been pressed forward and everything on earth is being visibly transformed. At last man is free to devote himself entirely to the mundane and to the ephemeral portion of himself. And this he does, not only with Herculean effort, but with a kind of religiosity. It is one of the salient features of our time that ephemeral goals and secular pursuits—down to the most trivial and inglorious—have become invested with a sacredness, one could almost say, which in bygone ages had been reserved for the worship of God. But why? What is it all about? "Equipped as he is by his very nature for worship," writes Martin Lings, "man cannot not worship; and if his outlook is cut off from the spiritual plane, he will find a 'god' to worship on some lower level, thus endowing something relative with what belongs only to the Absolute. Hence the existence today of so many 'words to conjure with' like 'freedom,' 'equality,' 'literacy,' 'science,' 'civilization,' words at the utterance of which multitudes of souls fall prostrate in sub-mental adoration."[22]

Everything depends on how we perceive the world, on the quality, one might say, of our knowledge. Is our vision of the universe centripetal? Is it oriented towards the spiritual center? Is it informed by a sense of verticality, by an intuition of higher spheres? Or is it, on the contrary, horizontal and centrifugal, a knowledge that faces away from the origin, away from the Source? Now that is the kind of knowing which perpetuates the Fall. Always mingled with delusion, it is a profane wisdom that scatters and leads astray. Moreover, it is something to which we have no right by virtue of what we are; like inassimilable food, its very truth becomes eventually a poison to us. Such a knowledge never enlightens us but only blinds our soul; it shuts the gates of Heaven and opens instead the way to the riches of this earth, along with the untold miseries there-

---

[22] M. Lings, *Ancient Beliefs and Modern Superstitions* (London: Perennial Books, 1965), p. 45.

of. The terrible fact is that a Promethean science, a science that would make man the measure and master of all things ("ye shall be as gods"), becomes in the end a curse ("cursed is the ground for thy sake, and in sorrow shall thou eat of it").

Spirituality and Science—
Convergence or Divergence?*

Seyyed Hossein Nasr

In a world torn by contention and strife at every level, from the spiritual and intellectual to the physical, those in quest of the creation of peace and harmony have often turned to the task of seeking accord between spirituality and science. The contemporary landscape is in fact filled by such efforts many of which, although based on the best of intentions, only contribute to further chaos in the present day world. Many such attempts substitute sentimental wishing for reality and ambiguous definitions and positions, for the clarity and rigor which alone can disperse the fog of ignorance that blurs the vision of present day humanity traveling on a road that becomes even more perilous thanks to a large extent to the lack of critical discernment in the relation between a knowledge derived from the senses and its consequences, and the wisdom which descends from revelation, intellection, or illumination. The "harmony" between science and spirituality, characteristic of much of the so-called New Age mentality in the West and also numerous Westernized Orientals who speak without a clear definition of the concepts involved and modes of knowledge and consciousness at play within the boundaries of what is to be harmonized and unified, is itself one of the sources of discord and cacophony in a world in which intellectual discernment, so long a hallmark of all metaphysical traditions especially those of India, is too easily sacrificed for ambiguous and disruptive accords which cannot but lead to discord as long as one mistakes the rope for a snake.

The subject of the relation between religion and science, and for those embarrassed by the use of the term religion, then between spirituality and science, remains for other reasons of paramount importance in a world in which, on the one hand, a science of nature

---

* Editor's Note: The text of an address given in New Delhi in July 1995 as part of a celebration of the sixtieth anniversary of the birth of His Holiness the Dalai Lama.

based upon power and dominance over nature, rather than the contemplation of its ontological and symbolic reality, reigns supreme as the only legitimate form of knowledge and is almost deified and certainly absolutized, while its practitioners appear more and more to the masses at large as priests wielding ultimate authority over human life and even determining its meaning. And on the other hand, the demands of the Spirit and the quest for the spiritual still continue unabated for they are woven into the very texture of human existence, and if anything the very threat to human life on earth brought about by the applications of modern science have only increased this yearning of late, as seen in the revival of religion throughout the world and the even greater flowering of "home-grown" and exotic forms of so-called spiritualities as well as aberrant mutations of Oriental teachings, in even the most secularized parts of Western society. In the light of this situation it is therefore necessary to ask before delving into the question of convergence or divergence exactly what we mean by science and spirituality in the context of the present discourse.

The definition of science might appear to be simple if one only uses the current understanding of the term in English, and not in fact French or German where the terms *science* and *Wissenschaft* have a more general connotation. In English the term science implies a particular way of knowing the natural world based upon empirical and rational methods and excluding by definition other modes of knowledge based upon other epistemological and ontological premises. Of course, even in English we do use such terms as Chinese, Indian, Islamic, or Buddhist science because such a basic term as science, derived from *scientia*, cannot become completely limited to its positivistic, operational, empirical, or rationalistic meaning. In the latter case, that is, if we were to think of let us say Chinese or Islamic science, then the relation of such a science to spirituality would be very different from what exists today when one limits the term science to its main current English usage. This difference is due to the fact that the traditional sciences are based on very different cosmological and epistemological principles from modern science. For the purpose of this discussion, however, we shall define science as that body of systematic knowledge of nature, combined with mathematics, which grew out of the Scientific Revolution of the seventeenth century on the basis of earlier Latin, Islamic, and Greek sciences. This limitation is quite unfortunate, especially in a discourse given here in India, and because so little attention has been paid by Oriental as well as Western scholars to the relation between spirituality and the traditional sciences of nature. And yet the crisis is not in that domain but is to be found in the confrontation between the modern Western scientific worldview, now spread over much of the globe, and the spirituality which has flowered over the millennia within the gardens of various religions of the world.

As for the definition of spirituality, it is even more problematic because of the very ambiguous manner in which it has been used during the past few decades. The origin of the usage of this term in European languages is fairly recent, that is, within the past century or two, where it was first used in Catholic circles. Only recently has it become widely used, often as a substitute for religion and for some in opposition to it. Words used in Oriental languages to denote spirituality usually reflect the etymology of the word as coming from *spiritus* or the Spirit. For example, in Arabic the term *ruhaniyyah* is a prevalent translation, the term coming from *al-ruh* which means precisely *spiritus*, without the meaning of the Arabic term having become in any way ambiguous. In the modern world, however, which is characterized by either the denial of the Spirit as an objective, ontological reality, or its confusion with the psyche, what can spirituality even mean? Most often it implies a vague yearning for meaning and the experience of the noumenal while settling for the psychological instead in forgetfulness of the truth that the Spirit manifests itself according to certain principles and only within the great traditions of celestial origin. And if the Bible asserts that "the spirit bloweth where it listeth," this only points to the exception which proves the rule.

Once traditional criteria of the reality of the Spirit and laws of its manifestation as contained in various traditions such as Hinduism, Buddhism, Christianity, and Islam are denied, then anything can be called spiritual and the term spirituality loses both its intellectual dimension and sacred quality. The vast labyrinth of the psychic world becomes confused with the luminous Heaven of the Spirit and the type of so-called spirituality resulting from this confusion can be made to converge with almost anything, including science. In this present discussion, therefore, we shall define spirituality as the inner, spiritual dimension of traditional religions dealing with the noumenal and the formless that can be experienced directly and is beyond mental categories but is not anti-intellectual. On the contrary if intellect is understood in its original sense as *intellectus* or the *buddhi* and not simply reason, spirituality and intellectuality are inseparable from each other.

The task of studying whether there is convergence or divergence between science and spirituality is in fact worthy of pursuit only if spirituality is understood in this traditional sense and not in an ambiguous manner which can embrace almost anything, including the psychic and even the demonic. Be that as it may, the discussion which follows confines itself to the traditional understanding of spirituality, one which is nevertheless vast beyond our imagination for it includes a Shankara as well as an Eckhart, a Rumi as well as a Honen, a Milarepa as well as a Chuang-Tzu, not to speak of the great masters of spirituality of other traditions such as Judaism, Zoroastrianism, Confucianism, and Shamanism.

Defined in this manner, one can at first ask what are the points of divergence between spirituality and science. Obviously there is first of all the question of the understanding of what constitutes reality. In traditional spirituality, reality is at once transcendent and immanent, beyond and here and now, but in all cases above every categorization and conceptualization of the mind. It is beyond the psycho-physical realm and yet encompasses this domain. One cannot comprehend it in the sense of its being encompassed because nothing can encompass that which is infinite. Yet it can be known by the Intellect which is a divine noetic faculty at the center of our being. Ultimate reality is absolute and infinite, the supreme Good and the source of all good. It is Beyond-Being as well as constituting Being, which is the origin of the cosmic hierarchy and levels of universal existence.

In contrast, for modern science reality, to the extent one still speaks of such a category, is that which can be empirically verified. Everything that is beyond the empirically verifiable cannot be treated or known "scientifically"; nor strictly speaking can it even be of scientific significance. To all extents and purposes it is nonexistent. To use the language of Hinduism, the Real is *Atman* while all modern science is a science of *maya*, or more exactly of its lower reaches; or in Buddhist terms, of samsaric existence, even if extended to the galaxies. The Real is known through the twin sources of revelation and intellection with the aid of the *buddhi*, while both of these sources, and along with them metaphysical and cosmological truths, are denied by the worldview of modern science, although not necessarily by individual scientists.

Authentic spirituality is always aware of the basic distinction between the Principle and Its manifestations, between *Atman* and *maya, nirvana* and *samsara,* the Divine Essence (*al-Dhat*) and the veils (*hijab*) which hide and yet reveal the theophanies of the Divine Names and Qualities from us and to us. The foundation of all traditional metaphysics is in fact the distinction between the Absolute and the relative, and knowledge of the relative in the light of the Absolute. By denying the Absolute in the metaphysical sense, modern science cannot but absolutize the relative, mistaking the cosmic "illusion," or *maya,* for reality. Its grave sin is what Buddhism calls the error of false attribution. As a result, the scientific worldview denies not only the Absolute in Itself but also the hierarchies and levels of being beyond the psycho-physical, the sensible, and the measurable. Many of its exponents then set about to reveal the mysteries of existence through the microscope, telescope, or some computer model, and a world dazzled by the glitter of modern technology, and having divinized modern science, stands with full anticipation for the revelation of the next "mystery of the universe" which does not usually go beyond adding or subtracting some purely quantitative element to or from the universe seen in a purely quantitative manner.

There is of course a metaphysical significance to those discoveries of modern science which correspond to some aspect of physical reality and are not purely conjecture, for all that is real is real to the extent that it symbolizes a reality beyond itself, and everything in the universe is ultimately symbolic except the Absolute Reality Itself. But this truth concerns precisely what lies beyond the confines of modern science and cannot be understood save by a metaphysician whether he be himself a scientist or not.

Before turning away from the question of divergence between spirituality and modern science, it is necessary to emphasize again that authentic spirituality depends ultimately upon a revelation from the Spirit on the basis of immutable principles. Modern science is also based on a set of premises, but the latter have not descended from Heaven. Rather, they are the creations of those philosophers who have woven together the elements that constitute the paradigm within which modern science has functioned since the seventeenth century. Strangely enough, it is only during the past few decades that the dependence of modern science upon a particular worldview and paradigm of physical reality is becoming accepted, at least in some circles, while the majority of modern educated people continue to believe that religion or spirituality is based on faith and certain assumptions about the nature of reality and science on the contrary is based upon reason and observation. Both in fact base themselves upon faith in a body of knowledge which for religion is considered to be the truth and for science premises and foundational assumptions. The great difference is that in one case the doctrines descend from the immutable Divine Order and the other from rational and empirical philosophies of a purely human order, whose consequences cannot of necessity transcend the purely human, and because of their denial of the supra-human, place man in the danger of falling into the sub-human. It is because of the radically different epistemologies, views of reality, and premises involved that science cannot confirm the Divine Origin of the world or its eschatological *omega point*, the reality of the spiritual worlds above the physical or the immortal nature of the soul of man, to use the terminology of the Abrahamic religions. Nor can it point to what constitutes the goal of human life here below.

Science is based in fact upon the idea that there is only one mode of perception and one level of external reality which that single level of consciousness studies. The world, according to it, is what we see if only we extend the word "see" to include what is shown by the microscope and the telescope, which do not represent a new mode or level of seeing but simply the extension, horizontally, of what the human eye perceives. In contrast authentic spirituality is based upon the basic thesis that not only are there levels of reality but also levels of consciousness which can know those levels of reality. What we perceive of the external world depends upon our mode of consciousness, not in the sense that a geologist looking upon a mountain sees certain geological structures which the non-geologist does not perceive; but rather, in the sense that other non-physical levels of reality of what taken only physically becomes the mountain, can be known if we possess higher levels of consciousness. And again this does not mean that this knowledge is based on some kind of subjectivism but means that when we possess a higher level of consciousness we have the preparation to "see" other dimensions and levels of the reality in question. In any case according to all traditional spiritual doctrines what we see depends upon our mode of consciousness and knowledge, and our mode of consciousness in turn depends upon our mode of being. Hence the centrality of spiritual discipline which transforms our mode of being as well as consciousness. Seeing is believing only if we extend the meaning of seeing beyond what the physical eyes perceive.

This great contrast becomes more evident when we consider the fact that to become educated as a modern scientist, it is not necessary to undergo any spiritual training but only to develop certain mental faculties and keenness of observation in total contrast to the case of spirituality when it is practiced seriously and not simply talked about, for authentic spirituality demands the transformation of our whole being and a change in how we think, perceive, evaluate, and act. The result of this basic difference is that there are some scientists who are interested in spirituality and some not at all. Even in the realm of ethics, modern science *qua* science demonstrates a relation very different from what we find in traditional spirituality. Ethical values are inseparable from the acts and deeds of spiritually realized men and women and spirituality has always been the fountainhead, the inner spring, and the life force of ethics in various religions. In contrast modern science as a system of knowledge is ethically neutral and in fact ethical questions are irrelevant to it. On the practical level there are many scientists who are very ethical and then of course there are many who are not, as the history of this century has amply demonstrated. In fact the whole idea of scientists being responsible for the consequences of the applications of their science within the societies in which they function has only recently become acceptable to a notable body of scientists, at a time when these applications threaten both the natural environment and the quality and possibly even continuity of human life on earth.

One could go on at length but the points mentioned should suffice to demonstrate that the facile convergence of science and spirituality championed in so many circles is based more on fervent desire than on reality. Also, it is often based on the one hand on the confusion of science with the views of some of its practitioners, and on the other on the dilution and distortion of authentic spiritual teachings. Nowhere is this more evident than in the question of evolution understood in its modern biological sense. All traditional doctrines which do deal with cosmogony, some like Taoism and Confucianism remaining silent about the genesis of the cosmos, speak of the descent of the world from the Divine Principle, the celestial archetypes, the logos, etc. God said, "Let there be light and there was light," the Bible asserts and the Quran states that Allah has said, "Be!" and all things came into existence. There is the primordial sacrifice of Purusa in Hinduism and of Gayomarth in Zoroastrianism to which numerous examples could be added from other traditions. The beings of this world have descended from the Divine, from the world of the Spirit, and the reality of all things in the cosmos resides in God, to speak in the language of Abrahamic faiths, or, according to Hinduism, is contained in the original cosmic egg, which far from being material is a spiritual reality containing all the possibilities to be manifested in a particular cosmic cycle.

In evolutionary theory, on the contrary, everything has ascended from below, from the original "soup of molecules" which somehow mysteriously produces a consciousness that can stand outside the process and understand and study it. Nothing in the world is more opposed to the spiritual understanding of the origin of man and other beings than nineteenth century evolutionary theory, which is a philosophy rather than science, but which is presented as science because it is the main support for the whole structure of the modern scientific worldview without which the whole secularist Weltanschauung would collapse. And nowhere is this sentimental attitude, so opposed to metaphysical discernment that has always characterized the intellectual life of the land of India, more evident than in the writings of an array of people, many from the Indian world, who would simply equate the traditional Hindu doctrines of descent and gradation of being with evolution and ascent of the higher from the lower through simple temporal processes of change and transformation.

To this century-old attempt at bringing about the convergence of totally divergent perspectives must now be added a recently written chapter by those who would reduce both science and religion or spirituality to a "story," claiming that each has a story about reality which can be made to converge. Of course this is done not only through the introduction of a certain degree of ambiguity and cloud, to cover the terrain which cannot be easily traversed intellectually, but also by a kind of subjectivism and psychologism which characterize much of the contemporary scene and especially what is called New Age spirituality. Moreover, to bring about convergence, it is usually the religious truths which are sacrificed because they are accused of being "dogmatic" and what is substituted for them is usually drawn from evolutionism itself, with some modifying factors to placate those who are still searching for a reality which is not simply material and physical. That such a thinking has entered even into writings that are taken seriously in certain religions, such as the works of Teilhard de Chardin in Catholic circles, only points out how far away the current understanding of spirituality has moved from that of the worlds which produced the Honens, Ramanujas, St. Theresas, and Rumis, as well as the Sankaras, Nagarjunas, Eckharts, and Ibn 'Arabis who, each in his or her own way and according to different modes and perspectives, have dominated the spiritual and intellectual lives of different human collectivities over the centuries.

Seeing how powerful science, or at least its image, is in modern society and also how persistent is man's need for spirituality, we must now ask what can be done to bring about a serious convergence and accord between science and spirituality, one which would not be apparent and only contribute further to the confusion and chaos that characterize so much of contemporary life. Needless to say there cannot be a convergence between the view which believes that we have descended from above and that which claims that we have ascended from below. But if one puts pseudo-science, or rather philosophical hypotheses parading as science aside on the one hand, and pseudo-spirituality, now so rampant in the West, on the other, then there are certainly significant steps that can be taken in bringing about, if not a convergence, at least an understanding between the principles of spirituality and the *dicta* of science as they exist today and might exist tomorrow, while being always mindful of the continuously changing nature of the latter at least in details if not always in Weltanschauung.

Let us begin by recalling the fact that today even the worldview or paradigm of modern science is beginning to change for the first time since the sixteenth and seventeenth centuries. There are scientists, especially physicists, who are turning to a worldview in which the reality of what is of concern to spirituality is not reduced to subjectivism or a secondary, derivative set of phenomena. It is as yet too early to foretell what will happen in this domain. At the present stage there are those who, groping for a new philosophy of nature, remain satisfied with superficial comparisons between the dance of Shiva and that of electrons or electro-magnetic polarity and the Yin-Yang principles of Far Eastern cosmology. This may, however, be but the first halting step, or series of steps, in the direction of the discovery, or rather rediscovery, of Reality in its vast amplitude and numerous dimensions, beyond the truncated version of it which is the subject of modern physics and which is then taken to be reality as such by the scientific mind.

Since it is not possible to discover higher levels of reality simply by means of even further analysis of matter and energy in a quantitative sense, such a discovery, if it ever comes, must of necessity draw from the metaphysical teachings of various traditions and be the result of the navigation through higher levels of reality by those who have been able to make such a journey, thanks to intellection and authentic spiritual techniques. If the shift of paradigm, so often discussed in the current philosophy of science, is to be anything more than the substitution of one limited view of reality for another, then recourse must be had to spiritual traditions, especially those of the East where a great deal of such teachings have been better preserved than in the modern West. If the substitution represents simply a "horizontal" shift, then accord between the new paradigm of science and spirituality will be as problematic as what one observes today. But there is some hope that a positive transformation of paradigm will come about. There are in fact a number of scientists, particularly physicists, who speak in such terms and who express serious theological and spiritual concerns, more than many theologians, who in fear of the onslaught of modern science, continue to surrender theology to the discoveries of the microscope and the telescope to an even greater degree.

In this process of the formation of a new paradigm, spirituality itself carries a heavy burden. What is called spirituality in various religions must be clearly defined, its roots in revelation, divine descent, or corresponding realities in other religions elucidated and its wedding to authentic metaphysics or *sophia* based upon the twin sources of intellection and revelation/illumination made manifest. It is for those knowledgeable in such metaphysics and molded by authentic spirituality to formulate a contemporary metaphysics of nature and cosmology, in the traditionally honored sense of this term, which could provide the intellectual background for the new paradigm being sought by modern science. Spirituality abdicates from its function and role when it simply repeats the current findings of modern science, which will not be current tomorrow, and then distorts its own millennial teachings to demonstrate that they are in accord with present day scientific theories or findings. Spirituality is based on the primacy of the Spirit, on the supreme reality of the One, the Tao, the Godhead, *Atman, Allah* and not on a reality discovered through the external senses alone. Spirituality envisages man as at once Spirit, soul, and body, and not only the mind and body of Cartesian dualism, and the cosmos also as a reality possessing not only a "body" which we can observe and study but also other dimensions corresponding to the psyche and Spirit. The more the basic metaphysical and epistemological differences between authentic spirituality and the current understanding of science are brought out, the more is there the possibility of the forging of a paradigm for science which could live at peace with the spiritual and not endanger the very existence of man on earth through its ever greater exertion of power over both the human psyche and the domain of nature. If representatives of authentic spirituality do not become aware of this grave responsibility, they will simply leave the field open to pseudo-spirituality and caricatures of authentic teachings to which many a well-meaning scientist, himself not trained in such matters, will turn for inspiration or guidance. The consequences cannot but be more catastrophic than an out-and-out rejection of all the claims of spirituality by this or that materialistic or agnostic scientist.

One might say that the most immediate task at hand is the creation of a sacred science of the cosmos which would not necessarily negate what modern science has discovered but provide another type of knowledge of the cosmos rooted in its sacred reality. Such a science, which had existed in various traditional civilizations but is rarely spoken of by current representatives of spirituality, would be the meeting ground between spirituality and science. It would provide a sacred view of nature, now being so mercilessly desecrated and one might say even murdered in the act which is now being called ecocide. It would also provide a knowledge of the cosmos which could discern between the aspects of modern science that correspond to some aspect of physical reality and those that are merely conjecture parading as science. It could also provide a domain of discourse between spirituality and science without destroying or mutilating the corresponding realities involved. Of course such an endeavor would require humility not only on behalf of certain individual men and women practicing science, for there are, to be sure, many humble scientists, but on behalf of science as a discipline. There must come the admission on behalf of the guardians and propagators of science in general, that modern science is a possible science and not *the* only legitimate science of nature. As long as such a totalitarian and monopolistic view of science exists, all talk of the harmony of spirituality and science remains mere talk, unless spirituality is diluted or transformed into something which has as little to do with the Spirit as do the discoveries in a physics laboratory. Once such a limitation is admitted, however, there is certainly the possibility of an *approchement* and even of the opening of the door to the metaphysical and symbolic significance of major modern scientific discoveries, a significance which lies beyond the realm and boundaries defined by science for itself, and therefore meaningless "scientifically" speaking, in the same way that the term sacred in "sacred science" is simply a meaningless word in the context of the way in which modern science defines and understands concepts and terms.

Let us hope that at this dangerous juncture of human history, when man's ever greater quantitative knowledge of nature, based on a definition of knowledge which excludes the numinous and the sacred, is threatening all human life, and in fact the whole of the natural ambiance, a deeper understanding will be attained of the infinitely profound and rich sources of authentic spirituality and the real nature and limitations of modern science. The *dharma* of those who know cannot but be to discern, to overcome the supreme sin of false attribution, to preserve a sense of proportion, and to remain faithful to the hierarchy of existence and the true relation between the spiritual and the physical based upon these realities. Only in the quest, preservation, and propagation of authentic spirituality and an honest and critical understanding of the premises, assumptions, findings, and gropings of modern science can one hope to avert the tidal wave that threatens what remains of traditional civilizations, authentic religions, and spiritual teachings, and that direct manifestation of Divine Wisdom and Power that is virgin nature. Also, this pursuit provides the opportunity to exercise to the highest degree the virtue of compassion of which the Buddhist Bodhisattva is such a compelling embodiment and image. The task is daunting but the end cannot but be witness to the victory of the Truth.[1]

---

[1] We have discussed more extensively the issues brought forth in this essay in *Knowledge and the Sacred* (Albany, NY: SUNY Press, 1991), *The Need for a Sacred Science* (Albany, NY: SUNY Press, 1993), and *Religion and the Order of Nature* (New York and Oxford: Oxford University Press, 1996).

THE THEORY OF EVOLUTION[*]

Titus Burckhardt

The least phenomenon participates in several continuities or cosmic dimensions incommensurable in relation to each other; thus, ice is water as regards its substance—and in this respect it is indistinguishable from liquid water or water vapor—but as regards its state it belongs to the class of solid bodies. Similarly, when a thing is constituted by diverse elements, it participates in their natures while being different from them. Cinnabar, for example, is a synthesis of sulfur and mercury; it is thus in one sense the sum of these two elements, but at the same time it possesses qualities that are not to be found in either of these two substances. Quantities can be added to one another, but a quality is never merely the sum of other qualities. By mixing the colors blue and yellow, green is obtained; this third color is thus a synthesis of the other two, but it is not the product of a simple addition, for it represents at the same time a chromatic quality that is new and unique in itself.

There is here something like a "discontinuous continuity," which is even more marked in the biological order, where the qualitative unity of an organism is plainly distinguishable from its material composition. The bird that is born from the egg is made from the same elements as the egg, but it is not the egg. Likewise, the butterfly that emerges from a chrysalis is neither that chrysalis nor the caterpillar that produced it. A kinship exists between these various organisms, a genetic continuity, but they also display a qualitative discontinuity, since between the caterpillar and the butterfly there is something like a rupture of level.

At every point in the cosmic web there is thus a warp and a woof that intersect one another, and this is indicated by the traditional symbolism of weaving, according to which the threads of the warp, which hang vertically on the primitive loom, represent the permanent essences of things—and thus also the essential qualities and

---

[*] Editor's Note: Taken from *The Essential Titus Burckhardt*, ed. William Stoddart.

forms—while the woof, which binds horizontally the threads of the warp, and at the same time covers them with its alternating waves, corresponds to the substantial or "material" continuity of the world.[1]

The same law is expressed by classical hylomorphism, which distinguishes the "form" of a thing or being—the seal of its essential unity—from its "matter," namely the plastic substance which receives this seal and furnishes it with a concrete and limited existence. No modern theory has ever been able to replace this ancient theory, for the fact of reducing the whole plenitude of the real to one or other of its "dimensions" hardly amounts to an explanation of it. Modern science is ignorant above all of what the Ancients designated by the term "form," precisely because it is here a question of a non-quantitative aspect of things, and this ignorance is not unconnected with the fact that modern science sees no criterion in the beauty or ugliness of a phenomenon: the beauty of a thing is the sign of its internal unity, its conformity with an indivisible essence, and thus with a reality that will not let itself be counted or measured.

It is necessary to point out here that the notion of "form" necessarily includes a twofold meaning: on the one hand it means the delimitation of a thing, and this is its most usual meaning; in this connection, form is situated on the side of matter or, in a more general sense, on the side of plastic substance, which limits and separates realities.[2] On the other hand, "form" understood in the sense given to it by the Greek philosophers and following them the Scholastics, is the aggregate of qualities pertaining to a being or a thing, and thus the expression or the trace of its immutable essence.

The individual world is the "formal" world because it is the domain of those realities that are constituted by the conjunction of a "form" and a "matter," whether subtle or corporeal. It is only in connection with a "matter," a plastic substance, that "form" plays the role of a principle of individuation; in itself, in its ontological basis, it is not an individual reality but an archetype, and as such beyond

---

[1] René Guénon, *The Symbolism of the Cross* (Sophia Perennis, Ghent, NY, 1996), chapter on the symbolism of weaving.

[2] In Hindu parlance, the distinction *nama-rupa*, "name and form," is related to this aspect of the notion under study, "name" here standing for the essence of a being or thing, and "form" for its limited and outward existence.

limitations and change. Thus a species is an archetype, and if it is only manifested by the individuals that belong to it, it is nevertheless just as real, and even incomparably more real, than they. As for the rationalist objection that tries to prove the absurdity of the doctrine of archetypes by arguing that a multiplication of mental notions would imply a corresponding multiplication of archetypes—leading to the idea of the idea of the idea, and so on—it quite misses the point, since multiplicity can in nowise be transposed onto the level of the archetypal roots. The latter are distinguished in a principial way, within Being and by virtue of Being; in this connection, Being can be envisaged as a unique and homogeneous crystal potentially containing all possible crystalline forms.[3] Multiplicity and quantity thus only exist at the level of the "material" reflections of the archetypes.

From what has just been said, it follows that a species is in itself an immutable "form"; it cannot evolve and be transformed into another species, although it may include variants, which are diverse "projections" of a unique essential form, from which they can never be detached, any more than the branches of a tree can be detached from the trunk.

It has been justly said[4] that the whole thesis of the evolution of species, inaugurated by Darwin, is founded on a confusion between species and simple variation. Its advocates put forward as the "bud" or the beginning of a new species what in reality is no more than a variant within the framework of a determinate specific type. This false assimilation is, however, not enough to fill the numberless gaps that occur in the paleontological succession of species; not only are related species separated by profound gaps, but there do not even exist any forms that would indicate any possible connection between different orders such as fish, reptiles, birds, and mammals. One can doubtless find some fishes that use their fins to crawl onto a bank, but one will seek in vain in these fins for the slightest begin-

---

[3] It is self-evident that all the images that one can offer of the non-separative distinction of the possibilities contained in Being must remain imperfect and paradoxical.

[4] Douglas Dewar, *The Transformist Illusion* (Dehoff Publications, Murfreesboro, Tennessee, 1957 [Editor's Note: Reprinted by Sophia Perennis, 1995.]). See also Louis Bounoure, *Déterminisme et Finalité* (Collection Philosophie, Flammarion, Paris).

ning of that articulation which would render possible the formation of an arm or a paw. Likewise, if there are certain resemblances between reptiles and birds, their respective skeletons are nonetheless of a fundamentally different structure. Thus, for example, the very complex articulation in the jaws of a bird, and the related organization of its hearing apparatus, pertain to an entirely different plan from the one found in reptiles; it is difficult to conceive how one might have developed from the other.[5] As for the famous fossil bird *Archaeopteryx*, it is fairly and squarely a bird, despite the claws at the end of its wings, its teeth, and its long tail.[6]

In order to explain the absence of intermediate forms, the partisans of transformism have sometimes argued that these forms must have disappeared because of their very imperfection and precariousness; but this argument is plainly in contradiction with the principle of selection that is supposed to be the operative factor in the evolution of species: the trial forms should be incomparably more numerous than the ancestors having already acquired a definitive form. Besides, if the evolution of species represents, as is declared, a gradual and continual process, all the real links in the chain—therefore all those that are destined to be followed—will be both endpoints and intermediaries, in which case it is difficult to see why the ones would be much more precarious than the others.[7]

The more conscientious among modern biologists either reject the transformist theory, or else maintain it as a "working hypothesis," being unable to conceive any genesis of species that would not be situated on the "horizontal line" of a purely physical and temporal becoming. For Jean Rostand,

---

[5] Dewar, *The Transformist Illusion*.

[6] *Ibid.*

[7] Teilhard de Chardin (*The Human Phenomenon*, p. 129) writes on this subject: "Nothing is by nature so delicate and fugitive as a beginning. As long as a zoological group is young, its characteristics remain undecided. Its dimensions are weak. Relatively few individuals compose it, and these are rapidly changing. Both in space and duration, the peduncle (or the bud, which comes to the same thing) of a living branch corresponds to a minimum of differentiation, expansion, and resistance. How then is time going to act on this weak zone? Inevitably by destroying it in its vestiges." This reasoning, which abusively exploits the purely external and conventional analogy between a genealogical "tree" and a real plant, is an example of the "imaginative abstraction" that characterizes this author's thought.

the world postulated by transformism is a fairy-like world, phantasmagoric, surrealistic. The chief point, to which one always returns, is that we have never been present, even in a small way, at *one* authentic phenomenon of evolution ... we keep the impression that nature today has nothing to offer that might be capable of reducing our embarrassment before the veritably organic metamorphoses implied in the transformist thesis. We keep the impression that, in the matter of the genesis of species as in that of the genesis of life, the forces that constructed nature are now absent from nature ...[8]

Even so, this biologist sticks to the transformist theory:

I firmly believe—because I see no means of doing otherwise—that mammals have come from lizards, and lizards from fish; but when I declare and when I think such a thing, I try not to avoid seeing its indigestible enormity and I prefer to leave vague the origin of these scandalous metamorphoses rather than add to their improbability that of a ludicrous interpretation.[9]

All that paleontology proves to us is that the various animal forms, such as are shown by fossils preserved in successive earthly layers, made their appearance in a vaguely ascending order, going from relatively undifferentiated organisms—but not simple ones[10]—to ever more complex forms, without this ascension representing, however, an unequivocal and continuous line. It seems to move in jumps; in other words, whole categories of animals appear all at once, without real predecessors. What does this order mean? Simply that, on the material plane, the simple or relatively undifferentiated always precedes the complex and differentiated. All "matter" is like a mirror that reflects the activity of the essences, while also inverting it; this is why the seed comes before the tree and the bud before the flower, whereas in the principial order the perfect "forms" pre-exist. The successive appearance of animal forms

---

[8] *Le Figaro Littéraire,* April 20, 1957.

[9] *Ibid.*

[10] The electron microscope has revealed the surprising complexity of the functions at work within a unicellular being.

according to an ascending hierarchy therefore in nowise proves their continual and cumulative genesis.[11]

On the contrary, what links the various animal forms to one another is something like a common model, which reveals itself more or less through their structures and which is more apparent in the case of animals endowed with superior consciousness such as birds and mammals. This model is expressed especially in the symmetrical disposition of the body, in the number of extremities and sensory organs, and also in the general form of the chief internal organs. It might be suggested that the design and number of certain organs, and especially those of sensation, simply correspond to the terrestrial surroundings; but this argument is reversible, because those surroundings are precisely what the sensory organs grasp and delimit. In fact, the model underlying all animal forms establishes the analogy between the microcosm and the macrocosm. Against the background of this common cosmic pattern the differences between species and the gaps that separate them are all the more marked.

Instead of "missing links," which the partisans of transformism seek in vain, nature offers us, as if in irony, a large variety of animal forms which, without transgressing the pre-established framework of a species, imitate the appearance and habits of a species or order foreign to them. Thus, for example, whales are mammals, but they assume the appearance and behavior of fishes; hummingbirds have the appearance, iridescent colors, flight, and mode of feeding of butterflies; the armadillo is covered with scales like a reptile, although it is a mammal; and so on. Most of these animals with imitative forms are higher species that have taken on the forms of relatively lower species, a fact which *a priori* excludes an interpretation of them as intermediary links in an evolution. As for their interpre-

---

[11] The most commonly mentioned example in favor of the transformist thesis is the hypothetical genealogy of the *Equidae*. Charles Depéret criticizes it as follows: "Geological observation establishes in a formal manner that no gradual passage took place between these genera; the last *Palaeotherium* had for long been extinct, without having transformed itself, when the first *Architherium* made its appearance, and the latter disappeared in its turn, without modification, before being suddenly replaced by the invasion of the *Hipparion*" (*Les Transformations du Monde animal*, p. 107). To this it can be added that the supposed primitive forms of the horse are hardly to be observed in equine embryology, though the development of the embryo is commonly looked on as a recapitulation of the genesis of the species.

tation as forms of adaptation to a given set of surroundings, this seems more than dubious, for what could be, for example, the intermediate forms between some land mammal or other and the dolphin?[12] Among these "imitative" forms, which constitute so many extreme cases, we must also include the fossil bird *Archaeopteryx* mentioned above.

Since each animal order represents an archetype that includes the archetypes of the corresponding species, one might well ask oneself whether the existence of "imitative" animal forms does not contradict the immutability of the essential forms; but this is not the case, for the existence of these forms demonstrates, on the contrary, that very immutability by a logical exhausting of all the possibilities inherent in a given type or essential form. It is as if nature, after bringing forth fishes, reptiles, birds, and mammals, with their distinctive characteristics, wished still to show that she was able to produce an animal like the dolphin which, while being a true mammal, at the same time possesses almost all the faculties of a fish, or a creature like the tortoise, which possesses a skeleton covered by flesh, yet at the same time is enclosed in an exterior carapace after the fashion of certain mollusks.[13] Thus does nature manifest her protean power, her inexhaustible capacity for generation, while remaining faithful to the essential forms, which in fact are never blurred.

Each essential form—or each archetype—includes after its fashion all the others, but without confusion; it is like a mirror reflecting other mirrors, which reflect it in their turn.[14] In its deepest meaning the mutual reflection of types is an expression of the metaphysical homogeneity of Existence, or of the unity of Being.

---

[12] On the subject of the hypothetical transformation of a land animal into the whale, Douglas Dewar writes: "I have often challenged transformists to describe plausible ancestors situated in the intermediate phases of this supposed transformation" (*What the Animal Fossils Tell us*, trans. Vict. Instit, vol. LXXIV).

[13] It is significant that the tortoise, whose skeleton seems to indicate an extravagant adaptation to an animal "armored" state, appears all at once among the fossils, without evolution. Similarly, the spider appears simultaneously with its prey and with its faculty of weaving already developed.

[14] This is the image used by the Sufi 'Abd al-Karim al-Jili in his book *al-Insan al-Kamil*, chapter on "Divine Unicity."

Some biologists, when confronted with the discontinuity in the paleontological succession of species, postulate an evolution by leaps and, in order to make this theory plausible, refer to the sudden mutations observed in some living species. But these mutations never exceed the limits of an anomaly or a decadence, as for example the sudden appearance of albinos, or of dwarfs or giants; even when these characteristics become hereditary, they remain as anomalies and never constitute new specific forms.[15] For this to happen, it would be necessary for the vital substance of an existing species to serve as the "plastic material" for a newly manifested specific form; in practice, this means that one or several females of this existing species would suddenly bear offspring of a new species. Now, as the hermetist Richard the Englishman writes:

> Nothing can be produced from a thing that is not contained in it; for this reason, every species, every genus, and every natural order develops within the limits proper to it and bears fruits according to its own kind and not according to an essentially different order; everything that receives a seed must be of the same seed.[16]

Fundamentally, the evolutionist thesis is an attempt to replace, not simply the "miracle of creation," but the cosmogonic process—largely suprasensory—of which the Biblical narrative is a Scriptural symbol; evolutionism, by absurdly making the greater derive from the lesser, is the opposite of this process, or this "emanation." (This term has nothing to do with the emanationist heresy, since the transcendence and immutability of the ontological principle are here in no wise called into question.) In a word, evolutionism results from an incapacity—peculiar to modern science—to conceive "dimensions" of reality other than purely physical ones; to understand the "vertical" genesis of species, it is worth recalling what René Guénon said about the progressive solidification of the corporeal state through the various terrestrial ages.[17] This solidification must obviously not be taken to imply that the stones of the earliest ages were soft, for this would be tantamount to saying that certain physical qualities—and in particular hardness and density—were then want-

---

[15] Bounoure, *Déterminisme et Finalité.*

[16] Quoted in the *Golden Treatise, Museum Hermeticum* (Frankfurt, 1678).

[17] René Guénon, *The Reign of Quantity and the Signs of the Times.*

ing; what has hardened and become fixed with time is the corporeal state taken as a whole, with the result that it no longer receives directly the imprint of subtle forms. Assuredly, it cannot become detached from the subtle state, which is its ontological root and which dominates it entirely, but the relationship between the two states of existence no longer has the creative character that it possessed at the origin; it is as when a fruit, having reached maturity, becomes surrounded by an ever harder husk and ceases to absorb the sap of the tree. In a cyclic phase in which corporeal existence had not yet reached this degree of solidification, a new specific form could manifest itself directly from the starting-point of its first "condensation" in the subtle or animic state;[18] this means that the different types of animals pre-existed at the level immediately superior to the corporeal world as non-spatial forms, but nevertheless clothed in a certain "matter," namely that of the subtle world. From there these forms "descended" into the corporeal state each time the latter was ready to receive them; this "descent" had the nature of a sudden coagulation and hence also the nature of a limitation and fragmentation of the original animic form. Indo-Tibetan cosmology describes this descent—which is also a fall—in the case of human beings under the form of the mythological combat of the *deva*s and *asura*s: the *deva*s having created man with a body that was fluid, protean, and diaphanous—in other words, in a subtle form—the *asura*s try to destroy it by a progressive petrification; it becomes opaque, gets fixed, and its skeleton, affected by the petrification, is immobilized. Thereupon the *deva*s, turning evil into good, create joints, after having fractured the bones, and they also open the pathways of the senses, by piercing the skull, which threatens to imprison the seat of the mind. In this way the process of solidification stops before it reaches its extreme limit, and certain organs in man, such as the eye, still retain something of the nature of the non-corporeal states.[19]

---

[18] Concerning the creation of species in a subtle "proto-matter"—in which they still preserve an androgynous form, comparable to a sphere—and their subsequent exteriorization by "crystallization" in sensible matter (which is heavy, opaque, and mortal), see Frithjof Schuon, *Light on the Ancient Worlds* (World Wisdom, Bloomington, IN, 1984), Chapter 2, "In the Wake of the Fall," and *Form and Substance in the Religions* (World Wisdom, Bloomington, IN, 2002), Chapter 5, "The Five Divine Presences."

[19] See Krasinsky, *Tibetische Medizin-Philosophie.*

In this story, the pictorial description of the subtle world must not be misunderstood. However, it is certain that the process of materialization, from the supra-sensory to the sensory, had to be reflected within the material or corporeal state itself, so that one can say without risk of error, that the first generations of a new species did not leave a mark in the great book of earthly layers; it is therefore vain to seek in sensible matter the ancestors of a species, and especially that of man.

Since the transformist theory is not founded on any real proof, its corollary and conclusion, namely the theory of the infra-human origin of man, remains suspended in the void. The facts adduced in favor of this thesis are restricted to a few groups of skeletons of disparate chronology: it happens that some skeletal types deemed to be more "evolved," such as "Steinheim man," precede others, of a seemingly more primitive character, such as "Neanderthal man," even though the latter was doubtless not so apelike as tendentious reconstructions would have us believe.[20]

If, instead of always putting the questions: at what point does humankind begin, and what is the degree of evolution of such and such a type regarded as being pre-human, we were to ask ourselves: how far does the monkey go, things might well appear in a very different light, for a fragment from a skeleton, even one related to that of man, is hardly enough to establish the presence of that which constitutes man, namely reason, whereas it is possible to conceive of a great variety of anthropoid apes whose anatomies are more or less close to that of man.

However paradoxical this may seem, the anatomical resemblance between man and the anthropoid apes is explainable precisely by the difference—not gradual, but essential—that separates man from all other animals. Since the anthropoid form is able to exist without that "central" element that characterizes man—this "central" element manifesting itself anatomically by his vertical position, amongst other things—the anthropoid form must exist; in other words, there cannot but be found, at the purely animal level, a form that realizes in its own way—that is to say, according to the laws of its own level—the very plan of the human anatomy; the ape

---

[20] In general, this domain of science has been almost smothered by tendentious theories, hoaxes, and imprudently popularized discoveries. See Dewar, *The Transformist Illusion.*

is a prefiguration of man, not in the sense of an evolutive phase, but by virtue of the law that decrees that at every level of existence analogous possibilities will be found.

A further question arises in the case of the fossils attributed to primitive men: did some of these skeletons belong to men we can look upon as being ancestors of men presently alive, or do they bear witness to a few groups that survived the cataclysm at the end of a terrestrial age, only to disappear in their turn before the beginning of our present humanity? Instead of primitive men, it might well be a case of degenerate men, who may or may not have existed alongside our real ancestors. We know that the folklore of most peoples speaks of giants or dwarfs who lived long ago, in remote countries; now, among these skeletons, several cases of gigantism are to be found.[21]

Finally, let it be recalled once more that the bodies of the most ancient men did not necessarily leave solid traces, either because their bodies were not yet at that point materialized or "solidified," or because the spiritual state of these men, along with the cosmic conditions of their time, rendered possible a resorption of the physical body into the subtle "body" at the moment of death.[22]

We must now say a few words about a thesis, much in vogue today, which claims to be something like a spiritual integration of paleontology, but which in reality is nothing but a purely mental sublimation of the crudest materialism, with all the prejudices this includes, from belief in the indefinite progress of humanity to a leveling and totalitarian collectivism, without forgetting the cult of the machine that is at the center of all this; it will be apparent that we are here referring to Teilhardian evolutionism.[23] According to

---

[21] Like the Meganthrope of Java and the *Gigantopithecus* of China.

[22] In some very exceptional cases—such as Enoch, Elijah, and the Virgin Mary—such a resorption took place even in the present terrestrial age.

[23] Teilhard's materialism is revealed in all its crudity, and all its perversity, when this philosopher advocates the use of surgical means to accelerate "collective cerebralization" in his *Man's Place in Nature* (Harper & Row, New York, 1966). Let us also quote the further highly revealing words of the same author: "It is finally on the dazzling notion of Progress and on faith in Progress that today's divided humanity can be reformed ... Act 1 is over! We have access to the heart of the atom! Now come the next steps, such as the vitalization of matter by the building of super-molecules, the modeling of the human organism by hormones, the control of heredity and of the sexes by the play of genes and chromosomes, the readjustment and liberation by direct action of the springs laid bare by psychoanalysis, the awakening and taking hold of the still dormant intellectual and emotional forces in the

Teilhard de Chardin, who is not given to worrying over the gaps inherent in the evolutionist system and largely relies on the climate created by the premature popularization of the transformist thesis, man himself represents only an intermediate state in an evolution that starts with unicellular organisms and ends in a sort of global cosmic entity, united to God. The craze for trying to bring everything back to a single unequivocal and uninterrupted genetic line here exceeds the material plane and launches out wildly into an irresponsible and avid "mentalization" characterized by an abstraction clothed in artificial images which their author ends up by taking literally, as if he were dealing with concrete realities. We have already mentioned the imaginary genealogical tree of species, whose supposed unity is no more than a snare, being composed of the hypothetical conjunction of many disjointed elements. Teilhard amplifies this notion to his heart's content, in a manner that is purely graphic, by completing its branches—or "scales," as he likes to call them—and by constructing a pinnacle in the direction of which humankind is supposed to be situated. By a similar sliding of thought from the abstract to the concrete, from the metaphorical to the supposedly real, he agglutinates, in one and the same pseudo-scientific outburst, the most diverse realities, such as mechanical laws, vital forces, psychic elements, and spiritual entities. Let us quote a characteristic passage:

> What explains the biological revolution caused by the appearance of Man, is an explosion of consciousness; and what, in its turn, explains this explosion of consciousness, is simply the passage of a privileged radius of "corpusculization," in other words, of a zoological phylum, across the surface, hitherto impermeable, separating the zone of direct Psychism from that of reflective Psychism. Having reached, following this particular radius, a critical point of arrangement (or, as we say here, of enrolment), Life became hypercentered on itself, to the point of becoming capable of foresight and invention ...[24]

human mass!" (*Planète III*, 1944), p. 30. Quite naturally, Teilhard proposes the fashioning of mankind by a universal scientific government—in short, all that is needed for the reign of the Antichrist. [Editor's Note: The reader is referred to Wolfgang Smith's *Teilhardism and the New Religion: A Thorough Analysis of the Teachings of Pierre Teilhard de Chardin* (Tan Books, Rockford, 1988), for a traditional critique of the views of the controversial Catholic priest and paleontologist.]

[24] *Man's Place in Nature*, pp. 62-63.

Thus, "corpusculization" (which is a physical process) would have as its effect that a "zoological phylum" (which is no more than a figure) should pass across the surface (purely hypothetical) separating two psychic zones ... But we must not be surprised at the absence of *distinguos* in Teilhard's thinking since, according to his own theory, the mind is but a metamorphosis of matter!

Without stopping to discuss the strange theology of this author, for whom God himself evolves along with matter, and without daring to define what he thinks of the prophets and sages of antiquity and other "underdeveloped" beings of this kind, we will say the following: if man, in respect of both his physical nature and his spiritual nature, were really nothing but a phase of an evolution going from the amoeba to the superman, how could he know objectively where he stands in all this? Let us suppose that this alleged evolution forms a curve, or a spiral. The man who is but a fragment thereof—and let it not be forgotten that a "fragment" of a movement is no more than a phase of that movement—can that man step out of it and say to himself: I am a fragment of a spiral which is developing in such and such a way? Now it is certain—and moreover Teilhard de Chardin himself recognizes this—that man is able to judge of his own state. Indeed he knows his own rank amongst the other earthly creatures, and he is even the only one to know objectively both himself and the world. Far from being a mere phase in an indefinite evolution, man essentially represents a central possibility, and one that is thus unique, irreplaceable, and definitive. If the human species had to evolve towards another more perfect and more "spiritual" form, man would not already now be the "point of intersection" of the Divine Spirit with the earthly plane; he would neither be capable of salvation, nor able intellectually to surmount the flux of becoming. To express these thoughts according to the perspective of the Gospels: would God have become man if the form of man were not virtually "god on earth," in other words, qualitatively central as well as definitive with regard to his own cosmic level?

As a symptom of our time, Teilhardism is comparable to one of those cracks that are due to the very solidification of the mental carapace,[25] and that do not open upward, toward the heaven of real

---

[25] René Guénon, *The Reign of Quantity and the Signs of the Times*, Chapter 15, "The Illusion of Ordinary Life."

and transcendent unity, but downward toward the realm of lower psychism. Weary of its own discontinuous vision of the world, the materialist mind lets itself slide toward a false continuity or unity, toward a pseudo-spiritual intoxication, of which this falsified and materialized faith—or this sublimated materialism—that we have just described marks a phase of particular significance.

Descartes' Angel:
Reflections on the True Art of Thinking*

Theodore Roszak

On the night of November 10, 1619, René Descartes, then an aspiring philosopher still in his early twenties, had a series of three dreams which changed the course of his life and of modern thought. He reports that in his sleep, the Angel of Truth appeared to him and, in a blinding revelation like a flash of lightning, revealed a secret which would "lay the foundations of a new method of understanding and a new and marvelous science." In the light of what the angel had told him, Descartes fervently set to work on an ambitious treatise called "Rules for the Direction of the Mind." The objective of his "new and marvelous science" was nothing less than to describe how the mind works. For Descartes, who was to invent analytical geometry, there was no question but that the model for this task was to be found in mathematics. There would be axioms ("clear and distinct ideas" that none could doubt) and, connecting the axioms in logical progressions, a finite number of simple, utterly sensible rules that were equally self-evident. The result would be an expanding body of knowledge.

Descartes never finished his treatise; the project was abandoned after the eighteenth rule—perhaps because it proved more difficult than he had anticipated. He did, however, eventually do justice to the angel's inspiration in the famous *Discourse on Method*, which is often taken to be the founding document of modern philosophy.[1] Descartes' project was the first of many similar attempts in the modern world to codify the laws of thought; almost all of them follow his lead in using mathematics as their model. In our day, the fields of artificial intelligence and cognitive science can be seen as part of this tradition, but now united with technology and centering upon

---

* Editor's Note: Chapter 10 of *The Cult of Information.*

[1] Jacques Maritain offers a lengthy analysis of Descartes' fateful dream in *The Dream of Descartes* (New York: Philosophical Library, 1944).

a physical mechanism—the computer—which supposedly embodies these laws.

The epistemological systems that have been developed since the time of Descartes have often been ingenious. They surely illuminate many aspects of the mind. But all of them are marked by the same curious fact. They leave out the Angel of Truth—as indeed Descartes himself did. For he never returned to the source of his inspiration. His writings spare no time for the role of dreams, revelations, insights as the wellsprings of thought. Instead, he gave all his attention to formal, logical procedures that supposedly begin with zero, from a position of radical doubt. This is a fateful oversight by the father of modern philosophy; it leaves out of account that aspect of thinking which makes it more an art than a science, let alone a technology: the moment of inspiration, the mysterious origin of ideas. No doubt Descartes himself would have been hard pressed to say by what door of the mind the angel had managed to enter his thoughts. Can any of us say where such flashes of intuition come from? They seem to arise unbidden from unconscious sources. We do not stitch them together piece by piece; rather, they arrive all at once and whole. If there are any rules we can follow for the generation of ideas, it may simply be to keep the mind open and receptive on all sides, to remain hospitable to the strange, the peripheral, the blurred, and fleeting that might otherwise pass unnoticed. We may not know how the mind creates or receives ideas, but without them—and especially what I have called the master ideas which embody great reserves of collective experience— our culture would be unimaginably meager. It is difficult to see how the mind could work at all if it did not have such grand conceptions as truth, goodness, beauty to light its way.

At the same time that Descartes was drafting his rules of thought, the English philosopher Francis Bacon was also in search of a radical new method of understanding. Bacon, who was a mathematical illiterate, preferred to stress the importance of observation and the accumulation of facts. He too was a man with a revolutionary vision—the intention of placing all learning on a new foundation of solid fact derived from the experimental "vexing" of nature. Before the seventeenth century was finished, these two philosophical currents—the Rationalism of Descartes, the Empiricism of Bacon—had formed a working alliance to produce the intellectual enterprise we call science: observation subjected to the discipline of an impersonal method designed to have all the logical rigor of mathematics. As Bacon once put it, if one has the right method, then "the mind itself" will "be guided at every step, and the business be done as if by machinery."

Since the days of Descartes and Bacon, science has grown robustly. Its methods have been debated, revised, and sharpened as they have thrust into new fields of study; the facts it has discovered mount by the day. But the angel who has fired the minds of great scientists with a vision of truth as bold as that of Descartes has rarely been given her due credit, and least of all by the computer scientists who seem convinced that they have at last invented Bacon's mental "machinery" and that it can match the achievements of its human original without the benefit of unaccountable revelations.

The gap that has so often been left by philosophers between the origin of ideas and the subsequent mechanics of thought—between the angel's word and the analytical processes that follow—simply reflects the difference between what the mind can and cannot understand about itself. We can self-consciously connect idea with idea, comparing and contrasting as we go, plotting out the course of a deductive sequence. But when we try to get behind the ideas to grasp the elusive interplay of experience, memory, insight that bubbles up into consciousness as a whole thought, we are apt to come away from the effort dizzy and confounded—as if we had tried to read a message that was traveling past us at blinding speed. Thinking up ideas is so spontaneous—one might almost say so instinctive—an action, that it defies capture and analysis. We cannot slow the mind down sufficiently to see the thing happening step by step. Picking our thoughts apart at this primitive, preconscious level is rather like one of those deliberately baffling exercises the Zen Buddhist masters use to dazzle the mind so that it may experience the unutterable void. When it comes to understanding where the mind gets its ideas, perhaps the best we can do is to say, with Descartes, "An angel told me." But then is there any need to go farther than this? Mentality is the gift of our human nature. We may use it, enjoy it, extend, and elaborate it without being able to explain it.

In any case, the fact that the origin of ideas is radically elusive does not mean we are licensed to ignore the importance of ideas and begin with whatever we *can* explain as if that were the whole answer to the age-old epistemological question with which philosophers have struggled for centuries. Yet that, I believe, is what the computer scientists do when they seek to use the computer to explain cognition, and intelligence.

The information processing model of thought, which has been the principal bone of contention in these pages, poses a certain striking paradox. On the basis of that model, we are told that thinking reduces to a matter of shuffling data through a few simple, formal procedures. Yet, when we seek to think in this "simple" way, it proves to be very demanding—as if we were forcing the mind to work against the grain. Take any commonplace routine of daily life—a minimal act of intelligence—and try to specify all its components in a logically tight sequence. Making breakfast, putting on one's clothes, going shopping. These common-sense projects have defied the best efforts of cognitive scientists to program them. Or take a more extraordinary (meaning less routine) activity: choosing a vocation in life, writing a play, a novel, a poem, or—as in Descartes' case—revolutionizing the foundations of thought. In each of these exercises, what we have first and foremost in mind is the whole, global project. We *will* to do it, and then—somehow, seemingly without thinking about it—we work through the matter step by step, improvising a countless series of subroutines that contribute to the project. Where something doesn't work or goes wrong, we adjust within the terms of the project. We understand projects: whole activities. They may be misconceived activities, but they are nevertheless the ends that must come before the means. When we get round to the means, we remain perfectly aware that these are subordinate matters. The surest way any project in life goes wrong is when we fixate on those subordinate matters and lose sight of the whole. Then we become like the proverbial centipede who, when he was asked to explain how he coordinated all his parts, discovered he was paralyzed.

What I am suggesting is that, in little things and big, the mind works more by way of gestalts than by algorithmic procedures. This is because our life as a whole is made up of a hierarchy of projects, some trivial and repetitive, some special and spectacular. The mind is naturally a spinner of projects, meaning it sets goals, choosing then from among all the things we might be doing with our lives. Pondering choices, making projects—these are the mind's first order of activity. This is so obvious, so basic, that perhaps we are only prompted to reflect upon it when a different idea about thinking is presented, such as that thought is connecting data points in formal sequences.

Now, of course, the mind takes things in as it goes along. We do register data. But we register information in highly selective ways within the terms of a project which, among other things, tells us which facts to pay attention to, which to ignore, which deserve the highest and which the lowest value. Thinking means—most significantly—forming projects and reflecting upon the values that the project involves. Many projects are simply given by the physical conditions of life: finding food, clothing the body, sheltering from the elements, securing help in time of danger. But all of us at least hope we will have the opportunity in life to function at a higher level than this, that we will spend as much of our time as possible beyond the level of necessity, pursuing what John Maynard Keynes once called "the art of life itself." Forming projects of this kind is the higher calling that comes with our human nature. Teaching the young how to honor and enjoy that gift is the whole meaning of education. That is surely not what we are doing when we load them down with information, or make them feel that collecting information is the main business of the mind. Nor do we teach them the art of life when we ask them "to think like a machine." Machines do not invent projects; they are invented by human beings to pursue projects. What Seymour Papert calls "procedural thinking" surely has its role to play in life; but its role is at the level of working out the route for a trip by the close study of a road map. It is an activity that comes into play only after we have chosen to make a journey and have selected a destination.

The substance of education in the early years is the learning of what I have called master ideas, the moral and metaphysical paradigms which lie at the heart of every culture. To choose a classic model in the history of Western pedagogy: in the ancient world, the Homeric epics (read or recited) were the texts from which children learned the values of their civilization. They learned from adventure tales and heroic exemplars which they could imitate by endless play in the roadways and fields. Every healthy culture puts its children through such a Homeric interlude when epic images, fairy tales, *chansons de geste*, Bible stories, fables, and legends summon the growing mind to high purpose. That interlude lays the foundations of thought. The "texts" need not be exclusively literary. They can be rituals—as in many tribal societies, where the myths are embodied in festive ceremonies. Or they may be works of art, like the stained glass windows and statuary of medieval churches. Master ideas may be taught in many modes. In our society, television and the movies are among the most powerful means of instruction, often to the point of eclipsing the lackluster materials presented in school. Unhappily, these major media are for the most part in the hands of commercial opportunists for whom nobility of purpose is usually nowhere in sight. At best, a few tawdry images of heroism and villainy may seep through to feed the hungry young mind. The rudiments of epic conduct can be found in a movie like *Star Wars*, but the imagery has been produced at a mediocre aesthetic and intellectual level, with more concern for "effects" than for character. At such hands, archetypes become stereotypes, and the great deeds done are skewed with an eye to merchandising as much of the work as possible.

Those cultures are blessed which can call upon Homer, or Biblical tales, or the Mahabharata to educate the young. Though the children's grasp of such literature may be simple and playful, they are in touch with material of high seriousness. From the heroic examples before them, they learn that growing up means making projects with full responsibility for one's choices. In short, taking charge of one's life in the presence of a noble standard. Young minds reach out for this guidance; they exercise their powers of imagination in working up fantasies of great quests, great battles, great deeds of cunning, daring, passion, sacrifice. They craft their identities to the patterns of gods and goddesses, kings and queens, warriors, hunters, saints, ideal types of mother and father, friend and neighbor. And perhaps some among them aspire to become the bards and artists of the new generation who will carry forward the ideals of their culture. Education begins with giving the mind images—not data points or machines—to think with.

There is a problem, however, about teaching children their culture's heroic values. Left in the hands of parents and teachers, but especially of the Church and the state where these institutions become dominant, ideals easily become forms of indoctrination. Idols of the tribe that can tyrannize the young mind. Heroism becomes chauvinism; high bright images become binding conventions. Master ideas are cheapened when they are placed in the keeping of small, timid minds that have grown away from their own childish exuberance.

In the hands of great artists like Homer, images never lose the redeeming complexity of real life. The heroes keep just enough of their human frailties to stay close to the flesh and blood. Achilles, the greatest warrior of them all, is nevertheless as vain and spoiled as a child, a tragically flawed figure. Odysseus can be more than a bit of a scoundrel, his "many devices" weakening toward simple piracy. It is the fullness of personality in these heroes that leaves their admirers balanced between adulation and uncertainty. The ideal has more than one side; the mind is nagged with the thought "yes, but ... " Where such truth to life is lost, the images become shallow; they can then be used to manipulate rather than inspire.

The Greeks, who raised their children on a diet of Homeric themes, also produced Socrates, the philosophical gadfly whose mission was to sting his city into thoughtfulness. "Know thyself," Socrates insisted to his students. But where else can self-knowledge begin but with the questioning of ancestral values, prescribed identities?

Here is the other significant use of ideas: to produce critical contrast and so to spark the mind to life. Homer offers towering examples of courage. Ah, but what is *true* courage? Socrates asks, offering other, conflicting images, some of which defy Homer. At once, idea is pitted against idea, and the students must make up their own minds, judge, and choose. Societies rarely honor their Socratic spirits. Athens, irritated beyond tolerance by his insistent criticism, sent its greatest philosopher to his death. Still, no educational theory that lacks such a Socratic counterpoint, can hope to free the young to think new thoughts, to become new people, and so to renew the culture.

In a time when our schools are filling up with advanced educational technology, it may seem almost perverse to go in search of educational ideals in ancient and primitive societies that had little else to teach with than word of mouth. But it may take that strong a contrast to stimulate a properly critical view of the computer's role in educating the young. At least it reminds us that all societies, modern and traditional, have had to decide *what* to teach their children before they could ask *how* to teach them. Content before means, the message before the medium.

The schooling of the young has always been a mixture of basic skills (whether literacy and ciphering or hunting and harvesting) and high ideals. Even if our society were to decide that computer literacy (let us hope in some well-considered sense of that much-confused term) should be included among the skills we teach in the schools, that would leave us with the ideals of life still to be taught. Most educators surely recognize that fact, treating the computer as primarily a means of instruction. What they may overlook is the way in which the computer brings with it a hidden curriculum that impinges upon the ideals they would teach. For this is indeed a powerful teaching tool, a smart machine that brings with it certain deep assumptions about the nature of mentality. Embodied in the machine there is an idea of what the mind is and how it works. The idea is there because scientists who purport to understand cognition and intelligence have put it there. No other teaching tool has ever brought intellectual luggage of so consequential a kind with it. A conception of mind—even if it is no better than a caricature—easily carries over into a prescription for character and value. When we grant anyone the power to teach us *how* to think, we may also be granting them the chance to teach us *what* to think, where to begin thinking, where to stop. At some level that underlies the texts and tests and lesson plans, education is an anatomy of the mind, its structure, its limits, its powers, and proper application.

The subliminal lesson that is being taught whenever the computer is used (unless a careful effort is made to offset that effect) is the data processing model of the mind. This model, as we have seen, connects with a major transition in our economic life, one that brings us to a new stage of high-tech industrialism, the so-called Information Age with its service-oriented economy. Behind that transition, powerful corporate interests are at work shaping a new social order. The government (especially the military) as a prime customer and user of information technology is allied to the corporations in building that order. Intertwined with both, a significant, well-financed segment of the technical and scientific community—the specialists in artificial intelligence and cognitive science—has lent the computer model of the mind the sanction of a deep metaphysical proposition. All these forces, aided by the persuasive skills of the advertisers, have fixed upon the computer as an educational instrument; the machine brings that formidable constellation of social interests to the classrooms and the campus. The more room and status it is given there by educators, the greater the influence those interests will have.

Yet these are the interests that are making the most questionable use of the computer. At their hands, this promising technology— itself a manifestation of prodigious human imagination and inventiveness—is being degraded into a means of surveillance and control, of financial and managerial centralization, of manipulating public opinion, of making war. The presence of personal computers in millions of homes, especially when they are used as little more than trivial amusements, does not in any meaningful way offset the power the machine brings to those who use it for these purposes.

Introducing students to the computer at an early age, creating the impression that their little exercises in programming and game playing are somehow giving them control over a powerful technology, can be a treacherous deception. It is not teaching them to think in some scientifically sound way; it is persuading them to acquiesce. It is accustoming them to the presence of computers in every walk of life, and thus making them dependent on the machine's supposed necessity and superiority. Under these circumstances, the best approach to computer literacy might be to stress the limitations and abuses of the machine, showing the students how little they need it to develop their autonomous powers of thought.

There may even be a sound ecological justification for such a curriculum. It can remind children of their connection with the lively world of nature that lies beyond the industrial environment of machines and cities. Sherry Turkle observes that, in times past, children learned their human nature in large measure by comparing themselves to the animals. Now, increasingly, "computers with their interactivity, their psychology, with whatever fragments of intelligence they have ... bid to take this place."[2] Yet it may mean far more at this juncture in history for children once again to find their kinship with the animals, every one of which, in its own inarticulate way, displays greater powers of mind than any computer can even mimic well. It would indeed be a loss if children failed to see in the nesting birds and the hunting cat an intelligence as well as a dignity that belongs to the line of evolutionary advance from which their own mind emerges. It is not the least educational virtue of the traditional lore and legends that so much of it belongs to the preindustrial era, when the realities of the nonhuman world were more vividly present.

[2] Sherry Turkle, *The Second Self,* p. 313.

How much ecological sense does it make to rush to close off what remains of that experience for children by thrusting still another mechanical device upon them?

There is a crucial early interval in the growth of young minds when they need the nourishment of value-bearing images and ideas, the sort of Homeric themes that open the adventure of life for them. They can wait indefinitely to learn as much as most schools will ever teach them about computers. The skills of unquestionable value which the technology makes available—word processing, rapid computation, data base searching—can certainly be saved for the later high school or even college years. But once young minds have missed the fairy tales, the epic stories, the myths, and legends, it is difficult to go back and recapture them with that fertile sense of naïve wonder that belongs to childhood. Similarly, if the taste for Socratic inquiry is not enlivened somewhere in the adolescent years, the growing mind may form habits of acquiescence that make it difficult to get out from under the dead hand of parental dominance and social authority.

As things now stand, there is a strong consensus abroad that our schools are doing a poor to mediocre job of laying these intellectual foundations. The reasons for the malaise of the schools are many. Teachers are often overworked and underappreciated; many students come to them bored, rebellious, distracted, or demoralized. Some of the children in our inner cities are too disadvantaged and harassed by necessity to summon up an educative sense of wonder; others may have been turned prematurely cynical by the corrupted values of commercialism and cheap celebrity; many, even the fortunate and affluent, may be haunted by the pervasive fear of thermonuclear extinction that blights all our lives. The schools share and reflect all these troubles; perhaps, at times, the troubles overwhelm the best efforts of the best teachers, driving them back to a narrow focus on basic skills, job training, and competitive grading. But it is at least worth something to know where the big problems lie and to know there is no quick technological fix for them. Computers, even when we reach the point of having one on every desk for every student, will provide no cure for ills that are social and political in nature.

It may seem that the position I take here about the educational limits of the computer finishes with being a humanist's conservative appeal in behalf of the arts and letters. It is that. Scientists and technicians, whose professional interests tend to make them computer enthusiasts, may therefore see little room for their values in the sort of pedagogy I recommend. But as the story of Descartes' angel should remind us, science and technology at their highest creative level are no less connected with ideas, with imagination, with vision. They draw upon all the same resources of the mind, both the Homeric and the Socratic, as the arts and letters. We do not go far wrong from the viewpoint of any discipline by the general cultivation of the mind. The master ideas belong to every field of thought. It would surely be a sad mistake to intrude some small number of pedestrian computer skills upon the education of the young in ways that blocked out the inventive powers that created this astonishing technology in the first place. And what do we gain from any point of view by convincing children that their minds are inferior to a machine that dumbly mimics a mere fraction of their native talents?

In the education of the young, humanists and scientists share a common cause in resisting any theory that cheapens thought. That is what the data processing model does by closing itself to that quality of the mind which so many philosophers, prophets, and artists have dared to regard as godlike: its inexhaustible potentiality. In their search for "effective procedures" that can be universally applied to all aspects of culture, experts in artificial intelligence and cognitive science are forced to insist that there is nothing more to thought than a conventional mechanistic analysis will discover: data points shuffled through a small repertory of algorithms. In contrast, my argument in these pages has been that the mind thinks, not with data, but with ideas whose creation and elaboration cannot be reduced to a set of predictable rules. When we usher children into the realm of ideas, we bring them the gift of intellectual adventure. They begin to sense the dimensions of thought and the possibilities of original insight. Whether they take the form of words, images, numbers, gestures, ideas unfold. They reveal rooms within rooms within rooms, a constant opening out into larger, unexpected worlds of speculation.

The art of thinking is grounded in the mind's astonishing capacity to create beyond what it intends, beyond what it can foresee. We cannot begin to shape that capacity toward humane ends and to guard it from demonic misuse until we have first experienced the true size of the mind.

Putting Nature in Her Place[*]

Mary Midgley

Wonder—The Mechanist Attack

To return, then to the contemplative tradition—was Aristotle right to encourage wonder, awe, and reverence towards the physical world? It is one of the points that the founders of modern science held against him. Thus Descartes wrote, "Know that by nature I do not mean some goddess or some sort of imaginary power. I employ this word to signify matter itself."[1] Similarly, Robert Boyle, in his *Enquiry into the Vulgarly Received Notion of Nature*, complained that "men are taught and wont to attribute stupendous unaccountable effects to sympathy, antipathy, *fuga vacui*, substantial forms, and especially to a certain being ... which they call Nature; for this is represented as a kind of goddess, whose power may be little less than boundless."[2] Accordingly, Boyle complained, "the veneration wherewith men are imbued for what they call nature, has been a discouraging impediment to the empire of man over the inferior creatures of God."[3]

This was an important element in the new notion then being forged of what it was to be scientific. With a similar disapproval of wonder, Descartes earlier expressed the hope "that those who have understood all that has been said in this treatise will, in future, *see nothing whose cause they cannot easily understand, nor anything that gives them any reason to marvel.*"[4] Wonder itself was to cease. Explanations

[*] Editor's Note: Chapter 7 of *Science as Salvation*.

[1] Descartes, *Le Monde*, in *Oeuvres philosophiques de Descartes*, ed. F. Alqui (Paris: Gamier Frères, 1973), vol. 1, p. 349. Quoted by Brian Easlea, *Science and Sexual Oppression* (London: Weidenfeld & Nicolson, 1981), p. 72.

[2] *The Works of the Honorable Robert Boyle*, ed. T. Birch (London, 1722), vol. 5, p. 532. Quoted by Brian Easlea, *Witch-Hunting, Magic, and the New Philosophy: An Introduction to the Debates of the Scientific Revolution* (Brighton: Harvester Press, 1980), p. 138.

[3] *Works*, vol. 5, p. 165. Quoted by Easlea, *Witch-Hunting*, p. 139.

[4] *Descartes on Method, Optics, Geometry, and Meteorology*, trans. P.J. Olscamp (Bobbs-Merrill, 1965), p. 361. Quoted by Easlea, *Witch-Hunting*, p. 117.

were to become so clear that there was to be no more mystery. Not only would everything on earth now be understood, it would also be demythologized—disenchanted—depersonified and seen, in the bleakest of daylight, as not specially impressive after all. Matter, fully debunked, was from now on to be recognized as what the New Philosophy declared it to be—mere inert, passive, mindless stuff, devoid of spontaneity, of all interesting properties such as sympathy and antipathy, and above all destitute of any creative power. All pleasing forms that might seem to belong to matter were to be credited, not to it, but directly to God the Creator.

God, seen as fully active and fully intellectual, was the beneficiary now credited with these powers, reft from Nature. Having intelligence as well as creative power, God could do directly—either at the moment of creation or through later miracles—all that had been previously thought to need special adaptations in matter itself. And that is what the men who founded the Royal Society (by and large) took him to do.

It is surely extraordinary that nineteenth and twentieth century thinkers have supposed that they could take over this attitude to matter unaltered, while eliminating the omnipotent Creator who gave sense to it, as well as the immortal soul which took its status from him. The metaphor of matter as machinery still continues to run around like a chicken with its head off, though the Designer who gave a sense to it has been removed.

Peter Atkins, echoing Monod, rejoices that "the Creator had absolutely no job to do" and "can be allowed to evaporate and disappear from the scene."[5] To make sure of that, it would be necessary both to understand much better what is involved in the idea of creation and to abolish the impoverished seventeenth-century ideas about mind and matter with a thoroughness that Atkins does not begin to conceive of. Before starting to raise any questions about a creating God, we need to make room for the creative powers of matter, to recognize once more the complexity of nature. The pre-adaptations that made life a possible option must, after all, still be lodged somewhere.

---

[5] Peter Atkins, *The Creation* (Oxford and San Francisco: W.H. Freeman, 1987), p. 17.

Nature and Her Tormentors

What went wrong? It may be easier to see that if we notice the way in which the pioneers of mechanism went about reshaping the concept of Nature. Very properly, they wanted to try the experiment of depersonalizing it. With that in view, the first step they surely needed to take was to stop using the feminine pronoun, or indeed any personal pronoun for "Nature" altogether. But this was not done. We come here to one more of the strange compensatory myths, dreams, or dramas that are my theme. The literature of early modern science is a mine of highly-colored passages that describe Nature, by no means as a neutral object, but as a seductive but troublesome female, to be unrelentingly pursued, sought out, fought against, chased into her inmost sanctuaries, prevented from escaping, persistently courted, wooed, harried, vexed, tormented, unveiled, unrobed, and "put to the question" (i.e., interrogated under torture), forced to confess "all that lay in her most intimate recesses," her "beautiful bosom" must be laid bare, she must be held down and finally "penetrated," "pierced," and "vanquished" (words which constantly recur).

Now this odd talk does not come just from a few exceptionally uninhibited writers. It has not been invented by modern feminists. It is the common, constant idiom of the age. Since historians began to notice it, they have been able to collect it up easily in handfuls for every discussion. I can't spend time on doing that here, but I will just give briefly a few well-known examples from Francis Bacon, who was something of a trail-blazer in the matter.

Bacon dismissed the Aristotelians as people who had stood impotent before Nature, destined "never to lay hold of her and capture her." Aristotle (said Bacon), being a mere contemplative, had "left Nature herself untouched and inviolate." By contrast, Bacon called upon the "true sons of knowledge" to "penetrate further" and to "overcome Nature in action," so that "passing by the outer courts of nature, which many have trodden, we may find a way at length into her inner chambers." Mankind would then be able, not just to "exert a gentle guidance over Nature's course," but to "conquer and subdue nature, to shake her to her foundations" and to "discover the secrets still locked in Nature's bosom." Men (Bacon added) ought to make peace among themselves so as to turn "with united forces against the Nature of Things, to storm and occupy her castles and strongholds." By these means scientists would bring about the "truly masculine birth of time" by which they would subdue "Nature with all her children, to bind her to your service and make her your slave."[6]

Just to show that this way of talking did not die with the crude manners of the seventeenth century, here are a couple of later echoes from Adam Sedgwick, that immensely respectable clerical professor of geology at Cambridge who was so disturbed by Darwin's theories. Sedgwick, describing true scientific method, explained how, after laws have been carefully formulated, investigators must always "again put nature to the torture and wring new secrets from her."[7] And, shifting to the military end of the spectrum, Sedgwick also described Newton as having "stormed the sky with mathematical artillery."[8]

The Cleansing Fire

As I say, these quotations are not exceptional. If we were just looking for absurdities, and trying to show the failure of the impersonal stance, we could spend many instructive hours sifting a crowd of still more picturesque examples. But the point is, of course, not just to collect them but to understand what is going on. In real life, most of these distinguished scholars were neither sex-maniacs nor soldiers sacking a city. Most of them, probably, would not normally have hurt a fly. Why, then, did they continually use this kind of language? Three explanations suggest themselves, one to be rejected, two to be seriously considered.

1. (Negative) They were *not* just exceptionally naïve. All ages, including our own, are naïve in their own way. Past errors only differ from present ones in being easier to see.

2. (Positive) They were trying to develop the very peculiar idea of matter as wholly inert, passive, and unproductive, without any

---

[6] B. Farrington, *The Philosophy of Francis Bacon* (Liverpool University Press, 1970), pp. 93, 92, 96, 92, 62.

[7] Adam Sedgwick, "Vestiges of the Natural History of Creation," *Edinburgh Review* 82 (1845): 16. Quoted by Easlea, *Science and Sexual Oppression*, p. 103.

[8] Sedgwick, "Vestiges," p. 23.

spontaneity or interesting qualities. This idea was far more entangled in traditional gender symbolism than they realized, because earlier, Aristotelian science—most bizarrely—deemed women also to be essentially inert, passive, and unproductive, mere vehicles for reproduction. As a piece of science, this notion of matter has gradually been shown up as inadequate and misleading by the later developments in physics. But as a drama, it has had enormous power, and derivatives of it still have a strong confusing influence, both in scientific and in everyday thinking. They are involved in most of the strange later fantasies we shall be looking at. So this is a point which still concerns us.

3. (Also positive) Besides this unsatisfactory doctrine about matter itself, and the gender symbolism, further trouble was introduced by the destructive gusto that, from the start, went with it. Wanting to emphasize experiment, the pioneers of modern science had an image of themselves which differed from most earlier images of learning in being more workmanlike, more suggestive of physical violence. This physicality, together with the fact that they really did want to make big changes, led them to revel in drastic language.

No doubt scholars proposing new schemes always have slashed at existing ones. But there really was a crucial shift of emphasis in the early Enlightenment towards making this destructive cutting and slashing central, and towards seeing the gusto that goes with it as a central motive for science. It began to seem that a scientist is typically a destroyer, one who sweeps away existing superstitions, rather than one who works to construct further on existing foundations. And among these superstitions, the former idea of Nature seemed an obvious target.

The difficulty about this destructive approach is of course how to keep some discrimination about what to destroy. Not all destruction is helpful. Almost any destructive move involves a positive one as well, and the gratifying sense that one has killed something bad can distract attention from the details of what one is promoting instead. Mechanistic seventeenth century scientists displayed a new purifying zeal, a passion for disinfection, at times a cognitive washing-compulsion, accompanied by a rather touching willingness to accept even a minor role in the great cleansing process. And these too came to be seen as essential to science.

The impersonality aimed at in modern science did indeed find its place here. Bacon said that experimental philosophy "goes far to level men's wits"[9] because it "performs everything by surest rules and demonstrations." Since anyone can scrub, scientists might offer themselves as humble fellow-workers without seeming to assume any pretentious role reminiscent of earlier sages, and without being held responsible for the main planning of the building. Thus Henry Power, celebrating the Royal Society in 1664, cried out:

> Methinks I see how all the old Rubbish must be thrown away, and the rotten Buildings be overthrown, and carried away with so powerful an inundation. These are the days that must lay a new Foundation of a more magnificent Philosophy, never to be overthrown ... a true and permanent Philosophy.[10]

John Locke showed the same spring-cleaning spirit in the famous Introduction to his *Essay on Human Understanding*:

> The commonwealth of learning is not at this time without masterbuilders, whose mighty designs in advancing the sciences will leave lasting monuments to the admiration of posterity. Everyone must not hope to be a Boyle or a Sydenham, and in an age that produces such masters as the great Huygenius and the incomparable Mr. Newton, with some other of that strain, it is ambition enough to be employed as an under-laborer in clearing the ground a little, and removing some of the rubbish that lies in the way of knowledge.[11]

It is tempting to set Locke's lively picture beside a less cheerful view of the academic building-site, as Conrad Waddington saw it three centuries later:

> Scientists have tended to refuse to see the wood for the trees. There have been an army of bricklayers piling brick on brick, even plumbers setting up super WCs, and heating and lighting engi-

---

[9] Francis Bacon, *Novum Organum*, vol. 4, p. 109. Quoted by Easlea, *Witch-Hunting*, p. 128.

[10] *Experimental Philosophy* , intro. M. Boas Hall (1664; reprint, London: Johnson Reprint, 1966), p. 192.

[11] "Epistle to the Reader," penultimate paragraph.

neers installing the most modern equipment; but they have all united to shoo the architect off the building site, and the edifice of knowledge is growing like a factory with a furnace too big for its boilers, its precision tools installed in a room with no lighting, and anyhow with no one who knows what it is supposed to manufacture.[12]

This situation might, of course, have something to do with the modest tendency, which Locke praised, to leave other people to take the big decisions, including the decision about what counts as rubbish to be carted away. Unfortunately, as things turned out, none of the great architects Locke named did come up with a comprehensive plan for science. And there is growing evidence that Newton, had he been asked to do so, would have produced a plan centering the edifice on alchemy ... In any case, however, it is doubtful policy to romanticize the destructive emphasis as Locke and his friends did—to cultivate the pugnacious zest that accompanies a release from positive choice.

Scientists Embattled

What, then, was all this destructiveness directed against? It is evident that, at this point, there did develop a sense of real alarm and disgust—a resolve to *écraser l'infâme*—directed against earlier views which were seen, not just as mistaken, but as odious because religiously wrong—as pagan and superstitious.

The campaign waged by members of the Royal Society, and by seventeenth-century mechanists generally, was not, as their atheistical successors often suppose, a campaign against religion as such. It was primarily a campaign against the *wrong* religion—against what seemed like nature-worship, against a religion centering on the earth, and apparently acknowledging a mysterious pagan goddess rather than an intellectual god. All the great scientific pioneers claimed to be campaigning on behalf of Christianity. And with most of them this was not just a political move—as again people now tend to think—but a matter of real conviction.

---

[12] C.H. Waddington, *The Scientific Attitude* (West Drayton: Penguin, 1941), p. 80.

Nor was the fight only against Aristotelian thinking. Aristotelianism was indeed the traditional orthodoxy that all scientific reformers wanted to change. But the contest was three-cornered, and the most bitter hostility was between two parties of reformers—between the mechanists, represented by Descartes, and the exponents of what was called "natural magic." This was a belief in an all-pervading system of occult forces, of mysterious sympathies and antipathies, the sort of thing that we do indeed now tend to think of as superstitious.

It was, however, by no means just a hole-and-corner affair used by sorcerers. It was a sophisticated system expounded by scientists, some of whom were not in any ordinary sense magicians at all, but were quite as learned, quite as experimental, and often quite as successful, as the mechanists. The contest was not a simple one between light and darkness.

Thus, Galileo in his *Dialogue* wrote with great respect of William Gilbert's book *De Magnete* (1600), accepting Gilbert's findings about magnets, though he differed from him about how to interpret them. Gilbert had attacked Aristotle for dividing the cosmos into a divine realm in the heavens and an inferior one on the earth, because this view dishonored the earth. The earth, wrote Gilbert, is not to be "condemned and driven into exile and cast out of all the fair order of the glorious universe, as being brute and soulless." "As for us," he continues, "we deem the whole world animate and all globes, all stars, and this glorious earth too, we hold to be from the beginning by their own destinate souls governed."[13]

Gilbert and Galileo thus both wanted to bring attitudes to the earth and heavens together again. But Galileo saw this as best achieved by withdrawing superstitious reverence from the heavens while exalting the earth. "We shall prove the earth to be a wandering body surpassing the moon in splendor, and not the sink of all dull refuse of the universe."[14] Gilbert, by contrast, proposed to do it by extending reverence to earth as well as heaven, by looking for

[13] William Gilbert, *De Magnete* (New York: Dover Publications, 1968), p. 309. Quoted by Easlea, *Witch-Hunting*, p. 91.

[14] Quoted in R. Dugas and P. Costable, "The Birth of a New Science, Mechanics," in *The Beginning of Modern Science*, ed. R. Taton (London: Thames & Hudson, 1964), p. 265.

explanations of its behavior in its own creative properties, and by the very significant image of the earth as mother. Gilbert wrote that all material things have "a propensity ... towards a common source, towards the mother where they were begotten."[15]

In some contexts, these ideas proved surprisingly useful for science. For instance, Gilbert argued that tides are produced by the attraction of the moon, working through sympathy. Johannes Kepler, accepting this idea, added that this was only part of a general system of attraction which explains all "heaviness (or gravity)." Heaviness, said Kepler, is simply a "mutual corporeal disposition between related bodies towards union or conjunction ... so that it is much rather the case that the earth attracts a stone than that the stone seeks the earth." Kepler suggested that the moon's attraction is what produces the tides, and he added, "If the earth should cease to attract its oceans, the waters in all its seas would fly up and flow round the body of the moon."[16] Kepler built this idea into his refinement of the Copernican system, by which he produced tables of the planetary motions which were some fifty to a hundred times more accurate than existing tables.

To us, who are used to Newton, all this seems reasonable enough, and Kepler may sound like a typical pioneer of modern science. But this is where our foundation-myths are so misleading. At the time, the mechanistic scientists who fill the rest of our pantheon rejected Kepler's view fiercely as superstitious. In particular Galileo, who might have been expected to welcome Kepler's support for the Copernican system, simply ignored it. The trouble was that, in the mechanists' view, "attraction" was no real explanation at all. It was just an unintelligible, vacuous name for an "occult force."

To mechanists, no explanation counted as intelligible unless it worked on the familiar model of push-pull, like the parts of the cog-driven machines with which they were familiar. Now it is hopelessly difficult to explain in this kind of way the well-known fact that things fall, or indeed how things stick together in the first place— how the hard particles, whose motion leads them only to bang

---

[15] *New Philosophy of Our Sublunary World,* quoted in P. Duhem, *The Aim and Structure of Physical Theory,* trans. P.P. Wiener (London: Athenaeum, 1962), p. 230.

[16] Kepler, "*Astronomia Nova,*" trans. A.R. Hall, in *Nature and Nature's Laws,* ed. M. Boas (New York: Harper, 1970), p. 73.

against each other, sometimes form solid stones rather than heaps of dust. Attraction was suggested here too, but it was still viewed as a vacuous superstition.

The mechanistic systems most widely favored, such as Descartes' theory of vortices, had no explanation for either of these things that looked even faintly plausible. In spite of this, not only was Kepler laughed out of court, but the same objection still told very strongly later against Newton. His theory of gravitation was resisted as empty and irrational well into the eighteenth century. As late as 1747, three most distinguished French scientists—Euler, Clairaut and d'Alembert—claimed to have disproved Newton's theory of gravitation, and it was some time before the resulting controversy was settled in his favor.

NEVER SAY DIE ... WITHOUT A CAUSE

Brian Coman

> The days of our years are threescore years and ten; and if by reason of strength they be fourscore years, yet is their strength labor and sorrow; for it is soon cut off, and we fly away.
> —Psalm 90:10

> Death is nature's way of telling us to slow down.
> —Anon.

In one of his shorter pieces, Jorge Luis Borges gives us an outline for a story he never wrote. That story outline concerns a young man called "Funes the Memorious." Funes dies young. He is a bit strange. He spends most of his short life in his bed just staring into space. At his wake, a few people begin to discuss his life. One of them suggests a startling reason for Funes' seeming lack of interest in the world when he was alive. Funes had perfect and unlimited memory. He could follow events or sensations back through the whole chain of causes so that when he saw a glass of wine on the table, his mind could recall the grapes, the vineyard, and the smell and texture of the soil where those vines were growing. He did not need continual sensory inputs and experiences like the rest of us do. I know why Borges never wrote the full story. It would not have been about a man called Funes at all, it would have been about God. And let's face it, people expect omniscience of God. The story would have been "old hat." In any case, I'm not sure that Borges believed in God.

I have a similar proposal for a story I will not write. It's about a very old man and it's called "O'Leary the Unclassified." O'Leary is a hermit, the last of the Australian swagmen. He is found dead in a shearers' hut. There are no records—no birth certificate, driver's license, or social security card. Even Diners Club International has no credit rating for him in its computers. No one can even be certain that O'Leary is his real name. That represents the first problem for the authorities. But things get worse. When an autopsy is carried out, the medicos can find no identifiable cause of death. There is no cancer, no signs of heart failure, or kidney failure. What can they put on the death certificate under "cause of death"? The awful truth dawns upon them. O'Leary simply died of old age. He just "wore out" and everything deteriorated at the same rate. His death is unclassifiable for he fits none of the allowed categories. He represents the statistician's ultimate nightmare.

Now, like the Borges story, mine is necessarily fictitious. There could be no O'Leary any more than there could be a Funes. Everyone today dies of some malady or malfunction; you cannot die of old age. Did I not read that the Queen Mother was weakened by a viral infection just before her death? But my story differs from that of Borges in this respect: his story would strike us as highly improbable in any age, past, present, or future, whereas my story would not have raised a single eyebrow as recently as a century ago. Back then, many people did die of old age—if not in the eyes of the medical profession of the day, then certainly in the eyes of ordinary people. There are two ways of reading those lines of Goldsmith:

> The doctors found, when she was dead—
> Her last disorder mortal.
> > (*Elegy on Mrs. Mary Blaize*)

What has changed in the last hundred years such that this category of death should have disappeared? The obvious answer is that advances in medical science have made the difference. That, of course, is true. But it is not the whole story. Implicit in the idea that every death is due to some identifiable malady or organ failure is the notion, at least in theory, that such an outcome is preventable. And from that comes the corollary that death can be postponed indefinitely. A couple of years ago one could see large, government-sponsored posters on city billboards which depicted (if I remember correctly) an "older person" in a tracksuit and runners. The caption read, "If old age is catching up, walk a little faster." The implication is pretty clear. And, of course, every other day there are television news bulletins which inform us that some new miracle cure for … [*insert rare disease here*] is just around the corner. Alas, most of these cures seem to sink without trace but, doubtless, not before the particular research institute involved has secured its funding for another year. We take it for granted that, one by one, these diseases will be overcome, just as smallpox and polio were. The men and women in the white coats are systematically denying the Grim Reaper access to his traditional tools and the day is not far off when the poor old beggar will be forced to hang up his scythe and join the dole queue. To put the matter another way, you get a distinct impression that parts of the health industry are not seeking a cure for illnesses but a cure for death itself.

It's fair to ask just how far we want to take this business. Are we going to be satisfied, some time in the future, when average life expectancy in the "developed" countries of the West is 100 years, or 120 years, or ... what? At what stage might we turn our attention away from ourselves and begin to look at the appalling conditions of life in many other countries? We apply the strict business principles of cost-benefit analysis to everything except human charity.

Aldous Huxley once said that death was the only thing that we haven't succeeded in completely vulgarizing (*Eyeless in Gaza*). He was wrong of course, but we ought to remember that he wrote those words before the world knew the full extent of Hitler's (and Stalin's) death camps. But we might have expected him to lob onto the *scientific* as distinct from the *organizational* vulgarization of death. He may have correctly presaged the scientific vulgarization of birth in *Brave New World*—growing embryos for spare parts is already possible and the technology needed to produce beta-minuses may be just around the corner—but he missed out completely on Robert C.W. Ettinger and his Cryonics Institute. The said institute, situated in Clinton, Missouri, offers "careful preparation, cooling, and long term patient [read cadaver] care in liquid nitrogen." All this for a one-time fee of twenty eight thousand American bucks, or thirty five thousand if you did not sign up beforehand. How you sign up afterwards is not explained. It's peanuts when you think about the benefits—"the sure and certain hope of the resurrection" as the good book says.

Ettinger is the author of two modestly titled books, *The Prospect of Immortality* and *Man into Superman*. The first-named, at least, is a bestseller. It has gone through several editions and has been published in several languages. The Cryonics Institute also has a website and I was visitor number 87059. Information is available in French, German, Italian, Portuguese, and Spanish. There is clearly a good deal of interest in the prospect of immortal life, at least of the particular type offered by Ettinger. I hasten to add that Ettinger's outfit is by no means the only one in existence. There are many others. I recall a news item some time ago reporting an unfortunate melt-down during a power failure at one such establishment. Very possibly, they purchased their electricity from Enron. The Cryonics Institute, though, claims to be a cut above the rest. They combine "the most affordable prices available anywhere" with "rapid on-the-spot care" and with "stability, safety, and security." "But please," they say, "don't wait too long. That can be fatal, and often has been." Well, I won't argue there. Death does tend to be fatal.

You can avail yourself of the services of the Cryonics Institute even if you fall off the twig in Europe (for rather obvious reasons, the word "die" cannot be used). F.A. Albin & Sons, London-based funeral directors, "are trained, practiced, equipped, and prepared to fly a team anywhere in Europe on short notice to help members or tourists and business travelers." It reminds me of a motto that my father proposed for the local undertaker in our town—"You die, we do the rest"! I am told that, just before her death in 1996, Jessica Mitford updated and republished her classic exposé of the American funeral industry in *The American Way of Death Revisited*. As far as I am aware though, the freezer people are not included. Their infant industry was still out in the cold, so to speak.

Before you dismiss these people as cranks, consider some comparable show starting up twenty-five years ago, say, with the aim of cloning humans or raising human embryos for cellular "spare parts." We would have laughed them out of court. I can remember solemn, scientific voices at the time: "look, that sort of thing is simply not possible. We are not mad scientists. We simply want to find a cure for … [*insert favorite disease here*]." Remember what they said about *in vitro* fertilization? The same solemn voices earnestly pleaded to be allowed to cure infertility in childless, married couples. Now we are debating whether lesbian couples should be denied the fruits of science, and there are frequent reports of court actions as surrogate mothers attempt to claim back children raised in their womb but "belonging" to some other couple. The whole thing is a legal and ethical nightmare.

It is unfortunate that those who are uneasy about issues like cloning, embryo harvesting, and human genetic engineering should have their arguments bundled under that phrase "slippery slope." It implies that once you take the first step down the slope, the rest will follow automatically and at an ever-increasing speed. It would be much more realistic if we replaced "slippery slope" with "high mountain." At the moment, the Cryonics Institute is perched atop Mount Impossible. Our current-day laboratory Strangeloves are far below at some base camp. They have no intention of climbing up to the top. They believe such a target to be both unrealistic and unpopular with the punters. They merely wish to reach the next staging camp where another research challenge can be ticked off the list. And when they get to that campsite, they will then set their sights on the next, and so on. They have to climb because that is the job we have given them. If they decide to plant the flag on some lesser peak and pull out, then the research grants dry up, the media camp followers desert them, and a once admiring public now ignores them. So, on they toil. One day, to their genuine surprise they will meet Mr. Ettinger and his frozen cadavers. And, make no mistake, he will be overjoyed. He has been waiting a long time for the gifts they bear.

As I write these words the TV in the next room brings news of the latest euthanasia case. The person in question—in a televised audience just before death—appears before the cameras and talks lucidly about her intentions to end a life which no longer has any hope. Twenty odd people are invited along for the death ceremony. I make the following prediction in all sincerity: if the pro-euthanasia people get their wish and euthanasia is legalized, then within a few years you will see it all on Big Brother or some similar show. It's the only place that "Reality TV" can go to maintain the ratings. As the Romans found out, bread and circuses just won't last the distance, you need blood. Nothing will draw them like a real-time snuff movie. What a mad world this is! Some people seeking approval of the law so that they might kill themselves or kill others and, at the other end, some people seeking to live the human life forever. Some lines of A.H. Clough come to mind:

> Thou shalt not kill; but needst not strive
> Officiously to keep alive.

The Cryonics Institute is just one of many manifestations of what the British philosopher, Mary Midgley, calls "science as salvation."[1] In a book of this title she puts the view that this so-called "post Christian era" in the West has not done away with the religious idea of salvation, it has merely transported that idea across to science. Midgley had detected, in her reading of the "popular" books on science, "a smell of incense and hymn books rather than of the laboratory." Salvation by freezer is just one modern manifestation of this sort of outrageous scientism. And because scientism is a pseudo-religion, certain of its followers tend towards the same fanaticism that can be found in some other religious sects. They demand total loyalty to their creed. That is why, when some people recently expressed their disapproval of embryonic stem cell research, one prominent researcher referred to them as "the Australian Taliban."

In fact, the crazy thing about the immortalists is not their religious faith in scientific technology and infinite progress. Some variant of their mad program may indeed come to pass in the manner I have suggested above. The crazy thing is their notion that living forever will bring some happiness or contentment to those thawed cadavers—heaven on earth. It is their supposition that infinite time and eternity are the same thing. But living forever in this world of space and time is not the same as living in eternity which is outside time. There can be no more terrible punishment than that of temporal immortality. Tennyson's *Tithonus* bears witness to it:

> The woods decay, the woods decay and fall,
> The vapors weep their burthen to the ground,
> Man comes and tills the field and lies beneath,
> And after many a summer dies the swan.
> Me only cruel immortality
> Consumes: I wither slowly in thine arms,
> Here at the quiet limit of the world,
> A white-hair'd shadow roaming like a dream
> The ever silent spaces of the East,
> Far-folded mists, and gleaming halls of morn.

I can see those poor survivors from the Cryonics Institute, fitted out with their bionic hands and plastic pudenda, forever roaming "at the quiet limit of the world"—tired of living but scared of dying. To them alone will heaven be denied as an option. Indeed, they will make their hell on earth. And none of Dante's wildest visions could approach its horror.

---

[1] Editor's Note: See her article in this volume entitled, "Nature in Her Place."

5

The Destruction of
Traditional Cultures

As on a gigantically raised stage we witness the
struggle between two worlds, which may be
interpreted, according to the standpoint of the
spectator, either as the struggle between the
past and the future, between backwardness and
progress, belief and science, superstition and
knowledge—or as the struggle between spiritual freedom and material power, between the wisdom of the heart and the knowledge of the
brain, between the dignity of the human individual and the herd-instinct of the mass,
between faith in the higher destiny of man
through inner development and the belief in
material prosperity through an ever-increasing
production of goods.

ANAGARIKA GOVINDA

MAKE YOUR CHOICE*

Thomas Yellowtail

In the olden-days the Indians had their freedom and they followed their traditional ways. Then the whites made us settle on reservations. People had to live close together and we were not free to live in our traditional way. People also lost sight of the true meaning of these ways. It was not long until a lot of the powers and sacred things that had been given to the Indians were taken back. That is what we were told by prophecies before the time of settlement on the reservations. Many medicine men who had had good medicine, good powers, lost them. This all happened gradually over the last one hundred years, until today there are fewer men with less spiritual power and understanding. Those who still have spiritual gifts or medicine—and there are a few left—don't have as strong a power as in the days when the Indians were still free to roam the country and live in the traditional manner. As time went on, the Indians became more "civilized" and learned to live in the white man's ways, and so all of the spiritual powers were diminished. People lost sight of religion and prayer, so it seems that the old prophecies were correct. Back in the days when we were free, when our people knew more about Nature and important things, almost every man had medicine powers and the only life people knew was centered on the sacred. The real medicine man could do wonders in those days. It is really the modern world and "civilization" that is causing us to lose all these things. In olden times, the people had their values centered on spiritual concerns. The spiritual Powers, the givers of medicines, are taking those sacred things back from us because we do not know how to care for them correctly.

Modern Indians care little for spiritual things and traditional ways, so there are very few traditional people remaining with real medicine or understanding. Modern civilization has no understanding of sacred matters. Everything is backwards. This makes it even more important that young people follow what is left today.

---

* Editor's Note: compiled and edited by Michael Fitzgerald.

Even though many of the sacred ways are no longer with us, what we have left is enough for anyone, and if it is followed it will lead as far as the person can go. The four rites that we have left form the center of the religion: the sweat lodge for purification; the vision quest for the spiritual retreat; the daily prayer with the offering of tobacco smoke; and the Sun Dance itself.[1] With all this, any sincere person can realize his inner spiritual center.

It is important that the young people understand the difference between the traditional ways and the modern world we live in today. I have spoken before about the sacred support that was always present for the traditional Indians. With this support everywhere, from the moment you arose and said your first prayer, until the moment you went to sleep, you could at least see what was necessary in order to lead a proper life. Even the dress that you wore every day had sacred meanings, such as the bead work designs on the clothing, and wherever you went or whatever you did, whether you were hunting, making weapons, or whatever you were doing, you were participating in a sacred life and you knew who you were and carried a sense of the sacred with you. All of the forms had meaning, even the tipi and the sacred circle of the entire camp. Of course the life was hard and difficult and not all Indians followed the rules. But the support of the traditional life and the presence of Nature everywhere brought great blessings on all the people.[2]

The world we live in is quite different. Young people today can't read the signs of nature and they do not even know the names of the different animals. When a bird calls, or we see the prints left by an animal, most of our people will not know the name of the animal that stands close by ... What is worse, many young people do not even look, or sometimes even care, where they are walking and do not observe the beautiful things that *Acbadadea*, The Maker of All Things Above, has created. It almost makes me cry to see how some

---

[1] These sacred rites are described in detail in *Yellowtail: Crow Medicine Man and Sun Dance Chief*, recorded and edited by Michael Oren Fitzgerald (Oklahoma: University of Oklahoma Press, 1991).

[2] In the vast expanses of Nature in which the traditional Indian roamed, he was in one sense without limits on this freedom; in another sense he was always confined to the strict role placed upon him by his religious universe. In every moment and in every place, everything reinforced the sacred obligations of his heritage.

young people waste precious gifts. They will let food spoil or waste water and electricity. People do not seem to realize the value of the gifts they have been given; they think things will always be there when they need something. These same people will have a big surprise someday, because sooner or later they will be shown their errors.

Look at the way people travel and work nowadays. You always hear people say, "We are in the fast age." Everything has to be fast, according to the way people want to do things nowadays. If we are going a great distance, the destination or place we are going to isn't going to move; it is standing still, so there is no need to be in such a hurry. In addition to not being safe, there are other dangers in this fast way of life. It is a problem with their entire way of living ... People should ask themselves what it is that they are doing and why it is that they are doing it. So many people today don't even think; they just do something.

Many of the modern things that we have now have made everything worse. We didn't have television until a few years ago, and since the television has come into use, people have just fallen crazy for it. It is something that I don't care for myself. It makes people lazy and gives them strange ideas about life. For instance, it seems as if there isn't any modesty anymore. When people see something on television, they think it is right. They don't think for themselves; they let the television think for them. Television is something that is not good for the world. It is too bad that most people don't realize how something like television can ruin all of our true values.

It seems as if everything in today's world is set up so that everyone can keep going so fast that they never have to consider why they were given the miracle of life. It is too bad that people waste their life and their intelligence by becoming part of this fast society. If they just stopped for a moment and considered that they will all die and meet their Lord, I wonder what they would do?

One of the reasons our society is so fast is the machine. Machinery has changed the manner in which we live, and all of our values regarding this world. In olden-days, it required manual labor for just about everything. Everyone had a responsibility and everyone helped each other. There was no money to keep and to possess, so you couldn't acquire more things than your neighbor. The olden-day Indians moved about the countryside and they couldn't carry more than what they needed. The qualities that a man possessed within himself were important, not what outward possessions he had.

In those days, everyone knew what was expected of him and the Indian Way taught him just how to do it. Not all olden-day Indians lived up to the tribal goals, even though the sacred center was present. Today some people still pray, as they should, even though the sacred center is almost gone. But the goals of the society in those days and today are different and this is something that everyone must understand. We have spoken about the manner in which we carry out our Sun Dance Religion and how everything has a meaning, a purpose. So it was with everything the olden-day Indians did, and so it should be today. You would begin to understand the mysteries of this world in which we have been placed and you would know what you must do to prepare yourself to meet death, to enter the world beyond that we cannot see.

Many of the Sun Dance ceremonies are difficult to endure; it is an ordeal to complete them. This is good and it helps us remember that there is a greater responsibility in life. Life is a gift that you are free to use as you see fit; but you also have to understand that your actions, your choices, are being observed by powers that you do not see. If everything is easy for us and if our concerns are only regarding our possessions, then we lose sight of what is important. In difficult times, we are always prepared to face death; it may come today. So it should be every day in everything we do. We must prepare ourselves today to meet *Acbadadea*, The Maker of All Things Above. People always think that there is plenty of time left to pray later. People who want to accumulate more wealth are always thinking, "I'll wait until later." The world today, and the way people do things, encourage people to be lazy in their spiritual duties.

Manual labor is not required anymore; it is all done by machinery. One man can now do a big field of hay all by himself. The hay is cut and baled by machines; they have even got machinery now that picks it up and brings it in. Without touching anything, the machine puts the bales there and they are already on the stack. Many men used to be required to work many days, but now it is practically done in one day with these machines. Sugar beet farming used to require several men; quite a few working people are all now eliminated by modern machinery. Men going around looking for farm jobs can hardly get any work now. No one needs them because the machinery they have takes care of all that.

Even in the cattle industry it is the same way. There used to be some good cowboys who would take care of the work on the cattle ranch. A lot of them cannot find jobs anymore. There are machines now that take their place. So it looks as if we get to the time when many good men cannot find any work at all. That is not like it should be.

Nowadays men want to accumulate money and then they use the money to buy machines so that all the work can be done more quickly; then they can accumulate even more money. That is all the rich man thinks about. What about the men who want to work for a living? They have no jobs and nothing at all to do. People end up working against each other, as the people without money and machines start to hate the others. Many of the wars in the world today result from this problem ...

Now what happens when one good Indian boy does go out and find a job with good, hard work? Everyone should be proud of him, but they are not. Jealousy is created by the fact that people are competing against one another. On our reservations today, people are jealous of each other. No one cooperates. People blame each other for all of the problems, and criticize people who do work hard and who try to help ... Maybe people can understand that what we see in this modern world is bad, that most of the values people have today are backwards. To follow the way of the machine world will not prepare you to meet your Maker either in this life or after death.

It is true that we cannot just go back to the olden-days either. What good does it do to wish you were an olden-day Indian? Why criticize your brother and try to find faults in everyone else? Will that make you a better person because you have decided that someone else has faults? Some Indians will face their problems with a bottle. This is very bad—drugs, too. It corrupts all of our youngsters. How can any of this solve problems? It just makes everything worse, because they don't try to make anything out of themselves. These same people expect that they will be given things by the tribe, the government. They think that it is the responsibility of others to take care of them ... They don't care at all about our children. All that matters is their own welfare today. These men will certainly receive their just reward when they meet their Maker.

We have spoken about the Sun Dance Religion and what it means for us today. You can see that everything is very different today and that many of the sacred things and sacred ways that were with our Indian people in the olden-days are lost. This was bound to come, for we did not deserve to keep them because we no longer had respect for them. But it does no good to blame any one person or country for our present-day situation. All these events were foreseen in sacred prophecies from all of the great religions.

No one person is to blame for our present state. Everyone who fails to live up to his spiritual duties causes further problems for everyone. Therefore, I tell people, "Don't criticize your neighbor; that will not help anyone. It is not good to fight Indian against Indian; it just makes matters worse. Work on yourself first; prepare yourself to meet your Lord."

Everyone can see how things have changed from the olden times, when sacred values were at the center of our life, up to the present day, when our society does not seem to have a sense of the sacred. So many young people wonder what may happen to this world that we are in, and what they should do if they want to follow a spiritual path. They may think, "Are there other people who want to follow a sacred way? Do I have an opportunity to lead a life in accordance with the traditional ways?"

If people continue on their present course, with no prayer and no respect for sacred things, then things will get worse and worse for everyone. Many prophecies from great religions all over the world speak of the end of time. The Crow have a prophecy about this time, too.

The Crow prophecy concerns an important Crow rite: the Beaver Dance or Tobacco Dance. It is the same thing, but is known by both names. It is a dance participated in by both men and women who are members of the Tobacco Dance Society. The society used to perform their ceremonies every year. We do not know of any other Indian tribe that has this same dance. You could call it a Crow Indian dance. The Tobacco Dance Society has an adoption dance to adopt new members into the society, so that the ceremonies can always be continued. Recently, very few new members have been adopted and the ceremonies are not held as often as they were in olden times ...

The plant they use in the ceremony is not really a tobacco. The Crow name for it is *Itchichea*. It is very holy. In olden-days, every year, they would plant the tobacco in a special ceremony in the spring, usually in May. They would harvest it in the fall and they would keep the plant and seeds and start the process over the next spring. Even when I was a young boy, they completed the planting and harvesting every year so that there would always be tobacco for special ceremonies and prayers. Today the Tobacco Society rarely plants and harvests the tobacco. Almost all of the old members are practically gone and very few new adoptions take place, so fewer people know about the correct way to perform the ceremony and care for the tobacco. I believe the last time they had a special planting ceremony was several years ago at my sister's place, just below where my brother lives now. They set up their tipis there and they held their ceremonies for a day or two. Then they came out and planted their tobacco plants. The plant grows all summer and they harvest it in the fall with another ceremony. I was not present at the time of the harvest ceremony of that planting, but I was told that the seed production and crop production were very poor. The plant is not a very strong plant and so it appears that it may be gone soon. There might not be any more of the plant left anywhere since this particular plant is only used by the Crow.[3]

The Crow Indian prophecy says that when this plant is gone, when it is not planted and harvested so that there is no reproduction of the seed, then finally, it will be the end of time and the world will end. It looks as if that time is near. I was not there that fall when they went to gather it, but they told me they did not get much production of seed that year. What they have on hand will finally get old and will not produce any more; it will not renew, and that will probably be the end.

There are prophecies from the other religions that also talk about the end of time.[4] The Hopi prophecies are very interesting

[3] In May 1984, Yellowtail and I [Michael Oren Fitzgerald.—*Ed.*] visited two of the oldest members of the Tobacco Society to inquire about recent ceremonies. Both informants verified Yellowtail's recollection that the last planting took place between 1976 and 1978. A severe frost killed all of the tobacco seed production that year, and the only known seed is from a previous planting. Two different society members are keeping this seed, but it is not known if the seed will germinate, and no plantings are scheduled at this time.

[4] The prophecies that Yellowtail discusses are not alone even among Plains Indians. For example, the Sioux have a symbolism of the buffalo and its four legs. Each year the buffalo loses a hair off one of the legs. The end of this cycle comes when the buffalo has no more hair on its legs. (The Hindus have an almost identical prophecy.)

to hear. I have met Thomas Banyacya several times, and he is very good at explaining the Hopi prophecies.[5]

It is important for the young people to understand and follow their traditional religion. We must help to educate our young ones

Moreover, the Indians feel that industrial civilization, since it ruptures the balance of Nature, cannot endure.

[5] This letter, signed by Thomas Banyacya on behalf of all Hopi Traditional Village Leaders, was sent to President Richard Nixon in 1970:

> We, the true and traditional religious leaders, recognized as such by the Hopi People, maintain full authority over all land and life contained within the Western Hemisphere. We are granted our stewardship by virtue of our instruction as to the meaning of Nature, Peace, and Harmony as spoken to our People by Him, known to us as *Massau'u*, the Great Spirit, who long ago provided for us the sacred stone tablets which we preserve to this day. For many generations before the coming of the white man ... the Hopi People have lived in the sacred place known to you as the Southwest and known to us to be the spiritual center of our continent. Those of us of the Hopi Nation who have followed the path of the Great Spirit without compromise have a message which we are committed, through our prophecy, to convey to you.
>
> The white man, through his insensitivity to the way of Nature, has desecrated the face of Mother Earth. The white man's advanced technological capacity has occurred as a result of his lack of regard for the spiritual path and for the way of all living things. The white man's desire for material possessions and power has blinded him to the pain he has caused Mother Earth by his quest for what he calls natural resources. And the path of the Great Spirit has become difficult to see by almost all men, even by many Indians who have chosen instead to follow the path of the white man ...
>
> Today the sacred lands where the Hopi live are being desecrated by men who seek coal and water from our soil that they may create more power for the white man's cities. This must not be allowed to continue for if it does, Mother Nature will react in such a way that almost all men will suffer the end of life as they now know it. The Great Spirit said not to allow this to happen even as it was prophesied to our ancestors. The Great Spirit said not to take from the Earth—not to destroy living things. The Great Spirit, *Massau'u*, said that man was to live in Harmony and maintain a good clean land for all children to come. All Hopi People and other Indian Brothers are standing on this religious principle and the Traditional Spiritual Unity Movement today is endeavoring to reawaken the spiritual nature in Indian people throughout this land. Your government has almost destroyed our basic religion, which actually is a way of life for all our people in this land of the Great Spirit. We feel that to survive the coming Purification Day, we must return to the basic religious principles and to meet together on this basis as leaders of our people.
>
> Today almost all the prophecies have come to pass. Great roads like rivers pass across the landscape; man talks to man through the cobwebs of

in the proper manner about our traditions. I always try to encourage the young to forget the other things that they have in mind: "Drop those things and try to learn something about your traditional Indian ways."[6] They should join these meetings that Indians are having and try to continue the use of the different ceremonies and of prayer according to the Indian heritage.

Some people might think, "It doesn't do any good to pray; it won't change anything." But there are many reasons to pray and those people are wrong. Only God knows when the end of this world will come, and when and how it comes will certainly depend on sincere prayers that are offered to Him in the correct way. Each man will pass from this earth in his own time. Some of the prophecies talk only about the end of time; others speak about the break-up of the modern world, as we know it, and a return to the traditional ways of our ancestors. I can't say what will happen and whether we will find the spiritual ways of our ancestors in this world or another; but I do know that in either case we still have to make a choice, each one of us must choose at this present moment which

telephone lines; man travels along the roads in the sky in his airplanes; two great wars have been waged by those bearing the swastika or the rising sun; man is tampering with the Moon and the stars. Most men have strayed from the path shown us by the Great Spirit. For *Massau'u* alone is great enough to portray the way back to Him.

It is said by the Great Spirit that if a gourd of ashes is dropped upon the Earth, that many men will die and that the end of this way of life is near at hand. We interpret this as the dropping of atomic bombs on Hiroshima and Nagasaki. We do not want to see this happen to any place or any nation again, but instead we should turn all this energy for peaceful uses, not for war.

We, the religious leaders and rightful spokesmen for the Hopi Independent Nation, have been instructed by the Great Spirit to express the invitation to the President of the United States and all spiritual leaders everywhere to meet with us and discuss the welfare of mankind so that Peace, Unity, and Brotherhood will become part of all men everywhere.

[6] Chief Fools Crow, Teton Sioux, commented on this same point:

I decided to go again to Bear Butte to fast and pray ... and do you know what happened? *Wakan Tanka* and *Tunkashila* gave me the same answer I was given on my trip there in 1927. The Sioux should go back and pick up the good things that our grandfathers, grandmothers, aunts, uncles, fathers, and mothers had taught us. Our only hope was to fall back upon our traditional way of life. It was the only foundation we had that would give meaning and purpose to us. I brought this message back to the elders ... (Thomas E. Mails, *Fools Crow* [Garden City: Doubleday, 1979]) path to follow. Each person's prayers can help everyone. The person who prays and remembers God will receive the greatest benefit for himself and for others.

Some people will not believe that they really have a choice in following a religion and in turning to prayer. This is a strange idea. Everyone has a free mind and at any moment each individual can choose to do one thing instead of another. Think about this. Even a child does not have to obey his parents; he can choose the punishment he will receive if he disobeys instead. So too, can each person choose whether to join a religion and way of prayer. There are different reasons why you should do this: Of course you can fear punishment just like the child who disobeys; or you can follow a sacred path because you know and love the sacred ways. Whatever your reason, you must choose one direction or another ... There is nothing more I can say except to raise my voice in prayer: During these next years, I need Your help to give me the knowledge and strength to carry our Sun Dance Religion to our people. I have been trying to speak out, so that all the young people will know what is expected of them. Help me to carry this message to their hearts. I am working with my grandson so that this message can be written down for many to see. Help us. Our Apsaroke people need to see that their own religion is good and that it can help them if only they open their eyes and hearts. Everyone needs to make a choice—each should choose a religion. Help them to understand that they must make that choice before it is too late.

You have told our people through our Apsaroke prophecies that the world will come to an end. The other religions that have been given to the white people also talk about the end of time. According to what we have been told, that time may be here soon. Help people see that they should select the religion of their choice. Then they must pray every day and live straight.

There was a time when all the different denominations used to stay away from each other or there was a little rivalry between them. It should not be that way. They should unite and pray together. All the people on the reservation should unite regardless of their beliefs. You have given different ways to different people all over the world. As we know, this earth is round like a wagon wheel. In a wagon wheel, all the spokes are set into the center. The circle of the wheel is round and all spokes come from the center and the center is You, *Acbadadea*, The Maker of all Things Above. Each spoke can be considered as a different religion of the world, which has been given by

You to different people and different races. All of the people of the world are on the rim of the wheel and they must follow one of the spokes to the center. The different paths have been given to us but they all lead to the same place. We all pray to the same God, to You. There are different places on the wheel so each way may look strange to someone following a different path. It is easy for people to say that their way is the best if they know all about their faith and it is good for them. But they should refrain from saying bad things about other ways that they don't know about. There should be no hard feelings about someone else if he is following a way that leads to You. Help us to see this wisdom.

A person should learn all about a path to You before he joins. It is not good to just enter a faith and then drop it. I tell this to the young people: "You must choose a religion, but before you enter one, you should know which one is the best for you. Take the time and find out all you can about the method of prayer and about what that religion tells you about The Maker of All Things Above. You should understand the rules and know what is expected of you. Find a path that provides you with the way you need to live a good life every day!" ... *Acbadadea,* Medicine Fathers, help all young people to know these things.

Some people don't want to know what religion requires of them. As soon as they don't like something—because it may not be easy or it may require some sacrifice—they leave in a hurry without asking themselves what You expect of them. They can't get anything out of a religion if they leave every time something hard is asked of them. If they ever do find a way that is so easy that they can always perform everything without any trouble, then they should know they have found a bad thing. That is the time they should leave that false religion. Maker of All Things Above, give people the wisdom to see these things and the strength to resist those who will not follow You.

I have tried to speak my mind and my heart in the best way I know. Thank You for helping guide my words. Now I have completed my responsibility of speaking about the sacred ways of our Apsaroke people, and I feel good about this. Thank You for the help that You have given me already so that I could carry out Your wishes until now. Help me to keep working and praying so that this position as Sun Dance Chief can be fulfilled and my people will be able to live ... *Aho, Aho!*

THE FATE OF TIBET*

Anagarika Govinda

Why is it that the fate of Tibet has found such a deep echo in the world? There can only be one answer: Tibet has become the symbol of all that present-day humanity is longing for, either because it has been lost or not yet been realized or because it is in danger of disappearing from human sight: the stability of a tradition, which has its roots not only in a historical or cultural past, but within the innermost being of man, in whose depth this past is enshrined as an ever-present source of inspiration.

But more than that: what is happening in Tibet is symbolical for the fate of humanity. As on a gigantically raised stage we witness the struggle between two worlds, which may be interpreted, according to the standpoint of the spectator, either as the struggle between the past and the future, between backwardness and progress, belief and science, superstition and knowledge—or as the struggle between spiritual freedom and material power, between the wisdom of the heart and the knowledge of the brain, between the dignity of the human individual and the herd-instinct of the mass, between the faith in the higher destiny of man through inner development and the belief in material prosperity through an ever-increasing production of goods.

We witness the tragedy of a peaceful people without political ambitions and with the sole desire to be left alone, being deprived of its freedom and trampled underfoot by a powerful neighbor in the name of "progress," which as ever must serve as a cover for all the brutalities of the human race. The living present is sacrificed to the moloch of the future, the organic connection with a fruitful past is destroyed for the chimera of a machine-made prosperity.

Thus cut off from their past, men lose their roots and can find security only in the herd, and happiness only in the satisfaction of their ephemeral needs and desires. For, from the standpoint of "progress" the past is a negligible, if not negative, value, bearing the

* Editor's Note: The first part of the Foreword to *The Way of the White Clouds*.

stigma of imperfection and being synonymous with backwardness and "reaction."

What, however, is it that distinguishes man from the animal, if not the consciousness of the past, a consciousness which stretches beyond his short life-span, beyond his own little ego, in short, beyond the limitations of his momentary time-conditioned individuality? It is this wider and richer consciousness, this oneness with the creative seeds hidden in the womb of an ever-young past, which makes the difference, not only between the human and the animal consciousness, but between a cultured and an uncultured mind.

The same is true for nations and peoples. Only such nations are truly civilized, or better, truly cultured, which are rich in tradition and conscious of their past. It is in this sense that we speak of Tibet as a deeply cultured nation, in spite of the primitive conditions of life and the wildness of nature prevailing over the greater part of the country. In fact, it is the very harshness of life, and the unrelenting struggle against the powers of nature, that has steeled the spirit of its inhabitants and built their character. Herein lies the unconquerable strength of the Tibetan, which in the end will prevail over all external powers and calamities. This strength has shown itself throughout Tibet's history. Tibet has been overrun more than once by hostile powers and has gone through worse calamities than the present one—as in the times of King Langdarma, who usurped the throne of Lhasa and persecuted Buddhism with fire and sword. But the Tibetans never bowed to any conqueror or to any tyrant. When the hordes of Genghis Khan drowned half the world in blood and Mongols overran the mighty Chinese empire and threatened to conquer Tibet, it was the spiritual superiority of Tibet that saved its independence, by converting Kublai Khan and his people to Buddhism and transforming this warlike race into a peaceful nation. Nobody has yet entered Tibet without falling under its spell, and who knows whether the Chinese themselves, instead of converting the Tibetans to Communism, may not be subtly transformed in their ideas like the Mongolian hordes of yore.

One thing is sure, and that is, that while the Chinese are trying their utmost to crush Tibet by brutal force, the spirit of Tibet is gaining an ever increasing influence upon the world just as the persecution of the early Christians by the might of the Roman empire carried the new faith into the remotest corners of the then-known world, converted a small religious sect into a world religion and finally triumphed over the very empire that had tried to crush it.

We know that Tibet will never be the same again, even if it regains its independence, but this is not what really matters. What matters is that the continuity of Tibet's spiritual culture, which is based on a living tradition and a conscious connection with its origins, should not be lost. Buddhism is not opposed to change—in fact, it is recognizing it as the nature of all life—it is, therefore, not opposed to new forms of life and thought or to new discoveries in the fields of science and technique.

On the contrary, the challenge of modern life, the widening horizon of scientific knowledge, will be an incentive to explore the very depths of the human mind and to rediscover the true meaning of the teachings and symbols of the past, which had been hidden under the accumulated dross of centuries. Much that had been merely accepted as an article of faith, or that had become a matter of mere routine, will again have to be consciously acquired and resuscitated.

In the meantime, however, it is our task to keep alive the remembrance of the beauty and greatness of the spirit that informed the history and the religious life of Tibet, so that future generations may feel encouraged and inspired to build a new life on the foundations of a noble past.

Towards a New Dreaming*

James Cowan

Throughout this book no attempt has been made to establish Aboriginal spirituality as a cohesive theology capable of being broken down into a tidy system of belief. Aboriginal religion has been poorly served by this approach in the past—an approach that for too long has been the mainspring of anthropological and social scientific inquiry. It is plainly evident that this confinement of the exploration of Aboriginal culture to the academic environment has lead to a malnourished vision of what Aboriginal spirituality is all about. In the process genuine intellectual intuition has been replaced by scholastic techniques masquerading as "social science."

This is not to say that there is no clearly defined "creed" of belief among Aborigines. Far from it. The essential core of their spirituality is remarkably consistent throughout the country, in spite of the tribal isolation that has made communication so difficult in the past. In this respect one is constantly struck by the similarities existing in mythic data and ritual practice, even though there might be contrasts in surface nuance. Nevertheless, these contrasts make it difficult to render Aboriginal spiritual belief in any other way than as a vast body of localized myths, Sky Hero identities, and individual totemic environments. Yet it is this very diversity that makes Aboriginal belief such a multi-faceted jewel.

But, like the land from which it has sprung, the Dreaming as a viable metaphysic is under threat. Not only has the purity of religious practice as observed by Aborigines in the past all but been destroyed, but the mysteries surrounding those practices have been virtually drained of their *numen.* European culture, under the burden of its frenetic desire to transform the country into an economic environment, has caused a great deal of damage to what was once a sacralized landscape. Some Aborigines would say that the damage done to their country is irreversible, that the economic and agri-

* Editor's Note: Chapter 8 of *Mysteries of the Dreaming.*

cultural vandalism of the past two hundred years has made it impossible to redeem their land from its "fallen" condition.

Few observers would disagree that a great deal of damage has been done in the past. Clearly the Aboriginal social fabric is in tatters. The Rainbow Serpent of the northern waterholes has been dragged from its sanctuaries and allowed to rot on the beach-heads of racial prejudice. The luminous expressions on the Wandjina rock paintings of the Kimberley have been allowed to peel away through indifference. The Aborigines themselves have been allowed, even encouraged, to sink into a morass of self-pity in the hope that they might just "go away." In consequence, the Aboriginal "problem," a problem of continual resistance by an indigenous people to assimilation into the ways of the white man, has consumed countless millions of dollars and caused the growth of vast government bureaucracies throughout the country, all in the hope of ameliorating a race who simply refuse to be pacified in the way that others see fit.

What the Aboriginal people are crying out for and no government has had the courage to grant them is full title to their tribal lands. This is because economic values in Australia today are a more powerful force than the more fragile, nurturing values of Aboriginal sanctity. No white politician, no agriculturalist, no mining magnate in the current political environment has ever had the courage to stand up and state the subservience of economic aspirations to those of the human spirit. In a world of agnosticism, the idea that spiritual values might correctly hold precedence over the demands of material well-being is an unthinkable proposition. Modern man is hell-bent on the destruction of all numinosities, whether they be metaphysical, mythic, or totemic, in order that he might pave the way for his own material apotheosis.

This has led to a critical situation among surviving Aborigines. They are at a loss as to how to regain their stolen birthright, except in terms of confrontation and political activism. In turn this has led to a feeling of resentment among European Australians who see Aborigines as opportunists trying to gain for themselves more than their fair share. Aboriginal resentment is quickly dismissed as the whining of urban activists who are "more white than black." Accusations of funds misuse, nepotism, and the sheer waste of federal grants on uneconomic enterprises further reduces Aboriginal credibility in the eyes of Europeans. Indeed Aborigines and

Aboriginal groups are regarded by many as perpetual mendicants who deserve far less than they're already receiving.

What is the answer to this impasse? If Aboriginal culture is to survive at all, then it requires a far more serious examination of the Dreaming as a metaphysical reality than there has been so far. The Dreaming is at the very root of the Aboriginal heritage, and it is this that must be preserved as a living reality at all costs. Spending money on housing or medical projects, funding artistic communities or economic programs are extremely important, of course, but must remain as secondary to the re-affirmation of the Dreaming. The Dreaming is the *raison d'être* of Aboriginal culture. Until this is recognized and acted upon by government and bureaucrats alike, Aborigines will continue to survive in a state of fringe ethnicity, at the mercy of the more dominant European cultural values that surround them.

Recognizing the Dreaming as a living reality, however, demands a fundamental shift in the attitudes of everyone concerned. It requires, firstly, that the Dreaming is seen for what it is: a metaphysical statement about the origins of mankind as a spiritual being. So long as the Dreaming is regarded merely as an assortment of myths that have little more than a quixotic value for the rest of Australians, then the Dreaming will always be demeaned as a metaphysical event. Men and women of goodwill, both European and Aboriginal, must begin to regard the mysteries of the Dreaming as being important in their own lives in the here-and-now. They must begin to see the Dreaming as a spiritual *condition*, rather than simply as a word denoting the creation-time of Aborigines. Indeed the idea that the Dreaming is an on-going metaphysical, rather than an historical event is the only way that this change can be brought about.

In order for this transformation in consciousness to come about, however, it is important that Aborigines regain possession of their totems. To do that, they must have access to their land free from intimidation or interference from governments, mining lobbies, and graziers. Regaining possession of their land means that the sanctity of sacred places can be restored and the Dreaming renewed at a ritual level. This resacralization process will inevitably lead to Aboriginal man renewing once more his own commitment to the totemic environment of his forebears. For it is only through the totem that a man makes contact with his Dreaming, and so with the

Dreaming of the entire Aboriginal people. If this were to happen, then in the long term the Dreaming might become a sustaining metaphysical principle for all Australians.

This is the lesson that Aborigines can teach everyone. For too long the assumed primitivity of the Aboriginal people has created an environment whereby the relationship between the teacher and those who were being taught favored Europeans. It has been Europeans who have made judgments and formulated policy about how Aborigines should live and think. It has been Europeans who have studied Aboriginal society under the spell of Darwinian and post-Darwinian evolutionary theories in order to justify European encroachment on their culture—and more particularly, Aboriginal land itself. And in more recent years, it has been Europeans who have argued against the return of this land to its rightful owners, citing economic detriment as an inevitable result. To support these actions it has been important to maintain the illusion that Aborigines are a "stone-age" race who are ill-equipped to handle their own lives in the contemporary sphere. That is, in spite of the evidence of 40,000 years of continuous occupation of the country by Aborigines before the advent of Europeans.

There is no reason why the Dreaming cannot be renewed in the context of contemporary Australian society, in spite of the evidence to the contrary. But it does involve a collective acknowledgement that the land has a sacred dimension rather than a physical one only. Just so long as we are intent on pacifying the landscape and, in a sense, taming it so that its spirit is broken, then we will destroy any hope of the Dreaming as a metaphysical event ever becoming a reality again.

Environments have their own individual genesis, wrote one French writer.[1] This is very true of the Australian continent which has always been the epitome of wildness. It was this wildness that the Aboriginal people sought to preserve in its integrity. They had no desire to pacify their land because they knew that in doing so they would cut off access to its mysteries. A land that remains wild is a land that remains mysterious. Aborigines have always been extremely aware of the power of this mystery, this *numen*, as a regenerative force for good among men. They know, or have known, that once a

---

[1] R.A. Schwaller de Lubicz, *Nature Word* (Lindesfarne Press, 1982).

land is pacified it loses its power to heal not only itself, but men as well. A land yearns for its freedom just as men do. The Aborigines teach us that by making it a slave to our will, we destroy its ability to challenge us as a friend and colleague.

It was Gregory of Nyssa, one of Christianity's early Church Fathers, who best reflects the Aboriginal's respect for his land. "What you see on earth and in the heavens, what you behold in the sun and contemplate in the sea, apply this to yourselves and your own nature." And again: "As you look upon the universe, see it in your own nature."[2] Goethe also remarked, "Man knows himself insofar as he knows the world, becoming aware of it only in himself, and of himself only within it."[3] Clearly there is a time-honored tradition demanding of mankind that he equate the integrity of his own nature with that of the land he inhabits. For it is in mutual recognition, mutual acceptance, and mutual reverence that the dualities of existence are eliminated, just as the male and female *Churinga* are bound together, or the tiny *Chichurkna* bird wings its way to its double, the *Arumburinga*, at the totem site at death. Spiritual man knows that he cannot survive without due regard for wildness as a reflection of the metaphysical exuberance of earth.

Aborigines who maintain a deep, reverential contact with the Dreaming are true Doctors of the Spirit. It is they who understand the power of land as a principial force and teach us how to respect it. They are true environmentalists who have carried on a tradition of husbandry for countless millennia. For them, true imagination is the power to see subtle processes of nature and their angelic prototypes in the form of spirits of the Dreaming. It is this capacity to reproduce in themselves the "cosmogenic unfolding,"[4] the permanent creation of the world in the sense in which all creation, finally, is only a Divine Imagination that makes Aborigines so unique. In this sense, they have attained to a state where *summa scientia nihil save* ("The height of knowledge is to know nothing").[5]

The challenge now is to translate this knowledge into some form of action and some form of acknowledgment of the Aboriginal her-

---

[2] St. Gregory of Nyssa, Commentary on Ecclesiastes, Homily I, in *The Cycle of Desire*.

[3] Goethe, *Botanical Writings*.

[4] See Maurice Aniane's *Material for Thought* (Spring Books, 1976) for a more detailed analysis of this remarkable concept.

[5] Christian Rosen Kreutz.

itage. Granting Land Rights is only an initial step. It does not solve the problem of a renewal of the Dreaming. This can only come about in the form of a commitment to a new level of understanding and respect for Aboriginal traditions and their age-old spirituality. For this to happen, modern man must re-examine his own attitude towards his abhorrence of instinctivity and the power of the *numen* as a metaphysical exemplar. He must learn to accept the land on which he lives as an extension to himself, not as a separate entity that should simply be utilized for material gain. He must go beyond what Christopher Bamford calls "the idea of a single, unique act of creation and assume as well a creative state of continuous and recurrent creation, metaphysical in nature, outside space and time." When, and if, this happens, we will then begin to see a rebirth of the Dreaming as an extension to our own spirituality.

"When the course of nature goes its proper way, it is a sign that the government is good. But when there is some disturbance in nature there is some error in government." So said Raphael Pati in his commentary on the Chinese Annals of Confucius. He was merely affirming what an Aboriginal informant remarked to the author when explaining why Cyclone Tracy devastated the city of Darwin in the Northern Territory sometime in the early 1970s. According to Big Bill Neidjie, the cyclone appeared as a result of the destruction of the Kakadu environment by mining companies, in particular those mining uranium. The cyclone reflected a rupture of chthonic rhythms. As far as he was concerned, the earth around Kakadu had been "wounded" by this invasion of modern technology bent on absconding with its booty. There had been no ritual requests made of the land prior to commencement of mining, no libations poured on the earth, no corroborees performed to appease the spirit of the earth. It had simply been plundered. In response, Cyclone Tracy did not attack the Kakadu region which was for Aborigines a land still filled with *numen*, in spite of the presence of mining companies. Instead, the cyclone hit the largest population center in the North: Darwin. It wreaked havoc at the very center of urbanism where the spirit of earth had been enchained for some time. If the Territorians had listened to the Confucian injunction, "The world is a holy vessel. Let him who would tamper with it, beware," then Cyclone Tracy would never have appeared at all as far as Big Bill was concerned.

Furthermore, there must be an effort made by modern man to accept nomadism as an important human right. It is time to stop thinking of mankind as forever tethered to the one environment, as if "roots" were the only pre-requisite for existence. Aborigines have long understood the joy of movement about a landscape, just as that other benighted race, the Gypsies. The Oglala Sioux Indian chief, Chief Flying Hawk, best expressed it when he said that, "If the great Spirit wanted men to stay in one place he would make the world stand still. But he made it always change, so birds and animals can move and have green grass and ripe berries, sunlight to work and play in, and night to sleep. Always changing. Everything for good. Nothing for nothing." A Juki Gypsy of the Lebanon reiterated this point when he remarked, "I say that he should not become absorbed by a single land ... I wish him a long, long journey over wild wastes and harsh lands, in green places and cool preserves, over islands and unheard of cities, over the 'limits' of this whole age."[6] Clearly there is a primordial tradition of nomadism unconfined by too strong an association with one place—a tradition that the Aboriginal people have long ago made their own.

Perhaps René Guénon best expressed the dilemma facing the Aborigines and the revival of the Dreaming as a metaphysical principle in our modern age when he wrote:

> Let there be no mistake about it: if the general public accepts the pretext of "civilization" in all good faith, there are some for whom it amounts to no more than mere economic hypocrisy, a cloak for their designs of conquest and economic civilization; but what strange times indeed, when so many men allow themselves to be persuaded that they are making a people happy by reducing them to subjection, by robbing them of what is most precious in their eyes, namely their own civilization, by compelling them to adopt customs and institutions which were intended for another race, and by coercing them into assuming the most distasteful occupations in order that they may perforce come to acquire things for which they have not the slightest use! That however is the position today: the modern West cannot tolerate the idea that men should prefer to work less and be content to live on little; as quantity alone

---

[6] Douglas Halebi, "The World of the Juki," *Studies in Comparative Religion* (1983).

counts, and as everything that eludes the grasp of the senses is held moreover to be non-existent, it is taken for granted that anyone not producing material things must be an "idler."[7]

This is precisely the condition under which Aborigines have suffered for two hundred years. They have been subjected to prolonged hardship and human suffering as a colonized people under those who refused to acknowledge any spiritual kinship with them. As a result they have been diminished as a race not only in terms of numbers, but in terms of their own self-esteem. Although attempts are being made now to rectify this situation, very little attempt is being made to acknowledge the Dreaming for what it is. This is because few people understand, or wish to believe in what Giordano Bruno calls the "diverse spirits and powers"[8] within nature. As long as there is no wish to recognize the divinity in all things, then Aboriginal belief will always be regarded as a suspect philosophy grounded in superstition and strange ritual practices.

These times are precarious in terms of the survival of traditional peoples throughout the world. They are all succumbing like wheat to the blight of modern civilization. It is beholden on us all to arrest this serious devolution of minorities in the interest of social "uniformity." Numbarkala, Wandjina, the Rainbow Serpent, Ungud—whatever name the presiding spirit of the Dreaming goes under—they are all but a manifestation of man's need to maintain vigilance against the threat of spiritual extinction. It is not traditional man that will die out when the last Aborigine or Sioux or Kalahari Bushman quits this earth; it will be the spirit of man as nature's consort that will finally disappear. This alone is worth fighting for, not the economic hegemonies or industrial wastelands that now threaten to blight this earth.

The Dreaming still exists. The pure asceticism of nature as an attainable condition within every one of us is possible if we listen to

---

[7] René Guénon, *The Crisis of the Modern World* (Luzac, 1975).

[8] Cf. "For ... diverse living things represent spirits and powers, which beyond the absolute being which they have, obtain a being communicated to all things according to their capacity and measure ... thus one should think of Sol (Sun) as being in a crocus, a daffodil, a sunflower, in the cock, in the lion ... For as the divinity descends to a certain measure in as such as it communicates itself to nature, so there is an ascent made to the divinity through nature" (Giordano Bruno, *Spaccio dellabastia trionforte*, Dialogue 3).

what the Aborigine is saying to us. Reestablishing our links with totems, making our own Dream journeys, listening to the voice of our own Dreaming and acknowledging our ancestors as being primordially present, is the beginning of the process of renewal. When this is achieved, then the revival of the Dreaming as a metaphysical condition will be a reality. Then we will be able to say, along with Big Bill Neidjie, "Dreaming place ... you can't change it, no matter who you are. No matter you rich man, no matter you king. You can't change it." Indeed, it is this very unchangeability of the Dreaming that makes it so steadfast in the lives of all Aborigines—and us if we wish it to be so.

EPILOGUE[*]

Philip Sherrard

Can we overcome this process of dehumanization and desanctification? We cannot know. But we can at least point to certain conditions on whose fulfillment depends our survival as human beings. The first is that, however perilous our situation, we do not on that account regard it as inevitable that we are doomed and that there is no alternative except progressive materialization leading to the Armageddon and the coming of the Anti-Christ. One of the great dangers is precisely that we become spell-bound before the sphinx-like monster of the world we have brought into existence. We even forget that it is we who have produced it, not it which has produced us. In this way we are reduced to a kind of helpless passivity, lamenting the world of natural simplicities and sacred forms that has gone, and seeing in the present and the immediate future the necessary and inescapable declension of the cosmic cycles into a pre-ordained dark age ending in the emergence of the beast from the abyss. We commit a kind of apostasy. We surrender to the image of negation and purposelessness which we are summoned to overcome.

We surrender in fact to what is the most negative and ugly side of our nature. Certainly we must realize that the scope and purpose of the modern scientific and technological mentality are at the opposite pole to the Christian scope and purpose of transfiguring all human and natural life through prayer, sanctity, and loving compassion; and that not only can there be no reconciliation between these two orientations, but also that the pursuit of the first may well erase the significance of the second from our minds. But such erasure is not simply an automatic and inevitable matter. If it happens, it is because we allow it to happen. It is only man himself who can consent to the damning of his own soul, and nothing and no one can force him to give this consent, least of all the machine and other abstract and technical processes.

[*] Editor's Note: The Epilogue from *The Rape of Man and Nature.*

If we cannot see how to restore the traditional forms of a Christian society, or to be the type of man of the ages of faith, we do not because of that cease to be created in the image and likeness of God, or lose our capacity to realize this image and likeness in our personal lives. We demean our own dignity when we attribute either a final character to the present scientific and technological period, or regard it as fatally and necessarily leading to our own human and terrestrial deformation or extinction. It may well lead to this. But, it must be repeated, if it does, this is our own responsibility. We are faced with a challenge, an issue of life or death: either to affirm the eternal nature of our being—that image in us and the values that go with it which lie beyond all forms of society, whatever their character—or to acquiesce in our own dehumanization and eclipse in obedience to the forces that with our cooperation have fabricated the infernal and artificial forms of the contemporary world.

If, though, we choose not to acquiesce, then we must realize that the first step towards becoming disentangled from these forms is the step of repentance, or *metanoia*: change of mind. Such a conclusion must follow from all that has been said in this book. The thesis of the book has been that the forms of our society, from those of our educational system down to those in which most of us spend our working lives, are such that they frustrate and even negate the expression and fulfillment of our true humanity at practically every turn. But as it is the pursuit of the ideals and methods of modern science that has brought us into this catastrophic situation, clearly there can be no issue from it without the renunciation of these ideals and methods. We have to free ourselves from subservience to the type of mentality by which we have been increasingly dominated over the last three or four centuries.

This mentality is the mentality which has produced modern science; and we have to realize that scientists are specialists who within the confines of their specialities may possess a capacity for order and sense of a formidable kind but who outside these confines produce disorder and nonsense which are equally formidable. This is because the conceptual ground within which knowingly or unknowingly they think and act does not permit anything else. As we have already said, modern scientific thought has no complexity or depth whatsoever. It does not even acknowledge the crucial distinction between the order of wisdom and the order of mere hypothesis based on experiment. It proceeds with blind determination from the premises that underpin it to the conclusions that inevitably follow from those premises. It demonstrates the efficacy of these conclusions by totally ignoring their human and ecological consequences. Its attempts to justify the premises themselves in terms of value and to say that they are "good" are little more than extrapolations from its capacity to analyze and describe, in the most superficial manner, what works and how it works.

At the same time this experimental mentality protects itself from the disruption with which it is threatened by every form of knowledge less shallow than its own by building around itself the departmental structure of modern schools and universities and by securing the undivided allegiance of corporate industrialists, bankers, big businessmen, and the clients of these people, the politicians and officials of the modern state system. In this sense it is monolithic and potentially totalitarian, aspiring to a monopoly that will permit experimentally derived, technologically pure solutions to be imposed by force. To think and act without the constraint of any knowledge and values other than those of the modern scientific mentality is to commit oneself to a tyranny of an unprecedented maleficence. That is why the freeing of ourselves from subservience to this mentality constitutes the second condition whose fulfillment is a prerequisite of our survival as human beings.

Does this mean that there cannot be either any science of phenomena or any practical technology based upon such a science? This does not follow at all. But if the consequences of the pursuit of such a science are to be the fostering and not the destruction of our humanity, several things have to be recognized. The first is that knowledge and what is done under the influence of a particular form of knowledge can never in the nature of things be neutral. For knowledge is either true knowledge, based on a true recognition of the reality of things, or it is false knowledge, based on a mistaken idea of the reality of things. But if it is false knowledge it is also on that account a diabolic form of knowledge, the product of "the father of lies," and hence it is tainted with evil. Consequently what is done under its influence is likewise tainted with evil.

This means, in the context with which we are here concerned, that if a science of phenomena starts out, as modern science does start out, with a mistaken idea of the relationship between the divine and the human, or the divine and nature, or, quite simply, with no awareness of the divine at all, the conclusions it reaches as to the nature of both man and the natural world will necessarily be false and to that extent diabolic; and all that is implemented, whether by way of educational programs or of technology, under the influence of such a diabolic form of knowledge will be tainted with the same character. As such it will inescapably be destructive of both man and nature, however neutral it may appear to be. As modern science as a whole has developed on the basis of such false premises, its so-called knowledge is a false knowledge and its consequences in the sphere of practical application are therefore inevitably destructive.

Yet it is by no means itself inevitable that a science of phenomena or a practical technology based on it should develop from false premises—should develop, that is to say, from a mistaken idea of who man is or of the relationship between the divine and the natural worlds. Consequently it is by no means inevitable that the findings of such a science or their practical application should be destructive of both man and nature. But for a science of phenomena not to be based on false premises requires on the part of scientists themselves a double act of recognition: first, the recognition that the conceptual framework within which modern science has been and still is operating is a false one and that this has the inescapable consequences we have noted in the practical sphere; and, second, the recognition that there can be no true knowledge of the physical world that does not derive from an *a priori* acceptance of a metaphysical knowledge—of a metaphysical knowledge which it is quite impossible to attain through the investigation, in however subtle or sophisticated a form, of the phenomenal world itself.

In other words, for a science of phenomena not to be false and destructive, its theory and practice must be based on an *a priori* acceptance of ideas as to the ultimate and intrinsic nature of reality which derive from a religious or metaphysical tradition. This is to say that they have to be based on the recognition and assimilation of ideas whose origin lies not in the human mind but in the mind of God as this has been disclosed to man through revelation. Such recognition and assimilation will always elude us until and unless we raise our consciousness above the level of the reason, because in themselves the categories of the reason exclude the possibility of attaining a metaphysical knowledge. Without such knowledge—knowledge capable of providing a bridge linking the human and the divine—the reason merely formulates endless hypotheses that involve us ever more disastrously in the world of materialization and illusion.

The third and overriding condition of our survival as human beings is, then, the recognition that the primordial ideas of a religious or metaphysical tradition must constitute the conceptual framework within which a science of phenomena has to operate if it is not to result in a false knowledge and hence to have consequences that, instead of fostering, positively negate man's humanity and his ability to live in harmony with himself and the natural world. Indeed, one can go further and say quite simply that it is the recognition of such primordial ideas as the operative standards guiding not only science but every form of human activity that is the *sine qua non* of our survival as human beings and that without such a recognition we are inevitably doomed to a total deformation and even to extinction. This is the case because these primordial ideas are themselves the expression on the conceptual level of the divine principles in the image of which both man himself and the natural world are created. To align all forms of human activity with them is thus to ensure that one does not violate the norms of human and natural life; it is to prevent oneself from stepping over into those spheres of dehumanization and desanctification into which modern science, by ignoring the standards they establish, has stepped with a vengeance.

Yet if we are to recover an awareness of such ideas within the framework of the Christian tradition—and the thesis proposed in the opening chapter of the present study is that this is the only real possibility available to us who belong to the cultural orbit of the Western world—we have to turn to the doctrinal masters of this tradition who have most clearly and authentically understood and expressed them. In the works of these masters—and again in the opening chapter we specified some of the most important of them[1]—is enshrined the sole living heritage of spiritual wisdom

---

[1] Editor's Note: The author refers to such masters as: the Cappadocian Fathers (fourth century), St. Dionysios the Areopagite (fifth century), St. Maximos the Confessor (c. 580-662), John Scotus Erigena (c. 810-c. 877), St. Simeon the New Theologian (949-1022), William of St. Thierry (c. 1085-1148), Meister Eckhart (c. 1260-1327), Jan Van Ruysbroeck (1293-1381), St. Gregory Palamas (c. 1296-1359), Angelus Silesius (1624-1677), the Cambridge Platonists (seventeenth century), and the poets William Blake and W.B. Yeats.

which the Western world possesses, obscured though it may be by the developments we have been discussing. Our ignorance of them is consequently a measure of the degree to which we have betrayed our inheritance, an inheritance common to the whole of Christendom. Concomitantly, if we are to overcome this ignorance, and to rediscover and reaffirm the true dignity of both man and nature in a way capable perhaps of stemming, if not of turning, the tide of progressive materialization and disintegration on which we are all now carried, it can only be by rediscovering and reaffirming the spiritual principles on which these masters have based their life and their thought.

ACKNOWLEDGMENTS

We would like to thank the following authors, editors, and publishers for their consent to publish the articles in this anthology.

Frithjof Schuon, "'No Activity Without Truth'":
The Sword of Gnosis, ed. Jacob Needleman, Penguin, 1974, pp. 27-39. New, revised translation for this edition by Mark Perry in collaboration with Jean-Pierre Lafouge, Deborah Casey, and James S. Cutsinger.

René Guénon, "A Material Civilization":
The Crisis of the Modern World, Luzac, 1942, pp. 78-96.

Brian Keeble, "Tradition and the Individual":
Conversing with Paradise, Golgonooza Press, 2003, pp. 28-42.

Kathleen Raine, "India and the Modern World":
Lecture given at the Indira Gandhi National Center for the Arts, Delhi, 1989.

Rama P. Coomaraswamy, "Ancient Beliefs or Modern Superstitions: The Search for Authenticity":
Sacred Web, Volume 1, July 1998, pp. 73-90.

Karen Armstrong, "Faith and Modernity":
Sacred Web, Volume 4, December 1999, pp. 17-32.

Timothy Scott, "The Logic of Mystery and the Necessity of Faith":
Previously unpublished.

M. Ali Lakhani, "'Fundamentalism': A Metaphysical Perspective":
Sacred Web, Volume 7, July 2001, pp. 7-11.

Rodney Blackhirst, "Rudolf Steiner, Anthroposophy, and Tradition":
Sacred Web, Volume 5, July 2000, pp. 85-94.

Ananda K. Coomaraswamy, "The Bugbear of Democracy, Freedom, and Equality":
The Bugbear of Literacy, Perennial Books, 1979, pp. 125-150.

Patrick Laude, "One for All, All for One: The Individual and the Community in Traditional and Modern Contexts":
Sacred Web, Volume 11, July 2003, pp. 27-45.

Fatima Jane Casewit, "Islamic Cosmological Concepts of Femininity and the Modern Feminist Movement":
Sacred Web, Volume 7, July 2001, pp. 81-92.

Roger Sworder, "The Desacralization of Work":
Mining, Metallurgy, and the Meaning of Life, Quakers Hill, 1995, pp. 121-148.

Dorothy Sayers, "Why Work?":
Lecture given in Eastbourne, April 1942, Methuen, 1942.

Robert Aitken, "Envisioning the Future":
Original Dwelling Place: Zen Buddhist Essays, Counterpoint, 1996, pp. 138-152.

Wolfgang Smith, "'Progress' in Retrospect":
Cosmos and Transcendence: Breaking through the Barrier of Scientistic Belief, Sherwood Sugden, 1984, pp. 134-158.

Seyyed Hossein Nasr, "Spirituality and Science—Convergence or Divergence?":
Sophia 1:2, Winter 1995, pp. 23-40.

Titus Burckhardt, "The Theory of Evolution":
The Essential Titus Burckhardt: Reflections on Sacred Art, Faiths, and Civilizations, ed. William Stoddart, World Wisdom, 2003, pp. 28-40.

Theodore Roszak, "Descartes' Angel: Reflections on the True Art of Thinking":
The Cult of Information, Paladin, 1988, pp. 238-249.

Acknowledgments

Mary Midgley, "Putting Nature in Her Place":
Science as Salvation, Routledge, 1992, pp. 75-83.

Brian Coman, "Never Say Die ... Without a Cause":
Quadrant Magazine, July-August 2002, pp. 46-48.

Thomas Yellowtail, "Make Your Choice":
Compiled and edited by Michael Fitzgerald. Previously unpublished in this form.

Anagarika Govinda, "The Fate of Tibet":
The Way of the White Clouds, Shambhala, 1970, pp. xi-xiii.

James Cowan, "Towards a New Dreaming":
Mysteries of the Dreaming, Prism/Unity, 1989, pp. 117-126.

Philip Sherrard, "Epilogue":
The Rape of Man and Nature, Sri Lanka Institute of Traditional Studies, 1987, pp. 113-118.

CONTRIBUTORS

ROBERT AITKEN is one of the most widely respected Western teachers of Zen Buddhism. He first encountered Zen during World War II as an internee in a Japanese camp for enemy civilians in Kobe. Whilst in the camp he met and was much influenced by R.H. Blyth. Robert Aitken and his wife, Anne, founded the Diamond Sangha in Hawaii in 1959. Aitken Roshi is the author of many articles and nine books, including *Taking the Path of Zen* (1985) and *Original Dwelling Place: Zen Buddhist Essays* (1996).

KAREN ARMSTRONG is the internationally renowned author of *Through the Narrow Gate* (1981), an autobiographical account of her seven years as a Roman Catholic nun, *Muhammad: A Biography of the Prophet* (1992), *A History of God* (1993), *Jerusalem: One City, Three Faiths* (1996), *The Battle for God* (2000), and *Buddha* (2000). She teaches at the Leo Baeck College for the Study of Judaism and in 1999 received the Muslim Public Affairs Council Media Award.

RODNEY BLACKHIRST lives in Bendigo, Australia, where he has lectured in Philosophy and Religious Studies at La Trobe University for the past decade. He has diverse interests in philosophy, cosmology, and religion, specializing in the Greek tradition and the monotheistic faiths. His doctorate re-examined the mythical foundations of Plato's dialogue, *Timaeus*. Dr. Blackhirst is a regular contributor to *Sacred Web*.

TITUS BURCKHARDT, a German Swiss, was born in Florence in 1908 and died in Lausanne in 1984. He was one of the most authoritative exponents of the perennialist school. His lifelong task was the elucidation of timeless metaphysical, cosmological, and iconographical principles and the illumination of the manifold religious and cultural forms which gave them concrete expression. He was a major voice of the *philosophia perennis*, that "wisdom uncreate" that is expressed in Platonism, Vedanta, Sufism, Taoism, and other authentic esoteric or sapiential teachings. A compendium of his writings, entitled *The Essential Titus Burckhardt*, was published by World Wisdom in 2003.

FATIMA JANE CASEWIT holds a Master of Philosophy in education from the University of Manchester and studied Chinese language and literature at Durham University. She now lives in Morocco where she works on a girls' education project as an information and advocacy specialist. She has translated Abdul Wahed Radhu's book *Caravane Tibetaine* into English.

BRIAN COMAN is a former research biologist who worked for the Department of Natural Resources and Environment in Victoria, Australia. As well as numerous scientific publications, he is the author of *Tooth and Nail: The Story of the Rabbit in Australia* (1999). He has also published a number of essays, mainly in *Quadrant*. Dr. Coman is currently enrolled as a postgraduate research student at La Trobe University, Bendigo where his doctoral thesis argues a defense of the Judeo-Christian tradition against the criticisms of contemporary ecological historians.

ANANDA K. COOMARASWAMY was born in 1877 in Ceylon. He was a multi-talented researcher, scientist, linguist, expert on art and culture, philosopher, museum curator, and author. Coomaraswamy was the first well-known writer of the modern era to expound the importance of traditional arts, culture, and thought as more than simply relics of a bygone past. His elucidation of traditional arts and crafts, and his exegesis of classical, Christian, and Indian metaphysics marked him as one the twentieth century's most authoritative and influential exponents of the perennial philosophy.

RAMA P. COOMARASWAMY was educated in both England and India where he received a traditional education in Sanskrit and Hindi. He later studied medicine in the USA where he practiced as a surgeon. He is the author of many articles and books on theological subjects, including *The Destruction of the Christian Tradition* (1981). He is the son of Ananda K. Coomaraswamy and has edited his father's letters and several collections of his essays, including *The Essential Ananda K. Coomaraswamy*, published by World Wisdom in 2004.

JAMES COWAN is an Australian philosopher, novelist, traveler, and "cultural adventurer" whose work explores the continuum between past, present, and future. He is best known for a series of works on the culture and spiritual heritage of the Australian Aborigines, including *Mysteries of the Dreaming* (1989) and *Myths of the Dreaming* (1994), and for his prize-winning novels which include *A Mapmaker's Dream* (1996) and *A Troubadour's Testament* (1998). He recently spent several years in Italy where he completed *Francis: A Saint's Way* (2001).

ANAGARIKA GOVINDA was born as Ernst Hoffman in Saxony in 1898. He studied architecture and philosophy at Freiburg University where he also developed his interests in painting and archaeology. In 1928 Hoffmann entered the Sangha and moved to the Island Hermitage in Ceylon where he took his Buddhist name. Several years later he committed himself to the Tibetan tradition and spent thirty years in the sub-continent before moving to the USA. Lama Govinda died in 1985. He was the author of many works on Tibetan Buddhism, as well as an account of his pilgrimage through central and Western Tibet, entitled *The Way of the White Clouds* (1966).

RENÉ GUÉNON was a writer of extraordinary power and insight. In the early decades of the twentieth century, Guénon urged the imperative necessity of a recovery of integral metaphysics in the face of the onslaughts of modernity, and delivered an irrefutable indictment of the assumptions and values of the modern world, perhaps most powerfully in his master-work, *The Reign of Quantity and the Signs of the Times* (1945). Guénon died in 1951. His writings have exercised a profound influence on many later perennialists.

BRIAN KEEBLE has long been devoted to the promulgation of the traditional arts and his best known book is *Art: For Whom and For What?* (1998). His most recent work is entitled *Conversing with Paradise* (2003). Brian Keeble is the founder of Golgonooza Press and co-founder of Temenos Academy, which is sponsored by The Prince's Foundation of HRH The Prince of Wales. The Academy is a teaching organization dedicated to the same central idea that had inspired *Temenos Review*, a journal devoted to the arts of the Imagination.

M. ALI LAKHANI graduated from Cambridge University before moving to Vancouver where he has practiced as a trial lawyer for 25 years. In 1998 he founded the traditionalist journal, *Sacred Web*, with the aim of identifying the first principles of traditional metaphysics and promoting their application to the contingent circumstances of modernity. The bi-annual journal has included contributions by many leading traditionalists. In the words of Professor Nasr, "Along with *Sophia*, *Sacred Web* is the most important journal in the English language devoted to the study of tradition."

PATRICK LAUDE was born in 1958 in Lannemezan, Hautes Pyrénées, France, of Gascon and Basque stock. He studied history and philosophy at Paris-Sorbonne and was a Fellow at the Ecole Normale Supérieure in Paris (1979-1982). His academic career took him to the United States where he obtained a PhD in French literature, specializing in poetry and mystical literature. He is the author of numerous articles and several books dealing with the relationship between mysticism, symbolism, and literature, as well as important spiritual figures such as Jeanne Guyon, Simone Weil, Louis Massignon, and Frithjof Schuon. Among his most recent publications are *Frithjof Schuon: Life and Teachings* (with Jean-Baptiste Ayamard, 2004) and *Singing the Way: Insights in Poetry and Spiritual Transformation* (2005).

MARY MIDGLEY was Professor of Philosophy at Newcastle University and is the author of several books exploring the history and philosophy of modern science. Her special interests include the development of moral principles concerning the welfare of non-human species. Her contribution to this anthology comes from one of her best known works, *Science as Salvation* (1992). Her most recent work is *Science and Poetry* (2001).

SEYYED HOSSEIN NASR is University Professor of Islamic Studies at George Washington University. The author of over fifty books and five hundred articles, he is a former president of Aryamehr University in Iran, and the founder and first president of the Iranian Academy of Philosophy. He is widely recognized as the leading Islamicist scholar in the world today. His publications include *Sufi Essays* (1972), *Knowledge and the Sacred* (1981), *Religion and the Order of Nature* (1996), and *The Heart of Islam* (2002).

KATHLEEN RAINE was an internationally recognized English poet and Blake scholar. She was the founder of Temenos Academy, an organization that advocates the primacy of the Imagination and which promulgates a traditional view of the arts and crafts in Britain. As well as her many seminal works on William Blake she published other critical and autobiographical works including *Defending Ancient Springs* (1985), *Yeats the Initiate* (1986), and *India Seen Afar* (1990). Kathleen Raine passed away, at the age of ninety-five, in July, 2003.

THEODORE ROSZAK is a philosopher, social commentator, novelist, and teacher who has held positions at Stanford, San Francisco State, and California State Universities. He is currently Professor of History and Director of the Ecopsychology Institute at California State University, Hayward. Among his many well-known works are *The Making of a Counter Culture* (1969), *Where the Wasteland Ends* (1972), *The Cult of Information* (1986), and *Ecopsychology* (1995).

DOROTHY SAYERS, born in 1893, was an Anglo-Irish novelist, playwright, critic, and theological commentator. As well as achieving popularity with novels, detective stories, and plays she was widely respected for her translations of *Tristan, The Divine Comedy,* and *The Song of Roland.* Throughout her life she took a close interest in ecclesiastical and theological developments and was a sharp and perceptive critic of many contemporary follies. She died in 1957.

FRITHJOF SCHUON is best known as the foremost spokesman of the perennial philosophy and as a philosopher in the metaphysical current of Shankara and Plato. Over the past 50 years he has written more than twenty books on metaphysical, spiritual, and ethnic themes as well as having been a regular contributor to journals on comparative religion in both Europe and America. Schuon's writings have been consistently featured and reviewed in a wide range of scholarly and philosophical publications around the world, respected by both scholars and spiritual authorities. Born of German parents in 1907 in Basle, Switzerland, Schuon died in the United States in 1998.

TIMOTHY SCOTT is an Arts Honors graduate of La Trobe University, Bendigo. He is currently engaged in writing a doctoral thesis on "The Universal Symbolism of the Ark." His interests include traditional metaphysics, cosmology, and esoteric sciences within the Western tradition. He is a regular contributor to the traditionalist journals *Sacred Web* and *Sophia* and lives with his wife and daughter in Germany.

PHILIP SHERRARD was an English author and scholar educated at Cambridge. Among the works for which he is best known is his collaboration in the complete translation of the *Philokalia*. The combination of his interests in metaphysics, theology, art, and aesthetics led to his participation in the journal *Temenos Review*, of which he was one of the founders in 1980. He was also recognized as a leading Christian voice in the contemporary debate about the environment. He passed away in 1995.

WOLFGANG SMITH is an eminent scientist and traditionalist thinker, and was for many years Professor of Physics and Mathematics at Oregon State University. His recent work is largely concerned with a critique of the modern, scientistic worldview and with traditional Christian theology. He is the author of *Cosmos and Transcendence* (1984), *Teilhardism and the New Religion* (1988), *The Quantum Enigma* (1995), and *The Wisdom of Ancient Cosmology* (2004).

ROGER SWORDER is Head of the Department of Arts at La Trobe University, Bendigo where he lectures in Philosophy, Religious Studies, and Literature. His particular interests include the pre-Socratic philosophers and Plato, traditional theories of work and art, and Romanticism. He is the author of books on Homer and Parmenides, and *Mining, Metallurgy, and the Meaning of Life* (1995).

THOMAS YELLOWTAIL, born in 1903, was a Medicine Man and Sundance Chief of the Crow Indians and was one of the most admired American Indian spiritual leaders of the last century. As a youth he lived in the presence of old warriors, hunters, and medicine men who knew the freedom and sacred ways of pre-reservation life. As the principal figure in the Crow-Shoshone Sun Dance religion during the last half of the twentieth century, he has perpetuated the spiritual traditions of his Crow tribe as one of the last living links to the pre-reservation days. Michael Fitzgerald recorded his life story in *Yellowtail: Crow Medicine Man and Sun Dance Chief* (1991).

BIOGRAPHICAL NOTE

HARRY OLDMEADOW is Coordinator of Philosophy and Religious Studies in the Department of Arts, La Trobe University, Bendigo, Australia. He studied history, politics, and literature at the Australian National University, obtaining a First Class Honors degree in history. In 1971 a Commonwealth Overseas Research Scholarship led to further studies at Oxford University. In 1980 he completed a Masters dissertation on the work of the renowned perennialist author Frithjof Schuon and the other principal traditionalist writers. This study was awarded the University of Sydney Medal for excellence in research and was eventually published under the title *Traditionalism: Religion in the Light of the Perennial Philosophy* (2000). His principal intellectual interests include not only the traditionalist school of thinkers but the mystical and esoteric dimensions of the major religious traditions, especially Christianity, Hinduism, and Buddhism. He also has an abiding interest in the primal traditions of the American Plains Indians and the Aborigines of Australia. His latest work, entitled *Journeys East: 20th Century Western Encounters with Eastern Religious Traditions*, was published by World Wisdom in 2004. Over the last decade he has published extensively in such journals as *Sacred Web*, *Sophia*, and *Asian Philosophy*. He currently resides with his wife and younger son on a small property outside Bendigo.

INDEX

For a glossary of all key foreign words used in books published by World Wisdom, including metaphysical terms in English, consult:
www.DictionaryofSpiritualTerms.com
This on-line Dictionary of Spiritual Terms provides extensive definitions, examples and related terms in other languages.

Titles in The Perennial Philosophy Series by World Wisdom